EARLIER BRITISH PAINTINGS

IN THE LADY LEVER ART GALLERY

ALEX KIDSON

Earlier British Paintings

IN THE LADY LEVER ART GALLERY

Copyright © Board of Trustees of the National Museums & Galleries
on Merseyside 1999

ISBN 0 906367 96 4

British Library Cataloguing in Publication data:
A CIP record is available from the British Library

Designed by Richard Hollis
Typeset by Trevor Gray
Printed in the U.K. by Balding + Mansell Ltd
Norwich

Contents

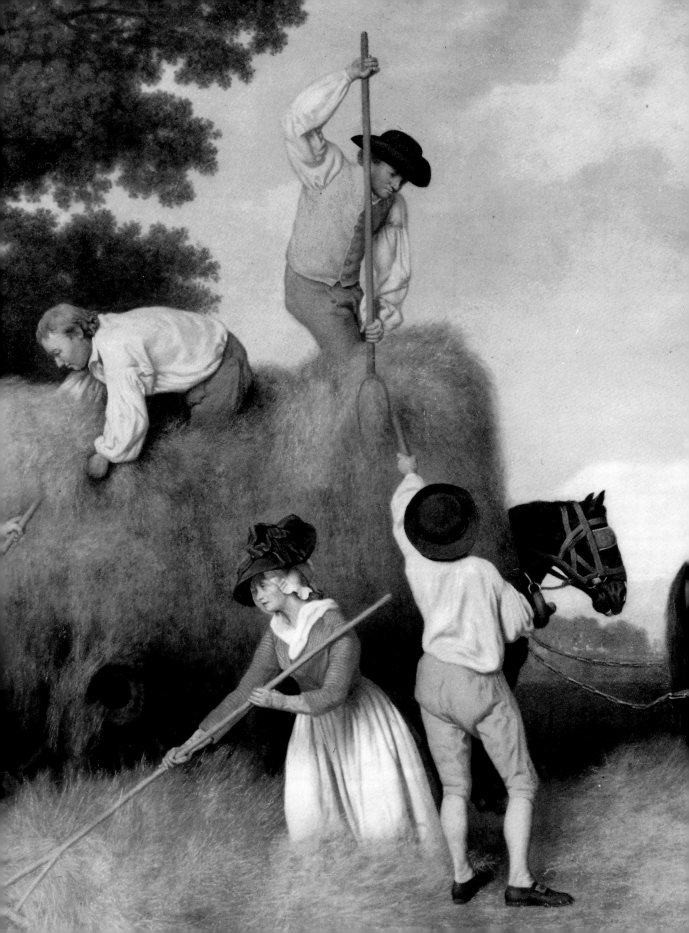

Foreword

This catalogue of one hundred and fifty paintings by artists born before 1810 completes the work of surveying all the British paintings in the Lady Lever Art Gallery, which began in 1988 with Mary Bennett's catalogue of the early Pre-Raphaelite works in the National Museums & Galleries on Merseyside, and was carried forward with Edward Morris's 1994 catalogue of the remaining Victorian and later paintings at the gallery. Making available the latest research on the collections is one of the Trustees of NMGM's key priorities in promoting the public's understanding and enjoyment of the works in our care, and we would like to thank Alex Kidson, Curator of British Art, who has a particular interest in late eighteenth-century portraiture, for compiling the present volume.

The gallery is famous today for its Victorian masterpieces, but as this catalogue reveals, Lord Leverhulme acquired earlier British paintings in surprising quantities. In his time, such currently unfashionable names as Romney, Hoppner and Raeburn were the equivalent of Van Gogh and Picasso today, and in buying their paintings and those of their contemporaries, Leverhulme was identifying himself as a collector with the highest pretensions. A second motive was more altruistic. With the Tate Gallery in its infancy, there was then no public gallery devoted to championing the national school across the whole range of its achievement. In buying the classic and representative works of the period from Reynolds to Turner which form the peaks in this catalogue, he aimed to illustrate for future generations the emergence of British painting onto the world stage – a process which had been paralleled in the growth of his own business empire.

The Lady Lever Art Gallery opened to the public in 1922 as an act of individual private patronage. Since 1986 it has been part of the National Museums & Galleries on Merseyside, which receive national funding in recognition of the quality and international significance of the collections. This assessment of our status is amply borne out by the works of art catalogued here.

Richard Foster
Director, NMGM

Julian Treuherz
Keeper of Art Galleries

George Stubbs:
Haycarting
LL 3683
(detail)

Acknowledgements

All catalogues of this kind are collaborative ventures; the result of gradual accumulation of information on the part of many scholars and curators past and present. I have depended enormously on the work of previous curators of the Lady Lever Art Gallery, notably A.C. Tait, Sydney Davison and Ralph Fastnedge; and I have also greatly benefited from discussions with my colleagues, especially Mary Bennett, Helen Brett, Xanthe Brooke, Nicola Christie, David Crombie, Frank Milner, Joseph Sharples, Timothy Stevens, Julian Treuherz and Lucy Wood. Above all I owe a huge debt to Edward Morris, whose knowledge of Lord Leverhulme is second to none, and who has guided my work on this catalogue with patience and generosity.

Many people have helped me over individual artists and specific enquiries. Their contribution is recorded in the footnotes, but my bare reference to a letter or conversation is a poor expression of a very real debt of gratitude. Three scholars in particular, David Mannings, Hamish Miles and Norma Watt, have been most generous in giving me information on Sir Joshua Reynolds, Sir David Wilkie, and Norwich School artists respectively. I should also like to thank Dick Kingzett at Agnew's; Kim Sloan and her colleagues in the Department of Prints and Drawings at the British Museum; Margie Christian and Jeremy Rex-Parkes at Christie's; Jane Cunningham, John Sunderland, Barbara Thompson and Sarah Wimbush at the Witt Library and Photographic Survey, Courtauld Institute of Art; Shelley Bennett and her colleagues at the Huntington Art Collections, San Marino; Olivier Meslay at the Louvre; Judy Egerton and her colleagues at the National Gallery; Peter Funnell, Catherine Macleod, Jacob Simon and their colleagues at the National Portrait Gallery; Tabitha Barber, Elizabeth Einberg and Andrew Wilton at the Tate Gallery; and the staffs of the National Art Library, Liverpool City Libraries and the other libraries and archives that I have consulted. To Duncan Robinson, then Director, and his colleagues at the Yale Center for British Art, New Haven, I am very grateful for the award of a Fellowship, which enabled me, longer ago than is decent to reveal, to begin work on this catalogue. I am also indebted to Brian Allen and the staff of the Paul Mellon Centre for Studies in British Art, not only for assisting my research, but also for a handsome grant towards the publication of this volume.

I should like to thank Sandra Penketh, who, as Assistant Curator of Fine Art, measured and checked the inscriptions on a number of the works; and also the three volunteers who, at different stages of this project, gave me very valuable assistance: Susan Jones at the beginning; Melanie Blake and Gareth Kemp at the end. Not least I thank Doris Robinson, who typed the catalogue with exemplary speed and accuracy, and its designer, Richard Hollis.

Notes to the User

The order of works in this catalogue is alphabetical by artist.

Sections devoted to individual artists contain four types of work,
placed in the following order:
(1) documented works and works where there is no reason to doubt
the traditional attribution. These are designated by the plain name of
the artist, and are grouped in order of date,
(2) works newly attributed to the artist, which are designated by
the prefix 'attributed to',
(3) versions of identified works by the artist, whether or not autograph,
which are designated by the prefix 'after', and
(4) works which fall into none of the above categories, which are designated
by the name of the artist in inverted commas. With these the decision has
been taken, in the absence of evidence of authorship, to retain the attribution of the work when it was acquired by Lever. The status of these works,
which are arranged in inventory number order, is discussed in the individual
entries. Finally, at the end of the catalogue is a small group of works, again
arranged by inventory number, which for one reason or another defy all
the above categories, and which are termed 'British School'.

Each work bears a new Lady Lever (LL) inventory number which dates
from the late 1970s and 1980s. Before the creation of the new inventory, each
work bore a number preceded by the letters WHL, or, if it was purchased by
the Gallery's trustees after Lever's death, LP. The WHL inventory, instituted
by Lever for his art collections in 1913, was applied both to all new
acquisitions after that date and also retrospectively to all the works he
already owned. These latter had existing inventory numbers with prefixes
designating which of his properties they belonged to: TM for Thornton
Manor, H for The Hill, Hampstead, and HH for Hulme Hall in Port Sunlight.
All the old inventory numbers (which in the case of the WHL sequence
are used in Tatlock's 1928 catalogue (see below), and are occasionally
found in other published references) are given in parentheses.

In the main body of each entry I attempt to summarise the current state
of information on the work, but I am conscious that in some respects this
is less complete than might have been expected. It has not been possible,
for example, to provide the full condition reports that are increasingly
a standard feature of permanent collection catalogues, and I generally
discuss the condition (and then briefly) only when it bears on the attribution
or historical status of the work. Similarly, I have made no study of frames,
and mention them only twice: once because it has some bearing on the
attribution, and once because a published reference exists to what is a
remarkable design. More critically, I have generally confined myself to
the view from the present, and have not attempted to survey, nor list, every

historical reference to the work in question, although I hope to have given, in the footnotes, enough signposts to enable users to find them for themselves. Many of the works in the catalogue are undocumented, and, without the luxury of an infinitely elastic deadline, I have found my task closer to raising the right questions about them than providing the answers.

Dots are used to indicate all gaps in provenances. Details of exhibitions, where known, are given in full for the period before works entered the gallery; however, some very minor loans thereafter have not been noted.

The following abbreviations have been used:

Lord Leverhulme: *Lord Leverhulme: Founder of the Lady Lever Art Gallery and Port Sunlight on Merseyside*, exhibition catalogue, RA (1980).

Tatlock: R.R. Tatlock: *English Painting of the XVIIIth to XXth Centuries with some examples of the Spanish, French and Dutch Schools, together with a collection of Historic and Modern Sculpture* (1928).

Webber: Byron Webber: *James Orrock R.I., Painter, Connoisseur, Collector*, 2 Vols (1903).

1904 Inventory: MS. *Inventory of Pictures, Watercolour Drawings, Furniture and China purchased by Mr. W. H. Lever from Mr. J. Orrock, November 1904, and, it is mutually agreed these remain at 48 Bedford Square at Mr. Orrock's risk, till April or May 1905* (Lady Lever Art Gallery archives).

1910 Inventory: Typed *Inventory & Valuation for Fire Insurance of Pictures, Watercolour Drawings & Decorative Furniture Purchased from James Orrock, Esqre., 48 Bedford Square* [by Tom Cox, dated 5 September 1910] (Lady Lever Art Gallery archives).

1912 Inventory: Typed *Inventory and Valuation of Pictures, Furniture, China, Silver and Glass removed from 48 Bedford Square July 1912* (Lady Lever Art Gallery archives).

BI: British Institution

DNB: Dictionary of National Biography

PRO: Public Record Office

RA: Royal Academy

Lever is referred to throughout under that name although he became, successively, Sir William Lever Bart, Baron Leverhulme of Bolton-le-Moors, and Viscount Leverhulme of the Western Isles.

Alex Kidson
July 1998

Introduction

The one hundred and fifty one works in this catalogue were collected by William Hesketh Lever between 1896 and 1925. In the former year, Lever was an energetic and successful forty-five year old businessman, whose expanding soap-manufacturing concern, located for the past nine years on the Wirral bank of the Mersey above Bromborough Pool, had just metamorphosed into the model village of Port Sunlight, built to house the factory's workers.[1] At the latter date Lever Bros. was one of Britain's largest and farthest-flung companies, and its founder, three times raised in the peerage, was one of the country's richest men, the owner of a dozen houses scattered throughout the British Isles and of a gigantic and celebrated art collection, only part of which could be accommodated in the new state-of-the-art gallery which had been opened to display it three years earlier.[2] Within that collection, which encompassed outstanding groups of English furniture, Chinese porcelain, Wedgwood wares and classical and contemporary sculpture as well as pictures, Lever's historical British paintings constituted a numerically significant element, and were a key to the understanding of his taste, its operation and fluctuations.[3]

Lever had graduated as an art collector in the second half of the 1880s by buying, sometimes off the walls of the Royal Academy summer exhibitions, pretty paintings to be used to market Sunlight Soap.[4] By the mid-1890s he had acquired a feel for the Victorian art scene, and a taste for the works of Leighton, Millais, and Burne-Jones in particular.[5] His move into historical British painting, signalled by the purchase of a portrait by Lawrence and four studies by Etty (including the *Bathers*, LL 3595 and 3596 below) may have been partially linked to his acquisition of new houses and the extension of his main property, Thornton Manor, in the second half of the 1890s;[6] but it was almost certainly the result, in the first instance, of a growing friendship with the amateur collector and dealer James Orrock (1830-1913). Orrock, a Scotsman who had studied medicine in Edinburgh and practised as a dentist in Nottingham for some years before moving to London to concentrate on his artistic interests,[7] played the decisive rôle in forming Lever's taste for and understanding of British art in its 'classic' period (then – as still so often now – generally regarded as beginning with the visits of Reynolds and Wilson to Italy in the early 1750s and ending with the death of Turner in 1851). Of Orrock the *Art Journal* wrote in 1892:

> '…it is doubtful whether he is best known as an artist,
> a connoisseur, a collector, a buyer, a seller, an enthusiastic advocate
> of the merits of the English School of Painting, a trusted Councillor
> of the Royal Institution of Painters in Watercolours, or a promoter
> of his patriotic scheme …of a real National Gallery, devoted
> entirely to the masterpieces of his country's art.'[8]

Lever's purchase of the Etty *Bathers* from him in June 1896 is the first

1. See E. Hubbard and M. Shippobottom: 'Architecture' in *Lord Leverhulme*, pp.150-175, especially pp.154-5; also E. Hubbard and M. Shippobottom: *A Guide to Port Sunlight Village* (1988).
2. For Lever and Lever Bros. see especially Viscount Leverhulme: *Viscount Leverhulme* (1927) and C. Wilson: *The History of Unilever* (1954-68) 3 Vols, especially Vol. 1, pp.290-96.
3. See especially E. Morris: 'Paintings and Sculpture' in *Lord Leverhulme*, pp.14-37; and A. Kidson: 'Lever and the Collecting of Eighteenth-Century British Paintings', *Journal of the History of Collections* (1992) Vol. 4, no.2, pp.201-9 for more detailed traversals of the ground covered by this introduction. For a visual overview of the collection see especially Lucy Wood, ed.: *The Lady Lever Art Gallery* (1996).
4. *Lord Leverhulme*, pp.14-16; also E. Morris: *Victorian and Edwardian Paintings in the Lady Lever Art Gallery* (1994) pp.xiii-xiv; A. Kidson: 'Lord Leverhulme's Soap Pictures', *Antique Collector* (March 1985) pp.64-69.
5. *Lord Leverhulme*, pp.44,60,64; Morris (1994) pp.xiv-xv.
6. *Lord Leverhulme*, p.16.
7. For Orrock see especially Webber; also *Lord Leverhulme*, pp.22-25, and Lucy Wood: *The Lady Lever Art Gallery Catalogue of Commodes* (1994) pp.33-38.
8. Cosmo Monkhouse: 'A Connoisseur and his Surroundings', *Art Journal* (1892) p.17.

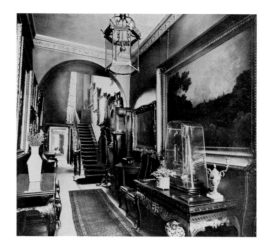

The entrance-hall of
James Orrock's house
at 48 Bedford Square.
Richard Wilson's
Villa of Maecenas, Tivoli (LL 3548)
hangs on the right-hand wall.
Photograph from
W. Shaw Sparrow, ed.:
The British Home of Today
(1904)

recorded point of contact between the two men, but the tone of their
correspondence at this time[9] suggests they were already more than polite
acquaintances. Lever had presumably visited Orrock's house at 48 Bedford
Square and absorbed the aesthetic which lay behind his collecting, which
consisted in combining, in a personal if somewhat anachronistic way,
English seventeenth and eighteenth-century furniture, late eighteenth
and early nineteenth-century oils and nineteenth-century watercolours,
together with Chinese blue-and-white porcelain, into what he perceived
as a harmonious whole. Orrock's attitude to the oils can be gauged by his
description of the British School as 'the third great school of colour';[10] he
owned pictures with generic subjects which did not distract attention from
their painterly qualities – Hollands and Hoppners rather than Hogarths –
and whose effect was chiefly sensual and decorative. Although Lever
later came to operate on a much larger scale, as a result of which some
diversification was inevitable, he nevertheless remained under the spell
of Orrock's approach for the rest of his life, favouring the same cluster of
artists and echoing Orrock's pre-occupation with decorative coherence
in his interiors.

Lever's collecting of historical British paintings falls into three distinct
phases. In the first, which lasted from 1896 until 1903, his main achievement
was to build up a small collection of late eighteenth-century portraits by
the best-known names of the period: Reynolds and Gainsborough, Romney
and Hoppner in particular. His purchases included Hoppner's *Lady
Elizabeth Howard* (LL 3128 below), Romney's *Mrs. Mary Oliver* (LL 3132),
Reynolds's *Mrs. Mary Fortescue* (LL 3541) and finally, Romney's elegant and
informal full length, *Sarah Rodbard* (LL 3539) for which he paid £12,000 in
1903. Although it is perhaps not too fanciful to see in these young women a
distant echo of the pretty girls in their white frocks which he had sought out
in the late 1880s and early 1890s for his soap advertisements, the names that
he went for, the prices that he paid and the dealer that he used – Agnew's –

9. Letter of 25 June 1896 quoted by Wood,
op. cit., p.36, note 188.
10. Webber, Vol. II, p.213.

suggest above all the standard initiation of a conventional 'Age of Duveen' collector.[11] He was, at this stage, as much a competitor for Orrock as he was a disciple.

In 1903, however, perhaps aware that he had paid nearly five hundred pounds in mark-up for *Sarah Rodbard*, Lever parted from Agnew's. Over the next decade his main pre-occupations were quantity and value for money. Twice, in 1904 and 1910, he found himself wanting pictures to decorate properties now ready to receive them: in the former case The Hill, Hampstead, in the latter, Hulme Hall, Port Sunlight; and on both occasions he met his difficulty by purchasing Orrock's own collection *en bloc*. In this way he obtained a handful of good pictures: Constable's *Cottage at East Bergholt* (LL 3120); three large Wilsons (LL 3122, 3548 and 3549) one Gainsborough (LL 3562) and one Reynolds (LL 3542) in 1904; one Wilson (LL 3550), Raeburn's portrait of Thomas Telford (LL 3147) and Reynolds's *Venus Chiding Cupid for Learning to Cast Accounts* (LL 3543) in 1910; but also – and this was even more the case with a third bulk purchase from Orrock in 1912 – an enormous number of minor and even suspect paintings whose attributions, as Charles Holmes put it at the time of Orrock's sale at Christie's in 1904, offered 'in a good many cases only a very general indication of authorship'.[12] Many of these attributions were to landscapists of the early nineteenth century: Constable first and foremost, followed by Turner, Cox, Bonington and artists of the Norwich School; but there were over thirty Morlands, and all the major portraitists of the late eighteenth century were also well represented. The sources of these dubious pictures remain obscure. Orrock does not seem to have bought at auction; in a few cases he is known to have purchased works from other dealers (among them the contested Hoppner of the Misses Fanning which Lever returned to him in 1908, after the work had been vilified in the press at an exhibition, and which Orrock had earlier bought from Partridge.)[13] But his dealings with Agnew's, for example, which accounted for several of the works in the 1904 sale to Lever, tailed off entirely after that date, and the indications are that many of the works in the 1910 and 1912 sales especially, he had purchased from private individuals. Others he had undoubtedly painted himself or employed associates to paint for him[14] or had obtained some time earlier from known forgers such as Joseph Paul or James Webb and kept up his sleeve.[15] Typical of his operation was the offer to Lever, at the time of the 1910 sale but in a contractually separate deal, initially for £5000 but soon reduced to £3000, of Reynolds's *Venus Chiding Cupid* along with a bizarre painting of lambs in a forest attributed to Gainsborough (LL 3690). This seems to have been an elaborate, but as far as Lever's collecting psychology was concerned, well-judged scam designed to conceal from the descendant of a former partner in the Reynolds how much he had realised

11. For a detailed survey of the eighteenth-century revival in collecting which formed the background to Lever's interest, see Morris's discussion in *Lord Leverhulme*, pp.17-22.

12. C.J. Holmes: 'Notes on Mr. Orrock's English Pictures', *Burlington Magazine* (July 1904) p.414.

13. Letter from Orrock to Lever 9 February 1908, gallery files.

14. That Orrock forged at least one Turner was stated by W.G. Rawlinson; quoted by C.J. Holmes: *Self and Partners* (1936) pp.207-8; for the suggestion that James Orrock had a 'studio' which executed (at least) Constable forgeries see C. Rhyne: 'Constable Drawings and Water-colours in the Collections of Mr. & Mrs. Paul Mellon and the Yale Center for British Art', *Master Drawings* (Winter 1987) pp.406-7.

15. See below under Paul (LL 3694 and 3712) and John Sell Cotman (LL 3614, note 3) respectively.

on it.[16] Orrock professed to Lever that he was unconcerned with the
provenances of his works and preferred to appreciate them on their merits
as paintings, but what this expression of self-confidence in his eye for
a picture concealed was a system for selling bad paintings under spurious
attributions at apparently cheap but actually inflated valuations. Orrock saw
Lever coming – yet Lever remained friendly with him all his life, and indeed,
with his ingrained businessman's mentality, no doubt admired the principle
by which Orrock survived, of buying cheap and selling dear.

Partly owing to business reverses, Lever bought very few paintings
between 1904 and 1910 (one major exception being Stubbs's *Self-Portrait
on a White Hunter* (LL 3684), which came in 1905 with the Tweedmouth
collection of Wedgwood wares). But from the later date he began to
purchase increasingly at auction. In 1913, with Orrock's death and the
foundation of the Lady Lever Art Gallery, the third phase of Lever's
collecting of historical British paintings opens, which witnesses an at least
partial effort on his part to broaden the range of the collection and to
seek out types of work more suitable for that national gallery of British
art for which Orrock had campaigned many years before.[17] Among the
key acquisitions of the period 1913-25 were Reynolds's two Grand Manner
full-lengths, *Elizabeth Gunning, Duchess of Hamilton and Argyll* (LL 3126)
and *Mrs. Peter Beckford* (LL 3125), both from the Hamilton Palace sale of
1919, in which the classicism of much of the later British figure painting
admired by Lever might be deemed to break through into the native
tradition; a quintessential Gainsborough, supposedly of a royal personage
(LL 3140 – Lever was always fond of pictures of royalty); one of Crome's
then acknowledged masterpieces (LL 3585) and a magnificent late Turner
(LL 3584). He extended the scope of his collection of the works of Etty, which
had already been transformed from the faintly gamey to the historic in
1910-11 by his purchase of *The Judgment of Paris* (LL 3588) and *The Triumph
of Cleopatra* (LL 3589). He also acquired interesting and major pictures
(which however had not passed into the gallery's collection at the time of his
death; and never did so) by Cipriani, Peters and Shee.

That these latter paintings, and many others, are not part of the collection
today is owing to the series of sales which were held, firstly in 1925-26, of
many of the works still in Lever's private homes, and then in 1958-61, of
what were then perceived as weaker examples of artists well-represented in
the gallery.[18] But if what remains of Lever's collection of historical British
pictures is a microcosm, it is nevertheless a microcosm which preserves
a true impression of his taste: its strengths, its fallibilities and its flavour.
It is very much a collection of its epoch: snobbish, sexist and sentimental
by turns; but to today's art historian, weaned on an alternative canon
of masterpieces, it is also full of unexpected surprises and delights.

16. Auctioneer's copy of the Christie's
sale catalogue 8 July 1910, and associated
day-book entries (Christie's archives).
17. Webber, Vol. II, pp.55-6.
18. For details see Appendix I below.

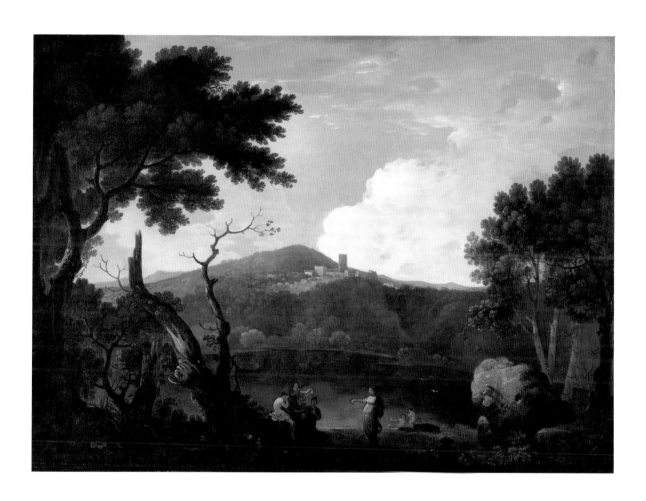

Plate 1
Richard Wilson: *Landscape with Diana and Callisto*
LL 3122

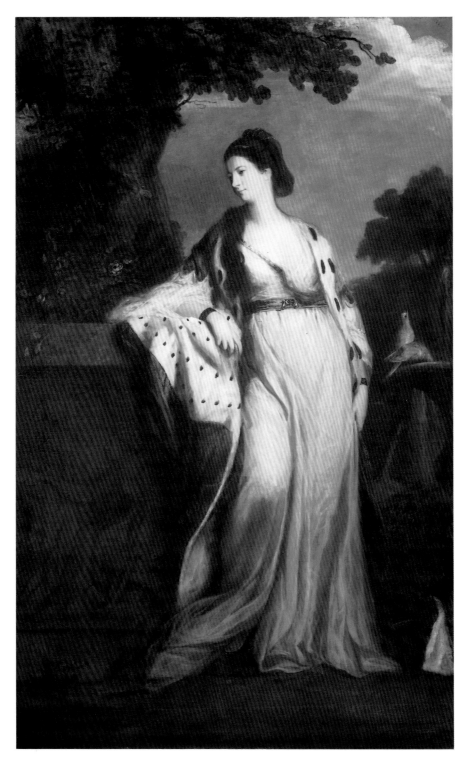

Plate 11
Sir Joshua Reynolds: *Elizabeth Gunning, Duchess of Hamilton and Argyll*
LL 3126

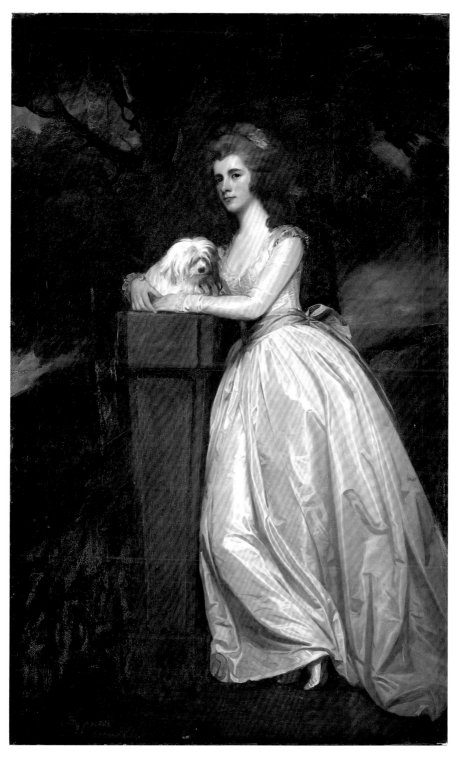

Plate III
George Romney: *Sarah Rodbard*
LL 3539

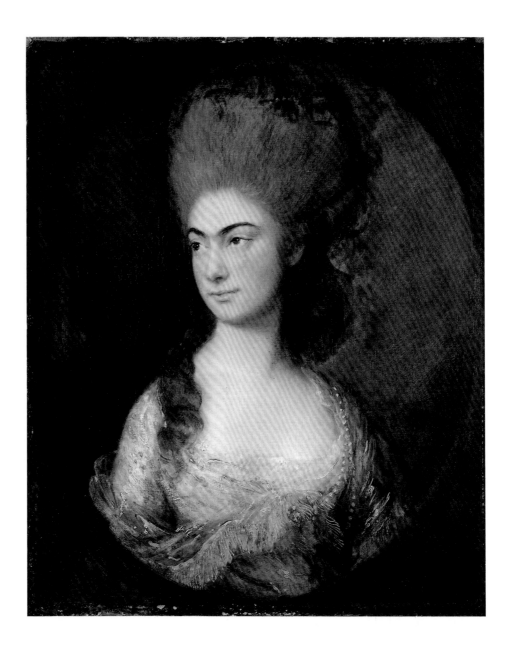

Plate IV
Thomas Gainsborough: *Anne Luttrell, Duchess of Cumberland*
LL 3140

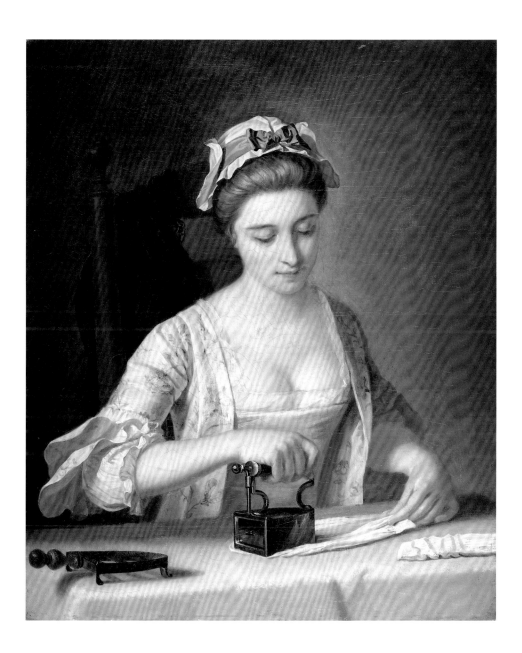

Plate v
Henry Morland: *Domestic Employment: Ironing*
LL 3538

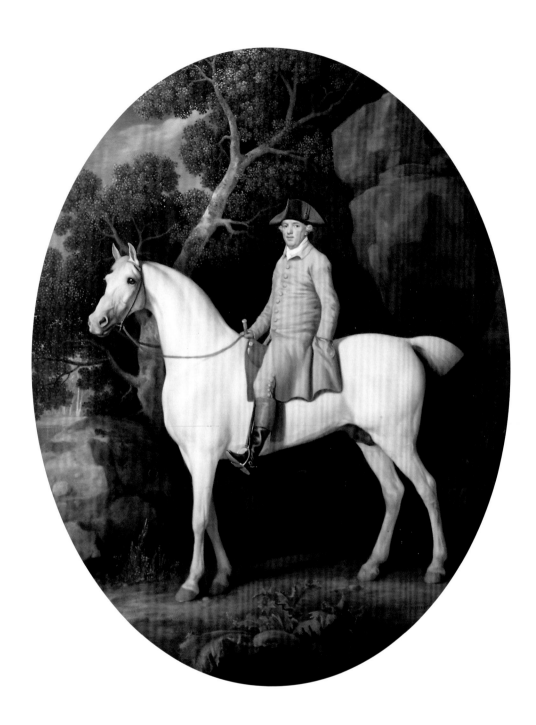

Plate VI
George Stubbs: *Self-Portrait on a White Hunter*
LL 3684

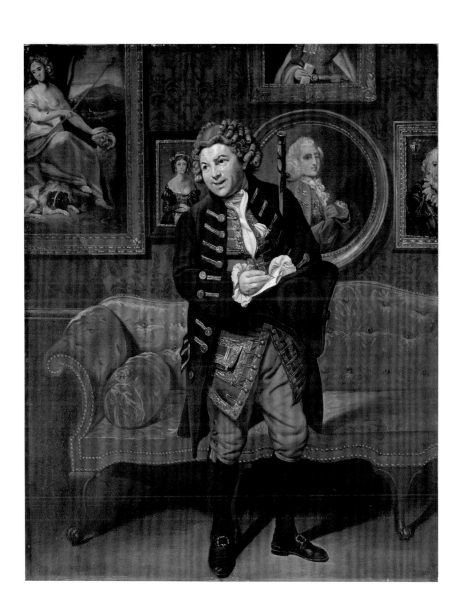

Plate VII
Johann Zoffany: *Robert Baddeley as Moses in 'The School for Scandal'*
LL 3534

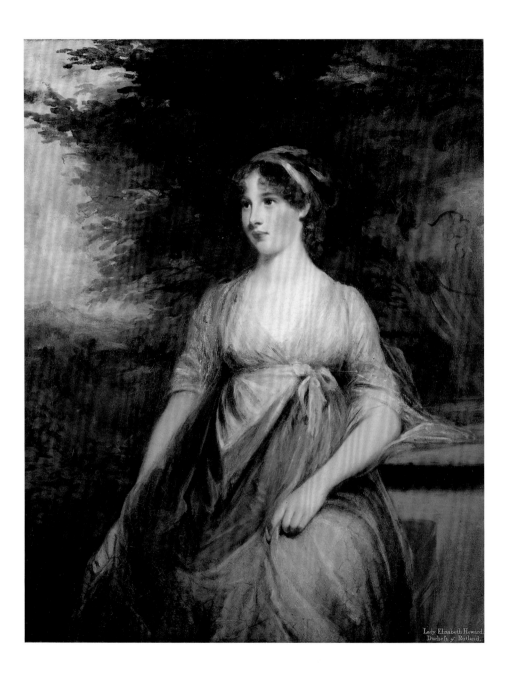

Plate VIII
John Hoppner: *Lady Elizabeth Howard*
LL 3128

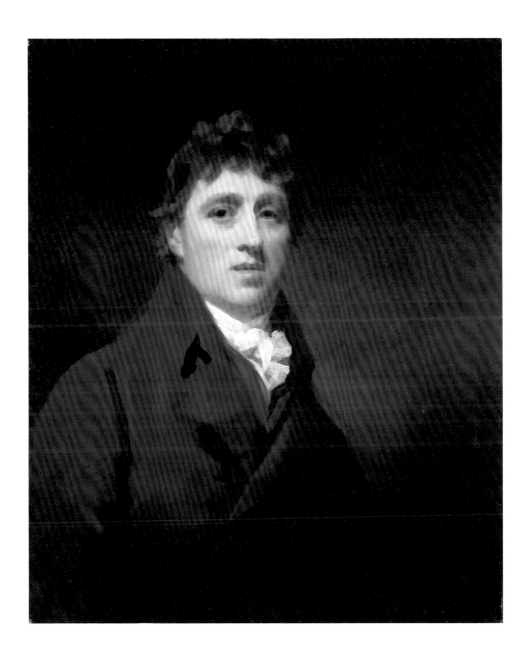

Plate IX
Sir Henry Raeburn: *Thomas Telford*
LL 3147

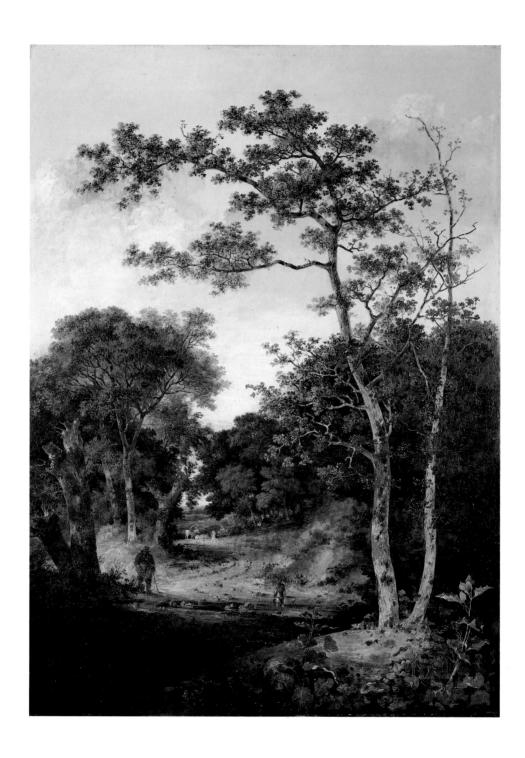

Plate x
John Crome: *Marlingford Grove*
LL 3585

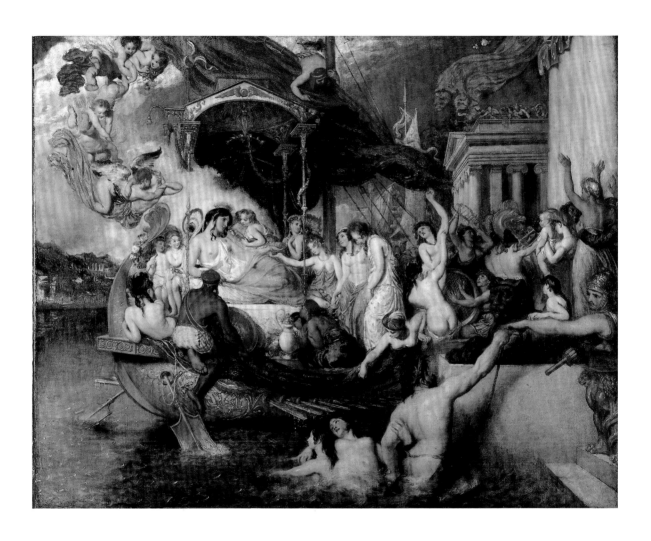

Plate xi
William Etty: *Cleopatra's Arrival in Cilicia*
LL 3588

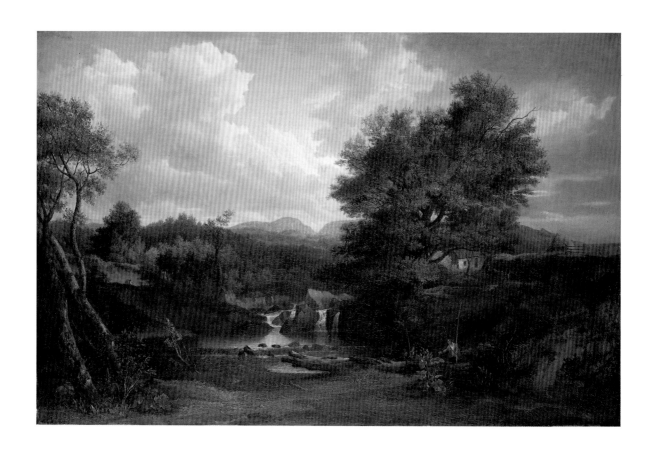

Plate XII
Patrick Nasmyth: *The Miller's Linn, Inveraray*
LL 3572

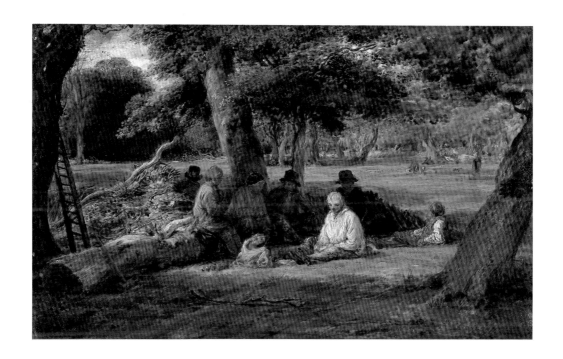

Plate XIII
John Linnell: *The Woodcutters' Repast*
LL 3738

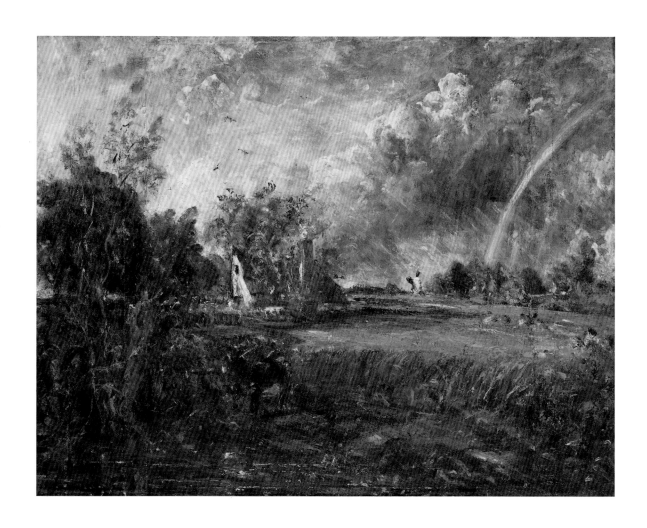

Plate XIV
John Constable: *Cottage at East Bergholt*
LL 3120

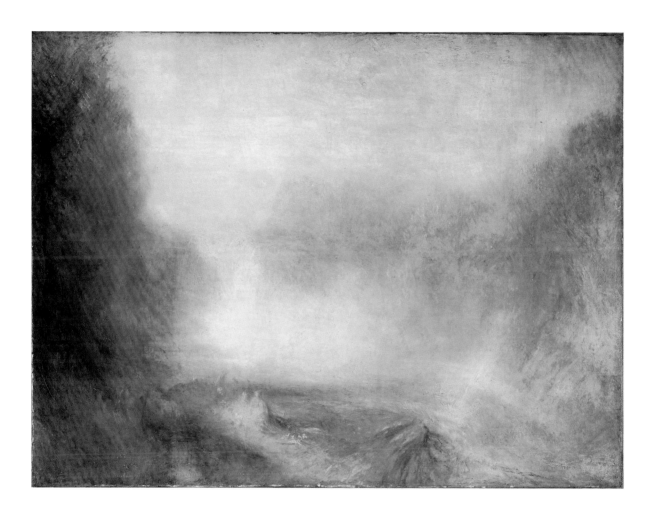

Plate xv
Joseph Mallord William Turner: *The Falls of the Clyde*
LL 3584

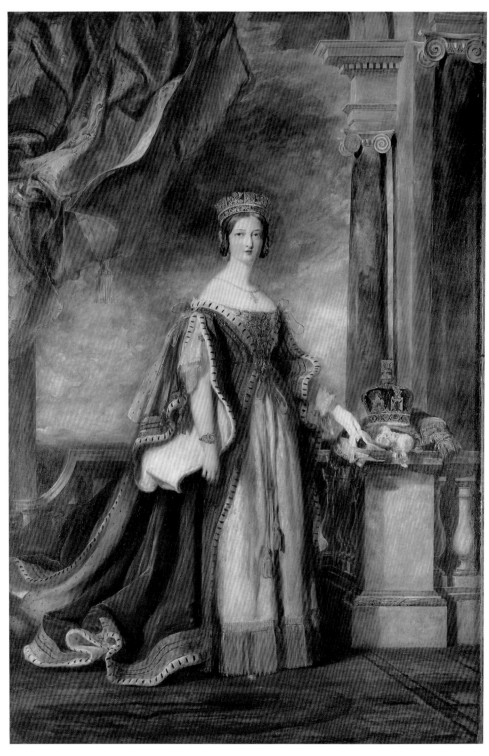

Plate x v i
Sir David Wilkie: *Queen Victoria in Robes of State*
LL 3598

Lemuel Francis Abbott
1760-1803

Horatio, Lord Nelson
LL 3551 (WHL 706, HH 113)
oil on canvas, 76.5 × 63.5 cm

When it was purchased by Lever, LL 3551 was attributed to Romney, probably because of his and Nelson's close association with Lady Hamilton. In fact, it is a version of the portrait for which Nelson sat to Abbott at Greenwich in the autumn of 1797. Nelson wears a Rear Admiral's undress uniform, the Star of the Bath and a Naval Gold Medal (St. Vincent) on a ribbon; his empty right sleeve is just visible fixed to the uniform below the medal.[1]

A preliminary study made by Abbott and kept by him during his lifetime was bought after his death by his friend and patron Francis Grant of Kilgraston, Perthshire, the father of Sir Francis Grant, PRA. According to the latter, Abbott frequently told his father that 'every portrait he painted of Nelson was done from that portrait'.[2] The first two versions of the portrait which Abbott made from this study were painted for Captain William Locker, who had originally asked Nelson to sit to Abbott, and for Lady Nelson; the latter was finished by the summer of 1798.[3] In the remaining five years of his life Abbott is said to have 'repeated the picture some 40 times or more',[4] and the quality of LL 3551 suggests that it is one of these later repetitions. Comparison with the version painted for Lady Nelson (National Portrait Gallery, fig. 1) suggests a gradual process of idealisation: Nelson's brow has become loftier, his nose has been straightened, and the sardonic expression made more beatific. The rendition of the uniform is much more perfunctory, particularly the shirt front and waistcoat.[5]

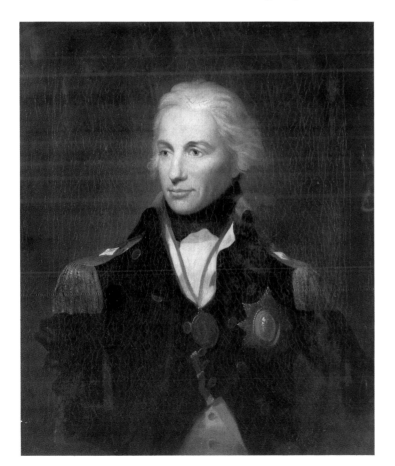

L.F. Abbott: *Horatio, Lord Nelson*
LL 3551

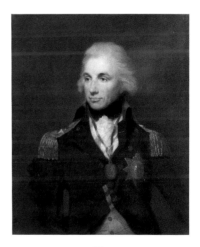

Fig. 1
L.F. Abbott: *Horatio, Lord Nelson*
Courtesy the National Portrait Gallery, London

PROVENANCE:
…James Orrock; bt. from Orrock by Lever 1910.[6]

REFERENCES:
1. R.J.B. Walker: *Regency Portraits* (1985) Vol. I, p. 358.
2. G. Callender: letter to *The Times*, 29 October 1932. This preliminary study is identified by Walker, *op. cit.*, p. 359, as probably the canvas sold at Sotheby, 23 March 1977 (91a).

3. Walker, *loc. cit.* The version painted
for Captain Locker is there identified as
that sold at Christie, 22 June 1979 (133).
4. F. Locker-Lampson: *My Confidences*
(1896) p.39, quoted by Walker, *loc. cit.*
5. For a discussion of the visual
differences between LL 3551 and another
of Abbott's replicas, now in the Scottish
National Portrait Gallery, see David
Phillips: *Exhibiting Authenticity* (1997)
p.147. Phillips suggests that both canvases
may be by 'a hack copyist working for
[Abbott]'.
6. 1910 Inventory p.41, valued at £300.

attributed to
George Balmer
1805-1846

The Black Gate, Newcastle-upon-Tyne
LL 2909 (WHL 2301, HH 72)
oil on canvas, 75 × 64 cm

The Black Gate, which survives
at the present day, was built in
1247-50 as the principal gateway to
Newcastle's 'new castle'. It stands
approximately fifty metres to the
north of the keep, which had been
erected in 1168-78; and is now
separated from it by the bridge
carrying the North-Eastern Railway
out of Newcastle Central railway
station, built in 1848. The two upper
storeys of the gate were added on in
the 17th century, and it was
completely restored in the mid-
1880s. The view is from the west.

Lever purchased LL 2909 as a
Street Scene, Norwich by John Sell
Cotman. The subject was correctly
identified – presumably in
consequence of the words TYNE
BREWERY being faintly visible on
the barrel in the centre foreground –
in the 1930s.[1] The attribution to
Balmer, who was native to Tyneside
and worked there between 1826 and
1834,[2] is attractive; but at the same
time it has to be admitted that

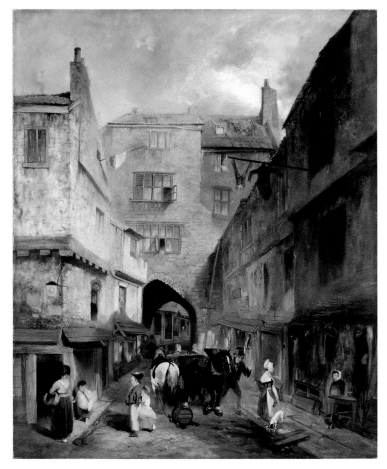

attributed to G. Balmer:
The Black Gate, Newcastle-upon-Tyne
LL 2909

LL 2909 is not wholly characteristic
of his known work and it does not
appear to be one of the paintings he
exhibited at the Northern Academy
in Newcastle.[3] The immature
character of the handling of the
figures suggests that it may be a
fairly youthful work.

PROVENANCE:
…James Orrock; Christie 4-6 June 1904
(77) bt. in; bt. from Orrock by Lever
1910.[4]

REFERENCES:
1. Tatlock, p.90, called the work 'after
John Sell Cotman'; A.C. Tait seems to
have re-identified the subject and made
the attribution in about 1935 (gallery
files). The painting was on loan to the
Laing Art Gallery, Newcastle-upon-Tyne
from 1937 to 1995.
2. For Balmer see Marshall Hall: *The
Artists of Northumbria* (1982) pp.11-12.
3. Sarah Richardson, Laing Art Gallery,
letter, 3 April 1998, gallery files.
4. 1910 Inventory p.38, valued at £80.

after
George Balmer
1805-1846

*Sunderland: The Lighthouse
on the South Pier*

LL 3700 (WHL 544, HH 229)
oil on canvas on board, 37 × 30.5 cm

An engraving of this subject 'drawn by G. Balmer' was published in 1842 in *Finden's Views of the Ports, Harbours and Watering Places of Great Britain* (fig.2). The term 'drawn' suggests that Balmer's original was a watercolour, a supposition reinforced by some of the effects reproduced in the engraving. What may have been

a related oil, titled *Entrance to the Port of Sunderland*, was exhibited by Balmer at the Society of British Artists, Suffolk Street, in 1837 (cat. 71), and it is tempting to think that LL 3700 is that work. However, evidence of an inscription (see below), as well as LL 3700's feeble quality, on balance militate against this.

The text written to accompany Finden's engraving observes that the view is from the south-east, the entrance to the harbour lying beyond the pier-head at the right; that the south pier, with its lighthouse, was built following a grant of royal letters patent to Edward Andrew of Sunderland in 1669, and that the

lighthouse on the more recent north pier, visible to the left, was erected in 1803. The large D on the fore-topsail of the collier 'is a distinguishing mark adopted by the owner that his vessels may be more readily known'.[1]

Lever acquired LL 3700 as *Lighthouses on the Dutch Coast* by John Sell Cotman. Some credence to this otherwise wildly optimistic attribution was perhaps thought to be given by an inscription, legible with difficulty as *J.S.C.32*, on the plank in the left foreground. This inscription is now very faint, but the first digit of the number seems to be an 8 rather than a 3, and LL 3700 has every appearance of being a later 19th-century copy of Balmer's design.[2]

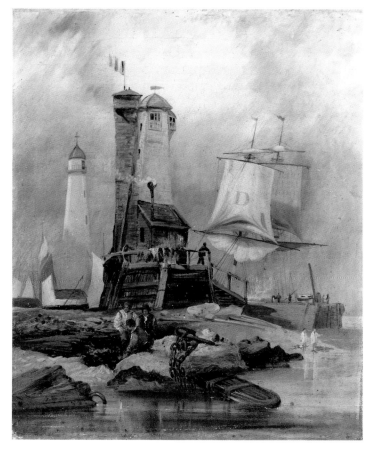

after G. Balmer:
Sunderland: The Lighthouse on the South Pier
LL 3700

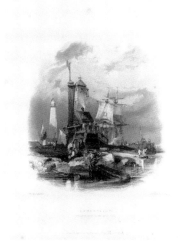

Fig.2
E. Finden, after G. Balmer:
*Sunderland: The Lighthouse
on the South Pier*
Photograph Courtauld Institute of Art

PROVENANCE:
...James Orrock; bt. from Orrock by Lever 1910.[3]

REFERENCES:
1. *Finden's Views of the Ports, Harbours and Watering Places of Great Britain* (1842) p.55.
2. Tatlock, p.117, re-attributed LL 3700 to Jock Wilson (1774-1855).
3. 1910 Inventory p.60, valued at £15.

after
Sir George Beaumont
1753-1827

The Forest
LL 3546 (WHL 3200)
oil on canvas, 76.5 × 63.5 cm

When purchased by Lever this work was attributed to Sir Joshua Reynolds,[1] but more recently it has been identified as a version of *The Forest* by Sir George Beaumont (Ashmolean Museum, Oxford, fig.3), which Beaumont presented to Oxford University in 1801.[2] The latter is said to be based on a landscape by Fouquières which Reynolds had owned, and to have been exhibited at the Royal Academy in 1797.[3] It was engraved by John Browne (1741-1801) (fig.4).

This work is smaller and more freshly painted than the Oxford painting. It lacks the group of gypsies in the middle ground and is a conscious re-interpretation of the landscape rather than a copy. Beaumont is not known to have made multiple versions of his paintings, and it is agreed that LL 3546 is not itself by him.[4]

An earlier attribution to Constable is no longer considered plausible.[5] One theory is that it is the work of S.W. Reynolds (1773-1835), who was an associate of Beaumont's and who is known to have made corrections to Browne's print.[6]

PROVENANCE:
...Charles Heath Warner; Christie 28 November 1879 (88) bt. Ferry (£11.-.6); R.E. Ferry; Christie 22 November 1912 (113) bt. Huggins (£78.15.-);...Gooden & Fox; bt. Lever 25 June 1917 (£400).

REFERENCES:
1. A. Graves and W.V. Cronin: *A History of the Works of Sir Joshua Reynolds P.R.A.* (1899-1901) Vol.III, p.1240, list LL 3546 as 'A Woody Landscape'.

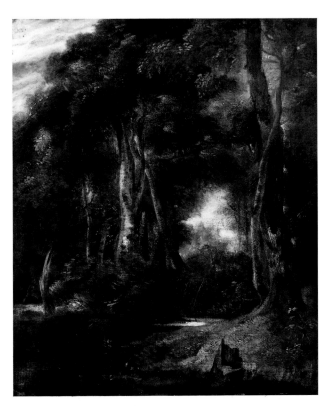

after Sir G. Beaumont: *The Forest*
LL 3546

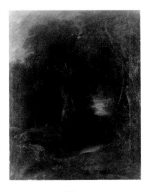

Fig.3
Sir G. Beaumont: *The Forest*
Ashmolean Museum, Oxford

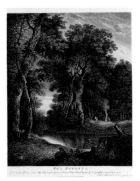

Fig.4
J. Browne, after Sir G. Beaumont:
The Forest
© The British Museum

2. F. Owen and D. Blayney Brown: *A Collector of Genius: Sir George Beaumont* (1987) p.148.
3. F. Owen: *From Gainsborough to Constable*, exhibition catalogue, Gainsborough's House, Sudbury (1991) pp.62-64. Owen here revises her earlier

suggestion that *The Forest* was one of the landscapes exhibited by Beaumont at the Royal Academy in 1800.
4. F. Owen, verbally, 1984; C. Rhyne, letters 14 and 15 March 1984, gallery files.
5. Rhyne, *loc. cit.*; the attribution had originally been proposed by C. Peacock

for a further version of the subject (formerly private collection London; repr. C. Peacock: *John Constable, The Man and His Work* (1965) p.116).
6. F. Owen: *From Gainsborough to Constable*, p.64; however, Owen's argument depends in part upon the mistaken assumption that LL 3546 was owned by Beaumont's friend Samuel Rogers and in his sale, Christie 2 May 1856 (as stated by Tatlock, p.65). This work (listed by Graves and Cronin, *op. cit.*, Vol.III, p.1234-5, as *A Romantic Woody Landscape*, and measuring 28½ × 28 in.) is not related to LL 3546.

Charles Brocky
1807-1855

Spring
LL 3580 (WHL 2893)
oil on canvas 99.5 × 121.5 cm

Summer
LL 3581 (WHL 2894)
oil on canvas, 99 × 121 cm

Autumn
LL 3582 (WHL 2895)
oil on canvas, 99 × 121 cm

Winter
LL 3583 (WHL 2896)
oil on canvas, 99.5 × 122 cm

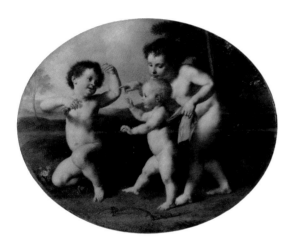

C. Brocky: *Spring*
LL 3580

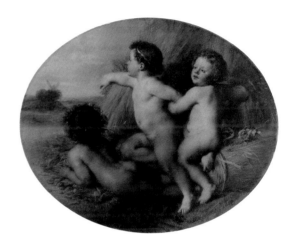

C. Brocky: *Autumn*
LL 3582

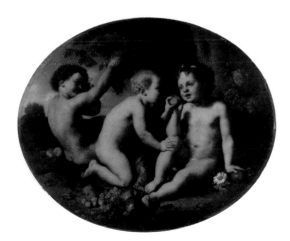

C. Brocky: *Summer*
LL 3581

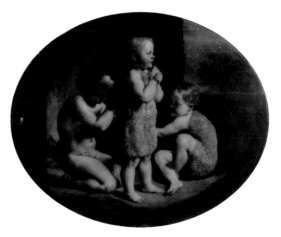

C. Brocky: *Winter*
LL 3583

These works have been described as typical of Brocky's later mythological and allegorical paintings, in which he regularly employed children as models.[1] The cycle was Brocky's exhibit at the 1852 Royal Academy, and is said to have been singled out for praise there by the Duke of Wellington.[2] However, the paintings seem to have received no attention from the more mainstream critics.

All four works have suffered from chronic flaking caused by old water damage. *Winter*, the worst affected, was restored in 1933 to remedy substantial paint loss in the lower part of the canvas.[3]

PROVENANCE:
....Gooden & Fox; bt. by Lever August 1916 (£200).[4]

EXHIBITION:
RA 1852 (235, 322, 329, 409)

REFERENCES:
1. Marianna Gergely, Hungarian National Gallery, letter, 12 December 1997, gallery files. For Brocky, who was Hungarian-born but spent much of his working life in England, see N. Wilkinson: *Charles Brocky, the Artist* (1870); *DNB*, Vol.VI, p.375.
2. 'When the Royal Academy opened, the Duke of Wellington went there, and afterwards went to Messrs Colnaghi in Pall Mall East and said, 'I can see no paintings there at all, excepting, indeed, 'The Seasons', four pictures painted by Brocky, which are very fine'.' (Wilkinson, *op. cit.*, p.22).
3. Conservation records in gallery files.
4. The sale was privately negotiated by F.W. Fox on behalf of the anonymous vendor who accepted Lever's offer for the works: Fox-Lever correspondence, 7, 8, 11 August 1916, gallery files. The identity of the vendor has not emerged from a search in Hazlitt, Gooden & Fox's archives.

John Constable
1776-1837

Cottage at East Bergholt
LL 3120 (WHL 557, H 14)
oil on canvas, 87.5 × 112 cm

The title used above is that given to the work at the Tate Gallery's Constable exhibitions of 1976 and 1991. The painting has been known under a variety of other titles, including *The Keeper's Cottage*,[1] *East Bergholt Mill*,[2] and *Dedham Mill*.[3] Although it has been suggested that the work is a topographically accurate rendition of a place that remains to be identified,[4] it has not conclusively been established that the location is East Bergholt (nor that the cottage belonged to a specific individual); and the opinion more frequently expressed is that it is an imaginary scene, based on Constable's recollections of East Bergholt.[5] That the work draws upon and adapts particular motifs from a number of earlier paintings and drawings reinforces this view.[6]

X-radiographs taken at the Tate Gallery in 1991 reveal that Constable began LL 3120 on an already painted canvas measuring 80 × 80 cm, which appears to have been used for figure studies (fig.5).[7] The tacking margins of this original canvas were incorporated into the new painting at the top and bottom, whilst at the sides, Constable twice added strips of new canvas, enabling him to extend the composition by including the dark tree on the left-hand side and giving increased prominence to the rainbow.[8] The additions are comparable to those in his full-size sketch for *Hadleigh Castle* (Tate Gallery),[9] and it seems probable that LL 3120 was a trial run for a large exhibition picture which was never carried out. It is very freely and rapidly painted, largely with a palette-knife.

The work has not been securely dated although it is clearly from the last phase of Constable's career. Grounds exist for a dating of around 1833[10] but recent commentators have preferred to see it as one of his very last works.[11] The painting remained out of the public eye until its first exhibition in 1893, when it acquired immediate notoriety as a result of being denounced as a forgery and 'mere palette-scrapings' by the artist G.D. Leslie, son of Constable's friend and biographer C.R. Leslie. The work's then owner, James Orrock, rebutted Leslie's claims and threatened him with libel proceedings, extracting from him an apology;[12] since when critical consensus has been almost uniform in the work's favour.[13]

PROVENANCE:
[?…] by descent in the Engleheart family;[14] bt. (?through Sir J.C.Robinson)[15] from an unidentified member of the Engleheart family in or shortly before 1892 by James Orrock; Christie 4-6 June 1904 (64) bt. in for Orrock by Agnew (£1050); bt. from Orrock by Lever November 1904.[16]

EXHIBITIONS:
Old Masters RA 1892-3 (10); *VII Internationale Kunstausstellung* Munich, June-October 1897 (287); New Gallery 1897-8 (205); *The Romantic Movement* RA 1959 (75); *Constable* Tate Gallery 1976 (329); *Lord Leverhulme* RA 1980 (6); *Constable* Tate Gallery 1991 (217).

REFERENCES:
1. It was exhibited under this title at the Royal Academy, 1892-93. According to Webber, Vol.II, p.169, this title was invented by Orrock at the time of the loan. G. Reynolds: *The Later Paintings and Drawings of John Constable* (1984) p.292 titles the painting *A Cottage at East Bergholt, The Gamekeepers Cottage*. M. Rosenthal: *Constable: The Painter and His Landscape* (1983) p.236 titles it *Cottage, Rainbow, Mill* but he returns to *A Cottage at East Bergholt* in his *Constable* (1987) p.196.
2. Webber, *loc. cit.*, states that the painting bore a label with this title, overlooked by Orrock when he furnished

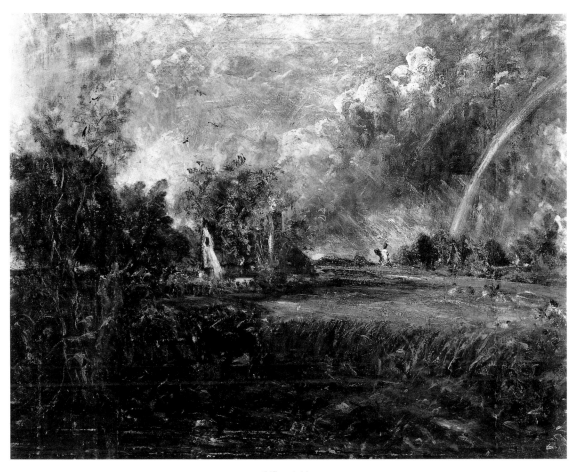

J. Constable:
Cottage at East Bergholt

the work with his alternative title. A label from the back of the painting with the title *East Bergholt Mill* in Orrock's autograph, preserved in gallery files, suggests that Orrock returned to this title (presumably in time for the Munich International (see exhibitions above), where the painting was shown as *Bergholt Mühle*). Webber, *loc. cit.*, discusses the *Times* correspondence on the issue during the 1893 exhibition.

3. Caption to the illustration in Webber, Vol. II, fp. 174.

4. C. Rhyne, letter, 5 February 1980, gallery files.

5. Reynolds, *op. cit.*, p.293; L. Parris and I. Fleming-Williams: *Constable*, exhibition catalogues, Tate Gallery (1976) p.186 and (1991) p.378.

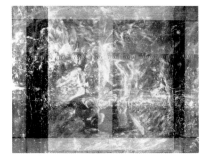

Fig.5
J. Constable: *Cottage at East Bergholt*;
x-radiograph
NMGM Conservation Department

6. The motif of the double rainbow has been identified as deriving from the oil sketch *Landscape and Double Rainbow* of 1812 (Victoria and Albert Museum; G. Reynolds: *Collection of the Constable Collection in the Victoria and Albert Museum* (1960) p.75, cat.117, repr. pl.69); this suggestion was first made in a 1976 lecture by C. Rhyne. The donkey is close to the one which appears in *The Cottage in a Cornfield* (Reynolds (1984) cat.33.3, exhibited in 1833 but a work originally of 1817); Reynolds is alone in observing ((1984) p.293) a ferryman similar to those in the late sketches of *A Farmhouse near the Water's Edge*; and a reminiscence of East Bergholt rectory in the background of the right-hand side. Rosenthal ((1983) p.236) sees the composition as originating

in the pencil drawing *Cottage and Road at East Bergholt* (Victoria and Albert Museum; Reynolds (1960) p.113, cat.157; repr. pl.128).

7.   Constable's large sketch for *The Lock* (1824, Philadephia Museum of Art) is painted on the reverse of a canvas previously used for an oil sketch of the figure of a girl (Reynolds (1984) p.135 and letter, 25 May 1995, gallery files).

8.   For a discussion of the importance of the rainbow motif in Constable's last works see for example Rosenthal (1987) *loc. cit.*

9.   Reynolds (1984) p.200, cat.29.2.

10. See note 6 above for LL 3120's relation to *The Cottage in a Cornfield* exhibited in that year.

11. Parris and Fleming-Williams (1976) *loc. cit.* suggested '?circa 1835'. Reynolds (1984) lists the work under 1836. Parris and Fleming-Williams (1991) *loc. cit.* imply a similar date through their catalogue numbering although dating the work only to the 1830s (in this following Rosenthal (1983) *loc. cit.*). However Rhyne (*loc. cit.*) felt that the most telling stylistic comparison was with the sketch for *Hadleigh Castle* (1829).

12. *Lord Leverhulme*, pp.44-45. For the initial exchange between Leslie and Orrock see *Athenaeum* (1893) Vol.I, pp.60, 128-9, 161, 191, 706. For a fuller exposition of Orrock's opinions, see his article 'John Constable', *Art Journal* (1895) p.369. See also C.J. Holmes: *Constable and his Influence on Landscape Painting* (1902) p.236 and 'Notes on Mr. Orrock's British Pictures', *Burlington Magazine* (July 1904) p.416; also Webber, Vol.II, pp.168-170. For a summary of the episode in the wider context of late 19th-century Constable forgeries see I. Fleming-Williams and L. Parris: *The Discovery of Constable* (1984) pp.102-104.

13. A single dissentient note was sounded in 1959 when the work was shown at the RA *Romantic Movement* exhibition as 'attributed to Constable'.

14. Reynolds (1984) p.293, citing a letter from Mr H.F.A. Engleheart to the Lady Lever Art Gallery, 19 April 1969, gallery files, proposes that LL 3120 was acquired by Henry Engleheart (1801-1885), son of the miniaturist George Engleheart (1752-1829), probably soon after 1834. The basis of this suggestion is an annotation in the Engleheart family record book of the picture collection at Henry's house, Bedfont Lodge (in which the work is referred to as *The Cornfield*). Parris and Fleming-Williams (1991) p.379 argue that Constable would have been unlikely to have parted with a sketch of LL 3120's nature to someone he apparently hardly knew and that Engleheart probably acquired LL 3120 at Constable's studio sale. The name Engleheart, however, is not recorded among the buyers at the sale, and it is not possible positively to identify LL 3120 amongst the titles there. The most promising lot, no.52, *Cottage in a Cornfield*, which fetched the relatively large sum of 26 guineas and must therefore have been a work of substance, is identified as the *Cottage in a Cornfield* in the Victoria and Albert Museum (see note 6 above). All that can be established from the annotation in the Engleheart record book is that the work came into the family's possession after 1834, and was certainly at Bedfont by 1861 (Henry Engleheart, letter, 13 June 1995, gallery files).

15. H.F.A. Engleheart letter, *cit.* Reynolds (1984) p.293.

16. 1904 Inventory p.1, no.21.

after
John Constable
1776-1837

Hampstead Heath, Branch Hill Pond
LL 3689 (WHL 66, H 30)
oil on canvas, 69.5 × 102.5 cm

The remains of a label on the reverse read: …*acquainted with it*/[signed] *Clifford Constable*. Clifford Constable (1864-1904), the grandson of John Constable, played a significant role in the dispersal of the remnants of the family's collection of Constable's work in the 1890s and he and his siblings were regularly approached by dealers anxious to have works authenticated.[1]

The present canvas, which is a crude pastiche, is based on Constable's painting *Hampstead Heath, Branch Hill Pond*, exhibited at the Royal Academy in 1828 (Victoria and Albert Museum, fig.6).[2] As part of the Sheepshanks Gift to the South Kensington Museum, this was one of the most familiar of Constable's works during the later 19th century. However, LL 3689 appears to derive still more closely from the print, *A Heath*, which David Lucas had engraved from Constable's painting for *English Landscape Scenery* in 1831;[3] as is suggested both by the handling of the sky, with its contrasting masses of white and dark cloud, and by the inclusion of wheeling birds, absent from Constable's original. The subject seems to have become a popular one for fakers around the turn of the 20th century.[4]

PROVENANCE:
…[?Mr Whitker[5]];…James Orrock; Christie 4-6 June 1904 (65) bt. in; bt. from Orrock by Lever November 1904.[6]

REFERENCES:
1.   I. Fleming-Williams and L. Parris: *The Discovery of Constable* (1984) pp.94-101.
2.   G. Reynolds: *The Later Paintings and Drawings of John Constable* (1984) p.190, cat.28.2.
3.   Reproduced in L. Parris and I. Fleming-Williams: *Constable*, exhibition catalogue, Tate Gallery (1991) p.320, fig.95.
4.   This may date to the *éclat* enjoyed by a *Hampstead; Stormy Noon* (one of the alternative titles proposed for Lucas's print) at the dealer Leggatt's Constable exhibition in 1899, which 'received special treatment' in the catalogue and was sold to the American collector J.H. McFadden in 1900 (Fleming-Williams and Parris, *op. cit.*, p.96). Sold to Leggatt by Hugh Constable, this work itself has been regarded as inauthentic. LL 3689 appeared in 1904, and in 1907 Hugh Constable was asked and refused to authenticate a *Branch Hill Pond, Hampstead* owned by the dealer Joseph Cahn, an associate of Orrock (Fleming-Williams and Parris *op. cit.*, p.100). In 1910 Orrock himself sold Lever the inauthentic works

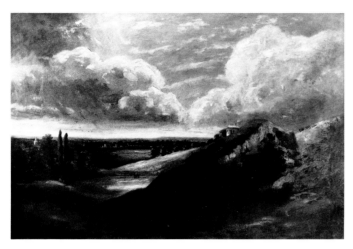

after J. Constable:
Hampstead Heath, Branch Hill Pond
LL 3689

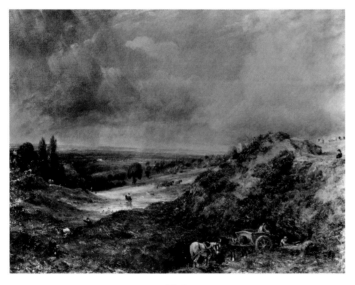

Fig.6
J. Constable: *Hampstead Heath,
Branch Hill Pond*
V & A Picture Library

Hampstead Heath, Stormy Day and *Storm over Hampstead Heath* (see Appendix 1 for Lever's other bogus Constables, which included further Hampstead subjects).
5. An inscription in chalk on the reverse reads *SOLD/MR WHITKER*.
6. 1904 Inventory p.1, no.24.

'John Constable'
1776-1837

A Lock on the Stour
LL 3691 (WHL 622, HH 48)
oil on canvas, 96 × 126.5 cm

To judge by the valuation given to it at the time of its acquisition by Lever (see below), LL 3691 then passed as an authentic work. It is, however, a pastiche: a good example of the kind associated with James Orrock.[1] The work combines and adapts motifs from such classic works as *Flatford Mill* (Tate Gallery), *A View on the Stour near Dedham* (Huntington Art Collections, San Marino), and *A Boat Passing A Lock* (Royal Academy of Arts).[2]

PROVENANCE:
…James Orrock (? by 1895);[3] bt. from Orrock by Lever 1910.[4]

REFERENCES:
1. C. Rhyne:'Constable Drawings and Watercolours in the Collections of Mr & Mrs Paul Mellon and the Yale Center for British Art', *Master Drawings* (Winter 1981) pp.406-7, has pointed out the close relationship of the bridge and cottage motif in the centre of the painting, derived from Constable's watercolour *Flatford Cottage*, to the painting *On the Stour near Bergholt*, given by Orrock to the Castle Museum, Nottingham as by Constable in 1909. The latter, and a preparatory pencil drawing in the Yale Center for British Art (B.1973.3.238) (*loc. cit.*, p.416, cat. II, 20) are attributed by Rhyne to 'studio of James Orrock'.
2. Reproduced in L. Parris and I. Fleming-Williams: *Constable*, exhibition catalogue, Tate Gallery (1991) pp.181, 195 and 291 respectively.
3. LL 3691 is perhaps the *Lock on the Stour* included in the Orrock-Linton sale, Christie, 25-27 April 1895 (288) bt. in. (£100). It is possibly also to be identified with the 'large painting of Flatford Lock' which Hugh Constable, grandson of John Constable, was asked to authenticate at Orrock's house in April 1907, although Hugh Constable's description ('I should say a picture by J.C. but foreground left

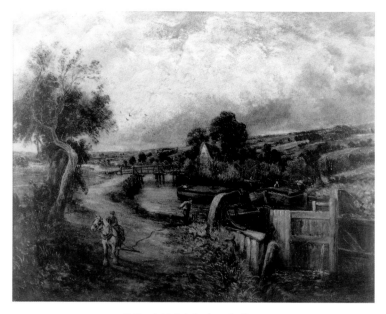

'J. Constable': *A Lock on the Stour*
LL 3691

unfinished and done up by someone else') is by no means conclusive (I. Fleming-Williams and L. Parris: *The Discovery of Constable* (1984) p.100).
4. 1910 Inventory p.35, valued at £2000.

'John Constable'
1776-1837

A Pony
LL 3702 (WHL 644, HH 237)
oil on canvas, 31 × 40.5 cm

Lever acquired LL 3702 as *Study of a pony, in landscape* by Constable. The only possible excuse for this ludicrous attribution is the presence of horses, ponies and donkeys in some of Constable's best-known paintings. The handling of paint is entirely unlike Constable's, and furthermore there is an anec-dotal, even sentimental element (the guilty-looking pony appears to have upset the bottle of water or something stronger) which is wholly alien to his work. The painting was later attributed to George Armfield

(flourished 1840-75),[1] but this suggestion, to judge by Armfield's known animal pictures, is also unconvincing.[2]

PROVENANCE:
…James Orrock; bt. from Orrock by Lever 1910.[3]

REFERENCES:
1. Tatlock, p.86.
2. No satisfactory attribution for LL 3702 has so far emerged, and it is very hard to judge whether the work is a genuine if mediocre painting of the mid-19th century, or a canvas 'commissioned' by Orrock to pass off as a Constable.
3. 1910 Inventory p.62, valued at £15.

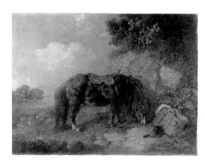

'J. Constable': *A Pony*
LL 3702

'John Constable'
1776-1837

River Scene with Barge and Cottages
LL 3710 (WHL 2060, HH 219)
oil on panel, 31 × 42 cm

Lever acquired LL 3710 as by Constable. The painting contains motifs to be found generally in Constable's work, but there is little effort to imitate his style closely, and the fact that a figure of a man has been painted out of the design (on the near riverbank, in the centre) suggests that the picture was executed in good faith rather than as a forgery.[1] It is in poor condition, with numerous losses and large areas of overpaint, especially in the sky.

PROVENANCE:
…James Orrock; bt. from Orrock by Lever 1910.[2]

REFERENCES:
1. The style of LL 3710 bears some resemblance to the later work of F.W. Watts (1800-70), an early sketch by whom is catalogued below (compare for example the figures and the cottage in the *Boys Fishing* sold at Sotheby, 27 March 1996 (62)). It seems, however, of too poor quality to be an autograph work by Watts.
2. 1910 Inventory p.60, valued at £30.

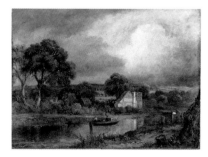

'J. Constable':
River Scene with Barge and Cottages
LL 3710

'John Constable'
1776-1837

Wooded Valley with Stream and Houses on a Hillside
LL 3711 (WHL 2009, HH 43)
oil on mahogany panel, 40.5 × 62 cm

The title used is that given to the work when it was purchased by Lever, as by Constable. The panel is in very poor condition, which makes it hard to assess. It has two horizontal splits extending across its whole width, the second of which was caused by the cradle constructed to repair the first. It is also extremely abraded following an earlier cleaning, and has been very substantially re-painted. It can never have been more than a feeble pastiche of Constable's style.

PROVENANCE:
…James Orrock; bt. from Orrock by Lever 1910.[1]

REFERENCE:
1. 1910 Inventory p.34, valued at £80.

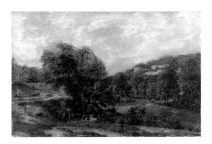

'J. Constable':
Wooded Valley with Stream and Houses on a Hillside
LL 3711

Thomas Sidney Cooper
1803-1902

A Study of Seven Sheep
LL 3718 (WHL 1440, TM 32)
oil on panel, 14 × 11 cm
signed and dated: *T.S. Cooper 1861* (bottom left)

This small sketch was probably undertaken as a compositional trial for a grouping of sheep in a larger oil, and is likely to have been carried out in the studio. No larger work, however, is known in which this precise configuration of sheep occurs.[1] Two of them, the one lying down in the right foreground and the one at the top turned away from the spectator, recur almost identically posed in a painting of 1865 titled *On the Kentish Coast near Folkestone*.[2] The roughly indicated landscape at left, with a river and distant church tower, appears in a pen and ink drawing of a group of five differently posed sheep which is inscribed *Sidney Cooper RA/Canterbury/Augt. 1861* (Cecil Higgins Art Gallery and Museum, Bedford).

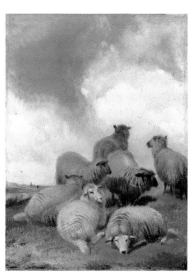

T.S. Cooper:
A Study of Seven Sheep
LL 3718

Roughly half of Cooper's thirty-four known oils of 1861 were small paintings and studies.[3]

PROVENANCE:
…F.O. Kirkby; bt. Agnew 16 Dec 1901; bt. from Agnew by Lever January 1902 (£40).[4]

REFERENCES:
1. Kenneth J. Westwood, letter, 24 February 1998, gallery files. Westwood notes that 'the sketch demonstrates Cooper's method of first drawing the outline of the animals in pencil prior to painting (visible around the forms of those sheep silhouetted against the sky)'. See also S. Sartin: *Thomas Sidney Cooper, CVO, RA* (1976) p.65, cat.157.
2. Sotheby, Belgravia 24 March 1981 (188).
3. Westwood, *loc. cit.*
4. Westwood, *loc. cit.*, points out that Cooper did not intend such preparatory sketches as for sale, and that the majority were only dispersed in the studio sale held after his death in 1902. LL 3718 was evidently an exception and was perhaps marketed by the addition of the landscape on the left and by the repainting of the sky which seems unnecessarily dramatic for a compositional study.

Thomas Sidney Cooper
1803-1902

Six Cows on the Banks of a River
LL 3576 (WHL 696, TM 323)
oil on panel, 40 × 61 cm
signed and dated *T. Sidney Cooper R.A. 1872* (bottom right)

Many of Cooper's paintings of cattle watering of the period 1867-1875 are set in the marshy landscape of East Kent, and have titles such as *In Fordwich Marshes*, *On the Stour* and *On the Banks of a River, East Kent*. The right-hand cow in LL 3576 is almost identical to one in Cooper's *Evening, Canterbury Meadows* of 1870.[1]

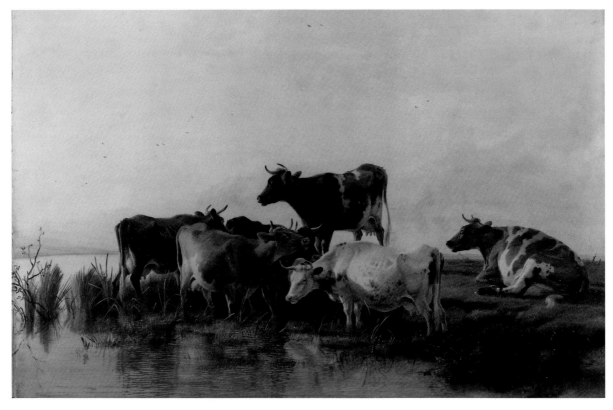

T.S. Cooper: *Six Cows on the Banks of a River*
LL 3576

The reverse of LL 3576 is inscribed with the number *279 1872*. The precise significance of this is unknown.[2]

PROVENANCE:
...James Nuttall; Christie 20 March 1897 (59) bt. Agnew (125 gns.) for Lever.[3]

REFERENCES:
1. Christie 7 June 1996 (662).
2. Kenneth Westwood, letter, 24 February 1998, gallery files, suggests that the figures refer to the date 27 September 1872 (the day following Cooper's sixty-ninth birthday). It is uncertain that the inscription is Cooper's own. See also S. Sartin: *Thomas Sidney Cooper, CVO, RA* (1976) p.67, cat.202.
3. In Agnew's stockbooks LL 3576 is given the title *Summertime*.

'John Sell Cotman'
1782-1842

Shipping in a Storm
LL 3614 (WHL 1208)
oil on canvas, 89.5 × 135 cm

Lever acquired LL 3614 as by Cotman and it is said to have been signed and dated *J.S. Cotman 1804*,[1] although no such inscription is now visible. The work bears very little stylistic resemblance to Cotman's known marine paintings[2] and it is quite inconceivable that the work dates from the first decade of the 19th century. Despite its eclectic character (the handling of the sun emerging from behind a dark cloud recalls Turner's *Hannibal Crossing the Alps* (1812, Tate Gallery) while

the fishing boat on the right-hand side is reminiscent of the mid-century works of E.W. Cooke), it seems unlikely that such an ambitious painting was made as a deliberate forgery, and much more probable that a work executed in good faith was later passed off as by Cotman.[3]

PROVENANCE:
...James Orrock; bt. from Orrock by Lever 1912.[4]

REFERENCES:
1. Note on the gallery's record card.
2. Many marine paintings formerly attributed to J.S. Cotman are now regarded as at best suspect, including the *Galiot in a Gale* in the Tate Gallery, and the *Small Craft and Hulks off Portsmouth* formerly in the Lady Lever Art Gallery, de-accessioned in 1961 (see Appendix I).

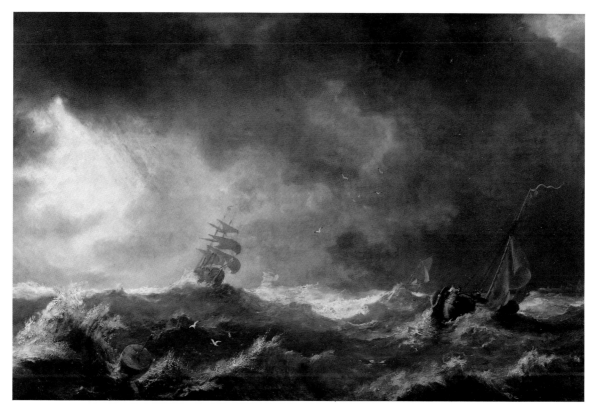

'J.S.Cotman': *Shipping in a Storm*
LL 3614

The two best-known works which remain above suspicion are the *Sea View* and *After the Storm* in Norwich Castle Museum which are both there dated to the 1820s, and are characterised by a thick application of paint, flat areas of colour and a subtle tonality wholly at variance with the style of LL 3614.

3.   Perhaps the most plausible attribution of LL 3614 is to James Webb (1825-1895), who besides painting large marines of just this type under his own name was notorious in his own lifetime as a forger of Constable and Turner. The degree to which he was associated with James Orrock remains obscure, but forged Constables in the Orrock sale at Christie in 1904 were identified at the time as the work of Webb, and Webb's ability to imitate a wide variety of artists has a clear bearing on Orrock's activities as a dealer. On this aspect of Webb's career see I. Fleming-Williams and L. Parris: *The*

Discovery of Constable (1984) pp.241-3. Marine paintings by Webb which bear some stylistic resemblance to LL 3614 include the *Boats leaving a Harbour* signed and dated 1868 at Shipley Art Gallery, Gateshead and the *Shipping off a Harbour* signed and dated 1867 sold at Christie 23 March 1984 (23).

4.   1912 Inventory p.12, valued at £450.

'John Sell Cotman'
1782-1842

Sailing Ships in a Harbour
LL 3703 (formerly HH 106[1])
oil on canvas, 76 × 63.5 cm

Lever acquired LL 3703 as by John Sell Cotman but neither the subject matter nor the handling of paint is characteristic of his work, and it is unlikely that the painting is by any Norwich School artist.[2] It can be dated to the second quarter of the 19th century. The view, which appears to be of an actual location rather than invented, has not been identified.

PROVENANCE:
…James Orrock; bt. from Orrock by
Lever 1910.[3]

REFERENCES:
1. There are labels on the reverse of
LL 3703 with the inventory number
WHL 43 on them; however, in the W.H.
Lever inventory book this number is
allotted to a work by Constable.

2. No satisfactory attribution for LL 3703
has emerged. The work is pleasing in its
handling of light and in the play of light
and dark shapes. However, the faulty
relationship in the foreground between
the size of the ropes and the size of the
figure on the barge indicates an artist of
relatively minor standing.
3. 1910 Inventory p.41, valued at £60.

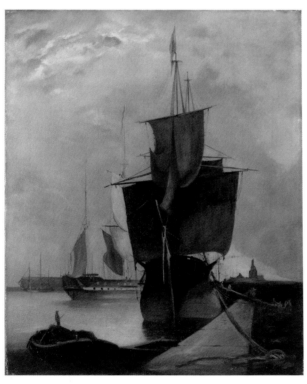

'J.S. Cotman': *Sailing Ships in a Harbour*
LL 3703

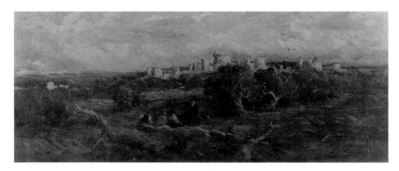

'D. Cox': *Windsor Castle*
LL 3707

'David Cox'
1783-1859

Windsor Castle
LL 3707 (WHL 568, H 88)
oil on canvas, 25 × 61 cm
inscribed: *1850* (lower left)

The subject is associated with Cox
but the very broken, vigorous
application of paint is only
superficially characteristic of his
style. The painting is probably a
deliberate attempt to imitate Cox's
work in oils.

PROVENANCE:
…James Orrock; Christie 4-6 June 1904
(79) bt. in (£210); bt. from Orrock by
Lever November 1904.[1]

REFERENCE:
1. 1904 Inventory p.2, no.53.

'David Cox'
1783-1859

A Woody River Scene, with a Fisherman and Two Cows Reposing
LL 3708 (WHL 652, HH 202)
oil on canvas[1] on board, 33 × 48.5 cm

The title above is that given to the
work at the time of its purchase by
Lever. The view nevertheless seems
to be of a specific, unidentified
location. A date of 1846 may once
have been visible on the canvas but is
so no longer.[2] The work is quite fresh
in quality and bears some stylistic
resemblance to Cox's oils but the
attribution must remain doubtful.[3]

The work was badly damaged in
1962 whilst on loan. A vertical tear
approximately 7 inches from the left
edge, running from the bottom to
about two thirds up the canvas,
and a horizontal tear joining this
approximately 3 inches from the
bottom of the canvas and running

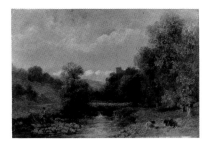

'D. Cox': *A Woody River Scene, with
a Fisherman and Two Cows Reposing*
LL 3708

approximately 9 inches to the right,
were repaired and the canvas backed
to board at this time.[4]

PROVENANCE:
…James Orrock; bt. from Orrock by
Lever 1910.[5]

REFERENCES:
1.   G. Roberson stamp on reverse of
canvas.
2.   This date is given on a typed receipt
for LL 3708, gallery files. It is not however
given in the 1910 Inventory (see note 5
below) in which dates were frequently
noted.
3.   Cox's name does not appear in the
records of Roberson's clients for the
year 1846 (Sally Woodcock, Hamilton
Kerr Institute, Cambridge, verbally,
16 February 1998).
4.   Copy invoice dated 1 October 1962
from J.C. Witherop to Ralph Fastnedge,
curator, gallery files.
5.   1910 Inventory p.58, valued at £15.

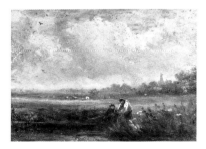

'D. Cox': *Pastoral Landscape
with Sheep and Figures*
LL 3714

'David Cox'
1783-1859

Pastoral Landscape with Sheep and Figures
LL 3714 (WHL 565, HH 257)
oil on panel, 15 × 22.5 cm

An inscription *David Cox* on the
reverse of the panel appears to be in
James Orrock's hand. The painting
is of low quality and bears little
resemblance to Cox's work.

PROVENANCE:
…James Orrock; bt. from Orrock by
Lever 1910.[1]

REFERENCE:
1.   1910 Inventory p.63, valued with its
pair at £10. The second work, HH 256/
WHL 2064, of virtually identical
dimensions, was sold under the title
*Pastoral landscape with Sheep and
Flowers* at Knight Frank and Rutley,
15 June 1926 (263), and was identified
in the catalogue as a drawing.

'David Cox'
1783-1859

Landscape with Cottage and Flock of Sheep
LL 3716 (WHL 556, H 452)
oil on canvas, 43.5 × 54 cm

The signature *David Cox* in the
bottom left-hand corner appears to
be a well-executed forgery. A few
sensitively handled areas such as
the dog and the hills on the horizon
apart, the work is a weakly designed
and crudely painted imitation of
Cox's oils. There is considerable
overpainting in all areas of the
canvas.

PROVENANCE:
…James Orrock; bt. from Orrock by
Lever 1912.[1]

REFERENCE:
1.   1912 Inventory p.14, valued at £80.

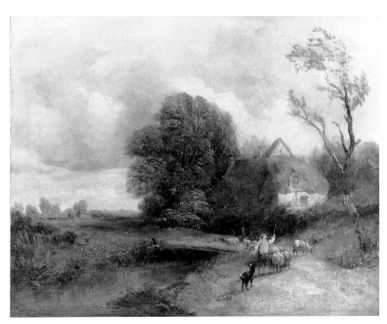

'D. Cox': *Landscape with Cottage and Flock of Sheep*
LL 3716

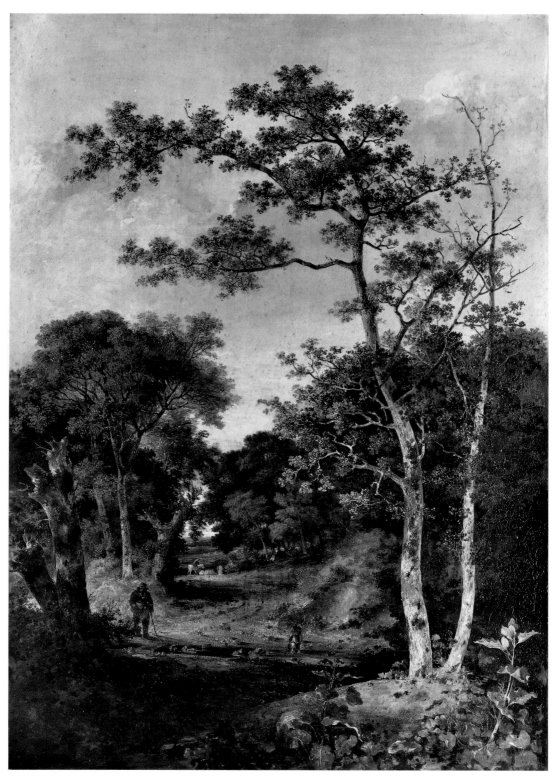

J. Crome: *Marlingford Grove*
LL 3585

John Crome
1768-1821

Marlingford Grove
LL 3585 (WHL 4636)
oil on canvas, 136.5 × 100.5 cm

Generally regarded as one of the artist's finest and most characteristic masterpieces, this large painting is thought to have been a commission from Samuel Paget of Yarmouth, who with other members of his family owned a number of Crome's works and to whose wife and daughter Crome gave weekly drawing lessons from 1817.[1] Its early history, however, has become confused with that of a second, smaller, version of the work (Norwich Castle Museum, fig.7), and the relative status of the two works is at present the subject of some controversy. In the early part of the 20th century, the reputation of LL 3585 was reflected in the enormous prices the work made at auction; but more recently, the suggestion has been made that it is no more than a copy of the Norwich version by Crome's son John Berney Crome (1794-1842).[2] Close inspection of LL 3585 does suggest that parts of the sky and the upper branches of the trees on the right may have been repainted in order to thin out the foliage.[3] The bright blue of the sky, particularly in the upper right corner, the crude and impasted white clouds, and the flatness in parts of the upper branches are not wholly characteristic of John Crome's work, and it seems possible that John Berney Crome or another artist did re-touch the picture at the request of one of its early owners.[4]

The Paget family lent their *Grove Scene Near Marlingford* to the Crome memorial exhibition held in Norwich in 1821 where it was dated in the catalogue to 1815. The work does not seem to have been exhibited in Crome's own lifetime (unless it is to be identified with the *Lane Scene* shown at the Norwich Society in 1815, cat.90). Marlingford on the outskirts of Norwich had been sketched and painted by Crome at least from 1808,[5] and since no later Marlingford subject is known, it may perhaps be suggested that LL 3585 is a distillation of his feelings for the place.[6]

Two copies from LL 3585 are recorded.[7]

PROVENANCE:
Samuel Paget, Great Yarmouth 1815; bt. from Paget by J.N. Sherrington;[8] bt. from Mrs Sherrington by Louis Huth[9] by 1862;[10] Charles Huth; Christie 20 May 1905 (44) bt. Agnew (3150 gns.); bt. from Agnew by Sir Joseph Beecham, November 1908; Christie 3 May 1917 (25) bt. Smith (5300 gns.); J.A. Mango; Mrs J.A. Mango; Christie 11 May 1923 (118) bt. Thomas (5000 gns.) for Lever.

EXHIBITIONS:
Crome Memorial Exhibition Norwich 1821 (12); B I 1862 (179); *Old Masters* RA 1871 (35); Burlington Fine Arts Club 1871 (44); Grosvenor Gallery 1888 (152); Burlington Fine Arts Club 1912 (31); *British Empire Exhibition* Wembley 1924 (26); *Liverpool Autumn Exhibition* Walker Art Gallery Liverpool 1933 (32); *British Art* Manchester City Art Gallery

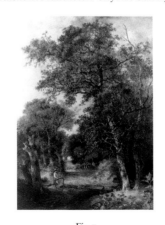

Fig.7
Attributed to J. Crome:
Marlingford Grove
Norfolk Museums Service (Norwich Castle Museum)

1934 (55); *A Hundred Years of British Landscape Painting 1750-1850* Leicester 1956 (16); *Primitives to Picasso* RA 1962 (302); *Crome* Norwich Castle Museum and Tate Gallery 1968 (15); *English Landscape Painting of the 18th and 19th Centuries* Tokyo and Kyoto 1971 (16); *La Peinture Romantique Anglaise et les Preraphaelites* Petit Palais Paris 1972 (89).

REFERENCES:
1. N. Goldberg: *John Crome the Elder* (1978) Vol.I, pp.64, 208-9; see also E. Paget: 'Old Crome', *Magazine of Art* (1882) pp.221-6.
2. D. & T. Clifford: *Crome* (1968) pp.229-30 cast the initial doubts on LL 3585; the adverse opinions of J. Newton (*Cambridge Quarterly* (Autumn 1968)) and M. Kitson (*Times Literary Supplement* (27 March 1969)) were cited in an exchange between the Cliffords and F. Hawcroft in *Burlington Magazine* (July 1970) pp.466-68, following the latter's defence of LL 3585 in his review of the Cliffords' book, *Burlington Magazine* (December 1969) pp.765-66. N. Goldberg, *op. cit.*, Vol.I, p.209, citing the opinions of Hawcroft and Miklos Rajnai, regarded LL 3585 as entirely autograph. None of the later apologists for LL 3585 has entirely disposed of the evidence cited by the Cliffords, which is as follows:
(i) an early etching of the subject by the Yarmouth-based Richard Girling follows the Norwich design, not LL 3585. This leads the Cliffords to conclude that it was the Norwich painting that was in Paget's collection, not LL 3585. (A further point, not made by the Cliffords, is that most known copies (e.g. one attributed to Colkett, 20 × 16 in., formerly with the Weston Gallery; one attributed to R. Ladbrooke, with Agnew about 1958; and a horizontal version attributed to J.B. Crome, 40 × 49 in., with Leggatt, 1956) also follow the Norwich design.) This argument, however, would lose force if it were proved conclusively that the visible differences between LL 3585 and the Norwich version were because LL 3585 had later been repainted.
(ii) It must have been the Norwich painting, and not LL 3585, which appeared in the Sherrington sale at Christie, 1 May 1858 (as lot 36, bought in for 76 guineas) since this work is described in the catalogue as having 'a peasant passing

over a small wooden bridge' – a feature which LL 3585 conspicuously lacks. Nevertheless, as the Cliffords concede, there is no doubt that Sherrington did also own LL 3585, since a watercolour copy he himself painted (still in family ownership in 1968) follows the latter in detail. Once this is accepted, the argument turns on which of the two versions Sherrington purchased from Paget. The Cliffords suggest that although Elise Paget, in her article on Crome describes and reproduces LL 3585 as the work once owned by her grandfather, her memory may well have been at fault after such an interval. Nevertheless, Elise Paget distinctly states (*op. cit.*, p.223) that Samuel Paget's commission to Crome was for a 'large picture', whereas the Norwich canvas measures only 35 × 27 in. Furthermore, in endeavouring to prove that the Norwich picture was that owned by Paget, the Cliffords describe as 'unaccountable' the fact that Sir Henry Holmes, its last owner, derived its provenance from the Rev. E. Valpy (Headmaster of Norwich Grammar School in 1811); whereas the painting has a label on the reverse dated 19th January 1845, signed by the dealer Rought, stating that he bought it from Valpy's family and sold it to 'J.T. Dorrington Esq.' (gallery files, Norwich Castle Museum). The last name is surely meant for Sherrington.

One further point of evidence adduced by the Cliffords (*op. cit.*, p.277) seems suggestive. That is that Sherrington is known to have bought three Cromes, two of them large, from Paget, on 6 July 1847. It is tempting to assume that LL 3585 was one of these, in which case the Cliffords' notion that the work was painted for Sherrington by John Berney Crome, who died in 1842, falls to the ground. On this view, if LL 3585 was in fact re-painted at all, it could have been done by J.B. Crome for Paget; but if any such re-touching was carried out for Sherrington (or his widow), another artist must have been responsible. The best scenario, on the evidence currently available, seems to be that LL 3585 is the Paget painting; that it was bought by Sherrington in 1847; that it was copied by Sherrington in recognition of its superiority to the smaller version of the subject which he had acquired not long before; and that the

latter was deemed surplus to requirements and included in the 1858 sale. But this remains speculative. It should be added that the Cliffords later changed their minds and accepted that LL 3585 was by Crome (information from Edward Morris, verbally, 5 June 1998); while the Norwich version has been rejected as an autograph work by Crome by Miklos Rajnai, and is presently regarded at the Castle Museum as a copy (not necessarily after LL 3585) (Norma Watt, verbally, 20 April 1998).

3. It has not been possible to date to take x-radiographs of LL 3585, which might help resolve this issue.

4. See note 2 above.

5. The *Scene at Marlingford* lent to the 1821 memorial exhibition by Rev. J.H. Browne (cat. 54) is dated to 1808 in the catalogue. Crome exhibited a *Sketch at Marlingford* at the Norwich Society in 1813 (cat. 44); this is perhaps the same as cat.98 in the memorial exhibition (dated to 1812). *A Study of Trees and Broken Ground at Marlingford* was lent to the memorial exhibition by J.D. Palmer Esq. and was dated to 1815 (cat. 99).

6. D. & T. Clifford, however (*op. cit.*, p.229), question whether LL 3585 represents Marlingford at all. They point out that the design closely resembles that of an etching by Crome which has no title and is known simply as *Composition – Sandy Road through Woodland*.

7. Goldberg, *op. cit.*, Vol.I, p.208. The 20 × 24 inch oil sketch of the lower section of the painting recorded here was in a private collection, Tennessee, in 1998. For the watercolour copy by J.N. Sherrington see note 2 above.

8. Gustav Waagen describes a visit to Sherrington's collection in Yarmouth where he was struck by four Cromes in particular; of these No.1, 'an avenue of trees foreshortened, with noonday shadows, a man and a dog in the foreground' is probably identifiable with LL 3585 (G. Waagen: *Treasures of Art in Great Britain* (1854) Vol.III, p.438). Of Crome Waagen wrote: 'the truth, originality, and variety of his conception, the fine character of his trees, the great power of his generally warm colouring, and a careful execution give him a very honourable position among English landscape painters' (*loc. cit.*). The date of

Waagen's visit is uncertain. On internal evidence it seems to have taken place in 1850, two years after Sherrington's death. The collection had at that point been kept intact by Sherrington's young widow.

9. Paget, *op. cit.*, p.224, stated that Huth acquired the work after Sherrington's death and Sir Charles Sherrington, in a memorandum dated February 1908 (cited by D. & T. Clifford, *op. cit.*, p.276) named the *Grove Scene, Marlingford* as one of fourteen large Cromes 'sold by [Mr Sherrington's] Widow privately more than 45 years ago to Louis Huth Esq.'.

10. Lent by Huth to the 1862 British Institution exhibition. Paget, *loc. cit.*, is in error in saying that it was one of two Cromes shown at the 1862 International exhibition; this contained six Cromes, none of which was lent by Huth.

'John Crome'
1768-1821

A Wood, with Figures at a Gate
LL 3663 (WHL 615, HH 15)
oil on canvas, 117.5 × 129 cm

The valuation put upon LL 3663 shortly after its acquisition by Lever suggests that it then passed as an autograph work by Crome. The empty and decorative rendition of the left-hand tree and the upper branches of the central one, the pedestrian painting of the foliage and the uninspired handling of light and shadow militate against the work being by him. An ambitious picture, possibly painted for exhibition, LL 3663 can be attributed to an early follower of Crome. It has been attributed to his eldest son John Berney Crome (1794-1842),[1] but is not typical of his work.[2]

PROVENANCE:
…James Orrock; bt. from Orrock by Lever 1910.[3]

REFERENCES:
1. Tatlock, p.91.
2. Norma Watt, Norwich Castle Museum, verbally 20 April 1998.

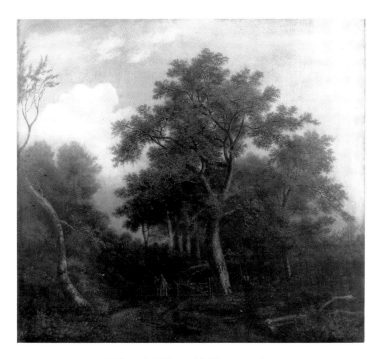

'J. Crome': *A Wood, with Figures at a Gate*
LL 3663

stamping-ground of Crome. He exhibited works with this name in their title at the Norwich Society of Artists in 1807 (pencil), 1808, 1812 and 1815, and others titled *St. Martin's River* in 1810, 1811 and 1816.[1] As his well-known views of the New Mills (which were located at St. Martin's) indicate, the area was relatively built up by 1810, and it is inconceivable that this work in fact represents the spot. Weak in conception and laboured in execution, LL 3697 appears to be a fanciful composition which betrays very little understanding of Crome and attempts to fabricate a standard and sentimental Norwich School scene. The use of a title so closely associated with Crome's *oeuvre* strengthens the likelihood that it is a deliberate forgery, probably dating from the later part of the 19th century.[2]

She tentatively proposed Crome's third son, William Henry Crome (1806-67), as the painter of LL 3663, citing his fussy painting of foliage and his tendency to expose the bifurcations of branches high up in his trees. Confirmation of this, however, must await further study of W.H. Crome's oeuvre, which is at present little known.

3.   1910 Inventory p.31, valued at £400.

'John Crome'
1768-1821

St. Martin's at Oak, Norwich
LL 3697 (WHL 540, H 17)
oil on canvas, 80 × 66.5 cm

An ink inscription on the centre stretcher bar which appears to date from the late 19th century reads as follows: *View in St. Martins at Oak/At Norwich by the [?late]/John Crome.* A district in the north-western part of the old city on the river Wensum, St. Martin's at Oak was a favourite

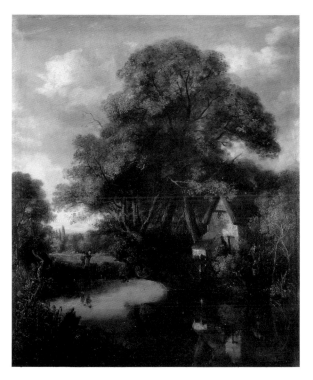

'J. Crome': *St. Martin's at Oak, Norwich*
LL 3697

PROVENANCE:
[…?]Thomas Churchyard; Spelman
2 July 1872(96) (*Bath House, St. Martin-
at-Oak*)³];…Gooden & Fox; bt. by Lever
November 1904 (£1,350).

REFERENCES:
1. N. Goldberg: *John Crome the Elder*
(1978) Vol.1, pp.128-31.
2. Tatlock, p.91, attributed LL 3697 to
John Berney Crome, but its quality is too
poor for it to be his work.
3. A. Graves: *Art Sales from Early in the
Eighteenth Century to Early in the
Twentieth Century* (1918-21) Vol 1, p.186.
LL 3697 is very conjecturally this work but
it has not apparently been identified as
any other St. Martin's subject.

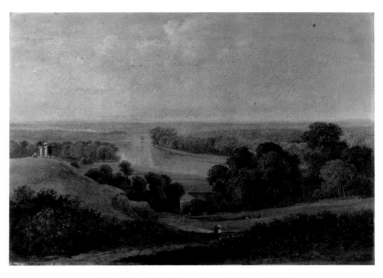

'P. De Wint:' *The Thames from Richmond Hill*
LL 3722

'Peter De Wint'
1784-1849

The Thames
from Richmond Hill
LL 3722 (WHL 693, H 68)
oil on canvas, 36.5 × 53 cm

Stylistic comparison of LL 3722 with
known oils by De Wint, especially his
Thames-side subjects,[1] suggests that
it is not autograph: the selection of a
'classic' landscape motif is highly
uncharacteristic, the response is
conventional and the handling
pedestrian. There are nevertheless
passages, notably the glassy stretch
of water and the tiny, rather distinct
figures, where the affinity to De
Wint's work is much closer. The
artist's grand-daughter, to whom
descended most of the oils discovered in De Wint's attic after his
death,[2] lent a *Thames, Richmond* to
the 1884 De Wint centenary
exhibition organised by J. and W.
Vokins.[3] Although it is not known
whether that work was an oil, it is
barely possible that LL 3722 may be
related to it.

PROVENANCE:
…James Orrock; Christie 4-6 June 1904
(322) bt. in; bt. from Orrock by Lever
November 1904.[4]

REFERENCES:
1. For two of these, *The Thames Near
Cliveden* and *Cliveden on Thames* see
H. Smith: *Peter De Wint* (1982) plates 70
and 71; other De Wint oils are reproduced
as pls.9, 69 and 72-76. Five oils in the
collection of the Usher Gallery, Lincoln
are reproduced in *Catalogue of the Usher
Art Gallery Collection of Works by Peter
De Wint* (1947); for reproductions of the
eight oils in the Victoria and Albert
Museum (which include one of the
Cliveden paintings) see R. Parkinson:
*Victoria and Albert Museum Catalogue of
British Oil Paintings 1820-1860* (1990)
pp.68-71.
2. W. Armstrong: *Memoir of Peter De
Wint* (1888) p.44.
3. Cat. 3. Smith, *op. cit.*, prints as
appendices the catalogue of the Vokins
exhibition, the artist's studio sale
catalogue, Christie 22-28 May 1850, and
a list of works by De Wint in public
collections; no other works titled *The
Thames, Richmond* (or similar) appear.
4. 1904 Inventory p.3, no.68.

Edward Duncan
1803-1882

Shrimpers, South Coast of Wales
LL 3704 (WHL 594, HH 152)
oil on panel, 25.5 × 35.5 cm
signed and dated *E. Duncan/1849*
(lower left)

From a label on the reverse it is
possible to identify LL 3704 as
Duncan's exhibit *Shrimpers, Coast
of Wales* at the Royal Manchester
Institution in 1849.[1] The exact
location of the view cannot certainly
be established, but Duncan painted
many oils and watercolours on the
coast of Gower, and around 1849
exhibited views of Rhosili Bay,
Llanrhidian Sands, Penclawdd and
Mumbles Head. The land mass in the
background of LL 3704 has been
described as fitting very well 'the
outline of Mumbles Hill behind
Southend, seen obliquely from
somewhere between Oystermouth
and Norton. The lighthouse island is
not obvious at this angle and would
be masked by the foreground when

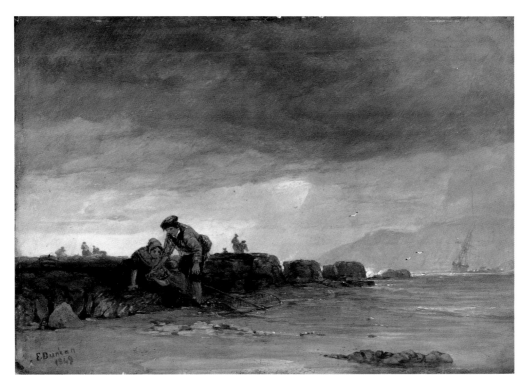

E. Duncan: *Shrimpers, South Coast of Wales*
LL 3704

seen from this low viewpoint'.[2] The ship in the right middle-ground has been beached rather than wrecked and a horse is loading or unloading coal or limestone: this was a practice common on the Gower coast until the late 19th century and certainly took place at Mumbles. The foreground, however, with its shelf of flat rocks, is likely to be invented.[3]

PROVENANCE:
[?Duncan's studio sale, Christie 9-12 March 1883 (386) (*Cockle Gatherers: Coast of Gower, South Wales, Dated 1849*) bt. Durham (£31.10.-)[4];...James Orrock; bt. from Orrock by Lever 1910.[5]

EXHIBITION:
Royal Manchester Institution 1849 (204).

REFERENCES:
1. The text of the label reads: *No.2 Shrimpers/South Coast of Wales/E. Duncan/ 2 Mornington Place/Hampstead Rd/London.*

2. Bernard Morris, letter, 7 May 1998, gallery files, communicated by Alison Lloyd, Glynn Vivian Art Gallery, Swansea.
3. Morris, *loc. cit.*
4. The only other possibility at this sale, rather less likely, is lot 385: *Cockle Gatherers, Llanrhidian sands, early morning, Dated 1849* bt. Vivian (£45.3.-.). Records of sales at the 1849 Manchester exhibition have not survived in the Institution's papers.
5. 1910 Inventory p.54, *Coast Scene with Figures*, valued at £10.

Gainsborough Dupont
1757-1797

The Gadshill Oak
LL 3586 (WHL 3846)
oil on canvas, 129 × 102.5 cm

Lever acquired LL 3586 as by Thomas Gainsborough. Although the work is closely dependent on Gainsborough's landscape idiom, both stylistic considerations and the nature of the painting technique[1] suggest it is not by him. It has now been convincingly re-attributed to his nephew, Gainsborough Dupont.[2]

The traditional title, which dates at least from the work's appearance at the Wynn Ellis sale, and was possibly already given to it at the (unknown) date when Ellis acquired it, has been retained. Gadshill is a small village in Kent near Gravesend

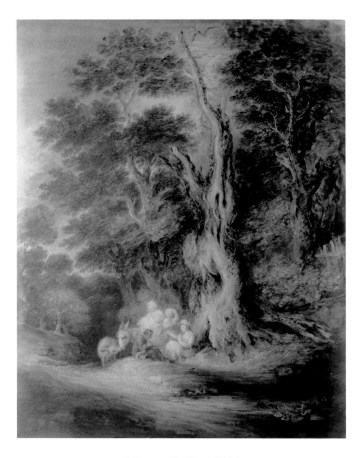

G. Dupont: *The Gadshill Oak*
LL 3586

with literary associations: Gadshill
Place was to be the house of Charles
Dickens, and Gadshill was the site
of the robbery, in which Falstaff was
tricked by Prince Hal, in Act 2
Scene 2 of Shakespeare's *King
Henry IV Part I*. Nevertheless,
neither Gainsborough nor Dupont is
associated with literary titles, and the
painting is really a straightforward
exercise in the late 18th-century
picturesque.

PROVENANCE:
…Wynn Ellis; Christie 6 May 1876 (62)
bt. Permain (310 gns.);…Sir Frederick
Thorpe Mappin; Christie 17 June 1910
(28) bt. Agnew (360 gns.); bt. from Agnew
by the Hon. Charles Lawrence, 2 August
1911;…T. McLean (Cremetti &
McLean);[3] bt. from McLean by Lever
5 June 1919 (£2,750).

REFERENCES:
1. LL 3586 was cleaned and restored in
1963 when it was noted that 'excessive use
of a lead drier' added to the paint medium
to shorten drying time (a practice
uncharacteristic of Gainsborough) had
caused severe cracking and continued
pliancy of the paint layer (condition
report, gallery files).
2. J. Hayes: *The Landscape Paintings of
Thomas Gainsborough* (1982) Vol.1,
p.194; catalogue of Dupont's works no.15.
Hayes titles the work *A Wooded
Landscape with a Peasant Family and
Animals Resting beside a Winding Track*.
In his view, it pre-dates the *Shepherd Boy*
exhibited by Dupont at the Royal
Academy in 1794.
3. McLean's copy invoice, gallery files,
states that the painting came from the
collection of [Charles] Fairfax Murray,
while a further note in gallery files

indicates that Lawrence sold the painting
privately in November 1917, but no
corroboration has been found for this
information.

William Etty
1787-1849

Cleopatra's Arrival in Cilicia
LL 3589 (WHL 169, H 350)
oil on canvas, 106.5 × 132.5 cm

Titled as above when exhibited at
the 1821 Royal Academy, LL 3589 has
also frequently been known as *The
Triumph of Cleopatra*.[1] In the RA
catalogue the title was accompanied
by the following quotations:
> 'She sailed along the river Cydnus in
> a magnificent galley; the stern was
> covered with gold, the sails were of
> purple and the oars were of silver;
> these, in their motion, kept time to the
> music of flutes, and pipes and harps.
> The Queen, in the dress and character
> of Venus, lay under a canopy
> embroidered with gold, while boys,
> like painted cupids, stood fanning her
> at each side of the sofa. Her maids,
> habited like the Nereids and the
> Graces, assisted in the steerage and
> conduct of the vessel. The fragrance of
> incense, vast quantities of which were
> burnt on the deck, was diffused along
> the shores, which were covered with
> people.'

Plutarch: *Life of Antony*[2]
> 'The sails were purple, and so
> perfumed, the Winds were love-sick
> with them'

Shakespeare:
Antony and Cleopatra[3]

The occasion is Cleopatra's arrival
for her momentous first meeting with
Mark Antony, which in history took
place in 42 BC at Tarsus, in Asia
Minor.

The painting was commissioned
by Sir Francis Freeling (1764-1836),
Secretary to the Post Office, after he
had failed to acquire Etty's chief
exhibit at the previous year's Royal
Academy, *The Coral Finder* (private
collection London in 1955).[4]

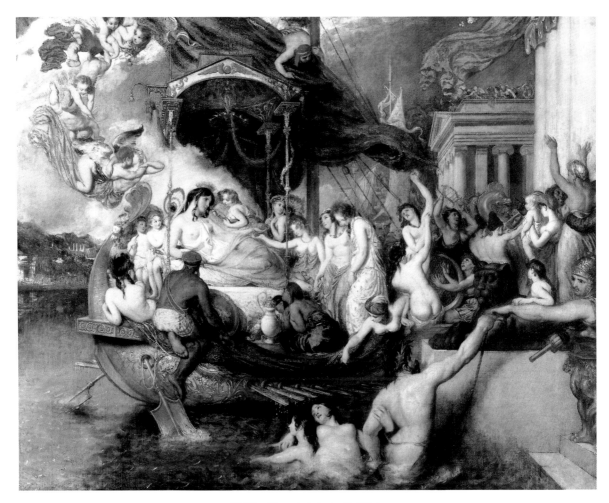

W. Etty: *Cleopatra's Arrival in Cilicia*
LL 3589

Freeling's commission may have specified a work of similar character, for although LL 3589 is a larger and far more ambitious painting, elements of the handling are notably similar. The imbalance of scale between the central figure and her vessel and companions; the treatment of the figures in the water, the putti in the sky, the flying drapery, and the distant cluster of classical buildings are all pre-figured in the earlier work. Etty is said to have had the subject in mind for some time previously and the example of Jean-Baptiste Regnault, with whom he

had studied briefly in Paris in 1816, has been proposed for his handling of a multi-figure composition in a shallow space.[5] The influence of Venetian painting generally and of Titian's *Rape of Europa* in particular, as well as of Rubens's *Landing of Marie de Medici* (Louvre), above all on the foreground figures, has also been noted.[6]

This was probably the single most significant work in the establishment of Etty's reputation. As Etty himself later put it in his *Autobiography*:

'It made a great impression in my favour. Sir Thomas (Lawrence)

jocularly said to me of it: 'They, *the public*, leave Marc Antony' – meaning himself – 'whistling in the market place, and go to gaze on your Cleopatra'. 'The Old Times' even deigned to notice me, though as much in the shape of a castigation as any other; but still the *Times* noticed me. I felt my chariot wheels were on the right road to fame and honour, and I now drove on like another Jehu'.[7]

In fact, *The Times* did not review the 1821 Royal Academy and Etty was probably recalling its article of 29 January 1822 which, after noting that Etty had 'got some reputation for painting *Cleopatra's Galley*', went on to criticise as indecent his next major work, *Cupid and Psyche Descending*. This work, as the *Cleopatra* had been, was a commission from Freeling; and it may have been owing to *The Times*'s remarks that Freeling asked Etty to paint drapery on some of the figures in LL 3589; although in 1829 he changed his mind and allowed the artist to return the work to its original state.[8]

At the Royal Academy, LL 3589 was noticed favourably by the *Morning Post*, which included it among 'the best of the fancy subjects'[9] and by the *Gentleman's Magazine*, which observed that 'in the school of painting, there are some pieces belonging to the highest class. Of these, the first is Etty's classical picture of Cleopatra's arrival in Cilicia'.[10] (*The Observer*, by contrast, thought that 'there is nothing which deserves the name of an historical picture, and indeed, not many which aspire to it').[11] The longest review, which appeared in the *Examiner*, began by pointing out the difficulty of the subject and comparing Etty unfavourably to Titian and Rubens, who themselves 'sometimes failed to give such subjects due effect. It would have been next to a miracle then, if an early practitioner amongst us in that school, were not found much wanting …'. After criticising the painting as defective in character and drawing, and Cleopatra for being 'scarcely voluptuous', the review conceded that the work had 'grace' and 'is well worthy of the possession, and must obtain the admiration of the tasteful for its composition and colour'. 'The opposition, agreement, and splendour of colour,' it concluded, 'cannot fail of affording much pleasure'.[12] C.R. Leslie, in a letter to Washington Irving, also described LL 3589 as 'a splendid triumph of colour', adding: 'It has some defects of composition, but is full of passages of that exquisite kind

of beauty which he alone can give.'[13]

Numerous preparatory works for LL 3589 are known. These include three sheets of studies in pencil for the figure of Cleopatra and her attendants,[14] and a study in sepia ink on tracing paper of the same subject,[15] which are in the Victoria and Albert Museum. Two oil studies, one 'for the sailor in his great picture of Cleopatra', and one of oval format have remained untraced since the last century.[16]

PROVENANCE:
Sir Francis Freeling; Christie 15 April 1837 (92) bt. Farrer (210 gns.); bt. from Farrer by Henry Labouchère, later Lord Taunton;[17] R.K. Hodgson; Christie 26 June 1880 (120) bt. in; Christie 2 April 1881 (279) bt. Marsden (430 gns.); J. Pearson; Christie 9 June 1883 (275) bt. Mrs Fielden (300 gns.); Christie 28 April 1888 (57) bt. McLean (? for Mrs Sanderson);[18] Arthur Sanderson; Knight Frank & Rutley 16 June 1911 (631) bt. Gooden & Fox (£252) for Lever.

EXHIBITIONS:
RA 1821 (261); BI 1825 (99); Royal Scottish Academy 1846 (342); *Modern Artists* Royal Manchester Institution 1846 (266); *Etty* Society of Arts 1849 (CV); *Art Treasures* Manchester 1857 (249); *International Exhibition* 1862 (374); *Old Masters* RA 1872 (23); *British Art 1830-1850* Whitechapel Art Gallery 1920 (27); *Bicentenary Exhibition* RA 1968-69 (225).

REFERENCES:
1. This title seems to have first been used at the Christie's sale in 1881 (see provenance above).
2. Plutarch: *Life of Antony*, XXVI 1-3.
3. Shakespeare: *Antony and Cleopatra*, Act 2, Scene 2, lines 193-4.
4. D. Farr: *William Etty* (1958) p.29. According to A. Gilchrist: *Life of William Etty RA* (1855) Vol.I, p.95, Etty's price for LL 3589 was 200 guineas but he actually received 'a much smaller sum'.
5. Farr, *loc. cit.*
6. Farr, *op. cit.*, p.30.
7. *Art Journal* (1849) p.37.
8. Farr, *op. cit.*, p.31; see also Gilchrist, *loc. cit.*

9. *Morning Post* (5 May 1821) p.3.
10. *Gentleman's Magazine* Vol.XCI (May 1821) p.446. Etty and his painting were the only artist and work to be mentioned by name in this brief note about the exhibition.
11. *The Observer* (11 June 1821).
12. *The Examiner* (3 June 1821) pp.346-7.
13. T. Taylor, ed.: *Autobiographical Recollections of C.R. Leslie* (1860) Vol.II, p.114.
14. Farr, *op. cit.*, p.141; two of these are his cats. 47(b) and (c); the third (V & A 7652.42, on a sheet with an 1817 watermark, which possibly confirms the notion that LL 3689 was as much as four years in gestation) is unlisted by Farr.
15. Farr, *op. cit.*, p.141, cat.47a.
16. Sold respectively at Christie 3 June 1842 (94) bt. Fuller (8 gns.); and Christie 15 February 1868 (304) bt. Vokins (22 gns.).
17. According to Gilchrist, *loc. cit.*, Labouchère paid Farrer 1000 guineas. The work was seen in Labouchère's collection, at Stoke near Windsor in 1851, by Waagen, who wrote: 'a rich and poetic composition, of great force and transparency of colour, which, in the Amorini floating in the air, approaches Rubens. Nor has the keeping of this picture lost by any subsequent darkening' (G. Waagen: *Treasures of Art in Great Britain* (1854) Vol.II, p.423). In 1866, on the other hand, the Redgraves wrote that the picture 'has suffered much since it was executed', pointing out that 'it is traditionally said to have been painted with a large addition of wax to the medium'. They concluded that 'even now the flesh painting maintains as happy a medium between the silvery hue and the rosy as it is possible to achieve.' (R. and S. Redgrave: *A Century of British Painters* (1947 edition) p.285).
18. Farr, *op. cit.*, p.141 states only that McLean was the purchaser; the provenance in gallery files gives 'Mrs. S.' as the purchaser.

William Etty
1787-1849

The Judgment of Paris
LL 3588 (WHL 642, HH 1466)
oil on canvas, 183.5 × 277 cm

This work was commissioned from Etty in 1825 by John, 4th Earl of Darnley, who had been impressed by the artist's *The Combat* (National Gallery of Scotland), shown at that year's Royal Academy exhibition. The subject was selected by Darnley from a number proposed by Etty; a price of £500 was agreed, and Etty devoted much of late 1825 and early 1826 to work on the painting[1]. It was exhibited at the Royal Academy in 1826 under the title *The Choice of Paris*, which was accompanied in the catalogue by the following quotation:

''The Goddess of Discord, insenced [sic] at not being invited to the marriage of Peleus and Thetis, threw into the assembly of the Gods who were at the entertainment, a golden apple, on which was inscribed 'To the fairest'. All the Goddesses claimed it as their own but at last only three, Juno, Venus and Minerva, wished to dispute their respective right to beauty, and the Gods unwilling to become arbiters in an affair so delicate, appointed Paris, a Phrygian shepherd, son of Priam, to adjudge the prize. Each tried by promises and entreaties to gain the attention of Paris, and influence his judgment. After he had heard their several claims and promises, Paris adjudged the prize to Venus and gave her the golden apple.' The figures in the background are Nymphs presiding over rocks and fountains; a Satyr &c'.

A number of visual sources for Etty's treatment of the subject have been identified.[2] The finished painting repeats, in the order of the central group of protagonists, the scheme of Raphael's *Judgment of Paris*, which was well-known through the engraving by Marcantonio Raimondi. These figures are, from left to right: Paris, offering the apple; Hermes (or Mercury), the messenger of the Gods; Athena (or Minerva), Goddess of Wisdom; Aphrodite (or Venus), Goddess of Love, accompanied by Eros in the form of a Cupid; and finally Hera (or Juno), Goddess of Marriage and Women. The pose of the latter, seen from the back and holding her robe to the right-hand side, is only slightly varied by Etty but the poses of the other figures, for which numerous preparatory studies are known,[3] have been more thoroughly re-invented. Also present in Marcantonio's engraving

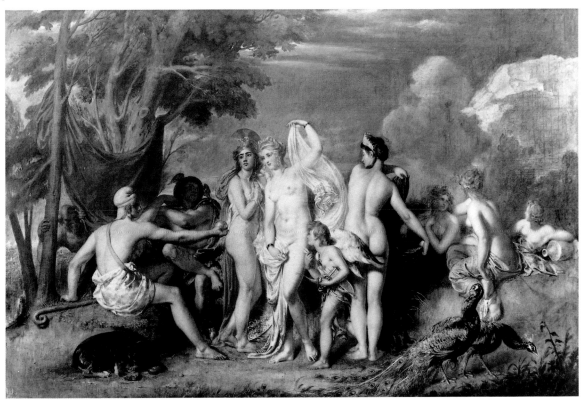

W. Etty: *The Judgment of Paris*
LL 3588

are a clump of trees on the left-hand side; a dog; a peacock; the Goddesses' attendants and a group of satyrs, elements which Etty has varied but retained.[4] Flaxman's engraving of the *Judgment of Paris* in his 1793 illustrations to Homer's *Iliad* (which Etty is known to have owned) may be the source for the treatment of Athena's helmet and Hera's diadem and straightened right arm. Etty is also thought to have drawn on Rubens's paintings of the *Judgment of Paris* (National Gallery, London and Prado, Madrid)[5] and, for the idea of the satyr peeping through the branches of a tree, on Mengs's *Judgment of Paris* (Hermitage, St. Petersburg) or a prototype by Poussin.[6]

Despite, or perhaps because of, the availability of such precedents, and perhaps also because Etty had had the subject in his mind for a long time already,[7] work on LL 3588 does not seem to have proceeded smoothly. Lord Darnley is said to have continually urged changes,[8] and the canvas gives the impression of having been worked on piecemeal. This is suggested by the existence of numerous pentimenti (for example in the positioning of Aphrodite's raised arm, of Athena's drape over her shoulder, and of the feet of the seated nymph at right); as well as by the unresolved appearance of several of the subsidiary figures and the large bare areas in the fore-ground and the right-hand side. It seems clear that Etty either lost patience or simply ran out of time before the sending-in day for the 1826 Royal Academy.

The painting's unfinished appearance seems however not to have been noticed at the exhibition and the work was generally admired. *The Times* praised its 'brilliant and harmonious colouring, combined with graceful and careful execution, such as no artist of the present day

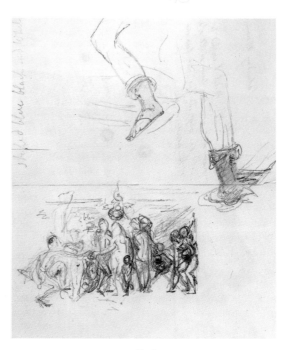

Fig.8
W. Etty: *Composition study for 'The Judgment of Paris', and other studies*
© The British Museum

can equal'.[9] The critic for the *Examiner* wrote that 'our ambitious painter has conquered nearly all with his masculine powers, for it not only provokes comparison with some fine old pictures – having been a favourite and frequent subject – but its large masses of flesh-colour and many naked figures demand great knowledge of the human form and its various tintings and character.' After observing that Etty's Venus was 'wanting in those potent charms, at which assembled Olympus was wont to gaze' and criticising the 'awkward' placing of her right hand ('to obviate a difficulty which might, we apprehend, have been otherwise subdued'), he concluded that: 'were the Muses to pass through the exhibition to see what Artists they have inspired, they would stop to admire this picture'.[10]

The work's reception may have persuaded Etty that he did not need to do any more work on the canvas,

but Lord Darnley remained unwilling to pay for the picture or take delivery of it. He allowed Etty to exhibit the work again at the British Institution in 1827 but told him that he wanted him to make alterations to it before he showed it again, and also hinted that he was already thinking of disposing of it. After the 1827 exhibition Etty had to store the painting in a warehouse. By 1829 he had received four hundred pounds from Darnley (after having written to him four times) but it was 1831 before Darnley agreed to take the work. After his death in the same year Etty wrote several times to his son to claim the balance due to him, eventually agreeing to take £75 in July 1834.[11] The work leapt to prominence in the following decade with its sale for £1500 in 1843 (see provenance) and it may have been this which led Joseph Gillott to commission from Etty a second *Judgment of Paris* (RA 1846; private collection, Yorkshire 1955)[12] for which the artist re-used some of his preparatory studies for LL 3588.[13]

PROVENANCE:
4th Earl of Darnley;'sold by auction, after the decease of Lord Darnley, at the gallery of Mr Rainy'[14] (in 1838; bt. in (£230));[15] bt. by C.W. Wass; bt. from Wass by Andrew Fountaine, 1843 (£1500);[16] Christie 7 July 1894 (2) bt. in (£500); Mrs Fountaine 1910;[17] bt. from Mrs Fountaine through the Corporation of York by Lever April 1911 (£500).

EXHIBITIONS:
RA 1826 (24); BI 1827 (312) *Etty* Society of Arts 1849 (CII); *Etty* York 1910 (118); *First Hundred Years* RA 1951-52 (240); *Etty* Arts Council 1955 (13, withdrawn); *Bicentenary Exhibition* RA 1968-69 (222).

ENGRAVING:
C.W. Wass, for *Art Union Journal* (1847) repr. fp.224.

REFERENCES:
1. A. Gilchrist: *Life of William Etty RA* (1855) Vol.I, p.233.
2. D. Farr: *William Etty* (1958) pp.49-50.
3. Farr, *op. cit.*, p.147, cats. 65a (private collection), 65c, 65d and 65e (British Museum).
4. Two oil studies of a peacock, one in the Tate Gallery, one in Manchester City Art Gallery (Farr, *op. cit.*, p.180, cats. 282 and 284) are likely to be associated with LL 3588 although the Tate one faces the opposite way and the pose of the bird in the Manchester picture is more exactly followed in Etty's 1846 *Judgment of Paris* (see main text above).
5. Of the two Rubens paintings of the subject in the National Gallery, the earlier and less familiar (No.6379, which was acquired by the Gallery only in 1966) had been offered and bought in at a sale at Christie in 1815. The fact that this painting re-appeared in the mid-20th century in a collection in York, Etty's home town, has led to some speculation that it might have been known to Etty there (see G. Martin: *National Gallery Catalogues: The Flemish School* (1970) p.215). The later and better-known work (No.194, acquired by the Gallery in 1844) had been part of the celebrated Orleans collection imported into England in 1792 and had been

offered for sale by its then owner, Lord Kinnaird, at Phillips in 1813. In contrast to the other picture, this one would have been available to Etty as an engraving (Martin, *op. cit.*, pp.156-158). Etty cannot have seen the Madrid painting in the flesh, and although A.C. Tait (note in gallery files) claimed that the main figures in LL 3588 derive from it, the relationship is not especially striking. The Orleans canvas reverses the direction of the figures so that the goddesses appear on the left and Paris and Mercury on the right, and the only obvious similarity between it and LL 3588 is the inclusion of a magnificent peacock, very similarly posed to the lower of Etty's two. The grouping and general disposition of the three goddesses in the early London Rubens, on the other hand, is distinctly reminiscent of that in LL 3588, as is the expression of the watching satyr; while one of Etty's preparatory sketches for the whole composition (British Museum, fig.8; Farr, *op. cit.*, p.147, cat.65b) includes a flying putto crowning Aphrodite whose place in the design recalls Rubens's treatment in the early painting (the motif itself, however, appears in both his other canvases, as well as the engravings by Raimondi and Flaxman). For the relation of Etty's interim sketches to Rubens's works, see Farr, *op. cit.*, p.147.
6. Farr, *op. cit.*, p.50.
7. Two sheets of preparatory sketches in the Victoria and Albert Museum (Farr, *op. cit.*, p.147, cats. 65f and 65g) are thought to date from around 1821-23. One (7650.125, Farr 65f) is a group of pencil studies drawn on an envelope addressed to Harry D'Orville, Consul in Venice during Etty's Italian journey of 1821-23; this includes whole-composition sketches considerably removed from the final 1826 design (although closer to the version Etty painted in 1846). The other (7653.35, Farr 65g) is a drawing in red waxed crayon on oiled paper, which has been identified (note in the Victoria and Albert Museum sheaf catalogue) as having been used originally in connection with the *Cupid and Psyche* of 1821. The sketches for the *Judgment of Paris* on this sheet are again much closer to the 1846 version.
8. Gilchrist, *op. cit.*, Vol.I, p.234.
9. *The Times* (29 April 1826); quoted by Farr, *op. cit.*, p.49.

10. *Examiner* (14 May 1826) p.306. John Constable, writing to his friend John Fisher on 26 April 1826, dryly observed of that year's newly-hung exhibition: 'Canning is over the fireplace, a dead Christ by Westall at the bottom of the Room, and a Group of Naked Women & peacocks on the west side centre' (R.B. Beckett, ed.: *John Constable's Correspondence*, Vol.6 (1968) p.220).
11. For the work's history 1826-1834 see Gilchrist, *op. cit.*, Vol.I, pp.234-5; see also Farr, *op. cit.*, p.50.
12. Farr, *op. cit.*, p.147, cat.66.
13. See note 7 above.
14. *Art Union Journal* (1847) p.224.
15. Gilchrist, *op. cit.*, Vol.II, p.80. It is unclear from Gilchrist's and the *Art Union Journal*'s accounts whether the work was bought in on behalf of the Darnley family or for Rainy himself. The 5th Earl of Darnley had died in February 1835 and his heir was still a child; presumably the work was consigned by the Countess of Darnley.
16. According to the *Art Journal* (1849) p.40 (in a footnote to Etty's *Autobiography*) Wass still owned the work then, but this is clearly an error; see *Art Union Journal* (1847) *loc. cit.*
17. Lent by Mrs Fountaine to the York exhibition (label on the reverse of LL 3588, stating also that the work was for sale at £500). Farr, *op. cit.*, p.147 states that the work was bought at the 1894 sale by Chester and subsequently re-acquired by Mrs Fountaine, but it seems most likely that the work was bought in on her behalf.

William Etty
1787-1849

Prometheus
LL 3590 (WHL 2849)
oil on oak panel, 70.5 × 77.5 cm

The traditional title of LL 3590 has been retained, although, as has been pointed out, Prometheus was not shot by an arrow: his liver was pecked by a griffon vulture.[1] The presence of pencil underdrawing around the outline of the figure, and the academic nature of the pose, suggest

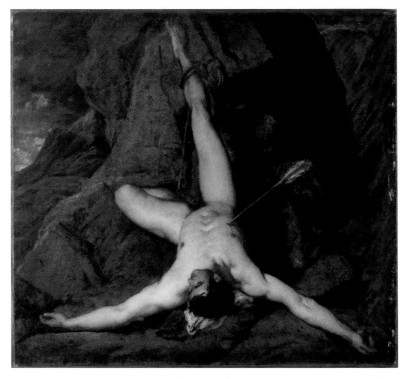

W. Etty: *Prometheus*
LL 3590

that the work originated as an exercise in the life-class. From the style, it has been dated to the second half of the 1820s.[2]

A long-standing tradition exists that (as with many of his academic studies) Etty did not finish the work and that the background was painted by John Linnell (1792-1882). This was stated in the E.M. Ward sale catalogue of 1879 and may well derive from Ward himself, who as a colleague of both men in the Royal Academy from the 1840s would have been in a good position to know the facts. Nevertheless, close examination of LL 3590 fails to yield clear-cut physical evidence of Linnell's involvement and the story may be apocryphal.[3]

PROVENANCE:
[? Etty's studio sale, Christie 7-10 May 1850 (5), (299) or (582)[4]]; ... E.M. Ward, RA; Christie 29 March 1879 (115) bt. Hooper (4 gns.); ... A.W. Pearce; Christie 5 March 1910 (37) bt. Wallis (10 gns.); Christie 14 July 1916 (100) bt. Gooden & Fox for Lever (7 gns.).

REFERENCES:
1. D. Farr: *William Etty* (1958) p.152, cat.81, noting that an arrow shot by Hercules killed the vulture.
2. Farr, *loc. cit.*
3. Farr, *loc. cit.*, observes that there seems little justification for it. Conceivably, Linnell may have enjoyed a reputation for painting in the backgrounds of works by his colleagues; he had for example repainted the sky in Constable's first version of *A Summerland* (for which see G. Reynolds: *The Early Paintings and Drawings of John Constable* (1996) p.189, cat.14.1). More noteworthy is a passage in Gilchrist's *Life of William Etty RA*, published in 1855 (Vol.II, p.309): 'even the landscape of a Linnell is beside the mark as the proxy of one of Etty's grandly

conceived, grandly coloured backgrounds ... the Promethean art to fix such shadows of Nature is not an everyday acquirement or endowment'; this seems as if it might be a veiled allusion to LL 3590. For the tradition that other artists completed Etty's studies '*pictorially*! for the dealers' see R. and S. Redgrave: *A Century of British Painters* (1866; 1947 edition) p.284.
4. Lot 5 was *A man transfixed by an arrow – foreshortened* bt. Roake (£3.12.-.); lot 299 was *Prometheus – finely foreshortened* bt. Weeks (5 gns.) (both of which are described as being on millboard, whereas LL 3590 is on a half inch-thick oak panel); lot 582 was *A man transfixed by an arrow – finely foreshortened* bt. Colls (7 gns.) None of these works is described as being completed by Linnell. The titles of lots 5 and 582 argue that Etty painted the arrow in LL 3590, and this certainly appears to be painted over the rock behind it.

William Etty
1787-1849

Andromeda

LL 3594 (WHL 2854)
oil on millboard, 67 × 50.5 cm

It has been suggested that LL 3594 may be a preliminary idea for Etty's *Britomart Redeems Faire Amoret* (Tate Gallery, fig.9; formerly in the Lady Lever Art Gallery), which was exhibited at the Royal Academy in 1833.[1] Although neither the scale nor the pose of the figure is comparable to that of Amoret, LL 3594 does seem closer in style to Etty's works of this period than to the thematically related *Andromeda – Perseus Coming to Her Rescue* exhibited at the Royal Academy in 1840.[2]

On the reverse of LL 3594 is a black chalk study of a male nude figure holding an arrow, together with two smaller female figures (fig.10). No painting by Etty has emerged which relates to these. Their presence, and the existence of pencil

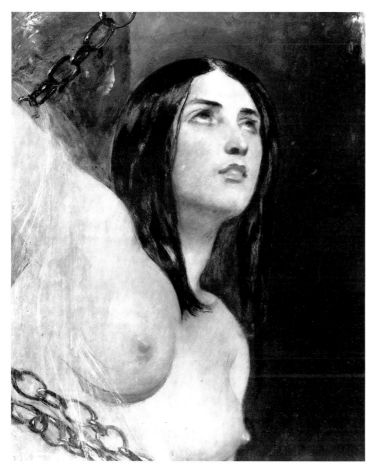

W. Etty: *Andromeda*
LL 3594

exhibited in *Etty*, York 1949 (19); c) *Andromeda, Perseus Coming to Her Rescue*, 32 × 25 in., RA 1840 (private collection) and d) *Andromeda and Perseus*, 30 × 24 in. (Manchester City Art Gallery). Perhaps to be identified with (b) are either *Andromeda Chained to the Rocks*, 27 × 20 in., sold at Sotheby 26 June 1968 (155) and again 26 July 1978 (98), or alternatively the *Andromeda*, 24 × 20 in. sold at Sotheby New York 23 October 1983 (246) both of which, from photographs, appear to be autograph works by Etty.

3.   That Huth's painting is identical with the one owned by Reade, and that this was bought in for 10 guineas at Reade's sale (*pace* Farr, *loc. cit.*) is confirmed by an annotation in the auctioneer's copy of the 1916 sale catalogue in Christie's archives. Three further 19th-century appearances of Ettys titled *Andromeda* probably do not relate to LL 3594: (i) the *Andromeda* sold from the estate of George Knott at Christie 26 April 1845 (52) bt. Rought (210 gns.) seems (title notwithstanding) certainly to have been the *Andromeda, Perseus Coming to Her Rescue* shown at the Royal Academy in 1840, since Gilchrist (*Life of William Etty RA* (1855) Vol.II, p.204) describes Knott's painting as having been 'obtained from the painter at first hand … five years before'. (ii) the *Andromeda* lent by Daniel Thwaites to the Royal Jubilee Exhibition in

underdrawing under the figure of Andromeda, suggests that Etty simply worked the painting up on a board originally taken to study in the life-class.

PROVENANCE:
… Charles Reade; Christie 18 May 1885 (243) bt. in (10 gns.); … Alexander Huth;[3] Christie 14 July 1916 (128) bt. Gooden & Fox for Lever (10 gns.).

REFERENCES:
1.   D. Farr: *William Etty* (1958) p.139.
2.   Farr, *loc. cit.*, lists a total four works by Etty titled either *Andromeda* or *Perseus and Andromeda*, as follows: a) LL 3594; b) *Andromeda*, panel, 25½ × 19½ in. [i.e. fractionally smaller than LL 3594] whose history is unknown prior to 1936; this was

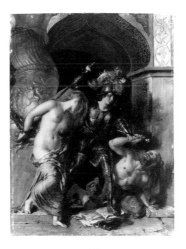

Fig.9
W. Etty: *Britomart Redeems Faire Amoret*
© Tate Gallery London

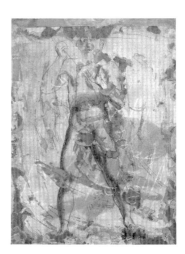

Fig.10
W. Etty: *Andromeda*; sketch on the reverse of a man holding an arrow
Lady Lever Art Gallery

Manchester in 1887 is identified by Farr, *loc. cit.*, as the same work, although the evidence for this does not appear watertight; (iii) an *Andromeda* was sold by Agnew on 23 May 1853 to Rought (Agnew's stockbooks) but the high price of £525 suggests a more ambitious work than LL 3594.

William Etty
1787-1849

Hesperus
LL 3592 (WHL 4111)
oil on canvas, 89.5 × 173.5 cm

In May 1843 Etty was one of eight artists commissioned by Prince Albert for frescoes to decorate the walls in his new garden pavilion in the grounds of Buckingham Palace. Etty fulfilled his commission in July with his fresco *Circe and the Sirens* (untraced; oil version in the Art Gallery of Western Australia, Perth, fig. 11); but by the following February, when he was still re-touching the work, he had become dissatisfied with it, and shortly afterwards applied to the Prince to be permitted to paint a replacement. LL 3592 is his full-scale oil version (including the spandrels) of this proposed replacement. It was exhibited at the Royal Academy in 1844.[1]

Both subjects, as the original commission required, are taken from Milton's masque *Comus* (1634). LL 3592 illustrates a passage from the Attendant Spirit's Epilogue (lines 981-985 and 998-1005; the first two lines were quoted in the RA exhibition catalogue):

'…All amidst the gardens fair
Of Hesperus and his daughters three
That sing about the golden tree;
Along the crisped shades and bowers
Revels the spruce and jocund
Spring…

Beds of hyacinth and roses
Where young Adonis oft reposes
Waxing well of his deep wound,
In slumber soft; and on the ground
Sadly sits the Assyrian queen;
But far above, in spangled sheen

Celestial Cupid, her famed son advanced
Holds his dear Psyche sweet entranced'[2]

In the centre of the composition the Hesperides (Etty has introduced a fourth daughter) dance in front of the apple tree; their father watches from behind on the left. Adonis and the Assyrian queen occupy the left foreground; Cupid and Psyche are on the right. The design is noticeably more sophisticated than that of the rather frieze-like and empty *Circe*.

Perhaps partly because it was accompanied at the Royal Academy by Maclise's and Leslie's studies for their frescoes, the three works dominating the East Room in the exhibition, LL 3592 received considerable attention from the critics. The most favourable reviews came from the *Examiner*, the *Illustrated London News* and the *Morning Chronicle*, the latter reporting: 'the painter has exhibited the gorgeous fancy and genius which distinguish him. The picture is full of

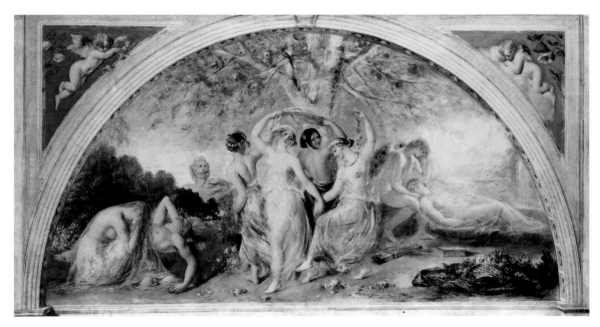

W. Etty: *Hesperus*
LL 3592

sunshine and a golden richness of voluptuous colour. The mystical notion conveyed in the lines is kept up somehow. You feel that you are looking at an enchanted ground; the colours are rich and indistinct, the figures dancing round in a haze and film, as one might see them in a dream of the enchanted place. The picture strikes us as being of the highest poetical order.'[3] Elsewhere, the response was more mixed. The *Spectator* described the work as 'sensual and smeary … with mannerism predominating',[4] while the *Observer* judged it as lacking sentiment, arrangement of parts and correctness of form, and said that 'were it not for the charm of the gorgeous but truthful colouring which is shed over all this incoherence and confusion, it would be, perhaps, one of the worst pictures in the collection'.[5] Perhaps the most balanced assessment came from the *Athenaeum*, which admired the 'luscious sweetness' of the central group and the 'fullness of sweet and melancholy grace' which had been lavished on the figures at either side, but also commented upon the 'meretricious slightness' of Etty's treatment and his 'recourse to effects and artifices of colour, … calculated we should imagine, seriously to impair the work, when it is abstracted from the transparencies and reflections of oil'.[6]

One further complimentary response to LL 3592, at the Royal Academy dinner in May 1844, came from Prince Albert himself,[7] whom Etty had primed by sending a preliminary sketch of his new idea for the fresco.[8] Although the chronological relationship between LL 3592 and the fresco is uncertain and it is possible that Etty had already begun work on the latter, it seems more likely that Etty took the Prince Consort's words at the dinner as encouragement to start. Whereas

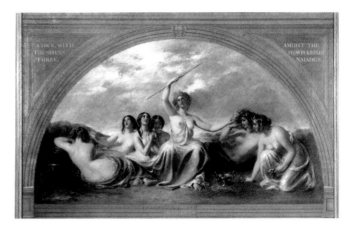

Fig.11
W. Etty: *Circe and the Sirens*
Art Gallery of Western Australia, Perth

most of the *Circe* fresco had been painted *in situ*, which had contributed to his difficulties, Etty executed the *Hesperus* fresco in his studio. In late June he was hoping to finish it, using wax, within a week; by early July it had been delivered to Prince Albert. It was rejected, and William Dyce was commissioned to replace Etty's fresco with one of his own.[9]

PROVENANCE:
bt. from Etty by Edwin Bullock;[10] Christie 21 May 1870 (116) bt. Agnew (1005 gns.); John Hargreaves; Christie 7 June 1873 (310) bt. Agnew (800 gns.); John Heugh;[11] … William Agnew 1891;[12] Mrs W. Agnew; Christie 27 February 1920 (133) bt. Gooden & Fox for Lever (£609).

EXHIBITIONS:
RA 1844 (152); Birmingham Society of Artists 1845 (107); *Old Masters* RA 1891 (13); *British Art 1830-1850* Whitechapel Art Gallery 1920 (77); *Yorkshire Artists 1600-1900* (CEMA) Leeds 1946 (12).

REFERENCES:
1. For the circumstances of the commission and Etty's difficulties with the fresco medium, see A. Gilchrist: *Life of William Etty RA* (1855) Vol.II, pp.149-153 and 162-171; W. Gaunt and F. Gordon Roe: *Etty and the Nude* (1943) pp.59-61; D. Farr: *William Etty* (1958) pp.95-97. See also L. Grüner and A. Jameson: *The Decorations of the Garden Pavilion in the Grounds of Buckingham Palace* (1846) and T.S.R. Boase: 'The Decoration of the New Palace of Westminster 1841-1863', *Journal of the Warburg and Courtauld Institutes*, Vol. XVII, Nos 3-4 (1954) pp.319-358. *Hesperus* is the title used by Etty in writing to Colonel Anson, Prince Albert's secretary (Gilchrist, *op. cit.*, Vol.II, p.166) but at the RA exhibition LL 3592 was titled *A Subject from Comus*.
2. An old label printed with these lines is stuck to the stretcher of LL 3592.
3. *Examiner* (18 May 1844) p.309; *Illustrated London News* (11 May 1844); *Morning Chronicle* (8 May 1844).
4. *Spectator* (11 May 1844) pp.450-1.
5. *Observer* (26 May 1844); compare *Art Union Journal* (June 1844) p.156: 'in considering this composition we are first struck by the extremely careless drawing everywhere prevalent, again by the total absence of grace in the Hesperides, and again by the extravagance of the entire composition … The proverb allowed Homer to sleep sometimes, but it must be feared that the slumbers of Mr Etty are mesmeric dozings.'
6. *Athenaeum* (11 May 1844) pp.432-3.
7. Etty to Robert Davies, York, letter, 12 May 1844 (Gilchrist, *op. cit.*, Vol.II, p.168).
8. Gilchrist, *op. cit.*, Vol.II, p.166 describes this as 'a sketch of great beauty, for the

group of *Daughters Three*'. It is presumably the lunette-shaped canvas (Farr, *op. cit.*, p.146, cat.63a as tempera on canvas, with oil on board spandrels) sold at Sotheby New York 12 May 1978 (311), there described as executed in gouache and chalk. Prince Albert is said to have glanced at the sketch and remarked: 'Poor man, he doesn't know what we want' (Gilchrist, *op. cit.*, Vol.II, p.169). A further small oil sketch of the whole composition (untraced), and four small sheets of sketches in pencil and pen, one for the whole composition and the others for details (Victoria and Albert Museum) are recorded (Farr, *op. cit.*, p.146, cats. 63b-f).

9. Gilchrist, *op. cit.*, Vol.II, pp.169-70; and see Farr, *op. cit.*, p.97 for Thackeray's response to the Prince Consort's conduct in *Fraser's Magazine*, 1845. The fresco itself is untraced since 1858, when it fetched 36½ guineas at William Wethered's sale (Farr, *op. cit.*, p.146).

10. Lent by Bullock to the Birmingham exhibition 1845.

11. Agnew's stockbooks.

12. Lent by Agnew to the Royal Academy exhibition 1891.

William Etty

1787-1849

Aurora and Zephyr

LL 3591 (WHL 4690)
oil on mahogany panel, 91 × 92.5 cm

Etty painted LL 3591 in 1845 and showed it at the Royal Academy that year. The subject is uncommon in Western art.[1] Etty may have intended a simple allegorical representation of daybreak: Aurora, the Goddess of Dawn, advances into the painting; Zephyrus, the personification of the west wind (and often said to be her son) ineffectually impedes her progress. In the RA exhibition catalogue however the title was accompanied by a quotation from Milton's poem *L'Allegro* (lines 18-20):

'The frolic wind that breathes the spring,

Zephyr with Aurora playing
As he met her once a Maying'

In Milton, the pair 'on beds of violets blue/And fresh-blown roses washed with dew' conceive a daughter, Euphrosyne, the Grace of Mirth. It has been pointed out that Etty's design reverses that of Titian's *Venus and Adonis*, which had been presented to the National Gallery with the Angerstein collection in 1824[2] (fig.12), and which Etty also copied separately.[3]

The work is painted on a solid, nearly square wood panel with the white ground left exposed at the four corners. Pencil underdrawing is visible, notably around the figures, suggesting that the design was established on the spot and that the gestation of the work was rapid. The circular format and exotic palette suggest Etty may have been looking closely at recent works by Turner: around this date he was commissioned by H. A. J. Munro of Novar (1797-1864) for a work to hang alongside one of the latter's Turners of Venice,[4] and it seems possible that this painting was originally conceived to that end. Munro, who was one of Etty's best patrons[5] and who later did acquire the work, also owned Watteau's *Le Printemps*, an amorous rendition of the related subject *Zephyrus and Flora*, and it may be suggested that Etty was thinking in terms of a

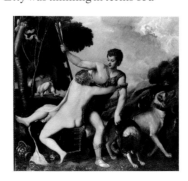

Fig.12
Titian: *Venus and Adonis*
© National Gallery London

companion work for this too (again he borrowed from the design by reversing the figures).[6]

At least two reviews of LL 3591 at the 1845 Royal Academy drew a comparison with Turner. The *Literary Gazette* described the work as with 'all the hues of Turner, employed in a different way',[7] while the *Examiner* noted: 'if his bodies are often like Titian, his heads have as frequently the indecision of Mr Turner's landscapes. Suddenly attracted by the beauty, we try to look closer; the faults of the drawing then appear; and we are obliged to retire and be content with the more distant view'.[8] A long notice in the *Observer* admitted that of Etty's seven exhibits, this was 'the least objectionable on the score of coarseness of feeling and ... almost animal grossness of expression: but unhappily it is also that which is least marked by that fine peculiarity of colour which has made [him] almost the rival of Titian ...'.[9]

A smaller version of LL 3591, 12½ inches in diameter, was last recorded in 1899.[10]

PROVENANCE:
[?bt from Etty by Joseph Gillott[11]]; ... William Wethered by November 1848;[12] Christie 7 March 1856 (148) bt. Rought (710 gns.); ... H. A. J. Munro of Novar;[13] Christie 6 April 1878 (27) bt. Vokins (460 gns.); Christie 8 June 1901 (88) bt. Agnew (200 gns.); William Lockett Agnew; Christie 15 June 1923 (28) bt. Gooden & Fox for Lever (240 gns.).

EXHIBITIONS:
RA 1845 (12); *National Exhibition of Works of Art* Leeds 1868 (1149); *British Art* RA 1934 (675); *Yorkshire Artists 1600-1900* (CEMA) Leeds 1946 (10).

REFERENCES:
1. The subject of Zephyr was however relatively popular in music and ballet about 1800-35; see J. D. Reid: *The Oxford Guide to Classical Mythology in the Arts* (1993) Vol.II, p.1059.
2. W. Gaunt and F. Gordon Roe: *Etty*

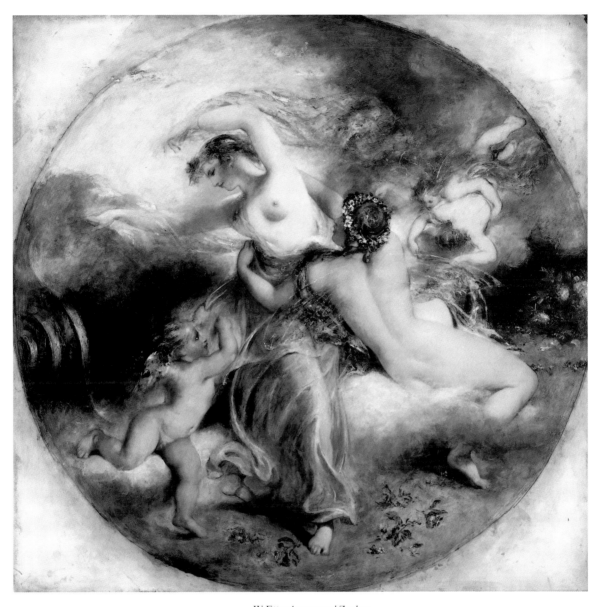

W. Etty: *Aurora and Zephyr*
LL 3591

and the Nude (1943) pp.73, 104; see also D. Farr: *William Etty* (1958) p.139, cat.40.

3. Farr, *loc. cit.*

4. Unpublished letter from Munro to Etty, mentioned by Selby Whittingham, letter, 20 July 1985, gallery files.

5. For the ten works by Etty owned by Munro in 1847 see the *Art Union Journal* (1847) pp.253-55. Etty's copy of Titian's *Venus and Adonis* (see main text above) was a later acquisition.

6. Selby Whittingham: ' 'What You Will'; or some notes regarding the Influence of Watteau on Turner and other British Artists', *Turner Studies*, Vol.5, No.1 (summer 1985) p.4 and notes 34-38.

7. *Literary Gazette* (1845) p.298.

8. *Examiner* (10 May 1845) p.293.

9. *Observer* (11 May 1845); for other reviews and mentions of Etty see for example *Art Union Journal* (June 1845) p.180; *Athenaeum* (1845) p.466; *Spectator*

(10 May 1845) p.450; *Illustrated London News* (10 May 1845) and *Morning Chronicle* (12 May 1845).

10. Christie 15 July 1899 (130) from the collection of Sir William Eden; bt. Maple (34 gns.); Farr, *loc. cit.*

11. According to Gilchrist (*Life of William Etty RA* (1855) Vol.II, p.204) *Aurora and Zephyr* was sold at the 1845 Royal Academy; the buyer is not specified. Farr, *loc. cit.* states that Gillott's

Account Book for 20 March 1849 records a payment for LL 3591, but elsewhere (*op. cit.*, p.99 note 2) Farr states that this account book ran from May 1843 to November 1846, so 1849 may be a misprint for 1845 (even though 20 March would have pre-dated the opening of the RA exhibition). See also note 12 below.
12. Etty's autobiography, in the *Art Journal* (1849) p.40, gives Wethered as the owner of LL 3591 at this date. It seems unlikely that he sold it to Gillott and bought it back again between then and 1856.
13. Farr, *loc. cit.*, places Munro's ownership of LL 3591 after that of Charles T. Maud, who was named as the owner at the 1868 Leeds exhibition. Clearly, however, Munro was in no position to acquire paintings by this date. Maud was presumably an agent for Munro's estate. LL 3591 is listed in W. Frost and H. Reeve: *A Complete Catalogue of the Paintings, Water-Colour Drawings, Drawings and Prints in the Collection of the late Hugh Andrew Johnstone Munro Esq. of Novar [...]* (1865) p.67, cat. 44. It is very likely Munro bought the painting directly from Rought.

William Etty
1787-1849

The Three Graces
LL 3593 (WHL 1381)
oil on board,[1] 90 × 68 cm

This work seems to have been painted in two phases. The three figures are painted on a board of about 68 × 52 cm; to this, six strips of varying dimensions have been added to all four sides enabling the composition to be worked up into its present state. The right heel of the right-hand figure, the coronet of the central one, and in places the foliage have been painted across the joins. It is unclear whether the figures were always intended for the present design or whether a simple academic study was extended at a later date.[2] Appearances would suggest, how-

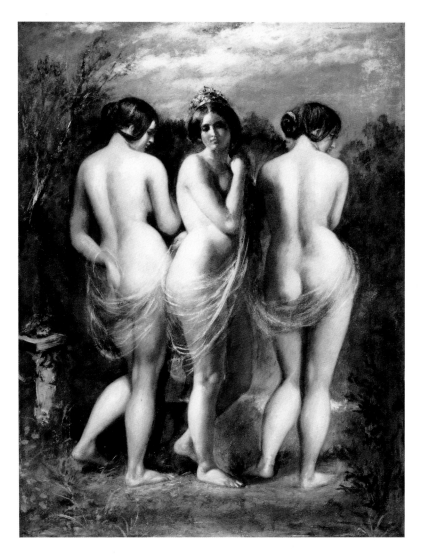

W. Etty: *The Three Graces*
LL 3593

ever, that the work's gestation period was a fairly short one.

Etty was especially concerned with the theme of the three Graces in the period 1843-47 and from its style LL 3593 may be dated to this period.[3] In 1847 he exhibited at the Royal Academy *Charites et Gratiae. The Graces, daughters of Venus by Jupiter or Bacchus, are three in number: Aglaia, Thalia and Euphrosyne. They were the constant attendants of Venus;* *and they were represented as three young and modest virgins.* LL 3593 was formerly identified as this work.[4]

PROVENANCE:
[? G.T. Andrews; Christie 23 June 1849 (45) bt. in (280 gns.); Christie 31 May 1851 (80) bt. Hatch (200 gns.)[5]]; ... A.M. Levy; Christie 28 June 1907 (51) bt. Tooth (34 gns.);[6] bt. from Tooth by Lever August 1914.

EXHIBITIONS:
Etty York 1910 (97); *Yorkshire Artists 1600-1900* (CEMA) Leeds 1946 (11); *Etty* York 1948 (1); *Etty* York 1949 (58).

REFERENCES:
1. Backed to a wood panel.
2. A Gilchrist: *Life of William Etty RA* (1855) Vol.II, p.57, cites a recollection of Etty setting models in the life-class by Maclise: 'I have known him set three or four models together. Now it was a group of Graces, now a composition of two or three gladiators …'. It is possible that LL 3593 derived from precisely such an occasion. Maclise, however, was a student in the 1830s, and the very similar looks of the three figures tends to suggest that here one model was studied in three separate poses.
3. See also *The Three Graces, Psyche and Cupid* (RA 1843); *The Three Graces* bought by John Singleton in 1849 (a photograph of what appears to be this work, in a private collection in 1956, is in gallery files in the Metropolitan Museum of Art, New York); and the *Study for Three Graces* (Agnes Etherington Art Centre, Queens' University, Kingston, Ontario). The Graces also appear in the earlier *Venus and Her Satellites* (RA 1835; Museo di Arte, Ponce, Puerto Rico; study in the Metropolitan Museum of Art, New York).
4. Tatlock, p.94. However, the painting exhibited at the 1847 Royal Academy was bought by Joseph Gillott, and included in his sale, Christie 27 April 1872 (259).
5. This provenance is given by D. Farr: *William Etty* (1958) p.154, cat.86. A *Three Graces* was included in Etty's studio sale, Christie 7-10 May 1850 (658) bt. Birch (£23.2.-). A painting of *The Graces* also appeared at Christie 18 May 1885 (?bt. in) (58 gns.).
6. According to the auctioneer's copy of the 1907 sale catalogue (Christie's archives) the purchaser was not Wright (as given by Farr, *loc. cit.*), but Tooth. Tooth lent the work to the York exhibition in 1910 (label on the back of LL 3593).

William Etty
1787-1849

A Bather turned to the left
LL 3595 (WHL 164, H 135)
oil on millboard, 25.5 × 25 cm

A Bather turned to the right
LL 3596 (WHL 165, H 136)
oil on millboard, 25.5 × 25 cm

Both works are circular compositions painted on nearly square boards and they are clearly a pair. Just possibly they were made in the Royal Academy life class, which Etty continued to attend even as a senior Academician; but they have a rather facile and decorative quality inconsistent with close observation of the model. Female studies of this type were much in demand among Etty's patrons towards the end of his life.[1]

PROVENANCE:
…James Orrock by 1886;[2] bt. from Orrock by Lever June 1896 (£100 the pair).[3]

EXHIBITIONS:
International Exhibition of Industry, Science and Art Edinburgh 1886 (1432 and 1435); *A Century of British Art 1737-1837* Grosvenor Gallery 1888 (196 and 255); *Etty* York 1910 (110 and 113); *Etty* York 1949 (56 and 57).

REFERENCES:
1. A. Gilchrist: *Life of William Etty RA* (1855) Vol.II, p.210; D. Farr: *William Etty* (1958) p.174, cats. 222 and 223, dated about 1845-49.
2. Lent by Orrock to the 1886 Edinburgh exhibition.
3. Lever's first purchase from Orrock and one of his earliest purchases of historical, rather than contemporary, British painting. For a discussion of the large collection of Etty's work assembled by Lever between 1896 and 1923 see M.C. Salaman: 'Etty's Pictures in Lord Leverhulme's Collection', *The Studio* (January 1923) Vol.LXXXV, pp.3-13. At this date only *The Judgment of Paris* had entered the Lady Lever Art Gallery and at Lever's London house, The Hill, Hampstead, around the spacious Arcade landing and up the staircase leading to it, the walls were hung with some thirty of Etty's works 'in which beauty of the nude female form is characteristically the dominant artistic motive' (p.3).

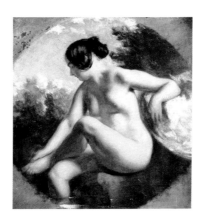

W. Etty: *A Bather turned to the left*
LL 3595

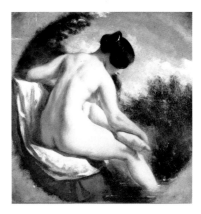

W. Etty: *A Bather turned to the right*
LL 3596

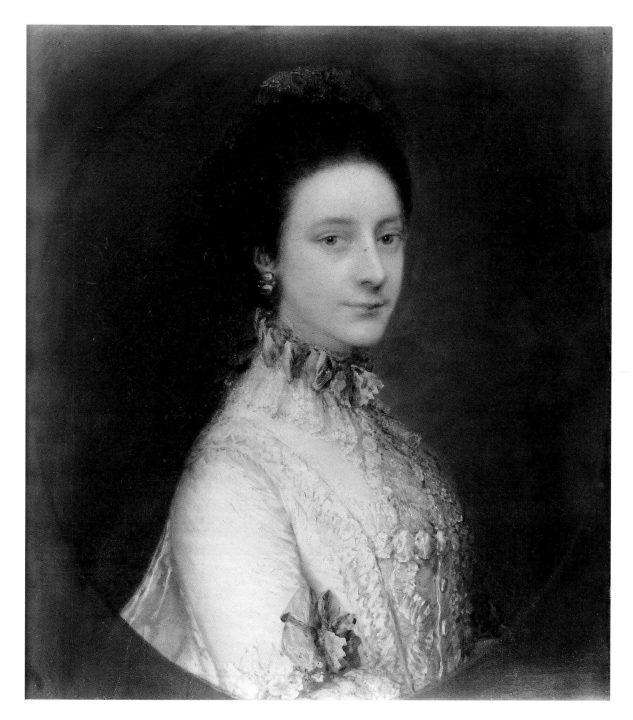

T. Gainsborough: *Mrs Charlotte Frere*
LL 3562

Thomas Gainsborough
1727-1788

Mrs. Charlotte Frere
LL 3562 (WHL 78, H 4)
oil on canvas, 76.5 × 63.5 cm

The sitter was the third daughter and fifth child of Sir George Trevelyan Bt., of Nettlecombe, Somerset (1707-68), who married Julia Calverley in 1733.[1] Charlotte's date of birth is unknown,[2] but it can perhaps be assigned to about 1739-40 from the fact that she married Tobias Frere of Shute, Devon, a widower, in Bath Abbey on 16 May 1757. Little is known about the Freres, except that Tobias is listed in the Bath Rate Books as the first tenant of 24, Circus (a house formerly believed to have been lived in by Gainsborough himself) in December 1767 and 1768, and again in December 1770. His name is erased in December 1771, and since his furniture is advertised as for sale in the *Bath Chronicle* of 20 February 1772, it can be assumed that he died in the latter part of the previous year.[3] Charlotte's own family, the Trevelyans, are listed regularly among the arrivals in the town by the Bath press in the late 1750s and early 1760s, and between 1766 and 1768 Sir George lived at 16, Circus, next door to Gainsborough at no.17.[4] Of Charlotte's later life, except that she married a M. de Coleseaue,[5] nothing is known.

This portrait was almost certainly painted in the first half of the 1760s. It is thought to be the companion of a three-quarters portrait by Gainsborough of her first husband (untraced).[6] Tobias was formerly believed to have died in 1763,[7] and both works, accordingly, have been assumed to date from about 1760 to 1762, (which seems plausible given the sitter's youthful appearance). It has been pointed out that Charlotte's hair is very high on top for this date,

but also that Gainsborough did repaint hairstyles in his portraits as they became outdated.[8] There is no obvious indication of this in LL 3562; but the continuation of the dress visible at bottom left indicates that the portrait was not originally conceived as a painted oval, and further alterations can be seen along the right-hand edge of Mrs Frere's face and along her back, which seems originally to have been further over to the left.

PROVENANCE:
…James Orrock by 1903;[9] Christie 4-6 June 1904 (93) bt. in; bt. from Orrock by Lever November 1904.[10]

EXHIBITIONS:
Gainsborough Arts Council 1949 (13); *Gainsborough* Cecil Higgins Art Gallery and Museum Bedford 1954 (9).

REFERENCES:
1. P.J. Hocking, Somerset Archive and Record Service, letter, 19 January 1998, gallery files.
2. She was born neither in the parish of Nettlecombe (Hocking, *loc. cit.*) nor in that of Bath Abbey (Susan Sloman, letter, 16 December 1997, gallery files).
3. Sloman, *loc. cit.*
4. Sloman, *loc. cit.*
5. Note in gallery files. The source of this information is unknown.
6. Ellis Waterhouse: *Gainsborough* (1958) p.68, cat.270. The emergence of this work in 1897 in the ownership of the dealer Wallis may suggest that it and LL 3562 left family ownership at this time.
7. Ellis Waterhouse: 'A Preliminary Checklist of Portraits by Thomas Gainsborough', *Walpole Society*, Vol.33 (1953) p.41.
8. Sloman, *loc. cit.*
9. Repr. Webber, Vol.I, fp.196.
10. 1904 Inventory p.2, no.29.

Thomas Gainsborough
1727-1788

Anne Luttrell, Duchess of Cumberland
LL 3140 (WHL 4242)
oil on canvas, 71.5 × 59.5 cm

Lever purchased LL 3140 as a portrait of Princess Augusta Sophia (1768-1840), second daughter of King George III. This identification, which appears to date from the work's appearance on the London art market in 1911, is unacceptable. The likeness is not close to that in other portraits of the Princess by Gainsborough;[1] and furthermore, given the sitter's apparent age, the portrait would have had to be painted at the very end of the artist's life, whereas it clearly dates, on grounds of style, from the 1770s.

The sitter was re-identified as the Duchess of Cumberland at the suggestion of Queen Mary, following a royal visit to Port Sunlight in 1929,[2] on the basis of her likeness to Gainsborough's portraits of the Duchess in the Royal Collection.[3] Although this suggestion has not found universal favour,[4] comparison with the full-length portrait exhibited at the Royal Academy in 1777 (fig.13), as well as with Gainsborough's earlier portrait of her, made shortly after her first marriage in 1765 to Christopher Horton of Catton Hall, Derbyshire (National Gallery of Ireland, fig.14), seems to confirm it. Even more closely comparable are the head and shoulders of the Duchess in Sir Joshua Reynolds's whole length portrait of her (now at Waddesdon) of which the engraving by James Watson was published 1 December 1773 (fig.15). The Duchess seems about the same age as in the Reynolds portrait, a little younger than in Gainsborough's Royal Collection portrait, and somewhat

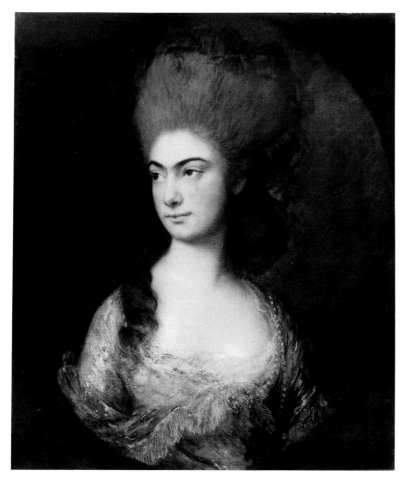

T. Gainsborough:
Anne Luttrell, Duchess of Cumberland
LL 3140

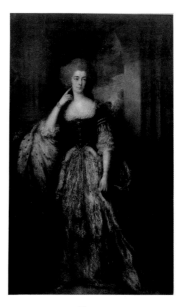

Fig. 13
T. Gainsborough:
Anne Duchess of Cumberland
The Royal Collection
© Her Majesty Queen Elizabeth II

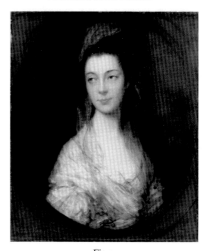

Fig. 14
T. Gainsborough: *Mrs. Anne Horton*
Courtesy of the National Gallery of Ireland

older than in his Dublin one, which argues a dating for LL 3140 of about 1772-75.

The sitter (1743-1808) was the eldest of three daughters of Simon Luttrell of Four Oaks Hall, Warwickshire. Her marriage in 1771 as a commoner and a widow to Henry Frederick, Duke of Cumberland, scandalised the King (the Duke's elder brother) and led in the following year to the passing of the Royal Marriage Act. Horace Walpole described the Duchess in a letter to Horace Mann at the time of the scandal as 'extremely pretty, not handsome, very well made, with the most amorous eyes in the world and eyelashes a yard long. Coquette beyond measure, artful as Cleopatra, and completely mistress of all her passions and projects.'[5] Following the death of the Duke in 1790 she lived a life of retirement in Switzerland.[6]

PROVENANCE:
[? ... Scott & Fowles; bt. by Agnew October 1911; bt. by Wallis & Sons 18 October 1911[7]]; ... G. Harland Peck; Christie 25 June 1920 (59) bt. Gooden & Fox for Lever (£6510).[8]

EXHIBITIONS:
Annual Loan Exhibition on behalf of the Artists Benevolent Fund Agnew November-December 1913 (3); *Royal Treasures* 5 Great Stanhope Street, London 1937 (154); *Art In the Georgian Home* Arts Council 1949 (34); *Lord Leverhulme* RA 1980 (17).

REFERENCES:
1. Gainsborough painted the Princess in 1782 (22 × 16 in., oval, Royal Collection) and again, with her sisters Charlotte

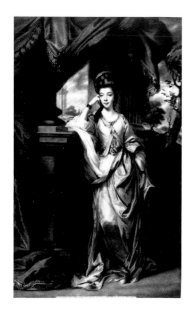

Fig. 15
J. Watson, after Sir J. Reynolds:
Anne Duchess of Cumberland
© The British Museum

Augusta Matilda and Elizabeth, in 1783-4
(formerly whole-length, cut down to
51 × 70 in., Royal Collection); Ellis
Waterhouse: 'A Preliminary Checklist of
Portraits by Thomas Gainsborough',
Walpole Society, Vol. 33 (1953) pp. 3 and
20, and Ellis Waterhouse: *Gainsborough*
(1958) p. 52, cat. 22 and p. 59, cat. 135.
2. See C.R. Grundy: 'A Discovery by Her
Majesty the Queen', *Connoisseur*, Vol. 84
(1929) pp. 245-6.
3. They are (i) 94 × 56 in., exhibited RA
1777 (132); (ii) 48 × 38 in., begun in 1783,
unfinished; (iii) (with the Duke of
Cumberland and Lady Elizabeth
Luttrell) 64 × 47 in., painted about 1785;
Waterhouse (1953) pp. 25-6 and (1958)
p. 62, cats. 178, 180 (repr.) and 181. A
further Gainsborough portrait of the
Duchess, thought to date from 1779, is in
the Huntington Art Collections, San
Marino (Waterhouse (1953) p. 26 and
(1958) p. 62, cat. 182.)
4. Waterhouse (1953) p. 4 described the
identification of LL 3140 as the Duchess of
Cumberland as 'certainly wrong'. In
(1958) p. 52 he stated merely that the
identification of the sitter (as Princess
Augusta Sophia) was doubtful.
5. W.S. Lewis et. al., eds.: *Horace
Walpole's Correspondence* (1937-83)
Vol. 23, p. 345.

6. *Complete Peerage*, Vol. III, pp. 24, 574.
7. Agnew's stockbooks. That this is the
same work as that exhibited by Agnew
in 1913 is conjectural, but is strongly
suggested by the identification of both
works as *Princess Augusta Sophia*. Agnew
had no Princess Augusta Sophia by
Gainsborough in stock in 1913 and
lenders to the 1913 exhibition are not
recorded (information from Dick
Kingzett, verbally, 9 June 1998).
8. A portrait attributed to Gainsborough
of the Duke of Cumberland, the same size
as LL 3140 and also an oval, was lot 64 in
the Harland Peck sale and also bought by
Lever. It was sold at the Anderson
Galleries New York, 17-19 February 1926
(104).

after
Thomas Gainsborough
1727-1788

*Surgeon-General
David Middleton*
LL 3662 (WHL 703, H 48)
oil on canvas, 77 × 64.5 cm

This is a copy of Gainsborough's
portrait of David Middleton now in
the Cincinnati Art Museum (fig. 16).[1]
Both canvases continued to be
identified into the 20th century as
portraits of the American statesman
and inventor Benjamin Franklin,[2]
despite the fact that a third version,
owned by Middleton's descendants,
had been exhibited as of Middleton

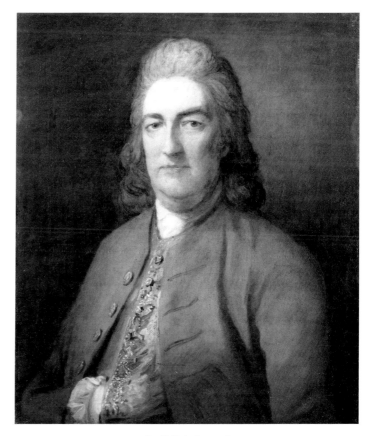

after T. Gainsborough:
Surgeon-General David Middleton
LL 3662

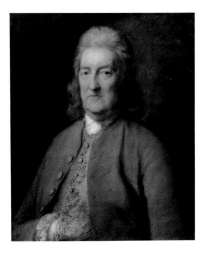

Fig.16
T. Gainsborough:
Surgeon – General David Middleton
Cincinnati Art Museum,
Bequest of Agnes S. and Murray Seasongood

in London in 1877 and again in 1885.[3] LL 3662 is the poorest in quality of the three versions. It is certainly not autograph; nor can it be attributed to Gainsborough's nephew and studio assistant, Gainsborough Dupont.[4]

The sitter (1703-1785) was surgeon to the Horse Guards 1732, and joined St. George's Hospital London as surgeon-in-ordinary 1733. He was Chief Surgeon with the army in Flanders during the War of the Austrian Succession, and during the Seven Years War, 1756-63, directed the military medical service as Surgeon-General. He resigned his commission at St. George's 19 December 1764 and died at Kensington Palace on 29 December 1785.[5] Gainsborough's original portrait can be dated, from Middleton's age and on stylistic grounds, to the second half of the 1770s.

PROVENANCE:
…T.H. Ward; Christie 25 March 1893 (369) (as *Benjamin Franklin*) bt. Davis (£73.10.-); Christie 10 July 1897 (71) (as *Benjamin Franklin*) bt. Turner (17 gns.); …James Orrock by 1903;[6] bt. from Orrock by Lever November 1904.[7]

REFERENCES:
1. Marquess of Lansdowne collection (as *Benjamin Franklin*) before 1844; Christie 7 March 1930 (41) bt. Meteyard (1300 gns.)…; Agnes and Murray Seasongood Bequest to the Cincinnati Art Museum 1983. See Ellis Waterhouse: 'A Preliminary Checklist of Portraits by Thomas Gainsborough', *Walpole Society*, Vol.33 (1953) p.75; Ellis Waterhouse: *Gainsborough* (1958) p.81, cat.485. For an argument that Gainsborough's portrait type represents Johann Christian Bach see Joan S. Reis: 'A Third Gainsborough Portrait of Johann Christian Bach?', *Musical Quarterly*, Vol.74, no.2 (1990) pp.295-302; Reis's proofs, however, are not convincing.
2. A label identifying LL 3662 as a portrait of Franklin dating from James Orrock's ownership is on the reverse. The Lansdowne version (see footnote 1 above) was first published as representing Middleton by W. Armstrong: *Gainsborough* (1898) p.199.
3. *Old Masters* RA 1877 (229); Grosvenor Gallery 1885 (203). This version descended to Mrs Hope Sutherland, 1972; thence to Old Hall Gallery, Iden, Rye, Sussex. Waterhouse (1953) *loc. cit.*, stated that this version was possibly by Gainsborough Dupont.
4. LL 3662 was accepted as by Gainsborough by Tatlock, p.53, and by W.G. Constable (note in gallery files). Waterhouse (1953) *loc. cit.*, describes LL 3662 as an early copy.
5. Biographical research by Millard F. Rogers, Cincinnati Art Museum, communicated by John Wilson.
6. Repr. Webber, Vol.II, fp. 121.
7. 1904 Inventory p.1, no.4.

after
Thomas Gainsborough
1727-1788

Horses Watering
LL 3660 (WHL 38, HH 47)
oil on canvas, 128 × 103 cm

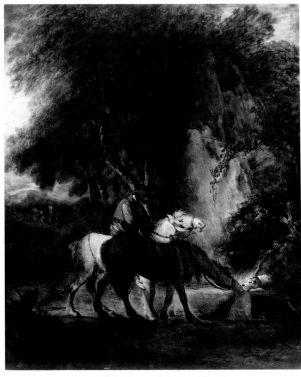

after T. Gainsborough: *Horses Watering*
LL 3660

This is a close copy of the landscape of virtually the same dimensions exhibited by Gainsborough at the Royal Academy in 1780. This painting marked a new departure for the artist in its use of large picturesque rocks as a key element of the composition, and its subject matter is unique in Gainsborough's work.[1] The painting appears to have enjoyed substantial exposure in the period 1797-1814[2] and it is probable that LL 3660, one of a number of known copies,[3] was executed in this period. Its authorship is unknown, although it has previously been ascribed to Thomas Barker of Bath (1769-1847)[4]. It is executed on a fine weave canvas; an area of damage measuring approximately 2×3 cm has been repaired at lower left.

PROVENANCE:
[? Sir William Knighton[5]];…Arthur Sanderson; Christie 3 July 1908 (61) bt. in (420 gns.);…James Orrock; bt. from Orrock by Lever 1910.[6]

REFERENCES:
1. J. Hayes: *The Landscape Paintings of Thomas Gainsborough* (1982) Vol.II, pp.481-2, cat.124.
2. A version was bought by J.W. Steers in 1797; another, or possible the same, was sold by Lord Robert Spencer at Christie 31 May 1799 (93) bt. Foster; this was exhibited at Parkes in Dean Street in March 1802; it then passed through the well-known collection of Sir John Leicester and that of Thomas Lyster Parker into that of William Earl of Lonsdale, who exhibited it at the British Institution in 1814 (Hayes, *loc. cit.*).
3. These include (i) Whitbread Collection, Southill Park, by S.W. Reynolds, executed before 1816 (a freer copy of the Gainsborough original than LL 3660, which on this evidence is not by S.W. Reynolds); (ii) Christie 2-6 August 1932 (912); (both of these are the same size as LL 3660); (iii) (of the lower portion of the design only) Victoria and Albert Museum.
4. Tatlock, p.50.
5. According to the 1908 sale catalogue, the work was 'from the collection of Sir

W.W. Knighton at Blendworth, near Horndean, Hants.' It was not among the contents of the Knighton sale at Christie 21-23 May 1885, but a manuscript note in the auctioneer's copy of the 1908 catalogue, preserved in Christie's archives (*451: at house June 5, 85*) suggests that the work was sold in a premises sale. No catalogue for such a sale has been traced.
6. 1910 Inventory p.34, valued at £600.

'Thomas Gainsborough'
1727-1788

The White Horse
LL 3602 (WHL 52, H 20)
oil on canvas, 103×129 cm

The painting is an unconvincing mixture of motifs adapted from Gainsborough's landscapes and executed in a rough approximation to his style by a later imitator.[1] It is not directly related to any autograph work. The canvas is said to have been signed and dated *T. Gainsborough 1773*[2] but no inscription is now visible.

PROVENANCE:
…James Orrock by 1903;[3] Christie 4-6 June 1904 (94) bt. in (520 gns.); bt. from Orrock by Lever November 1904.[4]

REFERENCES:
1. A number of large landscapes in a Gainsboroughesque idiom, dating from the period 1810-1830 and bearing some stylistic affinity to LL 3602, are attributed to Thomas Barker of Bath (1769-1847) and his brother Benjamin Barker (1776-1838) (photographs in the Witt Library). However, the *oeuvres* of the Barkers are at present insufficiently well defined for LL 3602 to be attributed to either of them with certainty. C. Holmes: 'Notes on Mr. Orrock's English Pictures', *Burlington Magazine* (July 1904) p.414 opined that the landscape in LL 3602 was by Hoppner.
2. Note in gallery files.
3. Repr. Webber, Vol.I, fp.150.
4. 1904 Inventory p.2, no.36.

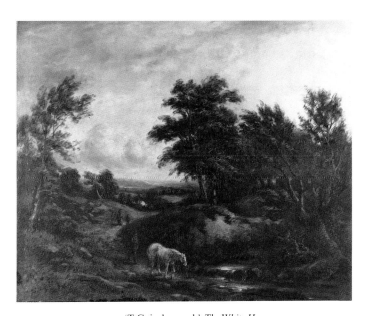

'T. Gainsborough': *The White Horse*
LL 3602

'Thomas Gainsborough'
1727-1788

Portrait of a Lady (called 'Mrs. Catherine Clements')

LL 3605 (WHL 621, HH 89)
oil on canvas, 73 × 61 cm

Lever acquired LL 3605 as a portrait by Gainsborough of Catherine Clements (1762-1836), second wife of Henry Theophilus Clements (1734-1795, MP for Co. Leitrim, Ireland). The work's very worn and repainted condition, thought to have resulted from an earlier relining, makes assessment problematic; but even after all due allowance has been made, it is inconceivable that the work is by either Gainsborough or Gainsborough Dupont.[1]

It is also most unlikely that the work does in fact represent Catherine Clements. The costume and hairstyle purport to date from the 1780s[2] but the sitter in LL 3605 appears at least thirty years old. Romney's portrait of Catherine Clements dating from 1788[3] is not obviously the same woman. Moreover, no connection can be established between Gerald Clements, from whose collection the portrait supposedly came, and Catherine Clements's descendants.[4] The work is probably a deliberate forgery dating from the late 19th or early 20th centuries.

A label on the reverse of LL 3605 which states that the sitter is Mary (née Webb; d. 1777) Clements's first wife, reflects a historic confusion between this portrait and LL 3666 (see below under Hoppner), which was said to come from the same source.

PROVENANCE:
[? by descent to Gerald Clements; bt. from Clements by James Orrock about April 1909[5]]; bt. from Orrock by Lever 1910.[6]

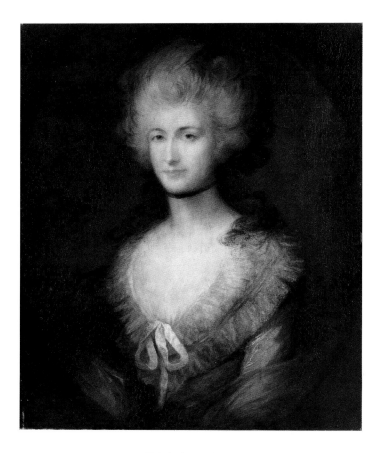

'T. Gainsborough':
Portrait of a Lady (called 'Mrs Catherine Clements')
LL 3605

REFERENCES:
1. Hugh Belsey, letter, 21 December 1996, gallery files.
2. Aileen Ribeiro, verbally, 26 February 1998.
3. Repr. T.H. Ward and W. Roberts: *Romney* (1904), Vol.I, fp. 68.
4. P.W. Clement: *Ancestors and Descendants of Robert Clements* (1927) Vol.II, pp.905-13 lists the descendants of Henry and Catherine Clements; no Gerald Clements appears either there or in the index of this work.
5. A supposed letter from Gerald Clements to James Orrock dated 3 April 1909, now untraced but partially recorded in gallery files, stated that the sitters in LL 3605 and LL 3666 were Mary and Catherine, the two wives of Henry Clements.
6. 1910 Inventory p.38, valued at £500.

'Thomas Gainsborough'
1727-1788

Portrait of a Lady (called 'Miss Fergusson')

LL 3667 (WHL 2342, HH 284)
oil on canvas, 76 × 63 cm

Lever acquired LL 3667 as by Gainsborough, but it bears no stylistic resemblance to his work. The costume and hairstyle appear to date from about 1775.[1] The portrait is in very worn condition.

PROVENANCE:
…James Orrock; bt. from Orrock by Lever 1910.[2]

REFERENCES:
1. Aileen Ribeiro, verbally,

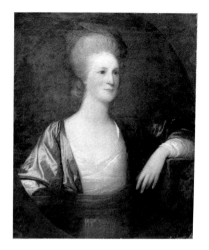

'T. Gainsborough':
*Portrait of a Lady
(called 'Miss Fergusson')*
LL 3667

26 February 1998. It remains moot whether LL 3667 is a *bona fide* work of the later 18th century (perhaps by a student or studio assistant, though it is not easy to propose a plausible master for such a portrait), or whether it is a later concoction. The sitters' files in the National Portrait Gallery include a number of Misses and Mrs Ferguson or Fergusson, of which the most plausible in terms of date is a *Miss Fergusson* engraved by Payrau after a portrait by Downman. She however bears little resemblance to the sitter in LL 3667.
2.   1910 Inventory p.65a, valued at £30.

'Thomas Gainsborough'
1727-1788

*Portrait of a Lady
(called 'Mrs. Elliott')*
LL 3668 (WHL 81, H 455)
oil on canvas, 75.5 × 63.5 cm

Lever acquired LL 3668 as by Gainsborough, but even allowing for the work's very worn condition, it seems of too poor quality to be autograph. Its subsequent re-attribution to Gainsborough Dupont[1] is equally unacceptable

on stylistic grounds, and it would appear to be a flimsy pastiche of Gainsborough's portraits of the late 1770s and early 1780s by a later artist.

When Lever obtained the picture, the sitter was identified as Georgiana Seymour (1782-1813), an obvious impossibility if the work was to be attributed either to Gainsborough (d.1788) or to Dupont (d.1797). Consequently, she was re-identified[2] as Georgiana's mother, Grace Dalrymple Elliott (c.1758-1823), whose well-known portrait by Gainsborough dating from 1782 (Frick Collection, New York, fig.17) may well have been the general inspiration for LL 3668.

PROVENANCE:
…James Orrock; bt. from Orrock by Lever 1912.[3]

REFERENCES:
1.   Tatlock, p.52. W.G. Constable nevertheless considered LL 3668 a genuine Gainsborough (note in gallery files). His opinion may perhaps have been

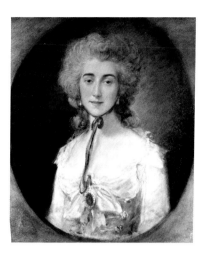

Fig.17
T. Gainsborough:
Mrs. Grace Dalrymple Elliott
Frick Collection, New York

coloured by the knowledge that Mrs Elliott was stated by W.T. Whitley (*Thomas Gainsborough* (1915) pp.243-4) to have sat to Gainsborough in 1785, and that no portrait is known to have resulted from such a sitting.
2.   Tatlock, *loc. cit.*
3.   1912 Inventory p.17, valued at £200.

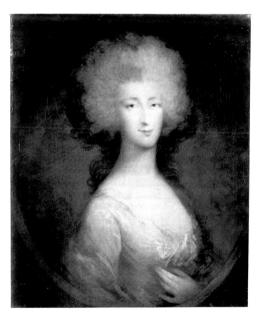

'T. Gainsborough':
Portrait of a Lady (called 'Mrs Elliott')
LL 3668

'Thomas Gainsborough'
1727-1788

A Forest Scene with Four Lambs
LL 3690 (WHL 624, H 24)
oil on canvas, 123 × 153 cm

Lever bought LL 3690, together with Reynolds's *Venus Chiding Cupid* (see below), for the combined price of £3000.[1] The work bears not the remotest resemblance, in terms either of subject or of style, to Gainsborough's work; and almost equally unacceptable on stylistic grounds[2] is its later re-attribution to Thomas Barker of Bath (1769-1847).[3] It appears to be a composite effort: the woodland by one hand and the gigantic lambs, totally out of place in the design, by another, possibly much later one.

PROVENANCE:
[? ... Sir William Knighton[4]]; ... James Orrock and Sir J.D. Linton, jointly; Christie 4-6 June 1904 (95) bt. in (£378); bt. from Orrock and Linton by Lever September 1910.

REFERENCES:
1. Contract dated 14 September 1910, gallery files.
2. Susan Sloman, letter, 2 March 1998, gallery files.

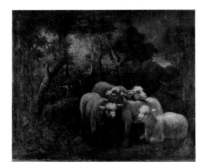

'T. Gainsborough':
A Forest Scene with Four Lambs
LL 3690

3. Tatlock, p.50.
4. Christie's sale catalogue of 4-6 June 1904 gives this provenance, but the work has not been traced in Sir William Knighton's sale, Christie, 21-23 May 1885. As with the copy of Gainsborough's *Horses Watering*, LL 3660 above, it may have been included in a premises sale held at Knighton's country estate, Blendworth, whose catalogue has not been traced.

James Holland
1799-1870

Venice
LL 3744 (WHL 695, HH 193)
oil on canvas, 55 × 40 cm
signed and dated: *JH 1840* (bottom left)

Holland made four trips to Venice, in 1835, 1845, 1851 and 1857.[1] One of the products of the first visit was a watercolour, exhibited at the Old Watercolour Society in 1836, titled *Venice*, which was purchased by John

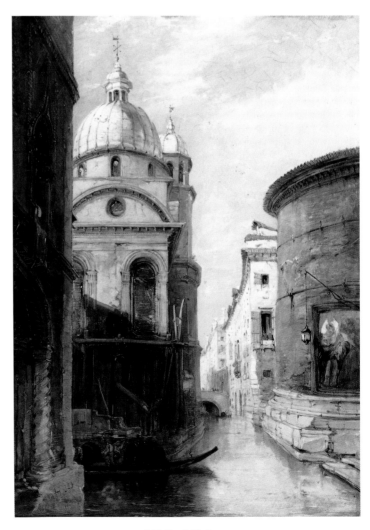

J. Holland: *Venice*
LL 3744

Ruskin's father J.J. Ruskin, and which is probably Holland's first treatment of the present motif.[2] The view is almost identical to that in LL 3744, except that the spectator is set slightly further back, permitting the inclusion of the whole of the door on the left and figures standing on the steps in the right foreground; the facade of the church is partly obscured by a wooden scaffold. An oil version of the same subject, 35 × 27 in., without the scaffold and with other small differences from the watercolour,[3] appears to represent an intermediate stage between the watercolour and LL 3744, which may be described as a repetition with minor variations. Another water-colour version,[4] horizontal in format, introduces further variations: the spectator is taken back still further and is placed on the stepped terrace of the building on the left (apparently an invented church).

Given its date, LL 3744 may be the *Venice* exhibited by Holland at the British Institution in 1840.[5] Alternatively, it may be the *At Venice* exhibited at the Society of British Artists in 1841.

For the church of Santa Maria dei Miracoli, see LL 3735 below. This view is taken from the (north) east,[6] probably from the bridge over the Rio dei Miracoli which leads on the right to the Campo Santa Maria Nova.

PROVENANCE:
…James Orrock; bt. from Orrock by Lever 1910.[7]

EXHIBITION:
[? BI 1840 (234)].

REFERENCES:
1. M. Liversidge and J. Farrington, eds.: *Canaletto & England*, exhibition catalogue, Birmingham Museum and Art Gallery (1993-4) p.184, cat.121; entry by Stephen Wildman.
2. 19 × 13½ in., with Ruskin provenance; Christie 9 November 1971 (56).

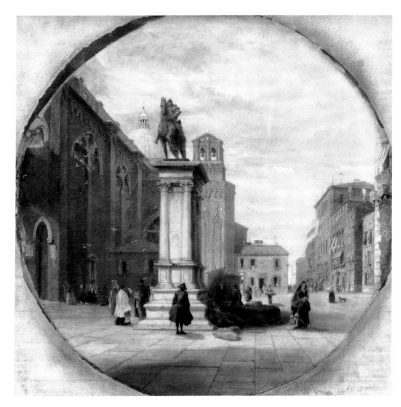

J. Holland:
*The Colleoni Monument and the Church of
Santi Giovanni e Paolo, Venice*
LL 3737

3. Formerly in the Dyson Perrins collection; exhibited at Agnew 1959; Christie 19 November 1976 (164).
4. 14½ × 18½ in., Christie 1 October 1973 (157) under the incorrect title *By the Church of San Simeone Piccolo, Venice*.
5. The (framed) size of the exhibited work is recorded as 2 ft 7 in. × 2 ft 4 in. (A. Graves: *The British Institution 1806-1867* (1908) p.276); the present frame of LL 3744 measures 2 ft 8 in × 2 ft 2 in.
6. The east end of the church is in the foreground, but the church is orientated on a north-east/south west axis.
7. 1910 Inventory p.57, valued at £50.

James Holland
1799-1870

The Colleoni Monument and the Church of Santi Giovanni e Paolo, Venice

LL 3737 (WHL 3564)
oil on canvas, 68.5 × 68.5 cm[1]
signed and dated: *JH* (monogram) *1848* (lower right)

Holland gave another version of this subject, exhibited at the Society of British Artists in 1845,[2] the following title: *The Monument of Bartolommeo Colleoni, a celebrated General of the Venetian Republic – the Scene where the Conspirators in Byron's Tragedy of 'Marine Faliero' met the Doge.*

'Doge – That warrior was the sire of my sire's fathers, and that statue was Decreed to him by the twice-rescued city'.

The subject can probably be associated with Holland's visit to Venice in that year.

The statue, by Andrea Verrocchio, and cast by Alessandro Leopardi, was begun in 1479 and completed in 1496; Ruskin wrote of it 'I do not believe that there is a more glorious work of sculpture existing in the world'. The brick Dominican church of Santi Giovanni e Paolo, burial place of twenty-five Doges of Venice, was begun in the late 13th century but only consecrated in 1430. It is one of the largest churches in Venice. The view is from the south west corner of the Campo Santi Giovanni e Paolo, by the eastern side of the Rio dei Mendicanti.

Holland exhibited a number of views of the monument and the church, as well as Marino Faliero subjects, but LL 3737 cannot be positively identified as any of these.

PROVENANCE:
…James Orrock by 1887;[3] …Hamilton Marr; bt. Agnew December 1898; G.H. Agnew November 1900; Christie 7 June 1918 (28) bt. Gooden & Fox for Lever (180gns).

EXHIBITION:
Royal Jubilee Exhibition Manchester 1887 (805).

REFERENCES:
1. LL 3737 has been lined to a square canvas of these dimensions and the painted overlap trimmed off. According to Tatlock, p.99, LL 3737 is the pair to LL 3736 (below); but although both are circular they are not of the same dimensions and entered the collection separately.
2. 38 × 49 in; bt. by Lever from Orrock in 1910 and in the Lady Lever Art Gallery till 1958; see Appendix 1 below. A further upright version of the subject is in the Hugh Lane Municipal Gallery of Modern Art, Dublin.

3. Lent by Orrock to the Manchester exhibition, whose label is on the reverse of the frame. (It is tempting to speculate that Orrock in fact exhibited the larger version of the subject which he also owned (see above) and contrived to transfer the label to LL 3737 in order to increase its sale value, but there is no real evidence for this.)

James Holland
1799-1870

Santa Maria dei Miracoli, Venice

LL 3735 (WHL 3565)
oil on board, 37 × 28 cm

The reverse of LL 3735 is inscribed in what appears to be the artist's writing: *S. Maria Dei Miracoli/ VENEZIA/James Holland 1855*. The church, which Ruskin called the most interesting and finished example in Venice of the Byzantine Renaissance style, and which has been described as one of the most beautiful small

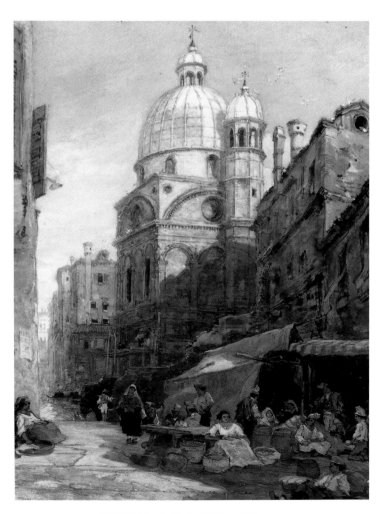

J. Holland: *Santa Maria dei Miracoli, Venice*
LL 3735

buildings in the world, was built by Pietro Lombardo between 1481 and 1489 to enshrine a miracle-working image of the Virgin. Giovanni Bellini's famous painting of the *Annunciation*, now in the Accademia in Venice, was originally for the organ doors of the church.[1]

Holland's view, which makes the church seem immensely large, is of the east end seen from the Campo Santa Maria Nova. The artist has taken liberties with topography in both this work and in LL 3744 (above, whose viewpoint is from behind the building on the extreme left in LL 3735).

PROVENANCE:
...T. Creswick RA; Christie 6-7 May 1870 (387) bt. Cox (£73.10.-); Joseph Gillott; Christie 19 April 1872 (26) bt. Rhodes (£86.2.-.); ...Frederick Nettlefold; Christie 5-6 June 1913 (123) bt. Agnew (£78.15.-.); Christie 7 June 1918 (29) bt. Gooden & Fox for Lever (£94.10.-).

REFERENCE:
1. H. Honour: *The Companion Guide to Venice* (1965) pp.83-4; see also *The Art Newspaper*, no.75 (November 1997) p.41.

James Holland
1799-1870

The Rialto Bridge, Venice
LL 3736 (WHL 48, H 436)
oil on canvas, 60 × 60 cm
signed: *JH* (monogram, lower left)

The bridge was built in 1588-92 by Antonio Da Ponte to replace an existing wooden structure, and until 1854 it was the only pedestrian crossing of the Grand Canal. It stood at the centre of the business quarter of Renaissance Venice, and the Rialto district is still today the city's main market and trading area.

The bridge was one of Holland's favourite Venetian subjects, and numerous watercolours of it are known in addition to oils. Of the

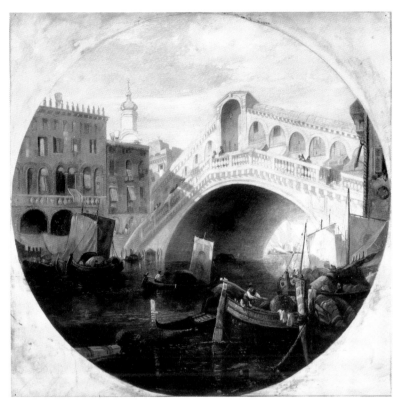

J. Holland: *The Rialto Bridge, Venice*
LL 3736

latter the largest, measuring 38 × 59 in., was presumably the work exhibited at the British Institution in 1849.[1] A square canvas titled *Near the Rialto Venice*, taken from the same direction as the view in LL 3736 but from further up the canal, with half the bridge cut off by the Palazzo dei Camerlenghi, is almost certainly the work exhibited at the British Institution the previous year.[2] Holland exhibited a further work titled *The Rialto*, not large to judge from its price, at the BI in 1855, for which LL 3736 is among several potential candidates.[3] The view in LL 3736 is from the western side of the Grand Canal, looking south east. The campanile of San Bartolommeo, rather schematically rendered, is visible in the background.

PROVENANCE:
...Charles Huth; Christie 20 May 1905 (53) bt. Agnew; James Orrock; bt. from Orrock by Lever 1912.[4]

REFERENCES:
1. This can probably be identified as the work with the Fine Art Society 1963 and exhibited in *The Victorian Vision of Italy*, Leicester Museum and Art Gallery 1968 (70) (with the date mis-read as 1859). The framed size of the work shown at the 1849 British Institution is recorded as 4 ft × 5 ft. 9 in. (A. Graves: *The British Institution 1806-67* (1908) p.276).
2. 19½ × 19½ in; Sotheby, Belgravia, 11 November 1975 (181).
3. Others are: (i) a canvas titled *Near the Rialto* signed and dated 1853 (18 × 25 in., untraced, photograph in the Witt Library); (ii) a circular canvas owned by Orrock in 1903 (Webber, Vol.II, fp. 200); this was in Orrock's sale, Christie, 4-6 June 1904 (73) and (iii) another circular work, with Barbizon House 1920.
4. 1912 Inventory p.16, valued at £200.

James Holland

1799-1870

Rotterdam

LL 3553 (WHL 582, HH 12)
oil on panel, 36.5 × 28 cm

The panel is inscribed on the reverse *Rotterdam 1856*.[1] The Dutch city was a favourite subject with the artist; his earliest known treatment is a watercolour dated 1838 and he showed oils of Rotterdam subjects at London exhibitions between 1846 and 1859 and at the Liverpool Academy in 1861. The present painting cannot be identified as an exhibited work and although no other version of this scene is known it is of decidedly pot-boilerish quality, as if Holland was repeating an existing design.

The view shows, in the foreground, the end of the Nieuwe Haven, looking across to the quay which divides it from the Oude Haven beyond. The Roobrug which divides the two is visible at the extreme left. The Oude Haven opens into the River Maas a short distance out of the picture to the left. The tower in the background seems to be intended for that of St. Lawrence's church. It appears in the majority of Holland's other Rotterdam compositions, although it cannot in fact be seen from the present point of view.[2]

PROVENANCE:
…James Orrock; bt. from Orrock by Lever 1910.[3]

REFERENCES:
1. Some words between title and date have been obliterated. The writing appears to postdate the painting.

2. Hans Brouwer, Gemeentelijke Archiefdienst Rotterdam, letter, 30 June 1998, gallery files.
3. 1910 Inventory p.31, valued at £100.

James Holland

1799-1870

The Doge's Palace, Venice, from the Grand Canal

LL 3734 (WHL 3548)
oil on board,[1] 41 × 74 cm
signed and dated : *J.H. 1862* (on the boat, right)

The Doge's Palace occupies the right background across the mouth of the Grand Canal; in the left foreground is the Custom House, built between 1676 and 1682, its tower surmounted by Bernardo Falcone's statue of *Fortune*. The viewpoint is closely comparable to that in Turner's *Venice, The Custom House with Canaletti Painting* (1833, Tate Gallery).

Holland's first treatment of this subject, which can probably be associated with his 1857 trip to Venice, appears to be a watercolour now in the collection of Eton College.[2] What is presumably the first oil version, signed and dated 1857, is very close to this in detail.[3] LL 3734, which introduces variations on the right-hand side, is the same size as, and very similar to, the undated version in the Tate Gallery. Another watercolour version, more horizontal in format, signed and dated 1864, is in the Huntington Art Collections, San Marino, California.

PROVENANCE:
[? Holland's studio sale, Christie 26-28 May 1870 (509) bt. Vokins (£65.2.-)];… William Cooke;[4] Miss Alice H. Cooke; Christie 24 May 1918 (28) bt. Gooden & Fox for Lever (£231.-.-.).

EXHIBITION:
[? BI 1863 (98)].

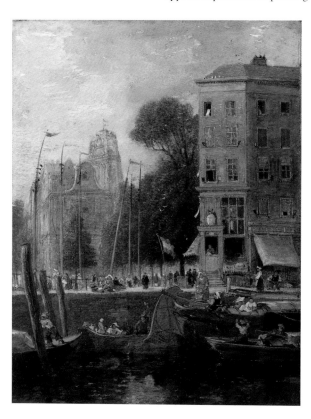

J. Holland: *Rotterdam*
LL 3553

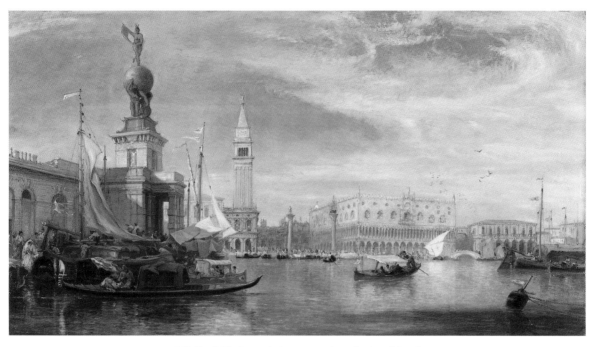

J. Holland: *The Doge's Palace, Venice, from the Grand Canal*
LL 3734

REFERENCES:
1. Backed to a second panel.
2. *Canaletto & England*, exhibition catalogue, Birmingham Museum and Art Gallery (1993-4) cat.121, p.184. In his entry Stephen Wildman suggests that the watercolour may derive from Holland's 1851 or 1857 visits to Venice but its closeness to the dated 1857 oil (see note 3 below) makes the latter date preferable.
3. 20 × 32½ in. (slightly bigger than LL 3734); Christie 7 October 1983 (24).
4. The painting may have been in France at some point since the word *combien* is written on the reverse of the frame.

John Hoppner
1758-1810

*Head of a Woman,
perhaps Sarah Siddons*
LL 3669 (WHL 68, HH 39)
oil on canvas on panel, 45.5 × 35.5 cm

Lever purchased LL 3669 as a portrait of the celebrated actress Mary 'Perdita' Robinson (1758-1800), but the sitter does not greatly resemble her as portrayed elsewhere by Hoppner or by other artists.[1] This title (or to be precise, the more evasive one of 'Mrs. Robinson') was given to the work by Agnew, who had acquired it shortly before as a portrait of the even more famous Sarah Siddons (1755-1831).[2] Why Agnew should have re-identified the work is unclear, since comparison with other portraits of Mrs Siddons confirms that it could very plausibly be of her;[3] and although no portrait of her by Hoppner is documented, she is said to have sat to him early in his career.[4]

The work has been dated to the 1780s.[5] Mrs Siddons conquered London as the new queen of tragedy in the winter season of 1782-83 and by 1785 had sat to Romney, Reynolds, Gainsborough and numerous other artists; in February 1784 she wrote of being 'under the hands of three painters which with her other avocations fully employs her'.[6] Hoppner, who had begun to exhibit at the Royal Academy in 1780, may well have been one of them. LL 3669 has been cut down and its paint surface flattened in the course of restoration,[7] but what remains does seem characteristic of him.[8] The work is a rapid sketch, almost certainly made at a single sitting, and must originally have had great freshness.

PROVENANCE:
…Mrs Hollins; bt. by Agnew November 1901; bt. from Agnew by Lever May 1902 (£385).

REFERENCES:
1. For the iconography of Perdita Robinson see J. Ingamells: *Mrs Robinson and her Portraits* (1978). Of the portraits reproduced in this volume, the closest to LL 3669 in terms of likeness is a drawing of about 1793 by George Dance (repr. p.28). W. McKay and W. Roberts: *John Hoppner RA* (1909) pp.217-8, list three 30 × 25 in.

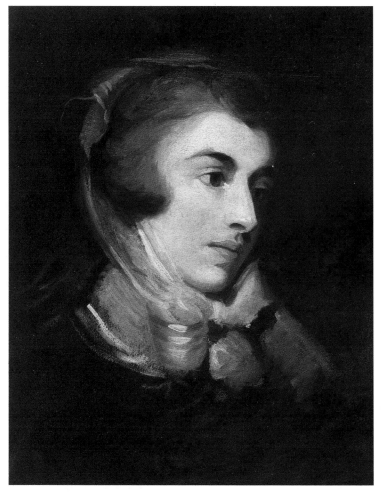

J. Hoppner: *Head of a Woman, perhaps Sarah Siddons*
LL 3669

San Marino) and half-length by Gainsborough (National Gallery, London) are also comparable. For an iconography of Mrs Siddons see P.H. Highfill Jr, K.A. Burnim and E.A. Langhans: *A Biographical Dictionary of Actors, Actresses, Musicians, Dancers, Managers and Other Stage Personnel in London, 1660-1800* (1973-93) Vol.XIV, pp.37-67.

4. W. Sandby: *The History of the Royal Academy of Arts* (1862) Vol.I, p.308, quoted by McKay and Roberts, *op. cit.*, p.236. McKay and Roberts mention 'a portrait of very fine quality painted on a millboard ... sold at Christie's in 1901' [presumably LL 3669, although it is not known to have been fixed to a millboard at that date, nor has the Christie's sale been traced] 'which we believe to be the portrait referred to by Sandby'. Highfill, Burnim and Langhans, *op. cit.*, Vol.XIV, p.43 list five other portraits of Mrs Siddons by or attributed to Hoppner; none of these, in terms of likeness or style, are especially close to LL 3669.

5. John Wilson, letter, 2 January 1997, gallery files.

6. Mrs Siddons to Lord Hardwicke, letter, 23 February 1784, quoted by Judy Egerton: *National Gallery Catalogues: The British School* (1998) p.119.

7. Approximately 7 cm was trimmed from each edge of the canvas, and the work backed to the panel, in 1963 (treatment report, gallery files).

8. Wilson, *loc. cit.*, is however more cautious: 'it doesn't jump right out as Hoppner'.

portrait types by Hoppner. One version was owned by James Orrock (Webber, Vol.I, fp.65), which may have prompted Lever to buy LL 3669 in a spirit of friendly rivalry. In neither the portrait dated to about 1782 formerly in the Los Angeles County Museum of Art (Sotheby New York 19 May 1995 (176)), nor the portrait formerly attributed to Hoppner in the National Gallery of Victoria, Melbourne, nor Hoppner's drawing in the British Museum, does the sitter remotely resemble the one in LL 3669. It should be added that a version of LL 3669 titled *Mrs. Robinson as Perdita* (60.5 × 51 cm, signed *W. Owen pinx*; showing the sitter

differently costumed and with foliage in the background) was sold from the Los Angeles County Museum of Art at Christie New York 16 May 1996 (73). Inscription notwithstanding, the attribution of this work to William Owen (1769-1825) does not appear convincing.

2. Agnew's stockbooks, and copy invoice to Lever, gallery files.

3. For the likeness, see especially Bartolozzi's 1785 engraving after the portrait by Horace Hone, and David Martin's portrait study in black chalk of about the same date (National Gallery of Scotland); the famous full-length by Reynolds (Huntington Art Collections,

John Hoppner
1758-1810

Francis Rawdon-Hastings, 2nd Earl of Moira
LL 3587 (WHL 85, H 7)
oil on canvas, 127 × 101.5 cm
inscribed, top left: *EARL OF MOIRA/by Hoppner*

Born in Dublin in 1754, Lord Moira entered the army at the age of 16 in 1771 and after a distinguished

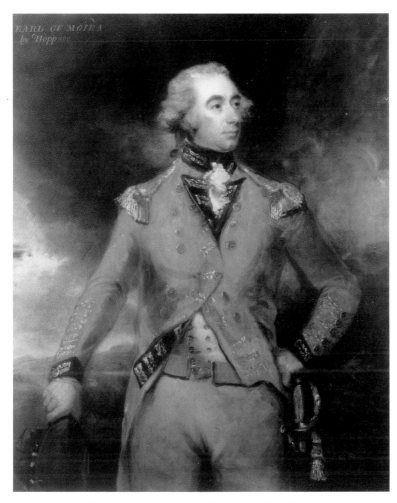

J. Hoppner: *Francis Rawdon-Hastings, 2nd Earl of Moira*
LL 3587

length by Hoppner's son in 1812.[3]
LL 3587 is stated in early inventories of the Lady Lever Art Gallery to have been painted in 1795,[4] but there is no evidence for this, and it is tempting to think that it is a character study undertaken by Hoppner in preparation for the full-length. The work is very rapidly and carelessly painted, as the pentimento of the right arm, which has been re-positioned closer to the body, suggests. Both arms remain badly drawn and modelled, while the relationship of head to body is awkward. Nevertheless the work has considerable spontaneity and *élan*.

Further portraits of Moira by Hoppner include a 30 × 25 in. half figure, currently untraced,[5] and the work engraved by Bartolozzi in 1804 which shows him as Acting Grand Master of the Freemasons; this seems to have been adapted by Bartolozzi himself from the 1794 type.

PROVENANCE:
[...Hon W. Vernon[6]]; Eyre & Sons; bt. Agnew June 1899; bt. by Lever 4 July 1899 (£1,150).

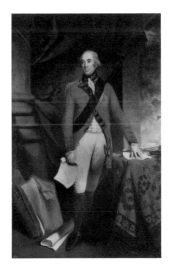

Fig. 18
J. Hoppner:
Francis Rawdon-Hastings,
2nd Earl of Moira
The Royal Collection
© Her Majesty Queen Elizabeth II

career in the American War of Independence had risen by 1793 to the rank of Major-General. For eleven years before this he had been ADC to King George III, and he had become the friend and confidant of the Prince of Wales. From 1790 (which may have made this portrait of particular interest to Lever) he was Acting Grand Master of the Freemasons of England. In 1793 he succeeded his father as 2nd Earl of Moira, and went on to enjoy a notable military and political career. He died as Governor of Malta in 1826.[1]

Hoppner's first portrait of Lord Moira is thought to have been the full-length commissioned by the Prince of Wales, exhibited at the Royal Academy in 1794 (Royal Collection, fig. 18). A half-length copy of this, 55 × 43 in., is at University College Oxford.[2] The relationship between this portrait type and LL 3587 (of which no other version is known) appears to be fairly close. Moira is about the same age in both, his hair is similarly dressed, and the costume is in effect the same, as the ribbon and Star of the Garter were added to the full-

REFERENCES:

1. *DNB*, Vol.xxv, pp.117-122; *Complete Peerage*, Vol.vi, pp.377-8; see also *Monthly Magazine* (January 1827) pp.107-9; and Oliver Millar: *Later Georgian Pictures in the Royal Collection* (1969) Vol.i, p.104.

2. W. McKay and W. Roberts: *John Hoppner RA* (1909) p.17.

3. Millar, *op. cit.*, Vol.i, p.52.

4. Repeated by Tatlock, p.54. C.R. Grundy, however, in 'Lord Leverhulme's Pictures at The Hill', *Connoisseur* (December 1917) p.190 dated the work to about 1806 and described it as 'illustrating in a singularly perfect manner Hoppner's attempt to free his art from the traditions of English 18th-century portraiture and evolve a new and original style of his own'.

5. McKay and Roberts, *loc. cit.*; owned in 1909 by Lady Arthur Russell. In it Moira is described as wearing a red uniform and having powdered hair, but the pose of the head is not that of LL 3587.

6. A note against the purchase in Agnew's stockbooks states that the work was in Vernon's collection.

John Hoppner
1758-1810

Lady Elizabeth Howard

LL 3128 (WHL 73, H 146)

oil on canvas, 127 × 102 cm

inscribed, bottom right: *Lady Elizabeth Howard/Duchess of Rutland*

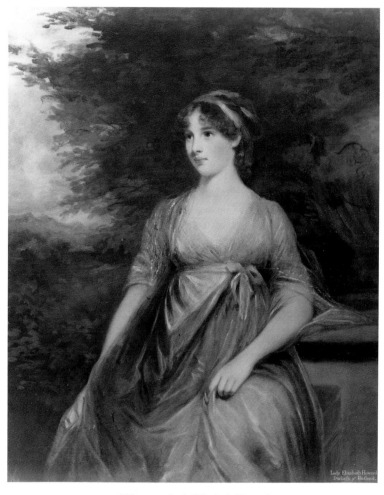

J. Hoppner: *Lady Elizabeth Howard*
LL 3128

The sitter's father, Frederick 5th Earl of Carlisle, one of the Whigs in the circle of the Prince of Wales whose patronage underpinned Hoppner's career in the 1790s, commissioned this portrait of his daughter in 1798, a few months before her marriage in April 1799 to the 5th Duke of Rutland. It is one of a cluster of portraits Hoppner made of the Carlisle and Rutland families,[1] and may be one of the works for which Hoppner was paid £102.15.- by Lord Carlisle on 9 August 1798.[2] The portrait was originally hung in the Carlisles' town house in Grosvenor Place, since it is recorded in manuscript notes on the pictures there made by the 5th Earl between 1800 and 1810: of LL 3128 he wrote 'the head well-coloured, spirited and like'.[3] It had been transferred to Castle Howard by 1814 and remained there for most of the 19th century.[4]

Lady Elizabeth, born on 13 November 1780, became one of the most admired women in Regency England. She was a noted patroness of artists and architects and herself an amateur artist;[5] she was the presiding genius of Belvoir Castle and of the improvement of the Belvoir estate, and was a celebrated farmer in her own right. On her death in November 1825 *The Times* observed that 'she produced in a few years changes which a mind less energetic would have required centuries to effect'.[6] She was also 'one of the brightest ornaments of the English court'[7] and formed a close friendship with the Duke of York.

The painting was formerly described as 'overcleaned and slightly repainted'.[8] There is now no evidence of overcleaning, but separation cracks, present especially in the lower part of the painting, have been extensively re-touched on more than one occasion.[9]

PROVENANCE:
by descent to George, 9th Earl of Carlisle; sold by him privately about 1892 to the dealer G. Donaldson;[10] bt. from Donaldson by Agnew December 1896; bt. from Agnew by Lever March 1897 (£3300).[11]

EXHIBITIONS:
New Gallery 1890 (207); *Guelph Exhibition* New Gallery 1891 (338); *International Exhibition* Paris 1900 (54); *International Exhibition* Glasgow 1901 (33); *Portraits by Sir Joshua Reynolds, Thomas Gainsborough etc* Birmingham Museum and Art Gallery 1903 (29); *Winter Exhibition* RA 1907; *Lord Leverhulme* RA 1980 (19).

ENGRAVINGS:
C. Wilkin (for *Ladies of Rank and Fashion*) May 1803; R. Cooper (for *La Belle Assemblée*) July 1809; A. Cardon.[12]

REFERENCES:
1. W. McKay and W. Roberts: *John Hoppner RA* (1909) record portraits of Lord Carlisle himself (1797), Lady Carlisle, and their son Viscount Morpeth (1798) (pp. 44, 175); two portraits of the Duke of Rutland, 1795 and 1799 (p. 222) and a second portrait of the Duchess of Rutland, whole length, painted after her marriage and completed by Matthew Wyatt (p. 223).
2. Carlisle family archives, J14/18, communicated by Christopher Ridgway, letter, 3 March 1998, gallery files.
3. Ridgway, *loc. cit.*
4. Ridgway, *loc. cit.*
5. Her drawings of the River Wye and Conway Castle, made from sketches by the Duke are referred to in Joseph Farington's Diary; see K. Garlick, A. McIntyre and K. Cave, eds.: *The Diary of Joseph Farington* (1978-84) Vol. VI, p. 2482. Her design for an entrance to Hyde Park Corner, and her involvement in the plans for a new proposed quay on the north bank of the River Thames and for a new Royal Palace are mentioned in her obituary in *The Times* (9 December 1825); for the latter see also F. Barker and

R. Hyde: *London as it might have been* (1982) p. 83.
6. *The Times* (3 December 1825) p. 2.
7. *The Times* (3 December 1825) *loc. cit.*
8. Tatlock, p. 54.
9. Condition and treatment report dating from 1979, gallery files.
10. Ridgway, *loc. cit.*
11. LL 3128 was Lever's first significant purchase of an 18th-century British painting; for an examination of the background to this aspect of his taste see *Lord Leverhulme*, pp. 17-25.
12. E. Evans: *Catalogue of Engraved Portraits, the Largest ever Submitted to the Public […]* (about 1853) Vol. 2, p. 344, cat. 20993.

John Hoppner
1758-1810

Jane, Countess of Oxford
LL 3670 (WHL 668, HH 120)
oil on canvas, 76 × 63.5 cm

With the difference that it is on canvas rather than a wooden support, LL 3670 is a close copy of what is assumed to be Hoppner's first version of the portrait (Tate Gallery, fig. 19).[1] That work is identified as the portrait of the Countess exhibited by Hoppner at the Royal Academy in 1798. The previous year he had shown a full-length of her, with her infant daughter Lady Jane Elizabeth Harley, which had been well-received,[2] and the present work may have been undertaken with an engraving in mind. S. W. Reynolds's mezzotint, published in 1799, was only the first of a large number of engravings and copies of the work which are testimony to the beauty and celebrity of the sitter.[3] (Hoppner himself, however, said of her that 'she wanted style and fashion'.)[4]

The condition of LL 3670 is mediocre. The paint is worn and flattened and there are many retouchings. Although it is not the version of the work used for

Reynolds's engraving, and probably post-dates the appearance of this,[5] it nevertheless appears of good enough quality to be autograph.

Jane Elizabeth, daughter of the Rev. James Scott, Chaplain in Ordinary to King George III, was born in 1774, and married Edward Harley, 5th Earl of Oxford in March 1794. She 'had so indifferent a reputation that her children were referred to as 'the Harleian Miscellany' and her own name was freely coupled with Lord Byron's and the Duke of Cumberland's, among others'.[6] At the time of Hoppner's portraits and for a considerable period afterwards she moved extensively in artistic circles.[7] She died in November 1824.

PROVENANCE:
… James Orrock by 1903;[8] bt. from Orrock by Lever 1910.[9]

REFERENCES:
1. M. Davies: *National Gallery Catalogues: The British School* (1946) p. 84.
2. W. McKay and W. Roberts: *John Hoppner RA* (1909) p. 192 and reproduced facing; this work is now in the Bass Museum of Art, Miami Beach, Florida, USA.
3. Further copies and versions include the canvas which appeared in the Harland Peck sale, Christie 25 June 1920 (84), which was wrongly supposed by Tatlock, p. 55, and Davies, *loc. cit.* to be identical with LL 3670. This was sold at Parke-Bernet New York 24 January 1951 (77). A version in a private collection, Hampshire in 1979 (Tate Gallery files), and one sold at Christie South Kensington 30 November 1995 (212) may be identical, and the same as the work above. A further copy by Solomon Coles was in a private collection, Wiltshire in 1975 (Tate Gallery files). A contemporary copy in miniature is in the Pierpont Morgan Library, New York. For further engravings after Hoppner, see McKay and Roberts, *loc. cit.*
4. K. Garlick, A. McIntyre and K. Cave, eds.: *The Diary of Joseph Farington* (1978-84) Vol. III, p. 843.

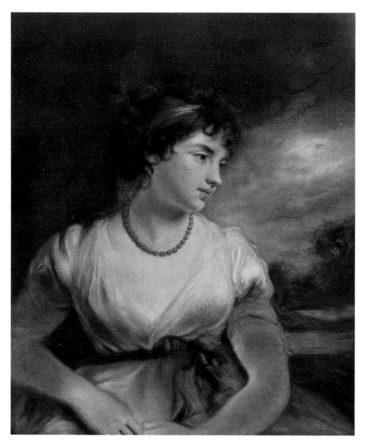

J. Hoppner: *Jane, Countess of Oxford*
LL 3670

between Uvedale Price and Richard
Payne Knight over a passage in the
latter's *Analytical Inquiry into the
Principles of Taste*.
8. Repr. Webber, Vol.II, fp.6. In the
Parke-Bernet sale catalogue, 24 January
1951 (see note 3 above), Orrock is stated
to have owned his version by 1895. The
work did not, however, appear in the
Orrock-Linton sale of that year.
9. 1910 Inventory p.42, valued at £800.

'John Hoppner'
1758-1810

*Portrait of a Lady
(called 'Maria Clements')*
LL 3666 (WHL 562, HH 88)
oil on canvas, 73.5 × 60 cm

At the time of its purchase by Lever
LL 3666 was described simply as
*Portrait of a Lady, a member of the
Leitrim family*. The portrait came
with the same provenance as LL 3605
(see above under Gainsborough) and
the two works were said to be the
two wives of the Rt. Hon. Henry
Theophilus Clements (1734-1795),
namely Mary (née Webb, d. 1777)
and Catherine (née Beresford, 1762-
1836).[1] More recently it has been

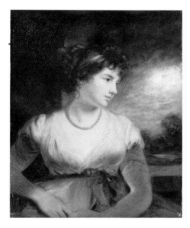

Fig.19
J. Hoppner: *Jane Countess of Oxford*
© Tate Gallery London

5. Davies, *loc. cit.*, points out that some
states of Reynolds's mezzotint illustrate a
large ribbon bow and others a small one,
and notes a pentimento in the Tate
painting which suggests that Hoppner
turned the bow from a large to a small
one, presumably while the print was being
worked on. In LL 3670 there is an
unaltered small bow.
6. *Complete Peerage*, Vol.X, pp.269-70;
see also McKay and Roberts, *loc. cit.*
7. Her name appears regularly in
Farington's Diary (see note 4 above);
apart from being on familiar terms with
Hoppner, she was also drawn by Richard
Westall and frequented his company; in
Paris in 1802 she sat next to Benjamin
West at a banquet given by West for
English and French colleagues; in 1806
she acted as a go-between in a quarrel

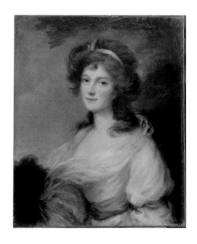

'J. Hoppner':
Portrait of a Lady (called 'Maria Clements')
LL 3666

recognised that neither portrait can be of a woman who died as early as 1777 and it has been proposed that LL 3666 instead represents Maria, Henry Clements's third daughter.[2] She was born in 1776, married the Rev. J. W. Keating in March 1799 and died in 1800.[3] However, whether the sitter is in fact any member of the Leitrim Clements family is open to question.[4]

The attribution of the portrait to Hoppner, although supported in the quite recent past,[5] is unacceptable. The work bears all the hallmarks of a late 19th-century pastiche of his style.[6]

PROVENANCE:
[? by descent to Gerald Clements; bt. from Clements by James Orrock about April 1909[7]]; bt. from Orrock by Lever 1910.[8]

REFERENCES:
1. The source of this information was a letter, supposedly from Gerald Clements, a descendant of the family, to James Orrock, dated 3 April 1909, untraced but partially recorded in gallery files. Tatlock, p.55, following this, identified the sitter in LL 3666 as Mary Clements. A gallery label on the reverse of LL 3666 identifies the sitter as Catherine Clements; this reflects a historic confusion within the gallery between LL 3666 and LL 3605.
2. Curatorial notes in gallery files.
3. See P.W. Clement: *Ancestors and Descendants of Robert Clement* (1927) pp.905-913 for outline biographies of this branch of the family.
4. Clement, *loc. cit.* and index, lists no descendant by the name of Gerald Clements, and the possibility cannot be discounted that the vendor, letter and portraits were 'manufactured' by Orrock himself.
5. W.G. Constable described LL 3666 to A.C. Tait as 'a genuine but inferior Hoppner'; note in gallery files.
6. This view was endorsed by John Wilson, letter, 2 January 1997, gallery files. No portraits of the Clements family are listed in W. McKay and W. Roberts: *John Hoppner RA* (1909).
7. See notes 1 and 4 above.
8. 1910 Inventory p.38, valued at £800.

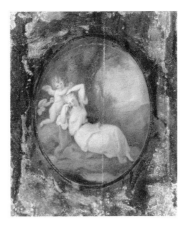

'A. Kauffman':
A Nymph and Cupid
LL 3610

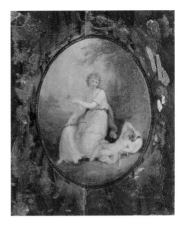

'A. Kauffman':
Cupid Disarmed
LL 3611

'Angelica Kauffman'
1741-1807

A Nymph and Cupid
LL 3610 (WHL 1418, TM 5)
oil on oak panel, 40 × 33.5 cm
(27 × 22 cm painted oval)

Cupid Disarmed
LL 3611 (WHL 1416, TM 3)
oil on oak panel, 40 × 34 cm
(27 × 22 cm painted oval)

These panels can be identified with a 'pair of paintings in oils attributed to Angelica Kauffman' purchased by Lever in 1901.[1] By May 1905, when they appear on an inventory of Lever's paintings at Thornton Manor, the attribution had been lost and the works were subsequently ascribed to William Hamilton, RA (1751-1801).[2]

It seems likely that LL 3610-11 were painted for an item of furniture.[3] X-radiographs reveal that under the present layer of brown overpaint there are laurel wreaths surrounding the oval images; while technical analysis reveals the use of a very thin metallic foil as a ground.[4]

Both these features suggest the work of a decorative artist. Even allowing for the very poor condition of both panels (they are split and heavily repainted) the quality of the works is not high, and the attribution to Hamilton, who is known to have decorated furniture, seems optimistic. Kauffman herself is not known to have made autograph works for furniture, but prints after her works were very popular in her own lifetime as source material for decorative artists.[5]

A Nymph and Cupid is based on Kauffman's *Cupid Binding Aglaia to a Laurel*, of which a stipple engraving by Thomas Burke (re-issued in

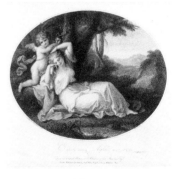

Fig.20
T. Burke, after A. Kauffman:
Cupid Binding Aglaia to a Laurel
© The British Museum

1816, fig.20) was published in 1784, together with its pair, *Cupid Disarmed by Euphrosyne*. The subjects are drawn from a festal piece, *Le Grazie Vendicate*, by the 18th century Viennese court poet Metastasio, whose works became very popular in England in the 1770s and 1780s.[6] However, LL 3611 is not based on Burke's companion print, and no direct source for it in Kauffman's work can be traced. Conceivably, whoever painted LL 3611 invented the design knowing what the companion subject was, but without a visual source to hand.

PROVENANCE:
…J.E. & E.K. Preston, Harrogate; bt. by Lever 22 August 1901 (£35).

REFERENCES:
1. Copy of dealer's bill, gallery files.
2. 1905 Inventory as *Portrait, Lady and Boy* (£2.-.-.) and *Portrait, Lady and Cupid* (£2.-.-.) (no artist) (it may be significant that they are the third and fifth items on this list although the (later) TM numbering does not otherwise follow the order of this inventory); 1906 Inventory as *Lady with Cupid's Bow* (£5.-.-.) and *Female under Tree sleeping with Cupid at back* (£5.-.-.) (no artist); 1911 Inventory (by Tom Cox) p.17, as by Hamilton; his attribution followed by Tatlock, p.53. The three inventories cited above are in gallery files.
3. Lucy Wood, verbally, 21 November 1996. It is significant that the firm from whom Lever bought the works were dealers in antiques, not paintings.
4. Conservation report, gallery files.
5. M. Forbes Adam and M. Mauchline: 'Kauffman's Decorative Work', in W. Wassyng Roworth, ed.: *Angelica Kauffman: A Continental Artist in Georgian England* (1992) pp.113-140.
6. Forbes Adam and Mauchline, *op. cit.*, pp.136-8. Kauffman's original paintings are in the Rosenbach Museum, Philadelphia. For the correct date of Burke's engravings see D. Alexander: 'Chronological Checklist of Singly Issued English Prints after Angelica Kauffman' in Roworth, *op. cit.*, pp.179-89.

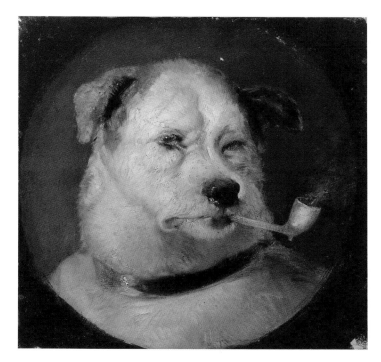

Sir E. Landseer: *A Jack in Office*
LL 3721

Sir Edwin Landseer
1802-1873

A Jack in Office
LL 3721 (WHL 3181)
oil on canvas, 28 × 30.5 cm

This is a much enlarged version of the dog's head in Landseer's *A Jack in Office*, first exhibited at the Royal Academy in 1833 (Victoria and Albert Museum, fig.21).[1] Although parts of the painting are weak, notably the pipe and the area around the collar (which, nevertheless, are not shown by technical examination to be significantly later additions or retouchings) it seems on balance likely to be authentic. It may be one of the works titled *Head of a Dog* which appeared in Landseer's studio sale in 1874.[2]

At least since 1887 up to the present, LL 3721 has gone under the title *Low Life*.[3] This is the name of another Landseer painting of a white

Jack Russell terrier (Tate Gallery, fig.22) perhaps taken from the same dog,[4] but clearly differently posed. The confusion may have arisen because of the pipe, which is one of the props in the Tate Gallery's painting; although a closer precedent, in which a very similar looking pipe is actually being smoked by the dog, occurs in Landseer's *Comical Dogs* of 1836 (also Victoria and Albert Museum, fig.23). In 1907

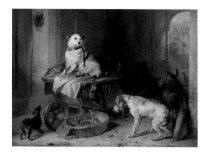

Fig.21
Sir E. Landseer: *A Jack in Office*
V & A Picture Library

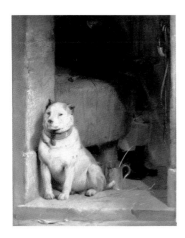

Fig.22
Sir E. Landseer: *Low Life*
© Tate Gallery London

A. & F. Pears issued with their Christmas Annual a print based on LL 3721 titled *A Quiet Pipe*, in which the dog wears a collar plate engraved with the word *Pears*). The print must have been familiar to Lever; and so must the painting itself from its presence until 1904 in James Orrock's collection.

PROVENANCE:
…James Orrock by 1887;[6] Christie 25-27 April 1895 (326) bt. in; Christie 4-6 June 1904 (268) bt. Grego (£110.5.-.); […? A. & F. Pears[7]]; ….Sir Joseph Beecham by 1913;[8] Christie 3 May 1917 (37) bt. Gooden & Fox for Lever (58 gns.).

EXHIBITION:
International Exhibition Glasgow 1888 (34)

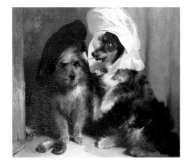

Fig.23
Sir E. Landseer: *Comical Dogs*
V & A Picture Library

REFERENCES:
1   R. Parkinson: *Victoria and Albert Museum Catalogue of British Oil Paintings 1820-1860* (1990) pp.144-45.
2.   It does not, however, appear to be either lot 40, *Head of a Dog*, bt. Agnew (£147), which Agnew sold to Lord Feversham, or lot 208, *Head of a Dog*, bt. Agnew (£94.10.-) which is described as being signed and dated 1821. The *Low Life: Portrait of Jack* dating from 1822 listed by A. Graves: *Catalogue of the Works of the Late Sir Edwin Landseer RA* (1876) p.7, cat.55 is not compositionally related to LL 3721.
3.   It was exhibited under this title in 1888 and was explicitly related to the Tate Gallery painting both by Tatlock, p.100, and by R. Ormond: *Sir Edwin Landseer*, exhibition catalogue, Philadelphia and London (1982) p.99, cat.58. See also notes 2 above and 6 below.
4.   Ormond, *loc. cit.*
5.   Photograph presented by C. Mason-Pope 1991, gallery files.
6.   LL 3721 bears an *Architects Conversazione* label on the reverse dated 1887, identifying the work's title as *Low Life* and its owner as James Orrock. No exhibition of this title has been traced but this was the name of an RIBA discussion group active in the second half of the 19th century which may well have held informal exhibitions of items owned by members (information from Eleanor Gawne, RIBA, verbally, 22 April 1998). The 'CONVERSAZIONE of members and their guests at the South Kensington Museum, by permission of the Lords of the Committee of Council on Education' held on 5 May 1887, referred to in the *Royal Institute of British Architects Journal of Proceedings*, New Series, Vol III (1887) p.v., may be the occasion concerned.
7.   Apart from the evidence of the print itself, (see main text), this is suggested by the name of the purchaser, Grego, presumably the Joseph Grego who was the author in 1898 of articles in the *Magazine of Art* on the collection of T. J. Barratt of Pears.
8.   LL 3721 is reproduced in C. R. Grundy: 'Sir Joseph Beecham's Collection at Hampstead II', *Connoisseur* (1913) p.106.

Sir Thomas Lawrence
1769-1830

Thomas Gataker
LL 3554 (WHL 3709)
oil on canvas, 76 × 63 cm

Thomas Gataker (1749-1844) was second cousin of the artist, his mother being Lawrence's mother's first cousin. At the date of his marriage in 1776 to Mary Swale he is described as 'of London, Hamburgh merchant' but he moved to Mildenhall, Suffolk, from where his wife's family came, and later lived at White Knights Park, Berkshire.[1]

Lawrence received 15 guineas for a portrait of Gataker 'soon after he came up to London',[2] presumably the work which appears in the 'List of Portraits painted by Mr. Lawrence about the years 1792, 1793 etc' included in the biography of the artist published the year after his death.[3] In a letter written in 1827, Lawrence alludes to finding a portrait of Gataker 'painted many years since' which, when cleaned, he will send to his son.[4] After Lawrence's death George Gataker claimed from the artist's executors a portrait of Mr Thomas Gataker 'painted some yrs ago & paid for and lent to Sir Tho L.'.[5] It is unclear, but likely, that these references all refer to the same portrait. LL 3554 can perhaps be dated to 1793 or a little later,[6] and though this is some time after Lawrence's arrival in London, no other portrait of Gataker is known.[7]

The paint surface of LL 3554 has suffered badly from bituminous cracking which has been inpainted with limited success by a later hand.

PROVENANCE:
by descent to M. Leicester Swale Gataker; Christie 20 December 1918 (145) bt. Gooden & Fox for Lever (£420).

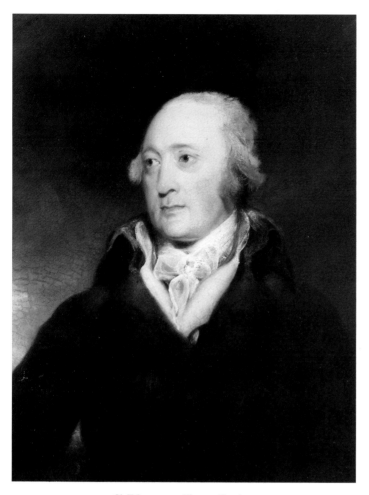

Sir T. Lawrence: *Thomas Gataker*

LL 3554

REFERENCES:
1. Sir W. Armstrong: *Lawrence* (1913) p.133; Swale and Gataker family papers deposited at Bury St. Edmunds Record Office (996/3/2).
2. Armstrong, *loc. cit.*
3. D.E. Williams: *Life and Correspondence of Sir Thomas Lawrence* (1831) Vol.I, p.129, *cit.* K. Garlick: 'A catalogue of the paintings, drawings and pastels of Sir Thomas Lawrence', *Walpole Society*, Vol.XXXIX (1964) Appendix I, p.268.
4. Armstrong, *loc. cit.*
5. Garlick, *op. cit.*, Appendix IV, p.293, no.197.
6. Garlick, *op. cit.*, p.84, dates LL 3554 'Early 1790s'. In *Sir Thomas Lawrence, A Complete Catalogue* (1989) he dates it '*c.*1795' (p.192, cat.322). The work is close in style to the celebrated portrait of Sir Richard Payne Knight exhibited at the Royal Academy in 1794 (Whitworth Art Gallery, University of Manchester).
7. A drawing dated 1795 hitherto identified as a portrait of William Brabazon Ponsonby, later 1st Baron Ponsonby, in the Ackland Art Museum, University of North Carolina, Chapel Hill, has been thought by Garlick to be of Gataker (C. Gillham, Assistant Curator, Ackland Art Museum, letter, 6 June 1997, gallery files). Despite considerable similarities in their pose and dress, and some of facial resemblance, it is not clear that the two works are related or are of the same man.

after
Sir Thomas Lawrence
1769-1830

Henrietta,
Countess of Harewood
LL 3555 (WHL 2787)
oil on canvas, 50.5 × 37.5 cm

Lever purchased LL 3555 as a portrait of Eliza Farren (the actress, later Countess of Derby, whose famous full-length portrait by Lawrence was exhibited at the Royal Academy in 1790). Subsequently, it was identified as a reduced copy of the unfinished portrait of the Countess of Harewood which Lawrence had begun 'before 1806'[1] and which was finally acquired by the sitter's husband at Lawrence's posthumous sale at Christie, 25 June 1831 (Harewood House; fig 24).[2] Henrietta, elder daughter of Sir John Sebright, 6th Bart, born in 1770, married Henry, Viscount Lascelles, later 2nd Earl of Harewood, in 1794. She was an accomplished artist, and drawings by her are in the collection at Harewood.[3] She died in 1840.

The early history of LL 3555 is unknown. Comparison with Hoppner's 1796 portrait of the Countess of Harewood (fig.25) – clearly the same person – suggests that she is a little older here, but not by as much as nine or ten years. LL 3555 is likely to be one of the canvases left in Lawrence's studio at his death, some of which were described at their sale as copies, and very few of which were identified. The work is of good quality. It is not an exact copy of the Harewood picture; the head is tilted fractionally differently and there are slight variations in the treatment of the hair and the costume. It is perhaps most likely to be a copy undertaken as an exercise by a student or assistant working in Lawrence's studio.

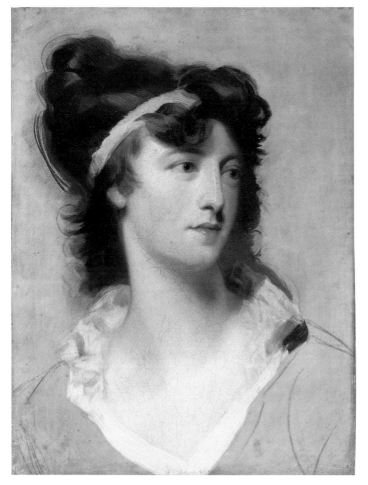

after Sir T. Lawrence: *Henrietta, Countess of Harewood*
LL 3555

PROVENANCE:
...T.J. Barratt by 1898;⁴ Christie 11 May 1916 (70) bt. Gooden & Fox for Lever (320 gns.).

EXHIBITIONS:
Loan Collection of Portraits Birmingham Museum and Art Gallery 1900 (9); *Lawrence* Brighton Art Gallery 1951 (12).

REFERENCES:
1. K. Garlick: 'A Catalogue of the Paintings, Drawings and Pastels of Sir Thomas Lawrence', *Walpole Society* Vol. XXXIX (1964) p.270 (Appendix II: *List of Pictures Painted and Painting by Thomas Lawrence Esqr.* [February 1806] no.92 ('Mrs. Lascelles')) probably refers to this portrait. When the Countess claimed the work after Lawrence's death, she said it had been begun 25 or 30 years previously (*ibid.*, p.274: Appendix IV: *Executors' List*, no.8).
2. K. Garlick: *Sir Thomas Lawrence, A Complete Catalogue* (1989) p.205, cat.388. The juxtaposition of LL 3555 with the Harewood picture at the Brighton exhibition of 1951 drew attention to the error in the identification (as noted by Garlick, *Burlington Magazine* (August 1951) p.250); thereafter, following T. Borenius: *Catalogue of the Pictures and Drawings at Harewood House* (1936) p.152, cat.366, the sitter was thought to be Lady Louisa Lascelles (1812-1886) until queried by Garlick (1964) p.121.
3. Information from Jane Sellars, Harewood House, letter, 2 February 1998.
4. J. Grego: 'The Art Collection at Bell Moor, The House of Mr Thomas J. Barratt III', *Magazine of Art* (1898) pp.261-8; repr. p.265.

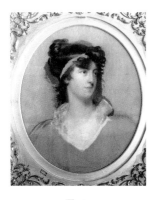

Fig.24
Sir T. Lawrence:
Henrietta, Countess of Harewood
Reproduced by kind permission of the Earl and Countess
of Harewood and the Harewood House Trust

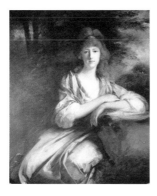

Fig.25
J. Hoppner:
Henrietta, Countess of Harewood
Reproduced by kind permission of the Earl and Countess
of Harewood and the Harewood House Trust

after
Sir Thomas Lawrence
1769-1830

*Portrait of a Lady
(called 'Eleanor,
Countess of Harborough')*
LL 3671 (LP 62)
oil on canvas, 61 × 51 cm

This work was purchased, and
has hitherto been identified, as
a portrait of Eleanor, Countess of
Harborough.[1] She was born in 1772,
the second daughter of the Hon. John
Monckton of Fineshade Abbey and
married in 1791 Philip, Lord Sherard,
who succeeded as 5th Earl of
Harborough in 1799. She died in
1809. The fact that the painting was
owned by E. Sherard Kennedy,[2] the
late 19th-century artist, and was
stated to have descended to him
from the Countess herself,[3] gave
credence to this identification.

Nevertheless, LL 3671 appears to
be a copy of the head in Lawrence's
portrait of *Charlotte Jerningham,
Mrs Fraser of Lovat* (California
Palace of the Legion of Honor, San
Francisco, fig. 26). This work, which
Lawrence started around the time
of the sitter's marriage in 1823, was
completed after his death by his
assistant John Simpson.[4] A further
version of the work has been
identified as of yet another sitter,
Lady Louisa Lucy Winterton, and
dated to 1809.[5]

The work is not easy to date either
in terms of Lawrence's stylistic
development or from hairstyle and
costume. On balance, it appears more
likely to show a woman in her
twenties than in her thirties, and to
date from the 1820s rather than two
decades earlier. An added complica-
tion is that the work has been
considerably retouched, especially
on the face, neck and bust, to the
extent that Lawrence's authorship
cannot be regarded as certain.[6]

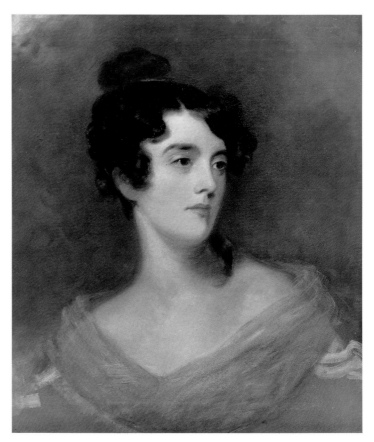

after Sir T. Lawrence:
Portrait of a Lady (called 'Eleanor, Countess of Harborough')
LL 3671

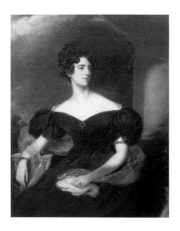

Fig. 26
Sir T. Lawrence:
*Charlotte Jerningham,
Mrs. Fraser of Lovat*
Fine Art Museums of San Francisco,
Mildred Anna Williams Collection

PROVENANCE:
[? by descent to] E. Sherard Kennedy; bt.
from his nephew by D. Croal Thomson,
Barbizon House; from whom bt. by the
Trustees of the Lady Lever Art Gallery,
December 1945 (£550).

REFERENCES:
1. K. Garlick: *Sir Thomas Lawrence,
A Complete Catalogue* (1989) p.204,
cat. 381.
2. Stencil on the reverse of the canvas:
E.S. KENNEDY/WALTON HOUSE/
BROMPTON.
3. Provenance given at the date of the
work's purchase, gallery files.
4. Garlick, *op. cit.*, pp.190-1, cat. 313.
5. F. Muller & Co., Amsterdam, 24 April
1906 (19); the date inscribed on the
reverse.
6. Garlick, *op. cit.*, p.204 observes that

'while the head appears to be autograph, the drapery and parts of the background are almost certainly late additions'. Inspection under ultra-violet light does not indicate that the gauzy drapery is significantly more recent than the rest of the canvas; but it does appear to have been added after the canvas was put in an oval mount (no longer present); broad strokes of white paint, approximating to the low cut of the dress in the portrait of *Mrs. Fraser of Lovat*, are visible underneath. The paint surface of LL 3671 continues on to the left and right-hand tacking edges.

'Sir Thomas Lawrence'
1769-1830

Portrait of a Lady (called 'Miss Tysson')
LL 3696 (WHL 2008, HH 40)
oil on canvas, 76.5 × 63 cm

Lever acquired LL 3696 as by Lawrence, but no part of the work can convincingly be ascribed to him.[1] The head, which is of higher quality than the rest of the portrait, is executed in a sub-Lawrentian idiom, but the torso and background are crudely painted, possibly by a later hand. No wholly convincing attribution for LL 3696 has emerged[2] but the costume suggests a date in the late 1820s or early 1830s.[3] Biographical information about Miss Tysson is lacking and the name may be an invention.[4]

PROVENANCE:
…James Orrock; bought from Orrock by Lever 1910.[5]

REFERENCES:
1. LL 3696 was however accepted as authentic by W.G. Constable, note in gallery files.
2. Tatlock, p.54, attributed LL 3696 to George Henry Harlow (1787-1819); on grounds both of style and likely date this is unacceptable. LL 3696 bears some resemblance to works attributed to Lawrence's assistant John Simpson (1782-1847) but this suggestion remains

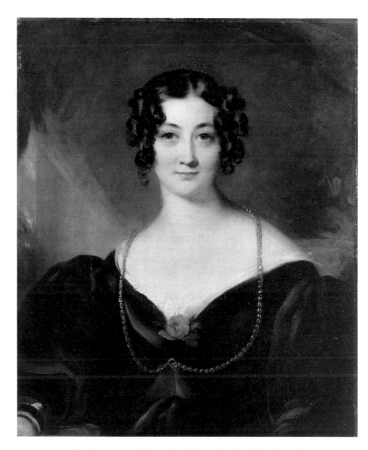

'Sir T. Lawrence': *Portrait of a Lady (called 'Miss Tysson')*
LL 3696

speculative.
3. Aileen Ribeiro, verbally, 26 February 1998.
4. The unorthodox spelling of the name with a double *s* may be a feature of names invented by James Orrock; compare *Miss Fergusson* (LL 3667 above, under Gainsborough).
5. 1910 Inventory p.34, valued at £200.

after
Sir Peter Lely
1618-1680

Barbara Villiers, Duchess of Cleveland
LL 3157 (WHL 2874)
oil on canvas, 76.5 × 71 cm

Lever purchased LL 3157 as a portrait of Mrs Beauchamp (later Countess of Chesterfield) by Lely[1] but the work has been shown to represent Barbara Villiers, Duchess of Cleveland (*c.*1641-1709), mistress of Charles II from the Restoration and mother of at least six of his children.[2] Lely painted her on many separate occasions from about 1662 into the 1670s; most of these portraits were much copied.[3] LL 3157 derives from Lely's full-length painted about 1664 when she was Countess of Castlemaine (private collection, Grand Bahama, fig.27);[4] it is of mediocre quality but may have been executed in Lely's studio.[5]

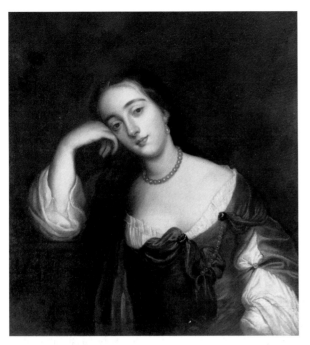

after Sir P. Lely:
Barbara Villiers, Duchess of Cleveland
LL 3157

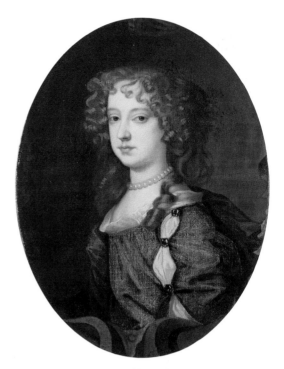

after Sir P. Lely:
Princess Mary, later Queen Mary II
LL 3165

PROVENANCE:
…Hugh Blaker; Christie 21 July 1916 (97, part);[6] bt. Gooden and Fox for Lever (11 gns.).

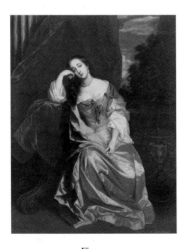

Fig. 27
Sir P. Lely:
Barbara Villiers, Duchess of Cleveland
Private collection; photograph courtesy the
National Portrait Gallery, London

REFERENCES:
1. An inscription on the reverse of the canvas reads *Countess of Chesterfield/by/Sir Peter Lely.*
2. E. Morris and M. Evans: *Lady Lever Art Gallery Port Sunlight: Catalogue of Foreign Works* (1983) pp. 12-13.
3. Oliver Millar: *The Tudor, Stuart and Early Georgian Pictures in the Collection of Her Majesty the Queen* (1963) p. 125, cat. 257; R. Beckett: *Lely* (1951) p. 40, cats. 100-109d; Oliver Millar: *Sir Peter Lely*, exhibition catalogue, National Portrait Gallery (1978) pp. 62-3, cat. 45.
4. Beckett, *loc. cit.*, cat. 102.
5. 'At the time of his death Lely's studio contained thirteen copies and one original portrait of the Duchess' (Millar (1978) *loc. cit.*).
6. LL 3157 was purchased with a portrait of Charles II in Garter Robes which was accessioned by Lever as WHL 2873 and is now in the Hall i' th' Wood collection, Bolton Museum and Art Gallery.

after
Sir Peter Lely
1618-1680

*Princess Mary,
later Queen Mary II*
LL 3165 (WHL 2858)
oil on canvas, 67.5 × 50.5 (oval)

This is a variant of Lely's earliest portrait of Princess Mary (1662-1694), who married William of Orange and became Queen Mary II of England.[1] The prime version (private collection, fig. 28) is likely to have resulted from the sitting mentioned in an undated letter from the Princess to her friend Frances Apsley, Lady Bathurst: 'My dear wil excuse me if my letter be not as it shoud be for I am in great hast to be drest for Mr Liley will be here at ten of the cloke …'.[2] The portrait has been dated to around 1672 (when the Princess was only ten),[3] perhaps

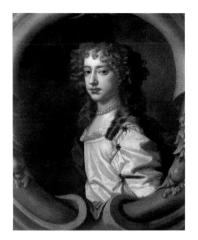

Fig.28
Sir P. Lely:
Princess Mary, later Queen Mary II
Private collection;
photograph Courtauld Institute of Art

History of the Apsley & Bathurst families
(1903) pp.62-63.
3. Beckett, *loc. cit.*
4. Beckett, *loc. cit.*, cat.326.
5. T. Borenius: 'Sir Peter Lely's
Collection', *Burlington Magazine* (1943)
pp.185-191.
6. Beckett, *loc. cit.*

'Sir Peter Lely'
1618-1680

Portrait of a Lady
LL 3153 (WHL 1207)
oil on canvas, 106 × 84 cm

from a comparison with her
appearance in Lely's second portrait
type, which dates from the period of
her marriage at the age of fifteen in
1677;[4] in this she certainly does
appear somewhat older, although
recognizably the same person.

The very abraded condition of the
paint surface makes assessment of
LL 3165 difficult, but its rather bland
and even quality suggests it is a
studio copy. The chief differences
between it and the original are its
smaller size, the actual rather than
feigned oval format and the green
rather than pale blue dress. LL 3165
is perhaps to be identified as the
bust length copy of the Princess of
Orange which was included in Lely's
posthumous sale.[5] Another version
of the portrait is recorded at Audley
End.[6]

PROVENANCE:
…Mrs Milbank; Christie 14 July 1916
(141, part) bt. Gooden & Fox for Lever
(£23.2.-.).

REFERENCES:
1. R. Beckett: *Lely* (1951) p.52, cat.325.
2. Cited by Earl Bathurst: *Catalogue of
the Bathurst Collection of Pictures* (1908)
pp.18-19; compare Hon. B. Bathurst:

Lever purchased LL 3153 as by Lely.
It has been pointed out that the
sitter's pose is close to Lely types
such as *Jane Scott, Marchioness of
Tweeddale* (private collection,
fig.29),[1] but stylistically the work is
not at all similar to Lely's and it
cannot be associated with his studio.
LL 3153 is a work of some quality: the
strongly modelled face and hands
and the rather finicky handling of the
ringlets and the background foliage
are distinctive.[2] It can be dated to the
early or middle 1660s.

PROVENANCE:
…John Ward, Blackburn; bt. by Lever
through Jonathan Simpson of Bolton,
July 1913 (£110).

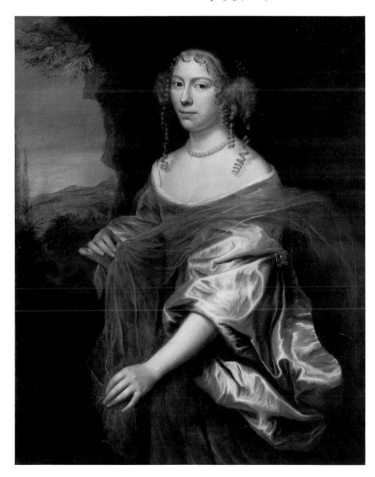

'Sir P. Lely': *Portrait of a Lady*
LL 3153

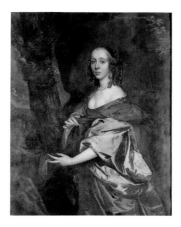

Fig.29
Sir P. Lely:
Jane Scott, Marchioness of Tweeddale
Collection of Hugo Morley-Fletcher;
photograph courtesy the Scottish National Portrait Gallery

REFERENCES:
1. E. Morris and M. Evans: *Lady Lever Art Gallery Port Sunlight: Catalogue of Foreign Works* (1983) p.12.
2. LL 3153 was restored in the early 1960s when a large amount of heavy overpainting was removed (Robin Ashton, letter, 23 January 1963, gallery files). No convincing attribution has been made.

John Linnell

1792-1882

Woodcutters' Repast

LL 3738 (WHL 142, H 105)
oil on panel, 24 × 37.5 cm
signed and dated: *J Linnell ft. 1831*
(bottom, left of centre)

A manuscript label on the reverse of LL 3738 reads: *Woodcutters, John Linnell/Snr. [...] of Richard Webster RA.* Linnell is known to have sold a version of *Woodcutters' Repast* to fellow-artist Thomas Webster for 40 guineas in 1846[1] and despite the error over the christian name the label seems to confirm LL 3738 is that work, which had been painted some fifteen years earlier. Linnell noted in his journal, 17 February 1830: 'Began a duplicate of the Woodcutter's

Repast 15 × 9 in.';[2] and continued to record his progress on the painting: he worked on it for two days in May 1830, and having laid it aside, completed it over six days between July and October 1831.[3]

Linnell's first treatment of this subject is a drawing, fractionally larger than LL 3738, in black and white chalks on grey paper, which is inscribed *Windsor Forest* and dated 1815.[4] Linnell etched the composition in reverse in 1818[5] and in 1819-20 painted a first oil version, which is presumed to be the work shown at the British Institution in 1827 and purchased by the Hon. Agar Ellis.[6] Also dating from 1827 is a watercolour version, which was commissioned from Linnell by Mrs Haldimand through George Fennel Robson.[7]

PROVENANCE:
bt. from Linnell by T. Webster RA, 1846; Christie 21 May 1887 (176) bt. Agnew (£246.15.-.); Keeley Halswelle;...James Orrock by 1895; Christie 25-27 April 1895 (295) bt. in (290 gns.); Christie 4-6 June 1904 (108), bt. in (380 gns.); bt. from Orrock by Lever November 1904.[8]

EXHIBITION:
Old Masters RA 1883 (19).

REFERENCES:
1. The price is noted in Linnell's sketchbook; information from D. Linnell, letter, 24 April 1997, gallery files.
2. John Linnell's journal, Linnell Trust and Ivimy papers, communicated by D. Linnell, *loc. cit.*
3. Linnell, *loc. cit.*
4. Exh. *John Linnell and His Circle* Colnaghi 1973 (46); sold Sotheby 14 April 1994 (354).
5. K. Crouan: *John Linnell, A Centenary Exhibition*, exhibition catalogue, Fitzwilliam Museum Cambridge and Yale Center for British Art (1982-3) p.18, cat.49.
6. K. Crouan: *John Linnell, Truth to Nature*, exhibition catalogue, Martyn Gregory Gallery (1982) p.31, cat.65; both this entry and the Fitzwilliam Museum catalogue entry (see note 5 above) identify LL 3738 as the 1819-20 painting. *A Story: The Life of John Linnell* (1893) Vol.II, p.263, describes LL 3738 as a replica painted in 1826 and lists a further replica painted in 1830, but there is no documentary evidence that Linnell painted a version in 1826. That he did in fact do so (the 1830 Journal reference to LL 3738 as a "duplicate" notwithstanding) is suggested by two pieces of evidence.

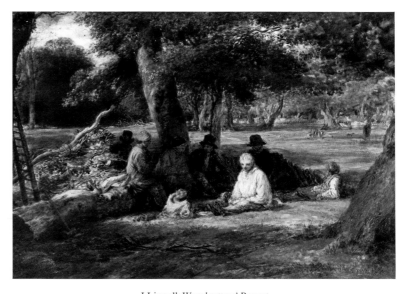

J. Linnell: *Woodcutters' Repast*
LL 3738

Firstly it is unlikely that Linnell would have waited till 1827 to exhibit a painting finished in 1820. Secondly, a version which appeared on the London art market in 1990, 28.5 × 45 cm, was stated to have been formerly in Linnell family ownership; if so, it can only have been the work sold to Agar Ellis on the improbable supposition that it was later re-purchased by the artist or his family. The fact that this work follows the original drawing and the etching in showing the woodcutters at a slightly greater distance, and in extending the design to left and right as compared with LL 3738, strongly suggests it is the 1819-20 version.

7. 6½ × 10½ in.; Christie 17 November 1981 (149); exh. Martyn Gregory Gallery 1982 as *Resting Woodcutters, Bray Wood, Windsor* (Crouan, *loc. cit.*, and repr. p.30).

8. 1904 Inventory p.2, no.44.

John Linnell
1792-1882

Woodcutters in a Forest Valley
LL 3730 (WHL 46, H 45)
oil on canvas, 37 × 53.5 cm

Linnell's note of this painting in his sketchbook (British Museum, fig.30) indicates that he called it simply *Woodcutter*. It is listed under the year 1850, and has been identified as the work referred to in Linnell's journal entry of 15 March of that year: 'Pro[ceded] small wood scene.'[1]

PROVENANCE:
bt. from Linnell by Joseph Gillott;[2] ... David Price; Christie's 2 April 1892 (88) bt. Agnew (£390) for James Orrock; Christie 4-6 June 1904 (109) bt. in (480 gns.); bt. from Orrock by Lever November 1904.[3]

REFERENCES:
1. Information from D. Linnell, letter, 24 April 1997, gallery files.
2. This is confirmed by the annotation *Mr. Gillott* in the sketchbook; however the painting has not been traced in Gillott's sale at Christie in 1872.
3. 1904 Inventory p.3, no.67.

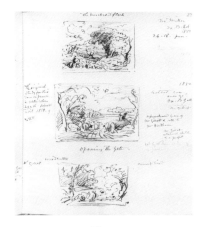

Fig.30
J. Linnell: *Sketchbook, fol. 82*
Photographed when in a private collection; now in the collection of the British Museum

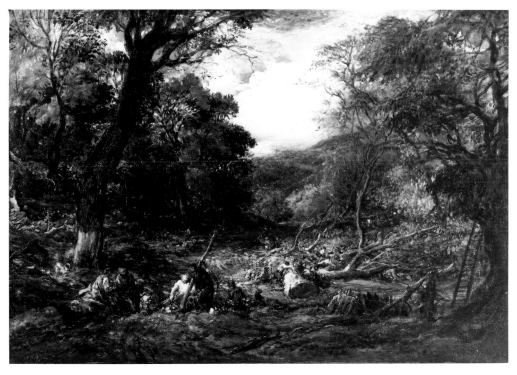

J. Linnell: *Woodcutters in a Forest Valley*
LL 3730

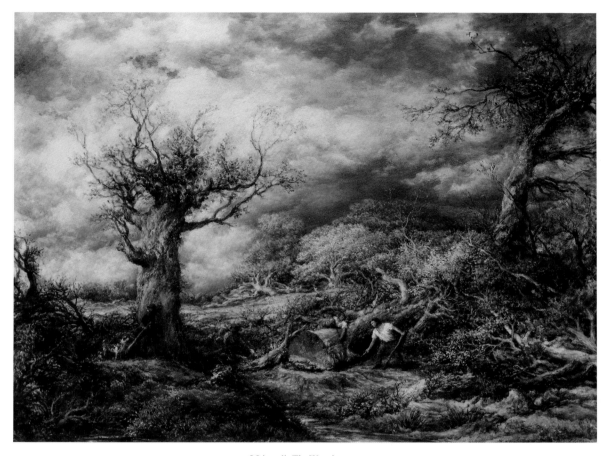

J. Linnell: *The Woodcutters*
LL 3688

John Linnell
1792-1882

The Woodcutters

LL 3688 (LP 13, WHL 3164)
oil on canvas, 77.5 × 109.5 cm
signed and dated *J. LINNELL/1876*
(bottom right)

Linnell's sketchbook refers to
LL 3688 under the title *Wood*.
According to his journal, he began
the painting on 14 November 1875
and worked on it for a further six
days that month and one day in
December. Three days were spent
completing it in February 1876.[1]

A horizontal tear approximately

six inches long, to the right of the
woodcutter in the white shirt, has
been repaired and patched on the
reverse.

PROVENANCE:
bt. from Linnell by Edward Fox White;[2]
...[? Agnew[3]]; ... Charles Churchill;
Christie 16 February 1917 (92) bt.
Gooden & Fox for Lever (320 gns.);
2nd Viscount Leverhulme; from whom
purchased by the Trustees of the Lady
Lever Art Gallery 1928.

REFERENCES:
1. Information from D. Linnell, letter,
24 April 1997, gallery files.
2. D. Linnell, *loc. cit.* The painting has
not been traced in White's sales at
Christie 6 March 1891 and 24 March 1900.
3. An annotation in the auctioneer's

copy of the 1917 sale catalogue indicates
that the work was in Agnew's possession
before Churchill's. A sale from Agnew to
Churchill has not been traced.

'John Linnell'
1792-1882

At the Cottage Gate

LL 3724 (WHL 90, H 57)
oil on panel, 16.5 × 22 cm

Lever acquired LL 3724 as by Linnell,
but its loose, hasty manner is only
very superficially reminiscent of
Linnell's work. It is of low quality
and was probably one of the many
imitations sold by dealers in the

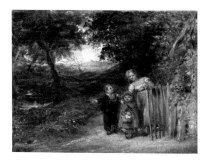

'J. Linnell': *At the Cottage Gate*
LL 3724

period between about 1860 and
Linnell's death.

PROVENANCE:
…James Lloyd, Dealer in Works of Art,
96 Gracechurch Street, London EC1;[1] …
James Orrock by 1895; Christie 25-27
April 1895 (289) bt. in; bt. from Orrock by
Lever November 1904.[2]

REFERENCES:
1. Label on the reverse of the painting.
2. 1904 Inventory p.2, no.45. LL 3724 is
identified in gallery files as possibly lot
274 in the Orrock sale, Christie 4-6 June
1904; although the dimensions match,
the title given in the sale catalogue is
A Landscape with cattle at a pool; nor
is lot 274 described as a panel.

John Lucas
1807-1874

The Duke of Wellington
LL 3446 (WHL 4505)
oil on canvas, 76.5 × 64 cm

An ink inscription on the back of the
canvas reads: *By permission of the
Duke of Wellington/this Portrait of
His Grace was copied by/Mr Lucas
from the one painted by him/for the
Trinity House 1839/A Clare*. The
Duke, here in his seventieth year,
wears the Star of the Garter. Lucas is
known to have made at least fifteen
versions and variants of his full-
length portrait of the Duke, which
was painted in 1838, not 1839 (Trinity

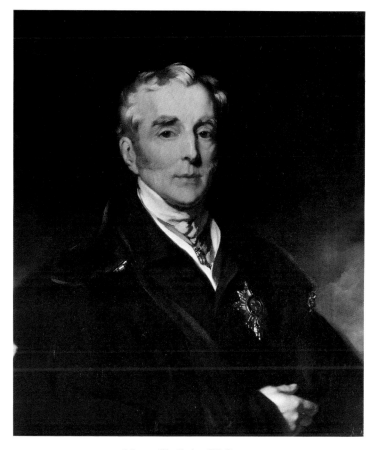

J. Lucas: *The Duke of Wellington*
LL 3446

House, fig.31).[1] The original was
a favourite with the Duke, who had
himself chosen Lucas for the commission having been taken to the
artist's studio by his niece, Lady
Burghersh.[2]

PROVENANCE:
Anne Countess of Clare; Dr Nevinson;[3]
…W. Lawson Peacock; Christie
14 November 1921 (265) bt. Hibbard
(£42); Christie 16 April 1923 (103) bt.
Gooden & Fox for Lever (20 gns.).

REFERENCES:
1. For a summary of these portraits see
R. Walker: *Regency Portraits* (1985) Vol.1,
p.539, which follows the list given in A.
Lucas: *John Lucas* (1910) p.115. LL 3446 is
presumably no.7 on Walker's list, where it
is stated to have been painted for the Earl
of Clare in 1842. The inscriptions imply,

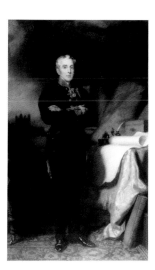

Fig.31
J. Lucas: *The Duke of Wellington*
By kind permission of the Elder Brethren, Trinity House,
London; photograph Courtauld Institute of Art

however, that LL 3446 was executed for Anne, Dowager Countess of Clare, the Earl's mother (d.1844).

2. Lucas, *op. cit.* p.20.

3. A label on the stretcher reads *The Duke of Wellington/given to Dr Nevinson by Lady Clare/at whose request the Duke sat/for it./by John Lucas [? Associate] of the/Royal Academy.* LL 3446 cannot be traced in Dr Nevinson's sales at Christie 3-4 June 1842 and at Phillips, 20 April 1847.

George Morland
1763-1804

The Piggery

LL 3558 (WHL 54, H 91)
oil on canvas, 46 × 62 cm
signed: *G. Morland* (centre right)

This was formerly described as a picture 'of the period just before Morland's death',[1] but has more recently been dated to 1790-1.[2] It has been known under a variety of titles (see below).

PROVENANCE:
… H. Haskett Smith, Goudhurst, Kent by 1872;[3] Christie 9 May 1896 (94) bt. Dowdeswell (£336);[4] … James Orrock by 1903;[5] [? W. Lockett Agnew 1904;[6] James Orrock;] bt. from Orrock by Lever November 1904.[7]

EXHIBITIONS:
Old Masters RA 1872 (43); New Gallery 1898 (156); *George Morland* Victoria and Albert Museum 1904 (69); *Liverpool Autumn Exhibition* Walker Art Gallery Liverpool 1933 (36); *Art in the Georgian Home* Arts Council 1949 (13).

REFERENCES:
1. Tatlock, p.57.
2. D. Winter: *George Morland* Ph.D

thesis, Stanford University (1977) cat. 75. Securely dated pig subjects occur in Morland's *oeuvre* from about 1790 to 1798.

3. Lent by Smith to the 1872 exhibition. The exhibition label on the reverse of LL 3558 gives the title as *Some Must Watch Whilst Some Must Sleep* (Tatlock, *loc. cit.*).

4. Lent by Dowdeswell to the 1898 exhibition.

5. Repr. Webber, Vol.I, fp. 66, as *Creature Comforts.*

6. A painting called *The Piggery* with dimensions corresponding to LL 3558 was lent by Agnew to the Morland exhibition at the Victoria and Albert Museum in 1904; LL 3558's absence from the Orrock sale in June 1904, while not conclusive evidence, suggests it may have been temporarily in Agnew's possession at that time.

7. 1904 Inventory p.3, no.87, as *Rural Felicity.*

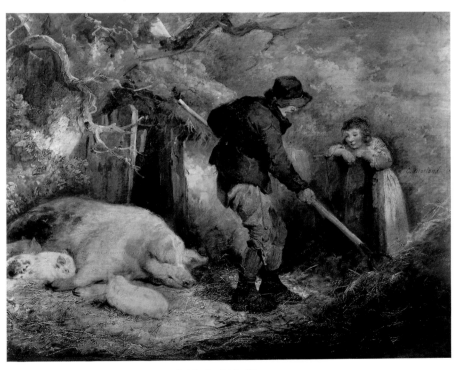

G. Morland: *The Piggery*
LL 3558

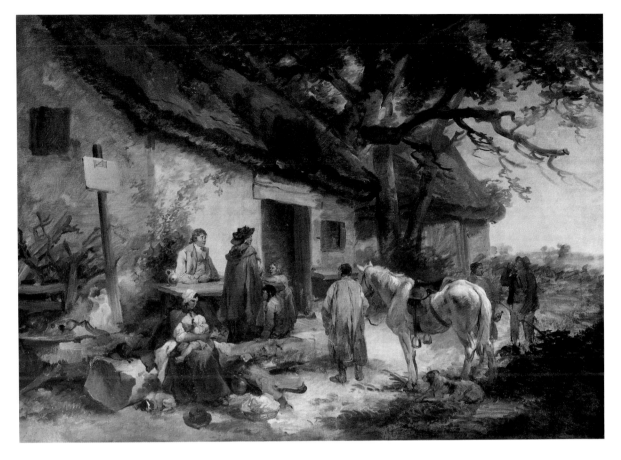

G. Morland: *The Roadside Inn*
LL 3557

George Morland
1763-1804

The Roadside Inn
LL 3557 (WHL 113, H 16)
oil on canvas, 101.5 × 142.5 cm

This work has been described as unfinished and dated to 1790-92.[1] To judge by the size of the canvas, and the care with which at least some of the figures have been laid in, Morland may originally have intended it for exhibition. Most of the design, including the inn itself, the sign announcing the neighbouring toll gate, the trees, and much of the foreground, has however been brushed in later in a much broader and more vigorous manner.

PROVENANCE:
…Sir W.G. Armstrong by 1876;[2] Christie 24 June 1910 (78) bt. Gooden & Fox for Lever (650 gns.).

EXHIBITION:
Old Masters RA 1876 (276).

REFERENCES:
1. D. Winter: *George Morland* Ph.D thesis, Stanford University (1977) cat. 84.
2. Lent by Armstrong to the 1876 exhibition.

George Morland
1763-1804

The Soldier's Departure
LL 3673 (WHL 87, H 81)
oil on canvas, 30.5 × 25.5 cm

The Soldier's Return
LL 3674 (WHL 88, H 82)
oil on canvas, 30.5 × 25.5 cm

These small, rather broadly handled canvases were probably commissioned from Morland by an engraver: perhaps to market a popular theatrical work (as with Singleton's

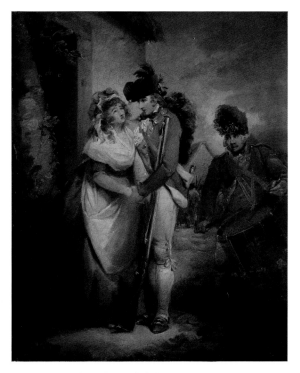

G. Morland: *The Soldier's Departure*
LL 3673

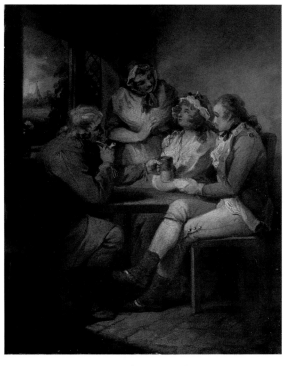

G. Morland: *The Soldier's Return*
LL 3674

Flora, LL 3680 below). Traditionally they have been identified as the works engraved as *The Soldier's Farewell* and *The Soldier's Return* by G. Graham and published in 1790, but Graham's prints derive from different compositions.[1] Engravings of both works are known (see below) but they are not a pair. At least one further version of LL 3674 is recorded.[2]

The date of LL 3673-4 is not known. Stylistically, they bear some resemblance to the (larger) paintings in the *Deserter* series which are signed and dated 1792 (although Keating's engravings of them were published the previous year). LL 3673-4 also recall *The Alehouse Door* whose engraving by Smith was published in January 1801. In the Coxe sale catalogue (see below) they were described as 'specimens of [Morland's] early genius'.

PROVENANCE:
…Charles Chatfield by 1805; Coxe, 7 May 1807 (5 and 6) bt. Gordon (£8.-.-.) and (£6.6.-.) respectively; …W.H. Cope; Christie 5 December 1903 (118);[3] James Orrock; bt. from Orrock by Lever November 1904;[4] sold to Agnew 19 February 1907 and re-purchased by Lever 22 February 1907.[5]

EXHIBITIONS:
Chatfield's Morland Gallery 1805-7;[6] *Morland* Tate Gallery 1954 (9 and 10); (LL 3673 only) *British Painting in the 18th Century* British Council exhibition touring USA and Canada 1957 (42) (LL 3673 and LL 3674) *Morland* Reading Museum and Art Gallery 1975 (7 and 8).

ENGRAVINGS:
LL 3673: A. Ragona, stipple, oval, in reverse; titled *Changing Quarters*; LL 3674: J. Hogg, stipple, in colour.[7]

REFERENCES:
1. This error seems to originate with the illustrations in J.T.H. Baily: *George Morland* (1906) pp.105 and 109; but in Baily's catalogue of published engravings after Morland's works, the Graham engravings are clearly identified as horizontal in format (*op. cit.*, p.129). Tatlock, pp.56-7, followed by the 1954 Tate Gallery exhibition catalogue and by D. Winter: *George Morland* Ph.D thesis, Stanford University(1977) cats. 67-8, perpetuated the mistake.
2. 10 × 7 in.; exh. Grosvenor Gallery 1888 (207) lent by W.W. Lewis.
3. This provenance is given by Winter, *loc. cit.*
4. 1904 Inventory p.1, nos. 7 and 8.
5. Agnew stockbooks and copy invoice, gallery files.
6. Winter, *loc. cit.*
7. Impressions in the Department of Prints and Drawings, British Museum. Neither is dated.

'George Morland'

1763-1804

Dragging the Trout Stream

LL 3672 (WHL 555, HH 170)

oil on panel, 14.5 × 16.5 cm

This very small painting has been regarded as authentic.[1] The bright, jewel-like colour is in its favour but the figures are very crudely drawn. It could conceivably be a product of Morland's last years (1801-1804) when he was turning out potboilers to satisfy his creditors, but seems more likely to be the work of an imitator.[2]

PROVENANCE:

…Mrs Doyle, Cricklewood Place;[3] … James Orrock; bt. from Orrock by Lever 1910.[4]

REFERENCES:

1. Tatlock, p.57; according to W.G. Constable 'probably genuine but unimportant', note in gallery files.
2. LL 3672 is omitted from D. Winter: *George Morland* Ph.D thesis, Stanford University (1977); the attribution to Morland is also doubted by R. Mitchell, letter, 7 July 1998, gallery files.
3. An ink inscription on the back of LL 3672, now no longer visible, was formerly recorded as *From Mrs Doyle's Collection, Cricklewood Place, 30* (gallery files).
4. 1910 Inventory p.56, valued at £15.

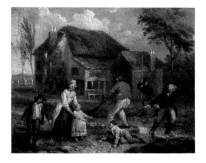

'G. Morland':
Dragging the Trout Stream
LL 3672

Henry Morland

c. 1719-1797

Lady's Maid Soaping Linen

LL 3118

oil on canvas, 76 × 64 cm

Domestic Employment: Ironing

LL 3538

oil on canvas, 77 × 64 cm

The titles used above are those given to the engravings by Philip Dawe which were published by Carrington Bowles, 69 St. Paul's Churchyard, on 2 October 1769 (figs. 32 & 33). Both compositions were much replicated,[1] often with slight variations, by Morland himself as well as by other artists, including Morland's son George. The fresh quality of LL 3118 and LL 3538 suggests that they are autograph, while the minor differences from the engravings imply that they are early but not original versions. Morland may have executed the first versions of both subjects in pastel.[2]

It has been suggested that Morland's inspiration for these and similar works were Philip Mercier's scenes of 'Domestic Employment' – women carrying out household tasks – which were engraved in the 1750s. Such works appealed to aristocratic tastes and probably had an erotic intention. The gowns have been identified as, respectively, painted silk and printed linen or cotton, materials too expensive to have been worn by laundry maids, and this suggests an element of the masquerade or dressing down on the part of the models.[3] Indeed, LL 3118 and LL 3538 bear old manuscript inscriptions on the reverse identifying the models as the famous Gunning sisters: respectively Elizabeth, Duchess of Hamilton and Argyll (1734-1790) (for whom see

LL 3126 under Sir Joshua Reynolds) and Maria, Countess of Coventry (1733-1760).[4] Although it seems inconceivable that these are authentic portraits,[5] many of the other versions of LL 3118 and LL 3538 have also been said to represent one or other of the sisters,[6] which suggests a tradition going back to the 18th century and an attempt to market the two subjects as a pair of 'beauties'. However, the fact that the subjects were exhibited separately in the late 1760s, and together in the mid-1770s,[7] suggests that it was only with the issue of Dawe's engravings that they came to be regarded as pendants.

These two works were purchased by Lever for immediate presentation to his soap works and were never part of his own personal collection.

PROVENANCE:

… 2nd Lord Tweedmouth; Christie 3 June 1905 (30) bt. Davis (480 gns.) (LL 3538) and (31) bt. Davis (350 gns.) (LL 3118); … Countess of Carnarvon; Christie 31 May 1918 (146) (a pair); bt. Gooden & Fox for Lever (200 gns.);[8] presented to Lever Bros; presented by Lever Bros. to the Lady Lever Art Gallery July 1983.

REFERENCES:

1. Versions of both subjects are in the Tate Gallery and at Scone Palace, Scotland. Many others are recorded.
2. A pastel version of *Domestic Employment: Ironing* measuring 22 × 17 in. inscribed with what appears to have been Morland's address in the period 1767-69 was sold at Christie 11 July 1995 (12). A same-sized pastel of *Lady's Maid Soaping Linen*, differing in detail to LL 3118 (but closer to an oil version thought to date from 1773 formerly in the Wertheimer collection) was sold at Sotheby 16 November 1989 (40).
3. See *Rococo: Art and Design in Hogarth's England*, exhibition catalogue, Victoria and Albert Museum (1984) p.233, cat. N.33; also Martin Postle: *Angels and Urchins*, exhibition catalogue, Iveagh Bequest, Kenwood (1998) p.85, cats. 69-70.

4. The inscription on LL 3118, which appears no later than early 19th century in date, takes the form of a biographical note. As it records the Duchess's death it must postdate 1790. The inscription on LL 3538, in the same hand, consists of an extract of two stanzas from William Mason's *Elegy on Maria Gunning, Countess of Coventry*.

5. If the subjects were both painted by Morland when Lady Coventry was alive, they must date from the 1750s, but the subjects were not exhibited nor engraved until the end of the 1760s, and then without any reference to the Gunning sisters. The Tate Gallery date their versions no earlier than 1765. According to H. Bromley: *A Catalogue of Engraved British Portraits from Egbert the Great to the Present Time* (1793) Vol.II, p.435, LL 3118 represents 'Miss [sic] Dawe, wife of the painter'. Bromley appears to have believed that Philip Dawe painted as well as engraved the subjects; he makes no mention of Henry Morland and describes *Lady's Maid Soaping Linen* as painted 'ad vivum'.

6. The models in the Tate Gallery and the Scone Palace versions have traditionally been identified as the Gunning sisters but the other way round to the Lady Lever pictures. The Tate Gallery subjects have been described as 'Lady Coventry soaping linen' and 'Miss Gunning [sic] ironing'. The Scone Palace pair were exhibited as the Gunning sisters at the 1867 National Portrait Exhibition (cats. 433 and 441).

7. The subjects were first exhibited separately at the Free Society of Artists: *A Servant Ironing* in 1768 (164), and *A Lady's Maid Soaping Linen* in 1769 (163); *A Lady's Maid Soaping Some Fine Linen* was exhibited with *A Girl Ironing Some Shirt Sleeves* at the Free Society in 1774 (209 and 215 respectively), in 1775 (169 and 174) and, slightly differently titled, in 1776 (250 and 251). *A Laundry Maid Ironing* was shown by itself at the Free Society in 1782 (40). A related subject, *A Girl Hanging Out Wet Linen* was engraved by Dawe in 1774, but it appears to employ the same model as *Domestic Employment: Ironing*. A pastel version of this (measuring 30 × 25 in.) was sold under the title *A Laundry Maid* at Christie 12 November 1996 (22).

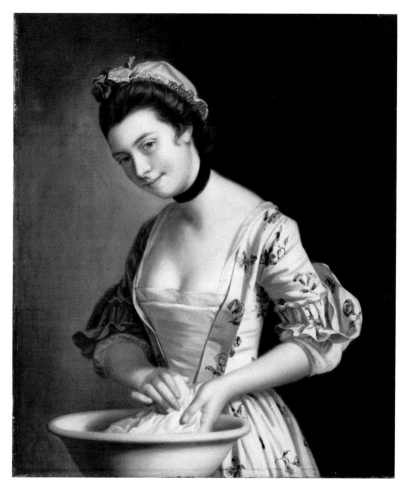

H. Morland: *Lady's Maid Soaping Linen*
LL 3118

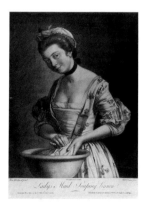

Fig.32
P. Dawe, after H. Morland:
Lady's Maid Soaping Linen
Yale Center for British Art, Paul Mellon Collection

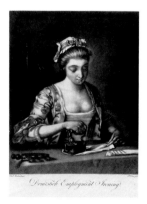

Fig.33
P. Dawe, after H. Morland:
Domestic Employment: Ironing
Yale Center for British Art, Paul Mellon Collection

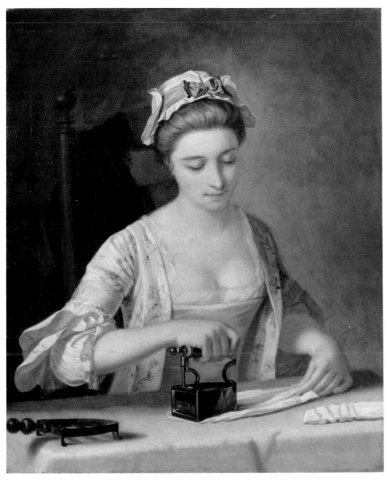

H. Morland: *Domestic Employment: Ironing*
LL 3538

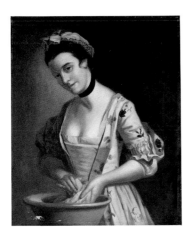

after H. Morland:
Lady's Maid Soaping Linen
LL 3117

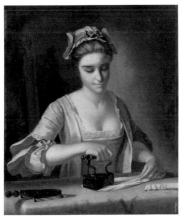

after H. Morland:
Domestic Employment: Ironing
LL 3119

8. They were almost the only pictures which Lever acquired at auction having deliberately set no limit bid. 'I wish to secure these pictures' he wrote to F.W. Fox, 30 May 1918, gallery files.

after
Henry Morland
*c.*1719-1797

Lady's Maid Soaping Linen
LL 3117
oil on canvas, 76 × 63 cm

Domestic Employment: Ironing
LL 3119
oil on canvas, 76 × 63 cm

These works are mediocre copies of Morland's compositions of which superior versions are LL 3118 and LL 3538 (above). There is no record of their acquisition by Lever.[1]

PROVENANCE:
…presented by Lever Bros., July 1983.

REFERENCES:
1. It is tempting to speculate that they were copied from LL 3118 and LL 3538 after the latter had been purchased by Lever, but this seems unlikely. There are a number of small differences in detail.

attributed to
John Hamilton Mortimer
1740-1779

*Portrait of a Lady
(called 'Mrs. Wells')*
LL 3552 (WHL 531, H 15)
oil on canvas, 72.5 × 60 cm

Lever purchased LL 3552 as by Sir Joshua Reynolds. It was later ascribed to Cotes[1] and has most recently been attributed to Mortimer.[2] The work is close in style to Mortimer's *Portrait of a Lady (called 'Lady Broughton')* of about

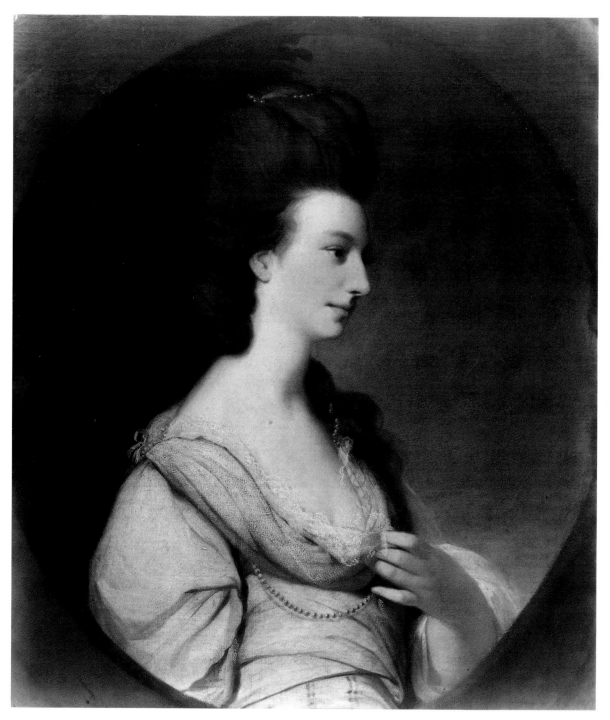

attributed to J.H. Mortimer:
Portrait of a Lady (called 'Mrs. Wells')
LL 3552

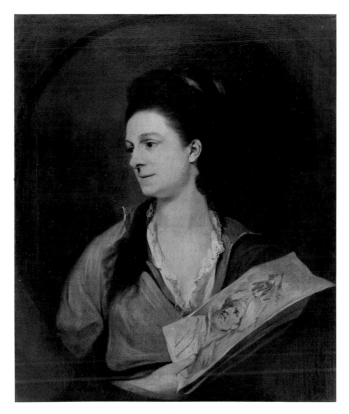

Fig.34
J.H. Mortimer:
Portrait of a Lady (called 'Lady Broughton')
Musée du Louvre

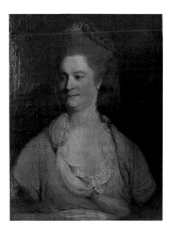

Fig.35
J.H. Mortimer: *Mary Lushington*
Towner Art Gallery and Local Museum,
Eastbourne

Mrs Mary Wells (d.1810) who is
mentioned occasionally by Farington in
his diaries. Both the Dr E. Wells referred
to in J. Nichols: *Literary Anecdotes of the
Eighteenth Century* (1813) Vol.VI, p.187,
are too early for LL 3552.
6.   A portrait of Elizabeth Wells by Cotes,
30 × 25 in., was sold by Christie 12 March
1898 (68) consigned by T. Wilkinson and
bought by McLean (110 gns.) but the
description in the catalogue suggests that
this is not the same work as LL 3552.
7.   1904 Inventory p.2, no.32.

Robert Muller
1773-after 1800[1]

George Morland
LL 3559 (WHL 2178)
oil on canvas, 77.5 × 65.5 cm

George Morland, the celebrated
painter of farm, tavern, gypsy and
smuggling scenes, was born in June
1763,[2] the son of Henry Morland,
whose apprentice he was from 1777
till 1784. (Works by both artists are
catalogued above.) After a colourful
and dissolute life he died in 1804.[3]

No other version of this portrait is
known but comparison with William
Ward's mezzotint, published

1776 (Musée du Louvre, Paris, fig.34)
and his *Mary Lushington* of 1777
(Towner Art Gallery, Eastbourne,
fig.35).[3] It is perhaps to be identified
as one of the three-quarters portraits
of ladies exhibited by Mortimer at
the Society of Artists in 1777 (cats. 85
and 87), although the height of the
sitter's hair suggests the work may
date from the following year.[4]

An inscription on the reverse,
not contemporary with the painting
itself, identifies the sitter as *Mrs.
Wells 1st wife of Dr. Wells*. Nothing
further is known of her.[5]

PROVENANCE:
…Commander H. Orpen, R.N.;
Christie 25 April 1903 (86) bt. McLean
(95 gns.);[6] …James Orrock; Christie
4-6 June 1904 (130) bt. in; bt. from Orrock
by Lever November 1904.[7]

REFERENCES:
1.   Tatlock, p.51.
2.   John Sunderland, ms. annotation to
photograph in Witt Library, about 1990.
The work was not included in his 'John
Hamilton Mortimer, His Life and Works',
Walpole Society, Vol.LII (1986).
3.   Sunderland, *op. cit.*, pp. 177-78, cats.
126 and 130; both works are in the same
feigned oval format as LL 3552.
4.   Aileen Ribeiro, verbally,
26 February 1998.
5.   Nobody by the name Wells is
associated with Mortimer or recorded
as sitting to him (Sunderland, *op. cit.*).
The best-known Dr Wells of the period,
William Charles Wells (1757-1817)
remained a bachelor (*Gentleman's
Magazine* (1817) Vol.II, pp.467-71); the
best known Mrs Wells (*c.*1759-1826), the
actress, who was painted by Romney,
Downman, Russell and Northcote, was
not married to a Dr Wells; nor was the

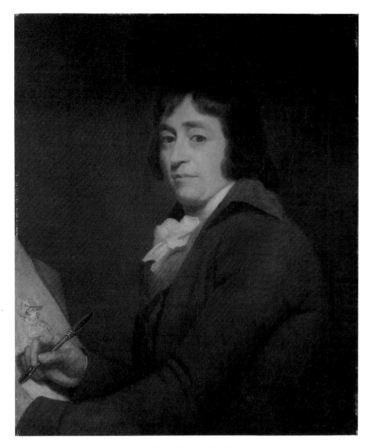

R. Muller: *George Morland*
LL 3559

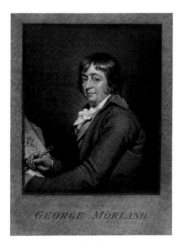

Fig.36
W. Ward, after R. Muller:
George Morland
Yale Center for British Art, Paul Mellon Collection

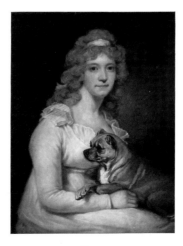

Fig.37
R. Muller: *Mrs. George Morland*
By permission of the Trustees
of Dulwich Picture Gallery

1 January 1805 (fig.36) suggests that LL 3559 may not be Muller's original. The shape of Morland's face, and the handling of his hair and neckcloth are noticeably different in the engraving. A drawing apparently based on the latter in the Huntington Art Collections, San Marino, California, shows Morland in a blueish green coat and a brown waistcoat, with red-brown hair; in LL 3559 he wears a brown coat and red waistcoat. However LL 3559 is in worn condition and this may be sufficient to explain the visual disparity with Ward's engraving.[4]

Little is known of Robert Muller except that he exhibited twenty-nine portraits at the Royal Academy in the period 1789-1800. An inscription on the frame of LL 3559 states that it was one of these exhibits, and the pendant portrait of *Mrs. Morland* (Dulwich Picture Gallery, fig.37) has been dated to before 1796 on the assumption that LL 3559 was shown at the Academy in that year.[5] No evidence has been found, however, to support the notion that LL 3559 actually was exhibited in 1796 or any other year.[6] The best evidence for the work's date is the costume in the portrait of Morland's wife, which has been placed around 1792-5.[7]

PROVENANCE:
Charles Chatfield; Coxe, 8 May 1807 (45) bt. in (£31.10.-.);[8] ... the dealer [?] Johnson after 1814; Foster 5 March 1818 (138) bt. in (£4.6.-.); ... T.H. Pearch;[9] Christie 19 July 1907 (72) bt. Agnew (£52.10.-.); bt. July 1907 by Sir Walter Gilbey; Christie at Elsenham Hall 11 June 1915 (362) bt. Gooden & Fox for Lever (£109).

REFERENCES:
1. Muller was described as 'the late' in Coxe's sale catalogue of 8 May 1807 (see provenance).
2. Or May 1762; see Ellis Waterhouse: *Dictionary of British 18th Century Painters* (1981) p.246.
3. See for example William Collins: *Memoirs of a Painter* (1805); George

Dawe: *The Life of George Morland* (1807), two of the numerous biographies which appeared immediately after his death. For a recent treatment see J. Barrell: *The Dark Side of the Landscape* (1980) pp.89-129.

4. Other engravings of LL 3559 include one by R. Page published by J. Robins, 1 October 1821 and one by E. Scriven published in *Arnold's Library of the Fine Arts* 1833. An oval miniature after LL 3559, 7.5 × 6.5 cm, watercolour on ivory, was with Spink in November 1980; another miniature version was sold at Sotheby 9 April 1992 (196).

5. P. Murray: *The Dulwich Picture Gallery: A Catalogue* (1980) p.84. Farington, however, does record Muller behaving rudely at a dinner to celebrate the King's birthday in 1796 (K. Garlick, A. McIntyre and K. Cave, eds.: *The Diary of Joseph Farington* (1978-84) Vol.II, p.570). Muller was evidently a close friend of Morland (see note 8 below); Tatlock, p.107, suggests that Morland himself added the little sketch to the left-hand side of LL 3559 and it is tempting to speculate that the dandyish young man is a portrait of Muller himself.

6. A. Graves: *The Royal Academy Exhibitors 1769-1904* (1905-6) Vol.v, p.320 lists six Muller portraits shown in 1796 of which three are identified as members of the Douglas family, and one as Dr Browning, with the remainder being of ladies. None of the portraits exhibited in other years seem, from the identifications or the titles, to be LL 3559. The claim that LL 3559 was shown at the Royal Academy was made by Tatlock, *loc. cit.*

7. Aileen Ribeiro, verbally, 26 February 1998.

8. LL 3559 was described in the sale catalogue, and thereafter in catalogues of the European Museum, where Chatfield placed the work 1808-14, as 'acknowledged to be the most exact likeness of that extraordinary character that has ever been taken, and executed in a most bold and masterly manner by the late Mr Muller, who was intimately acquainted with him.' (B. Fredericksen, ed.: *The Index of Paintings Sold in the British Isles in the Nineteenth Century* (1988-present) Vol.2, p.660; and compare Vol.3, p.674 for slightly different wording

in the 1812-14 catalogues).

9. Murray, *loc. cit.*, states that LL 3559 was sold 'by itself' in 1905; this sale has not been traced.

William Mulready
1786-1863

The Wedding Morning
LL 3715 (WHL 42, H 85)
oil on panel, 17 × 19.5 cm

This small study develops two pen and sepia wash drawings, one of the left-hand group of figures, and one of the whole composition, in the Victoria and Albert Museum.[1] It has been described as a sketch for a painting which was never undertaken.[2]

Its date is uncertain. The style of the preparatory drawings is close to others dateable to the period 1820-22,[3] but Mulready's drawing technique in works of this type does

not appear to alter greatly, and an earlier date of about 1808 has been proposed, partly on the basis that the subject is essentially humorous rather than sentimental, as Mulready's later treatments of courtship tended to be.[4] LL 3715's general kinship with the early work of David Wilkie, who had leapt to fame in London in 1806, is manifest.

The Wedding Morning has been described as an example of Mulready's most effective narrative subjects, in being constructed according to a strict principle of pictorial order: 'the dominant class of imagery is concerned with clothes, a rich terrain for classification'.[5]

PROVENANCE:
[? Mulready's studio sale, 28-30 April 1864 (493, part) bt. H. White (£1.5.-.)[6]]; ...Thomas Woolner; Christie 12 June 1875 (68) bt. Goupil (£30.9.-.);[7] ...James Orrock by 1904;[8] bt. from Orrock by Lever November 1904.[9]

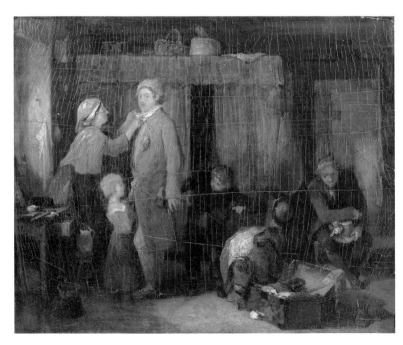

W. Mulready: *The Wedding Morning*
LL 3715

REFERENCES:

1. V & A 6051-2; A. Rorimer: *Drawings by William Mulready*, exhibition catalogue, Victoria and Albert Museum (1972) p.141, cats. 333-4, repr.
2. K.M. Heleniak: *William Mulready* (1980) p.192, cat.43.
3. See for example Rorimer, *op. cit.*, cat.323 (*The Street Preacher*, 1822) and cat.353 (*A Family introducing a Baby to a Dog*, 1820).
4. Heleniak, *op. cit.*, p.123.
5. M. Pointon: *Mulready*, exhibition catalogue, Victoria and Albert Museum (1986) pp.155-6.
6. Lot 493 (misprinted in the catalogue as 483) is described as two sketches in imitation of Ostade, and is the only item in the sale which seems a plausible candidate for LL 3715. It seems doubtful that Mulready would have sold or given the work to Woolner without noting the fact in his account book, which does not refer to LL 3715.
7. Heleniak, *op. cit.*, p.192.

8. Reproduced in C. Holme, ed.: 'The Royal Academy from Reynolds to Millais', *The Studio* (1904) fp. XVI, owned by Orrock.
9. 1904 Inventory p.2, no.41. The Christie's stencil of Orrock's sale, 4-6 June 1904, appears on the back of LL 3715, but it was not listed in the catalogue. A note in gallery files which states that Lever purchased LL 3715 from Gooden & Fox (ex Orrock) in 1907 (followed by Heleniak, *op. cit.*, p.192) is apparently incorrect.

Patrick Nasmyth
1787-1831

The Miller's Linn, Inveraray
LL 3572 (WHL 574, H 76)
oil on panel, 58 × 86.5 cm
signed and dated: *Patk. Nasmyth 1818* (bottom right)

The Miller's Linn is the name given to a stretch of the river Aray on the estates of the Dukes of Argyll at Inveraray Castle, where it flows over a number of small weirs before entering Loch Fyne. Nasmyth's view is looking north, away from the lake which is behind the spectator, towards the hills of Glen Aray which are visible in the background, treated with a good deal of artistic licence.[1] Both Patrick Nasmyth and his father Alexander, who worked for the 5th Duke of Argyll at the beginning of the 19th century and designed buildings on his estates,[2] painted Inveraray subjects over an extended period.[3] One of the buildings attributed to Alexander Nasmyth is a hexagonal structure on the left bank of the river opposite a meal mill which had stood on the right-hand bank since the 17th century,[4] giving

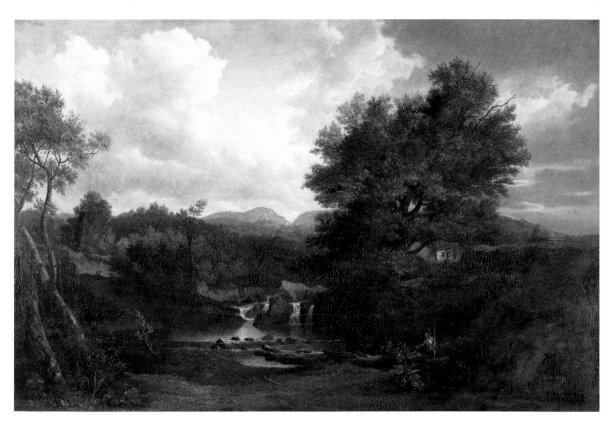

P. Nasmyth: *The Miller's Linn, Inveraray*
LL 3572

the water its name. Conceivably the cottage on the right side of LL 3572 is a fanciful treatment of the latter.

The present painting is the same size as another of Patrick Nasmyth's Inveraray canvases, *A View of Douglas Bridge*,[5] and both works are signed and dated 1818. They were clearly designed as a pair. Nasmyth showed LL 3572 at the 1818 British Institution and the companion picture at the same year's Royal Academy.

The former attribution of LL 3572 to Charlotte Nasmyth (1804-84), Patrick's sister,[6] is disproved by the authentic signature.

PROVENANCE:
…[? with Knoedler & Co.[7]];…Henry E. Kidson, Liverpool; bt. by Lever December 1898 (£350).

EXHIBITION:
BI 1818 (49).

REFERENCES:
1. Mrs R. MacGregor, Inveraray, letter, 21 February 1998, gallery files.
2. J.C.B. Cooksey: *Alexander Nasmyth, H.R.S.A., 1758-1840, A Man of the Scottish Renaissance* (1991) part I, pp.78-83.
3. The nature of the Nasmyth family operation, in which the same landscape subjects were repeated and varied by its different members (for which see P. Johnson and E. Money: *The Nasmyth Family of Painters* (1977)) makes the present day identification of specific works hazardous. Alexander Nasmyth had painted at Inveraray by 1801, and the *View of Inveraray from Loch Fyne* (attributed to Patrick when sold at Christie 2-3 April 1969 (17) but to Alexander when shown in *Painting In Scotland, The Golden Age*, Talbot Rice Art Centre Edinburgh and Tate Gallery (1986) cat.145), dates from then (Cooksey, *loc. cit.*). Alexander's view of the *Miller's Linn* signed and dated 1807 is catalogued by Cooksey as S29 (*op. cit.*, part II, p.133-4). The *View in Argyleshire* shown by Alexander at the British Institution in 1815 (105) is likely to be an Inveraray or Glen Shira subject (Glen Shira being a few miles away to the north-

east; see LL 3741 below) and further views of the district were shown by Alexander at the Royal Scottish Academy, the Society of British Artists and the Liverpool Academy in 1836-39. Patrick Nasmyth showed seven Inveraray or Glen Shira subjects (including LL 3572) in London and Manchester between 1818 and 1827.
4. MacGregor, *loc. cit.*
5. Christie 22 March 1968 (72).
6. Tatlock, p.108.
7. A Knoedler & Co. photograph in the Witt Library, annotated '57 × 86 inches' (but presumably an error for centimetres) appears to show LL 3572 but may be of a second, identical, painting.

Patrick Nasmyth
1787-1831

Wooded Landscape with Figures

LL 3560 (WHL 3059)
oil on panel,[1] 32 × 42 cm
signed and dated: *Patk. Nasmyth 1820* (bottom right)

The location of the landscape in LL 3560 has not been identified. Nasmyth moved from Edinburgh to London in 1814 and although he continued to paint Scottish subjects, the bulk of his landscapes thereafter were of places in the Home Counties. However, the generic nature of the present subject suggests it may well be an invented composition. An almost identical version, the same size and also on panel, was last traced in a private collection in Suffolk. An unpainted border of approximately 1.5 cm is present on all four sides of the work.

PROVENANCE:
[?…] Wynn Ellis;[2] Christie 6 May 1876 (81) bt. Lord Moray (£420); Dowell, Edinburgh, 22 February 1913 (48) bt. [?] (160 gns.);[3]…E. Cremetti; bt. from T. McLean by Lever 1 November 1916 (£330).

EXHIBITIONS:
[? BI 1832 (240); BI 1865 (151)].

REFERENCES:
1. Stamp: *R. LEEDHAM*.
2. If LL 3560 is the work lent by Wynn

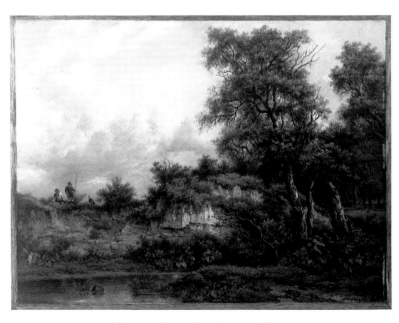

P. Nasmyth: *Wooded Landscape with Figures*
LL 3560

Ellis to the British Institution in 1832 (and although Ellis owned several works by Nasmyth, the vague title of *Landscape* given to the 1832 exhibit is a point in LL 3560's favour), the likelihood is that he acquired it directly from the artist.
3. The National Gallery of Scotland's copy of the sale catalogue is annotated with the price, but not the name of the purchaser.

Patrick Nasmyth
1787-1831

A Waterfall in Glen Shira near Inveraray
LL 3741 (WHL 618, H 98)
oil on canvas, 98.5 × 137 cm
signed and dated *Patk. Nasmyth/1822*
(lower left)

From its ambitious and formal nature, and from the apparently authentic signature and date, LL 3741 can very plausibly be identified as the work exhibited by Patrick Nasmyth at the Royal Academy in 1822: *A Waterfall in Glen Shirah* [sic] *near Inverary, the Seat of the Duke of Argyll*. The river Shira flows south-westwards down Glen Shira into the loch of that name at the northern end of Loch Fyne, a few miles above Inveraray. There are numerous waterfalls in the lower end of the glen. The artist and his father, Alexander Nasmyth, were closely associated with the area (see LL 3572 above) and both exhibited numerous Glen Shira subjects; two paintings by Alexander traditionally identified as of Glen Shira, one of them inscribed

to that effect, are very similar in design to LL 3741.[1]

It has however been pointed out that the landscape in the painting does not bear much actual resemblance to Glen Shira in reality,[2] and from its purchase by Lever down to the present LL 3741 has gone under the title *The Trossachs*. This too was an area regularly treated by members of the Nasmyth family and it may be significant that Alexander Nasmyth exhibited a *View of a Wooden Bridge near Loch Katrine* at the British Institution in 1823. Patrick Nasmyth showed a *Scene In The Trossachs* at the Royal Manchester Institution in 1828, which was purchased by the local collector John Greaves, and since the provenance of LL 3741 begins with

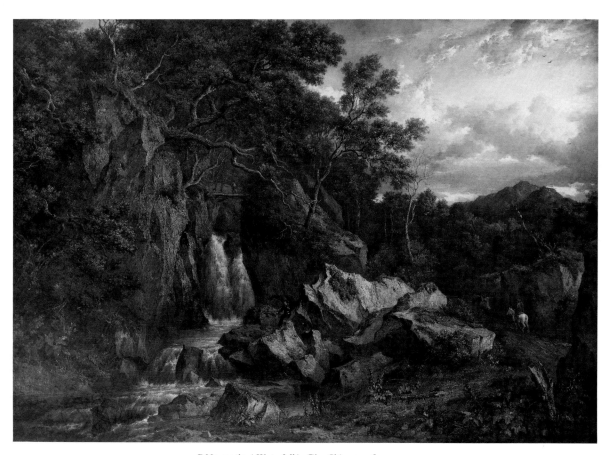

P. Nasmyth: *A Waterfall in Glen Shira near Inveraray*
LL 3741

the Manchester branch of Agnew, it is tempting to think it might be that picture. To complicate matters further, however, Patrick Nasmyth at the previous year's exhibition in Manchester showed a *View of Glenshirrah, Head of Loch Awe* [sic]; that painting remained unsold.[3]

It is difficult to judge how much weight to give to these respective points of evidence. Given that Nasmyth had been based in London since 1814, and that in any case fidelity to nature was never a significant feature of his art, it would be wrong to lay too much stress on the topographical inexactness of the view. The title proposed above seems on balance preferable to the traditional one.[4]

PROVENANCE:
…Agnew & Zanetti, Manchester; sold to Mr Roper in the mid-19th century; bt. from Mrs Roper by the Liverpool artist Harry Hime (1858-1933);[5] bt. from Hime by Lever 1904 (£600).

EXHIBITION:
[? RA 1822 (310)].

REFERENCES:
1.   (a) 26½ × 36 in., Sotheby 20 November 1963 (135); J.C.B. Cooksey: *Alexander Nasmyth HRSA 1758-1840, A Man of the Scottish Renaissance* (1991) Part II, pp. 136-7, cat. S35; (b) 25½ × 34 in., Sotheby 3 April 1996 (107).
2.   Mrs R. MacGregor, Inveraray, verbally, 9 March 1998.
3.   Royal Manchester Institution sales books 1827-1847, Manchester Central Reterence Library.
4.   No help is provided by reviews of the 1822 Royal Academy, which do not notice Nasmyth's work.
5.   Provenance given by F.W. Fox, letter to Lever 26 October 1904, gallery files. He reported 'in my opinion it is a perfectly genuine picture. It is cracked in places but these could be put right …The picture has been re-lined but I should think this was done at least twenty years ago …I do not think the price asked of you, viz. £1100 [sic] to be an excessive one …', Agnew and Zanetti's supplier has not been traced.

'Patrick Nasmyth'
1787-1831

Wooded Landscape near Iver, Uxbridge[1]
LL 3719 (WHL 2323, HH 160)
oil on panel, 29.5 × 40.5 cm

The signature *Patk. Nasmyth* on LL 3719 beneath the upper log appears to be inauthentic, and overall, the work does not display Nasmyth's tight, controlled brushwork, nor his characteristic intricate juxtaposition of light and dark strokes of paint. The foliage is mechanically painted and the work has the quality of a superior pot-boiler. After Lever had acquired LL 3719, the false signature seems to have become obscured, since for a time the work was re-attributed to Edward Williams (1782-1855).[2] Cleaning in 1936 recovered the signature and the attribution returned to Nasmyth.[3]

As a candidate for the artist, Edward Williams seems less promising than his son, Edward Charles Williams (1807-1881), a signed work by whom, dated 1841 and titled *Near Uxley, Kent*, bears considerable stylistic resemblance to LL 3719.[4] Another painting close in style to LL 3719, formerly in a private collection in Chicago attributed to Alexander Nasmyth, has been re-attributed to Henry Ladbrooke (1800-69).[5] In the current state of knowledge of these artists' works, however, it would be rash to ascribe LL 3719 to either of them. The work can certainly be dated to the second quarter of the 19th century.

PROVENANCE:
…James Orrock; bt. from Orrock by Lever 1910.[6]

REFERENCES:
1.   This title is given on an old ms. label on the reverse of LL 3719. S.L. Davison: 'A Lost Masterpiece', *Bebington News* (5 December 1936) seems to have been the first to notice this although it appears of much earlier origin.
2.   Tatlock, p. 116.
3.   Davison, *loc. cit.*
4.   20½ × 16½ in.; Sotheby Belgravia 20 June 1972 (22, part).

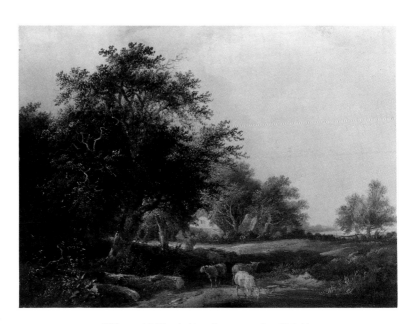

'P. Nasmyth': *Wooded Landscape near Iver, Uxbridge*
LL 3719

5. Annotation by Miklos Rajnai to a photograph in the Witt Library. Signed and dated 1830s works by J.B. Ladbrooke (1803–79) also seem close to LL 3719.

6. 1910 Inventory p.55, valued at £20.

attributed to
Joseph Paul
1804–1887

Freston Tower on the Orwell
LL 3694 (WHL 630, HH 39)
oil on canvas, 102 × 127.5 cm

Lever acquired LL 3694 as by John Crome, but it has since been identified as a work by his imitator, and possibly erstwhile pupil, Joseph Paul.[1] The antler-like branches of the trees are a noted stylistic feature of works believed to be by him. Two smaller variants of the same composition are known.[2]

The traditional title of LL 3694 has been retained, but Freston Tower, occupying an elevated site on the south bank of the Orwell estuary about three miles from Ipswich, is a six-storeyed folly built of brick,[3] whereas the tower in LL 3694 is that of a ruined church. The first owner of

LL 3694 (see below) is thought to have been the Rector of Trimley St. Martin, a parish on the north side of the Orwell estuary near Felixstowe, and it is just possible that the painting is a very fanciful rendition of his church (which, however, is orientated in the reverse direction in relation to the river, and is some distance inland from it, as well as being quite unrecognisable today from the ruined building portrayed by Paul). The adjoining church of Trimley St. Mary (which shares its churchyard with St. Martin) was in a ruined state in the mid-19th century, but a print dating from 1854

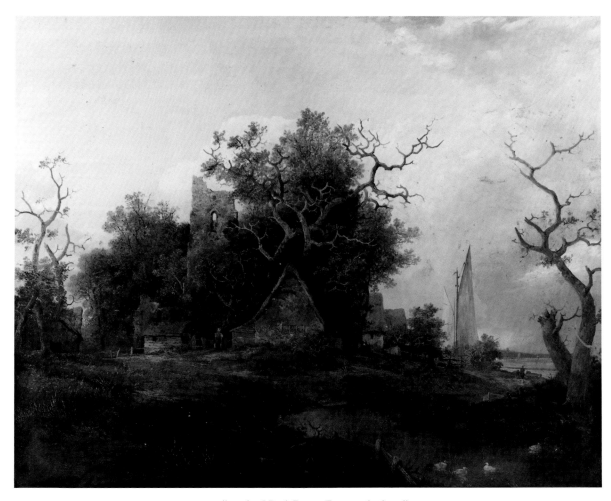

attributed to J. Paul: *Freston Tower on the Orwell*
LL 3694

preserved in parish records shows that its (now rebuilt) western tower was not standing at that period. LL 3694 has the character of a studio composition, and seems unlikely to represent an actual location.

PROVENANCE:
[? The Rector of Trimley St. Martin; Mr Gurney, of Overend Gurney & Co.; Capt. B. Hamilton by 1883[4];... [?Sir Cuthbert Quilter; Christie 16 June 1900(94) bt. Gribble (£220.10.-)[5];... [? C. Fairfax Murray[6];...James Orrock by 1906;[7] bt. from Orrock by Lever 1910.[8]

EXHIBITION:
Old Masters RA 1906 (45).

REFERENCES:
1. On Joseph Paul the best source of information is a Norfolk Museums Service typescript:*Joseph Paul (1804-1887)* prepared by the Art Department of the Norwich Castle Museum (no date). This points out that 'Paul never exhibited in London. He never signed his paintings, and in fact there is no known documented work by him. Every single painting that goes under his name is attributed to him on stylistic grounds based on a few pictures traditionally accepted as his work'. See also Miklos Rajnai:'Robert Paul the Non-Existent Painter', *Apollo* (April 1968) supplement pp.2-3. LL 3694 was attributed to 'John Paul' by Tatlock, p.59; the reproduction from Tatlock in the Witt Library is annotated by C.J. Holmes: 'a typical specimen of 'Old' Paul's work in youth when under the immediate influence of Crome', suggesting that LL 3694 should be dated to around 1830 (although at this period his exhibits with the Norwich Society of Artists consisted of portraits). Norma Watt, Norwich Castle Museum, verbally, 20 April 1998, endorsed the attribution of LL 3694 to Paul.
2. (a) untraced, 30×45 in. (photograph in the Witt Library); (b) Sotheby 20 July 1983 (71). Both of these are also attributed to Paul.
3. It was built in the mid-16th century by Lord Freston as a school for his daughter Ellen: on the ground floor she took lessons in the practice of charity; on the first she wove tapestries; on the second, studied music; on the third ancient

languages; on the fourth English literature; on the fifth painting, and on the sixth astrology (L. Parr: *Countryside Curiosities of England* (1990) p.244.)
4. This provenance is established by a manuscript label on the reverse of LL 3694, now largely illegible, but formerly recorded by A.C. Tait. Addressed to Captain B. Hamilton it read: *Sir, This picture was purchased by the late owner, Mr Gurney (Overend Gurney) from the Rector of Trimley St. Martin's Ipswich, for whom* [...] (Tait assumed this to have read 'it was painted') [...] *St. George's Square* [...] *again some 16 years afterwards he had to give up his big house where it held the post of honour on the mantelpiece of his dining room yours etc. E. Murton Feb 16th 1883.* A further label reads *Highfield House/Gt. Berkhamstead.* The Rectors of Trimley St. Martin in the period were Samuel Kilderbee from 1787 to 1847; John Ambrose, MA, from 1847 to 1860; and thereafter Thomas Palmer, MA.
5. C.H. Collins Baker: *Crome* (1921) p.157 states incorrectly that the work was consigned by C.W. Dawes; it was sold by Gooden on behalf of Quilter (Christie's day books). The dimensions recorded in the sale catalogue, 37½×47½ in., may indicate that it was not LL 3694 but a further, untraced, version. It was titled *Preston* [sic] *Tower* but the description is of the present composition.
6. Tatlock, *loc. cit.*, gives Fairfax Murray as the previous owner and adds 'not sold', but he did not record the earlier provenance.
7. Lent by Orrock to the 1906 exhibition. Paul evidently continued to be active, with his sons, into the 1880s (Norwich Museums Service, *op. cit.*) and there is a distinct possibility that Orrock would have known them personally and had dealings with them. The preponderance of Constables (known to have been imitated by Paul), and works of the Norwich School among the inauthentic works sold by Orrock to Lever is highly suggestive.
8. 1910 Inventory p.34, valued at £800.

attributed to
Joseph Paul
1804-1887

Wooded Landscape
LL 3712 (WHL 658, HH 253)
oil on canvas, 26×39 cm

Lever acquired LL 3712 as by John Crome, but at a valuation which implied that it was not a genuine work. It has been re-attributed to Joseph Paul on the basis of stylistic comparison with other paintings traditionally ascribed to him.[1] LL 3712 has the character of a Norwich School pastiche, with a Cromesque wooded lane being combined with the sail of a wherry, partially obscured on the right-hand side, and behind it, what may be intended as the spire of Norwich cathedral. The paint is very crudely and insensitively applied, much of it dragged on hastily by a knife.

PROVENANCE:
...James Orrock; bt. from Orrock by Lever 1910.[2]

REFERENCES:
1. Tatlock, p.59, attributed LL 3712 to 'John Paul'. A work copied from Crome's etching *Oaks Near Hingham* (photograph in the Witt Library) is traditionally attributed to Paul and is close in style to LL 3712. Norma Watt, Norwich Castle Museum, verbally, 20 April 1998, endorsed the attribution to Paul.
2. 1910 Inventory p.62, valued at £15.

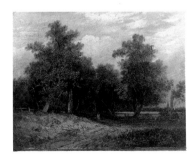

attributed to J. Paul:
Wooded Landscape
LL 3712

attributed to
Edward Pritchett
active 1828-1864

The Piazzetta, Venice
LL 3733 (WHL 96, HH 58)
oil on canvas, 35.5 × 30.5 cm

Lever acquired LL 3733 as by James Holland (other Venetian works by whom are catalogued above). The slick and flashy manner is, however, not especially close to Holland's more literal and fussy style, and comparison with a signed painting of the same subject by Edward Pritchett (Manchester City Art Gallery, fig.38) suggests that LL 3733 is also by him. Especially similar are the loosely brushed figures and the mannered handling of the white cloud. The slightly different angle of viewpoint accounts for the minor variations in the treatment of the buildings.

The view is dominated by the columns of Marco and Todaro at the open end of the Piazzetta next to St. Mark's Square. In the distance, across the mouth of the Grand Canal, is the little tower of the Dogana (the Customs House) and to the right are the domes and the campanile of Santa Maria della Salute. LL 3733 is obviously derived from Richard Parkes Bonington's *The Piazzetta, Venice* (Tate Gallery, fig.39) which, having been shown at the British Institution in 1828 and given to the nation by Robert Vernon in 1847, had been further popularised with the publication of J.W. Allen's engraving in the *Art Journal*, 1851.[1] Numerous contemporary copies of Bonington's work also attest to its popularity as a subject.[2]

PROVENANCE:
…James Orrock (? by 1895);[3] bt. from Orrock by Lever 1910.[4]

REFERENCES:
1. *Art Journal* (1851) fp. 192.
2. For Bonington's painting see P. Noon: *Richard Parkes Bonington: On the Pleasures of Painting*, exhibition catalogue, Yale Center for British Art, New Haven (1990) p.256, cat.131. It had been engraved while in Vernon's collection by Edward Finden and published in the *Book of Gems* (1837).
3. LL 3733 is probably lot 74 in the Orrock-Linton sale, Christie 25-27 April 1895 (Bonington: *The Piazzetta, Venice* bt. Smith [i.e. bt. in] (£29.8.-.)).
4. 1910 Inventory p.36, valued at £50.

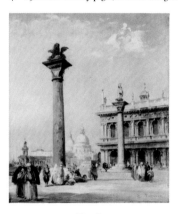

Fig.38
E. Pritchett: *St. Mark's Square, Venice*
© Manchester City Art Galleries

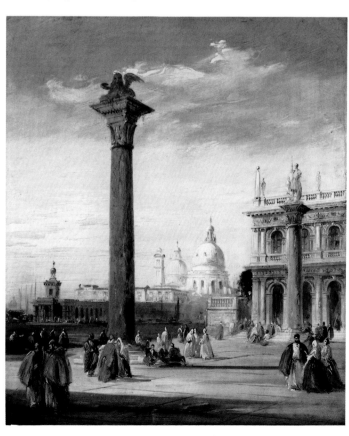

attributed to E. Pritchett: *The Piazzetta, Venice*
LL 3733

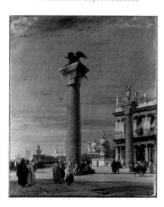

Fig.39
R.P. Bonington:
The Column of St. Mark
© Tate Gallery London

Sir Henry Raeburn
1756-1823

Thomas Telford
LL 3147 (WHL 619, HH 203)
oil on canvas, 76.5 × 63.5 cm

Thomas Telford (1757-1834)
was born near Westerkirk,
Dumfriesshire, the son of a shepherd.
A man of enormous energy, he
developed into one of the greatest
civil engineers of his day, a visionary
builder of bridges, designer of canals
and surveyor of roads and harbours.
His greatest achievements included
the Pont-y-Cysylte Aqueduct over
the River Dee (1796-1803),
described by Sir Walter Scott as the
most impressive work of art he had
ever seen, the Caledonian Canal
(1803-22), the Göta Canal in Sweden
(1808-32) and the Menai Bridge
(1819-26).[1]

   Although the attribution of
LL 3147 to Raeburn has not been
universally accepted,[2] the handling
does seem characteristic of his work
and the work's pedigree is strongly
in its favour. LL 3147 was lent to the
National Portrait Exhibition of 1868
and the great 1876 Raeburn
exhibition in Edinburgh by Mrs
Margaret Burge, the youngest
daughter of Rev. Archibald Alison,
one of Telford's closest friends.
Alison (1757-1839), the author of the
*Essay on the Nature and Principles
of Taste* (1790), had commissioned
Telford to make some alterations to
his Northamptonshire vicarage in
the mid-1780s and Telford had
thereafter become a kind of adopted
uncle to his children.[3] It is thus very
unlikely that any mistake should
have arisen over who painted the
portrait.

   The work has traditionally been
dated to around 1812,[4] when Telford
was fifty-five. It seems scarcely
possible that the sitter in LL 3147 is
this age although in Samuel Lane's

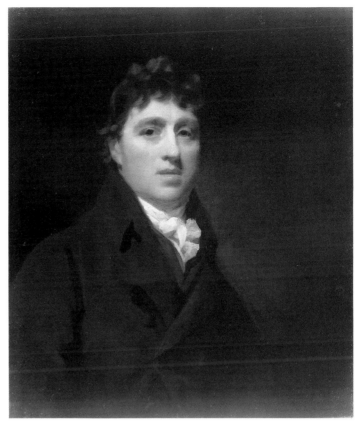

Sir H. Raeburn: *Thomas Telford*
LL 3147

full-length portrait of 1822
(Institution of Civil Engineers)
Telford also appears phenomenally
youthful.[5] There are, nevertheless,
indications that LL 3147 may date
from considerably earlier. Alison
and his family moved to Edinburgh
in 1800, and Telford himself began
visiting Scotland regularly after July
1801 in order to carry out his surveys
of the Scottish Highlands and
certainly stayed with the Alisons at
some point thereafter.[6] He was in
Edinburgh for a week in November
1801 and again in 1803 when he was
elected to the Edinburgh Royal
Society.[7] It is tempting to think that
Alison commissioned the portrait
from Raeburn at around this time.

PROVENANCE:
[? commissioned by or presented to
Rev. Archibald Alison]: Alison's youngest
daughter Margaret (Mrs Burge) of
Woodville, Colinton, Edinburgh, by 1868
and until after 1876;[8] her nephew, Sir
Archibald Alison (1826-1907);… James
Orrock; bt. from Orrock by Lever 1910.[9]

EXHIBITIONS:
National Portrait Exhibition 1868 (166);
Raeburn Edinburgh 1876 (314); *Lord
Leverhulme* RA 1980 (30).

REFERENCES:
1. For Telford see especially J. Rickman,
ed.: *Life of Thomas Telford* (1838);
Sir A. Gibb: *The Story of Telford* (1935);
L.T.C. Rolt: *Thomas Telford* (1979). For a
brief summary of his work in the Scottish
Highlands see J. Hulbert: 'Thomas
Telford, Highland Engineer', *Country
Life* (8 October 1970) pp. 906-7.
2. Tatlock, p.97, attributed LL 3147 to
Sir John Watson Gordon (1788-1864).
The work is not included in D. Mackie:
*Raeburn, Life and Art. A Complete
Catalogue of the Artist's Work*, Ph.D

thesis, University of Edinburgh (1994).
It is included in J.L. Caw's list of
Raeburn's portraits in W. Armstrong:
Raeburn (1901) p.113 and was accepted
by J. Greig: *Sir Henry Raeburn R.A.*
(1911)p.61; also by Dr L. Errington, letter,
24 September 1979, gallery files.
3. Lady Alison, ed.: *Sir A. Alison: Some
Account of my Life and Writings* (1883)
pp.15-17.
4. Armstrong, *loc. cit.*, and Greig, *loc. cit.*
5. J.L. Caw, in *Scottish Portraits* (1903)
Vol.2, p.101, compared LL 3147
unfavourably to Lane's portrait: 'it gives
a nearly front view, and for that reason
perhaps the characteristics of Telford's
face, the high straight-bridged, pointed
nose, and the somewhat peculiarly shaped
chin are less evident than in the other,
where a three-quarter view was chosen'.
6. Alison, *op. cit.*, p.31.
7. Rolt, *op. cit.*, pp.80-82.
8. Labels for both the 1868 and 1876
exhibitions, bearing Mrs Burge's name
and address, are on the reverse of LL 3147.
She wrote from the same address to
acknowledge her father's receipt of
Telford's *Life* in July 1838 (A. Penfold,
Ironbridge Gorge Museum Trust, letter,
10 January 1980, gallery files).
9. 1910 Inventory p.58, valued at £300.
The work is there stated to have been in
Sir Archibald Alison's collection. Orrock,
who came from Edinburgh, probably
purchased it privately from his estate.

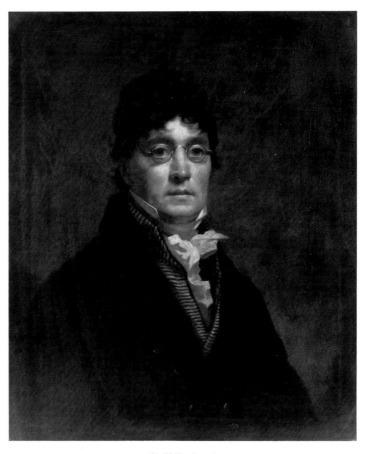

'Sir H. Raeburn':
Portrait of a Man (called 'James Edgar' or 'John Guthrie')
LL 3561

'Sir Henry Raeburn'
1756-1823

*Portrait of a Man
(called 'James Edgar' or
'John Guthrie')*
LL 3561 (WHL 3414)
oil on canvas, 77 × 64.5 cm

Both the attribution of LL 3561 to
Raeburn and the traditional
identification of the sitter as James
Edgar of Auchingrammont (d.1813)
are doubtful.

The painting is of good quality,
although not superior to a second
version (see below); nevertheless, the
handling of neither work is wholly
characteristic of Raeburn and doubts
have been expressed that LL 3561 is
by him.[1]

The identification of the sitter
presents difficulties which are
currently insoluble. There is some
evidence that LL 3561 is one of four
Raeburn portraits sold at Christie
in 1890 from the collection of Col.
James Handasyde Edgar, one of
which was of James Edgar of
Auchingrammont, yet it is certain
that LL 3561 is not the latter work
even though Lever subsequently
bought the painting as a portrait of
this man.[2] Of the three other
portraits in the 1890 Edgar sale,

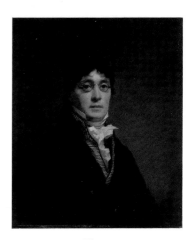

Fig.40
Sir H. Raeburn: *John Guthrie of Carbeth*
Felton Bequest 1934, National Gallery of Victoria,
Melbourne, Australia

the *James Edgar as a boy of four* and the *Alexander Edgar of Auchingrammont* cannot be LL 3561, but the *Handasyde Edgar M.D. F.R.S.* is presently unaccounted for and remains a possibility.[3] On the other hand, conflicting evidence has subsequently emerged that the sitter had nothing to do with the Edgar family, but is John Guthrie of Carbeth (1768-1834), a Glasgow merchant who returned from the West Indies in the first decade of the 19th century and who built up the Carbeth estate between 1808 and 1817. This re-identification was made on the basis of a second version of the portrait, purchased as a Raeburn in 1935 by the National Gallery of Victoria, Melbourne (fig.40), whose frame is inscribed John Guthrie and whose provenance is traceable directly back to the sitter himself.[4]

PROVENANCE:
[…?Col. J.H. Edgar; Christie 22 February 1890(74) bt. Vokins (£27.6.-.)[5];… Horsbrugh; bt. by Agnew October 1898; C.A. Barton November 1898 until November 1901; bt. by Agnew; bt. by H.L. Bischoffsheim January 1902 (£400); [? from whom] bt. by Lever through Gooden & Fox, privately, 11 February 1918 (£400).[6]

REFERENCES:
1. Tatlock, p.60, tentatively suggested that the style resembled Sir J. Watson Gordon's. LL3561 is referred to in D. Mackie: *Raeburn, Life and Art. A Complete Catalogue of the Artist's Work*, Ph.D thesis, University of Edinburgh (1994) under 'James Edgar' but Mackie doubts the attribution to Raeburn and notes the later identification of the sitter.
2. The reverse of LL 3561 bears the Christie's stencil 655b. Although that stencil does not relate to the property of Col. Edgar, it does relate to an item intended to be offered in the same 22 February 1890 sale (though in the event apparently never actually auctioned); and the implication appears to be that LL 3561 was stencilled in error at the same time (day books, Christie's archives). The

James Edgar of Auchingrammont sold as lot 75 in this sale was bought by Curtis Lampson and re-sold at Christie by Lampson 15 June 1901(94). The 1901 sale catalogue describes the sitter as wearing a blue coat; the sitter in LL3561 is not in a blue coat. The Lampson portrait is undoubtedly the work now in the Memphis Brooks Museum of Art, Tennessee.
3 Mackie, *op. cit.*, does not list the portrait of Handasyde Edgar.
4. U. Hoff: *European Paintings Before 1800 in the National Gallery of Victoria* (1995) p.222, and citing, for biographical information on Guthrie, J. Guthrie Smith: *The Parish of Strathblane* (1886) p.41 and his *Strathendrick and its Inhabitants from Early Times* (1896) pp.xviii-xix.
5. See main text and note 2 above.
6. 'I have submitted your offer for the Raeburn portrait of J. Edgar and it has been mailed on to America where the owner at present is' (F.W. Fox to Lever 21 December 1917) and 'I have just

received news that your offer for the Raeburn portrait of James Edgar is accepted' (Fox to Lever 30 January 1918), gallery files.

'Sir Henry Raeburn'
1756-1823

Lieutenant Thomas Gifford
LL 3676 (WHL 2130, H 31)
oil on canvas,[1] 76×63.5 cm

A 19th-century inscription on the reverse of LL 3676 reads: *Lieutenant Thomas Gifford/[the] Younger of Busta/Shetland/Por[trait af]ter Henry Raeburn*. The sitter is probably Thomas Gifford of Hillswick, born in 1789, third son of Gideon Gifford of Busta.[2] He was

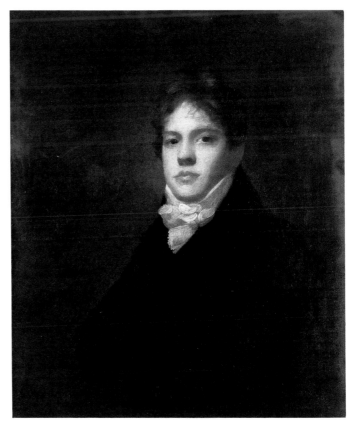

'Sir H. Raeburn': *Lieutenant Thomas Gifford*
LL 3676

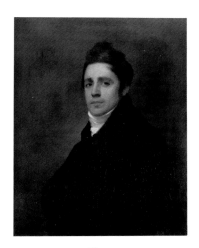

Fig.41
G.Watson: *Prof. Robert Jameson*
Private collection; photograph courtesy the
Scottish National Portrait Gallery

a lieutenant of the 25th Native Infantry, East India Company; married Jessie Scott, by whom he had two sons and six daughters, in June 1821 and died about 1836. He was the great-grandson of Thomas Gifford of Busta (about 1682-1773) which may account for his being termed 'the younger'.[3] Alternatively, rather less plausibly, the portrait may be of a younger Thomas, who has been identified as Lieutenant Gifford's illegitimate son, born before the latter's marriage in 1821; this man was not a lieutenant, but did live at Busta, where he worked as factor.[4] But this man is likely to have been too young for a portrait which must date from between 1815 and 1830.

The present canvas is thinly and perfunctorily painted. A second version, formerly at Busta House,[5] appears from a photograph to be of better quality, without being convincingly by Raeburn. LL 3676 has formerly been attributed to Raeburn's colleague and rival in Edinburgh, George Watson (1767-1837).[6] While it is very unlikely to have been executed by Watson himself, similarities with his portrait types, such as the *Professor Robert Jameson* engraved in 1819 (private

collection, fig.41), do suggest that it may be a copy of an original by Watson.

PROVENANCE:
…James Orrock; Christie, 4-6 June 1904 (127) bt. in (170 gns.); bt. from Orrock by Lever November 1904.[7]

EXHIBITION:
Loan Exhibition of Pictures and Engravings by British Artists Museum and Art Gallery Birkenhead March-April 1912 (98).

REFERENCES:
1.   The canvas has been glue-lined to a panel backed onto a conventional stretcher.
2.   Gideon was the notorious heir of the Giffords, born to a maid who claimed to have been secretly married to John Gifford of Busta; see M. Henderson: 'The Giffords of Busta House', *Scottish Field* (February 1985) pp.1-8.
3.   F.J. Grant: *Zetland Family Histories* (1907) pp.84, 88-9; the approximate date of Thomas Gifford of Hillswick's death (not in Grant) was communicated by Mrs Judith Jones, Busta House, letter, 10 January 1998, gallery files.
4.   I. Mead, letter to M. Henderson, 26 March 1985, communicated in Jones, *loc. cit.*
5.   This portrait was sold by previous owners of the house at an untraced sale in the mid-1970s (Jones, *loc. cit.*).
6.   Tatlock, p.68.
7.   1904 Inventory p.1, no.5.

'Sir Henry Raeburn'
1756-1823

A Boy Holding a Stick and Hoop
LL 3720 (WHL 2330, HH 225)
oil on canvas, 60.5 × 50 cm

Lever acquired LL 3720 as by Raeburn. On grounds of style, this attribution is unacceptable. The portrait purports to date from about 1800 and is of fair quality, but the handling of the boy's head in

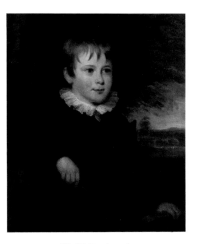

'Sir H. Raeburn':
A Boy Holding a Stick and Hoop
LL 3720

particular is not at all characteristic of Raeburn.[1]

PROVENANCE:
…James Orrock; bt. from Orrock by Lever 1910.[2]

REFERENCES:
1.   LL 3720 is conceivably a later pastiche carried out for James Orrock, but on balance seems more likely to be an authentic unattributed work of the period 1795-1810. Certain portraits ascribed to George Watson bear some stylistic resemblance to it, but Watson's work is not yet well enough defined for LL 3720 to be attributed to him with confidence.
2.   1910 Inventory p.60, valued at £35.

'Sir Henry Raeburn'
1756-1823

David Wilkie
LL 3731 (WHL 2129, H 6)
oil on canvas, 80 × 67 cm

Lever acquired LL 3731 as by Raeburn. This attribution is unacceptable on stylistic grounds, as is a later one to Sir John Watson Gordon (1788-1864).[1] The pedestrian handling suggests that the work is a copy, and since no other version of the portrait is known, the

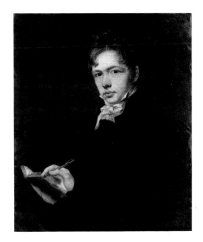

'Sir H. Raeburn':
David Wilkie
LL 3731

PROVENANCE:
…James Orrock;[3] Christie June 4-6 1904 (126) bt. in (£210); bt. from Orrock by Lever November 1904.[4]

REFERENCES:
1. Tatlock, p.97.
2. Hamish Miles, letter, 30 May 1998, gallery files.
3. The painting seems previously to have been in Manchester, since there is a stamp on the lining canvas of J.R. Taylor, 15 Brazennose Street. This firm is recorded under this name and at this address between 1858 and 1890 (information from Sandra Martin, Manchester City Art Gallery, 1995).
4. 1904 Inventory p.1, no.25.

'Allan Ramsay'
1713-1784

The Dinwiddie Sisters
LL 3547 (WHL 3838)
oil on canvas, 148.5 × 124 cm

The sitters are traditionally the two daughters of Robert Dinwiddie (1692-1770), Surveyor-General of the Southern Colonies 1738-51 and Lieutenant-Governor of Virginia 1751-8; and his wife Rebecca Auchinleck or Affleck (d.1793). Elizabeth, the elder, was born in 1738 and died unmarried at Clifton,

artist represented may not be David Wilkie, whose iconography is familiar. Nevertheless, certain similarities are apparent between LL 3731 and Sir William Beechey's portrait of Wilkie, shown at the Royal Academy in 1809 and engraved the following year by John Young. Besides the costume and the positioning of the figure these include more specific details such as the comma of hair above the left eye and the treatment of the left eyebrow. It is possible, therefore, that LL 3731 is an imaginary portrait of Wilkie confected from Beechey's type.[2]

Sir David Wilkie, born at Cults, Fife in 1785, became one of the most popular British artists of the early 19th century. His name was made by *The Village Politicians*, exhibited at the Royal Academy in 1806, which epitomised his gift for character-isation and the close observation of human types (as is suggested by the sitter's gaze in LL 3731). One of his last works, the state portrait of Queen Victoria, is catalogued below. He died at sea off Gibraltar in 1841, the event which moved J.M.W. Turner to paint *Peace: Burial at Sea* (Tate Gallery).

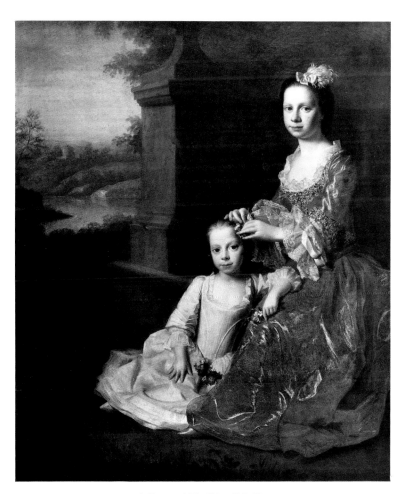

'A. Ramsay': *The Dinwiddie Sisters*
LL 3547

Bristol in 1773; Rebecca, the younger, was born in 1742[1] and in August 1771 married Archibald Hamilton of the Isle of Man.[2]

Although the old title of LL 3547 has been retained, the identity of the two girls cannot be regarded as established beyond question. In the first place, the attribution of the portrait to their fellow-Scot, Allan Ramsay, is highly doubtful.[3] The older girl's face is reminiscent of Ramsay types but otherwise the handling, especially of the costumes and the background, is not at all characteristic of his work. The older girl's costume has been described as probably foreign,[4] and the landscape background, with its round tower, also has a continental feel, raising doubts as to whether the artist was British at all.[5] Secondly, if the two girls are the Dinwiddie sisters, the work is quite awkward to date on the basis of their apparent ages. The costumes have been placed in the mid-1740s,[6] and this accords with the apparent age of the younger girl who is perhaps four or five. However, if the portrait was painted in 1746-7, Elizabeth Dinwiddie would have been only eight or nine; whereas both the looks of the older girl and the dress she is wearing would suggest she is somewhat older than this.[7] Finally, the work is traced to Dinwiddie ownership only in the late 19th and early 20th centuries, and cannot be proved to have descended in the family from the sitters themselves.

In 1920, shortly after its acquisition by Lever, LL 3547 was re-lined onto a canvas approximately 1 cm larger in dimension than the original and was cleaned. The retouchings which were carried out at this time have subsequently darkened considerably.[8]

PROVENANCE:
[? by descent to] General Gilbert Hamilton Dinwiddie, 1883;[9] [? his daughter] Miss Dinwiddie by 1894[10] and [?] until 1917;[11] … Dr W. Watson Griffin; Christie 30 May 1919 (123) bt. Gooden & Fox for Lever (£559.13.-.).

EXHIBITIONS:
Old Glasgow Glasgow 1894 (12); *Scottish Groups and Conversation Pieces* Scottish National Portrait Gallery Edinburgh 1956 (5).

REFERENCES:
1. *Old Glasgow*, exhibition catalogue, Glasgow (1894) p.7.
2. *Scots Magazine* (1771) Vol.33, p.445.
3. The attribution was first questioned by A. Smart: *The Life and Art of Allan Ramsay* (1952) p.183.
4. Aileen Ribeiro, verbally, 26 February 1998.
5. Both Alastair Laing and Elizabeth Einberg, verbally, have suggested that LL 3547 is not by a British artist, and indeed no obvious British candidates have suggested themselves. The portrait could conceivably have been executed when the Dinwiddies were in the colonies (although it is not known whether the girls accompanied their father abroad; nor does LL 3547 seem characteristic of colonial portraiture). Einberg tentatively proposed that LL 3547 may have been painted by Carl Tuscher (1705-51) who worked in England 1741-43; if so the sitters are certainly not the Dinwiddie sisters.
6. Ribeiro, *ibid*.
7. Ribeiro, *ibid*., described the dress as 'rather grown-up to be worn by a ten year-old English girl'.
8. A photograph of LL 3547 taken by A.J. Melhuish, 12 York Place, Portman Square, when it was owned by Miss Dinwiddie (Scottish National Portrait Gallery Library) indicates that the younger girl's face has been altered to make her pupils slightly larger and to give her a more smiling expression.
9. Information from Mrs Janet Dinwiddie, letter, 7 April 1932, gallery files, citing a letter to her of 1921 from Mr R. Dinwiddie Whittenbury-Kaye who was then writing a book on the Dinwiddie family.
10. Lent by Miss Dinwiddie to the 1894 exhibition. According to James Gourlay, Glasgow, letter, 26 October 1933, gallery files, LL 3547 was also lent by Miss Dinwiddie to the 'Industrial Exhibition held [in Glasgow] in 1900'. No such exhibition has been traced.
11. James Gourlay, letter, 18 October 1933, gallery files, states that 'since 1917 the whereabouts [of LL 3547] were unknown to local antiquarians like myself'. Miss Dinwiddie sold a portrait supposedly of the daughters' father, Governor Dinwiddie, also attributed to Ramsay, to the National Portrait Gallery in 1912 (the last year in which she is recorded at the address of 1 Gloucester Crescent London NW given in the *Old Glasgow* catalogue; Gourlay letter, 26 October 1933). That portrait, not by the same hand as LL 3547, is also not authentic.

Sir Joshua Reynolds
1723-1792

Lady Lepell Phipps and her Son
LL 3664 (WHL 3274)
oil on canvas, 90 × 69 cm

Lady Lepell Phipps (1723-1780), the eldest daughter of John, Lord Hervey, married in 1743 Constantine Phipps, later first Baron Mulgrave, by whom she had six children.[1] The boy in the portrait is traditionally her eldest son Constantine John, later 2nd Baron Mulgrave (1744-1792), whose chief claim to fame in later life was as an explorer of the Arctic. Reynolds's pocket books list five sittings from 'Master Phipps' in June 1757 and sittings from Lady Phipps on 21 and 24 February 1758, 16, 18, 19, 21, 22, 25 and 28 May 1758, and 28 April, 5 May and 22 and 24 June 1759. On the day after the last of these appointments another 'Master Phipps' sitting is recorded. A later note in Reynolds's ledger dating from before 23 January 1761 reads 'one guinea due: Lady Lapel Phips for altering a Child's Picture'.[2] On grounds of style LL 3664 can be dated to the late 1750s, and there seems no reason to doubt that LL 3664 was

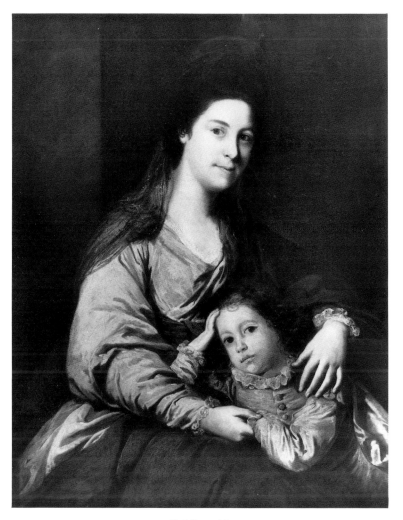

Sir J. Reynolds:
Lady Lepell Phipps and her Son
LL 3664

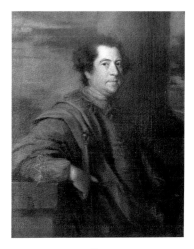

Fig.42
Sir J. Reynolds:
Constantine Phipps, 1st Baron Mulgrave
Private collection; photograph courtesy the owner

characteristic of many Reynolds portraits of the 1750s, were noted in 1894 when the work was first exhibited in public.[5]

PROVENANCE:
By descent to Constantine Henry, 3rd Marquess of Normanby; Christie 19 July 1890 (20) bt. Murray (£273); ... Samuel Joseph by 1894;[6] Mrs Joseph; bt. by Agnew September 1916; bt. from Agnew by Cremetti 1917; bt. by Lever 18 July 1917 (£2,250 plus exchanged painting).

EXHIBITION:
Old Masters RA 1894 (18).

REFERENCES:
1. *Burke's Peerage*, 105th ed. (1978) p.1983.
2. A. Graves and W.V. Cronin: *A History of the Works of Sir Joshua Reynolds P.R.A.* (1899-1901) Vol.II, p.751; further information from David Mannings, letter, 2 July 1997, gallery files.
3. Graves and Cronin, *op. cit.*, pp.751-2, list under 'Master Phipps' a portrait (for which no sittings are recorded) of Henry, third son of Lady Lepell Phipps. He was born in February 1755 and as described, the portrait does not seem to be of a two year old, as would be required by the 'Master Phipps' sittings in June 1757; however, this portrait may be the one which was altered later. Neither Graves and Cronin nor Ellis Waterhouse, in *Reynolds* (1941) record any portrait of

commissioned as a companion portrait to Reynolds's kit-cat portrait of Lady Lepell Phipps's husband Constantine, dating from 1757 (private collection, fig.42). However, the entries in the pocket books are hard to square with the visual evidence: the boy in the portrait cannot be as old as twelve, and it is most unlikely that Reynolds had five sittings from him as the basis of the present pose before receiving any from his mother. It is probable that the sittings of 1757 refer to a separate, hitherto unidentified, portrait,[3] in which case the boy in

LL 3664 might well be Lady Phipps's second son Charles (1753-1786) at the age of about five.[4] However, the awkwardness of the boy's pose, drawn with little concern for anatomical accuracy, and the alarming disparity in size between the mother's hands suggest that Reynolds may well have made substantial changes in this area of the canvas, and his note alluding to 'altering a Child's Picture' seems very likely to refer to LL 3664 rather than to the suppositious portrait proposed above.

The faded flesh tints in LL 3664,

Constantine John as a twelve year old; it is possible, however, that such a portrait was begun and abandoned; or conjecturally, converted into the supposed portrait of him of 1764 (Montreal Museum of Fine Art; for this see J. Watson: *Reynolds in Canada*, exhibition catalogue, Kitchener – Waterloo Art Gallery (1988) p.43, cat.11).

4.   As proposed by Watson, *loc. cit.*. Ellis Waterhouse, in his annotated copy of Graves & Cronin, citing a Mulgrave inventory of 1834, suggested that the child is William, a son who died young (information from Mannings, *loc. cit.*).

5.   *Athenaeum* (6 January 1894) p.22: 'its rosy tints have mostly vanished, leaving a solid and careful underpainting of bluish colour and grey quite sound ...'.

6.   Lent by Joseph to the 1894 exhibition.

Sir Joshua Reynolds
1723-1792

Mrs. Mary Henrietta Fortescue
LL 3541 (WHL 62, H 2)
oil on canvas, 76 × 63.5 cm

Mary Henrietta, eldest daughter of Thomas Orby Hunter of Croyland Abbey, Lincs, was born in 1734. She married the Rt. Hon. James Fortescue (1725-1782), MP for Louth, by whom she had six children; her second son William Charles, born in 1764, succeeding his uncle as 2nd Viscount Clermont in 1806. She died in 1814.

Mrs Fortescue sat to Reynolds four times between 1 and 4 June 1757,[1] and a memorandum in the artist's pocket book written in the week beginning 13 August 1759 reads 'send Mrs. Fortescue to be copied'.[2] This evidence appears to relate to LL 3541 and another version of the portrait at Fyvie Castle, National Trust for Scotland (fig.43). Clearly, however, the two canvases do not stand in a straightforward relation of original version to copy; they are not

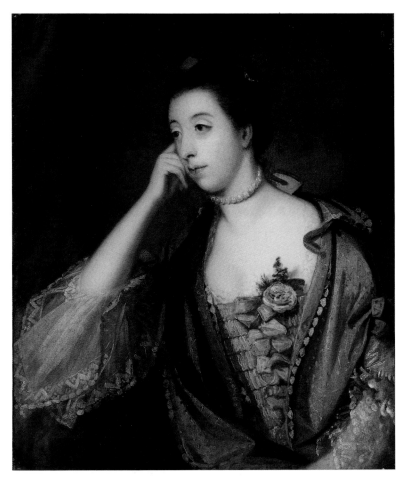

Sir J. Reynolds: *Mrs. Mary Henrietta Fortescue*
LL 3541

the same size, and more awkwardly, there are significant differences of facial feature, which has raised the possibility that LL 3541 could represent a different sitter altogether and that Reynolds simply used a particular pose and costume twice for two separate commissions.[3]

If this notion is rejected, it is not easy to define the relationship between the present canvas and the Fyvie one. LL 3541 does not have the look of a copy, and the handling generally seems characteristic of Reynolds himself. The treatment of Mrs Fortescue's left arm, admittedly, is feeble in the extreme, and in order to account for this it has been suggested that LL 3541 was later cut

down and repainted, especially on the right-hand side.[4] This hypothesis, for which there is no physical evidence, is open to the objection that LL 3541 is not an odd size but the standard 'three quarters' format; nevertheless, it seems the most convincing explanation of the differences between the two versions. The alternative idea that the larger Fyvie canvas was copied from LL 3541 seems plausible only if it is argued that Reynolds was dissatisfied with the effect of LL 3541 and solved his difficulties by extending the design; but in that case the second work would hardly have been executed by someone else, as Reynolds's memorandum suggests happened.

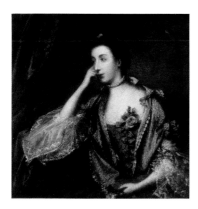

Fig.43
Sir J. Reynolds: *Mrs. Mary Fortescue*
Fyvie Castle, National Trust for Scotland

PROVENANCE:
[? the sitter's daughter, Charlotte
Fortescue, Lady Goodricke; her bequest
to her brother-in-law, George Barlow,
1842; his bequest to his relation] George
Howard, 9th Earl of Carlisle; sold by
the Earl of Carlisle about 1892;[5] …
C. Sedelmeyer; bt. by S. Gooden
18 November 1897; bt. by Agnew
December 1897; bt. from Agnew by
Lever 1 January 1898 (£1,100).

REFERENCES:
1. Information from David Mannings,
letter, 27 August 1997, gallery files.
A. Graves and W. V. Cronin: *A History of
the Works of Sir Joshua Reynolds P.R.A.*
(1899-1901) Vol.I, p.327 state that sittings
took place in 1761, but Mannings
concludes that the Mrs Fortescue
commission was done with by November
1759 when Reynolds noted in his pocket
book 'Mrs. Hunter and Mrs. Fortescue to
be sent to Weverly Abbey near Farnham
Surry' [another home of Mrs Fortescue's
parents].
2. Graves and Cronin, *loc. cit.*
3. Mannings, verbally, 20 September
1990; he drew attention to a photograph
in the Ellis Waterhouse archive, Paul
Mellon Centre for Studies in British Art,
London, of a version of LL 3541 on the
New York art market in the 1920s,
identified as *Mrs Aston*. For the possibility
that LL 3541 is also to be identified as a
portrait of this sitter see note 5 below.
4. Tatlock, p.62; also suggested by
Mannings (1997) *loc. cit.*

5. Two paintings by Reynolds inherited
from George Barlow are recorded in a
late 19th-century inventory of the
London home of the Earls of Carlisle,
where the sitters are identified as Frances
Murray, Countess of Clermont, (*c.*1733-
1822) and Mrs Hervey Aston. The precise
relationship of George Barlow to the
9th Earl has not been elucidated, but the
connection was through Cecilia Barlow,
Lady Wensleydale, the Earl's grand-
mother. George Barlow died in 1848,
but left a life interest in his possessions to
his wife, and the Earl is thought to have
received the inheritance only shortly
before the inventory (which however
gives the full provenance back to the
Fortescue family) was drawn up. The
description of *Frances, Countess of
Clermont*, together with the record of its
disposal (at Christie, 19 March 1892)
suggests that it cannot be identified with
LL 3541. *Mrs. Hervey Aston* is not further
described in the inventory, nor is its
disposal recorded, but it may well have
been sold privately at the same time
(information from C. Ridgway, Castle
Howard, letter, 3 March 1998, gallery
files). It is not clear whether LL3541 is
a third, uninventoried Reynolds
presumably deriving from the same
source, or whether it is identical with
the so-called *Mrs. Hervey Aston*; the
former seems on balance the more
probable, since LL3541 was titled
Miss [sic] *Fortescue* when it was in
Agnew's possession and on Agnew's
invoice to Lever (gallery files). The
latter states that the work came 'from
the Castle Howard Collection'.

Sir Joshua Reynolds
1723-1792

Elizabeth Gunning, Duchess of Hamilton and Argyll
LL 3126 (WHL 4093)
oil on canvas, 238.5 × 147.5 cm

Elizabeth Gunning was the second
daughter of John Gunning of Castle
Coote, County Roscommon, Ireland,
and his wife, Hon. Bridget Bourke,

daughter of the 6th Viscount Mayo.
Born in Hemingford Grey,
Huntingdonshire, in November 1733,
she was taken to Ireland at the age of
three and lived there until 1750
when, with her elder sister Maria, she
was brought back to England and
presented in London society. Thanks
to their beauty and unsophisticated
charm, the Gunning sisters 'became
the rage and the subject of conversation at every fashionable rout';[1]
public excitement reaching its
apogee early in 1752 when they both
married. Elizabeth became the wife
of James, 6th Duke of Hamilton in an
extraordinary ceremony, performed
with the ring of a bed-curtain at half
past midnight on St. Valentine's Day,
after a party at Bedford House at
which the Duke had lost £1200 at
cards. The two sisters continued to
exert an extraordinary fascination,
Horace Walpole writing to Sir
Horace Mann that 'there are mobs at
their doors to see them get into their
chairs, and people go early to get
places at the theatre when it is known
they will be there', and reporting of
the Duchess's presentation at court
that 'the noble mob in the Drawing
Room clamboured on tables and
chairs to look at her'.[2] The Duke of
Hamilton, by whom she had three
children, died on 17 January 1758
and early in the following year she
married John Campbell, Marquis
of Lorne, who in 1771 succeeded as
5th Duke of Argyll. She was created
Baroness Hamilton of Hambledon
in her own right in 1776. Lady of the
Bedchamber to Queen Charlotte
from 1761 to 1784, she was appointed
Mistress of the Robes in 1778 and
died on 20 December 1790.[3] She was
one of the most portrayed women in
Britain during the period 1750-1770;
besides Reynolds's portrait, there
exist well-known full-lengths by
Gavin Hamilton (1752)[4] and Francis
Cotes (1767),[5] two pastels by the
latter[6] and one by Catherine Read, as

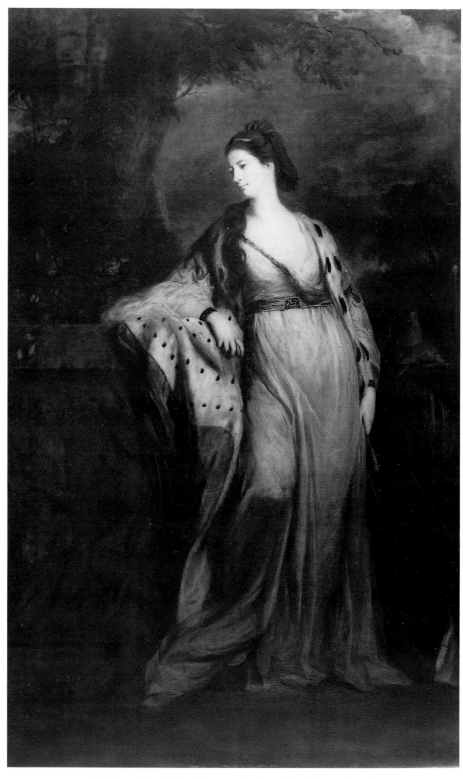

Sir J. Reynolds: *Elizabeth Gunning, Duchess of Hamilton and Argyll*
LL 3126

well as a number of unattributed portraits.[7] Many of these were engraved. A whole-length copy of LL 3126, presumably executed in Reynolds's studio, is now in the Yale Center for British Art, New Haven, and a small one, $19\frac{1}{2} \times 12\frac{1}{2}$ inches in dimensions, lacking the foliage above the Duchess's head, is in the California Palace of the Legion of Honor, San Francisco.

The Duchess of Hamilton began sitting for the portrait in January 1758, the month in which she was widowed (the sarcophagus-like plinth on which she rests has been interpreted as a reference to this).[8] It is tempting to imagine that the work was undertaken as a publicity venture, against a period of enforced withdrawal from society, but it has been pointed out that two sittings, one of which was cancelled, were scheduled in the Duke of Hamilton's lifetime; this and the painting's provenance indicate that it was in fact commissioned by the Duke, presumably in the last months of 1757.[9] After two visits to Reynolds's studio, the Duchess did not return until early in the following year, when seven further sittings[10] must have enabled Reynolds to complete the bulk of the portrait.

By the spring of 1760 it was sufficiently finished to be shown (as *A Lady, Whole Length*) at the first Society of Artists exhibition in London, where the reviewer for the *Imperial Magazine* noted: 'said to be the Duchess of Hamilton, but rather the Queen of all Grace and Beauty'.[11] Nevertheless, either the Duchess may not have been entirely happy with the portrait, or else Reynolds may have regarded it as not completed; it is noticeable that despite the celebrity it clearly enjoyed at the exhibition, it was not engraved, and it remained in his studio for four further years, until in April 1764 the Duchess finally paid

for it in full.[12] Over the previous three months she had given Reynolds three further sittings, and it seems possible that significant alterations were carried out at this stage. It has been noted that the ermine-lined robe is technically a peeress's Coronation robe and that the looped chignon of hair was also a style worn at the Coronation;[13] George III was crowned in 1761 and with that event a significant change had taken place in the Duchess's public image, from society beauty to Lady of the Bedchamber, which she may well have wanted the portrait to reflect.[14]

This painting has generally been regarded as a key work in Reynolds's oeuvre and as a classic embodiment of his theory of portraiture.[15] Among the elements of this are the generalisation of likeness; the choice of a pose and a costume which recall classical sculpture rather than contemporary fashion,[16] and the inclusion of doves at the right and the relief sculpture of the Judgment of Paris on the plinth, allusions to the mythological *persona* of Venus intended to be recognised, by educated viewers of the portrait, as applying to the sitter. The effect of Reynolds's approach is to emphasise the social and historical standing of the Duchess at the expense of her character or personality.

Cleaning of LL 3126 in 1964 revealed numerous damaged areas in the lower part of the costume which were thought to have been caused by an earlier relining. These were restored.[17]

PROVENANCE:
by descent in the collections of the Dukes of Hamilton;[18] Christie 6 November 1919 (49) bt. Gooden & Fox for Lever (£7350).

EXHIBITIONS:
Society of Artists 1760 (47); *Works by Old Masters and Scottish National Portraits* Edinburgh 1883 (208); Grosvenor Gallery 1883 (26); *Guelph Exhibition*

New Gallery 1891 (130); New Gallery 1899 (173); *Lord Leverhulme* RA 1980 (31); *Reynolds* RA 1986 (36).

REFERENCES:
1. R. M. Bleackley: 'The Beautiful Misses Gunning', *Connoisseur* (1905) Vol.12, p.162.
2. W. S. Lewis et al., eds.: *Horace Walpole's Correspondence* (1937-83) Vol.20, pp.302-3 and 311.
3. Bleackley, *op. cit.*, and see also H. Bleackley: *The Story of a Beautiful Duchess. Being an Account of the Life and Times of Elizabeth Gunning, Duchess of Hamilton and Argyll* (1907).
4. Repr. *Manners and Morals*, exhibition catalogue, Tate Gallery (1987) p.207, cat.194.
5. E. M. Johnson: *Francis Cotes* (1976) p.83, cat.219; and see Appendix v, p.163, cat.28.
6. Johnson, *op. cit.*, p.52, cat.16, and p.54, cat.31; see also Appendix v, p.164, cat.45.
7. Bleackley (1905) p.232.
8. See R. W. Jones: ''Such Strange Unwanted Softness to Excuse': Judgement and Indulgence in Sir Joshua Reynolds's Portrait of Elizabeth Gunning, Duchess of Hamilton and Argyll', *Oxford Art Journal*, Vol.18, no.1 (1995) p.39.
9. David Mannings, entry in N. Penny, ed.: *Reynolds*, exhibition catalogue, RA (1986) pp.197-9. Reynolds also painted the Duchess's daughter, Lady Elizabeth Hamilton in 1758 (National Gallery of Art, Washington DC; see J. Hayes: *British Paintings of the 16th through 19th centuries*, National Gallery of Art (1992) pp.210-2).
10. Sittings were on 14, 16 (cancelled) and 20 January 1758; 2, 3 (possibly), 9, 15 January, 2 February, 10 and 17 April and 2 June 1759; Penny, *op. cit.*, p.198, and Mannings, letter, 19 September 1997, gallery files. Edward Morris has suggested (verbally) that the gap between the 1758 and 1759 sittings was owing to her lack of a husband and consequent financial worries about paying for the portrait.
11. Quoted in W. T. Whitley: *Artists and their Friends in England 1700-1799* (1928) Vol.I, pp.167-8.
12. A final payment of 25 guineas, unlikely to represent the whole cost of the

portrait, is recorded in Reynolds's ledger on 13 April 1764 (Penny, *op. cit.*, p.199).

13. Penny, *op. cit.*, p.198.

14. To date no x-radiographs of LL 3126 have been taken, which would help establish whether the work was substantially altered.

15. Penny, *op. cit.*, pp.197-9 and see also Martin Postle: *Sir Joshua Reynolds, The Subject Pictures* (1995) p.3ff. and D. Shawe-Taylor: *The Georgians* (1990) p.147.

16. For a discussion of Reynolds's possible sources in earlier painting and sculpture see Penny, *op. cit.*, pp.197-8. For a discussion of the portrait in terms of contemporary male attitudes to the portraiture of women, see Jones, *op. cit.*

17. J.C. Witherop to R. Fastnedge, letter, 31 October 1964, gallery files.

18. Listed in the possession of the 8th Duke of Hamilton, the sitter's son, in an inventory of 4 September 1793 (Penny, *op. cit.*, p.199).

Sir JoshuaReynolds
1723-1792

Mrs. James Paine
and the Misses Paine
LL 3540 (WHL 3568)
oil on canvas, 126.5 × 103 cm

The sitters are Charlotte, youngest daughter of Richard Beaumont of Whitley Beaumont, near Huddersfield, Yorkshire, who in 1748 became the second wife of the architect James Paine (1717-1789); and their two daughters Charlotte, born in 1751, who in 1781 married St. John Charlton, and Mary (known as Polly), born in 1753, who married the painter Tilly Kettle in 1777 and died in 1798. They sat to Reynolds in July 1765.[1]

This is the pendant to Reynolds's portrait of the males of the family, James and James junior (1745-1829), for which the former had given sittings to Reynolds in January 1764 (Ashmolean Museum, Oxford,

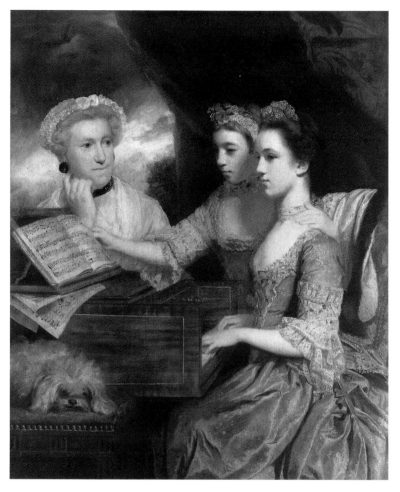

Sir J. Reynolds: *Mrs. James Paine and the Misses Paine*
LL 3540

fig.44).[2] The two works are of the same dimensions and are clearly designed to be viewed side by side, as a single family group, symmetrically ordered around the figure of Mrs Paine, and with Charlotte looking across at the figure of her father. Nevertheless, the two works were not exhibited together[3] and, perhaps owing to the death of Mrs Paine in 1766,[4] entered separate collections, LL 3540 passing to the Beaumonts, Mrs Paine's family. It is not known whether LL 3540 was completed by the time of Mrs Paine's death, but there is some reason to think that Reynolds had difficulties in resolving

the work; the figures are awkwardly integrated and the harpsichord (which has been identified as an unusual Shudi with a cross-banded spine and a stand added to the top[5]) seems to have been a late addition to the design and painted over the figures of Mrs Paine and her younger daughter. The music which Charlotte plays (without looking at it) is a song by Michael Arne, setting the words of the poem *Through the Wood Laddie* by Allan Ramsay, father of Reynolds's great rival; the musical notation has been faithfully rendered,[6] a degree of detail highly uncharacteristic of Reynolds. The

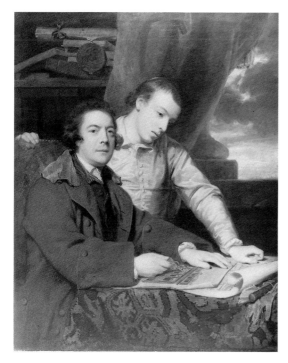

Fig.44
Sir J. Reynolds: *James Paine and his Son*
Ashmolean Museum, Oxford

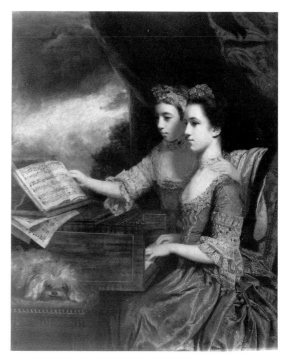

Fig.45
Sir J. Reynolds: *Mrs. James Paine and the Misses Paine*
former state, with Mrs. Paine painted out
Photograph in the Lady Lever Art Gallery archive

curly-haired white dog appears in several of Reynolds's portraits of the mid-1760s, for example *Nelly O'Brien* (Wallace Collection London).

Assessment of the quality of LL 3540 is complicated by the fact that the figure of Mrs Paine was overpainted and then re-instated earlier in the 20th century. The portrait was exhibited at the Royal Academy in 1908 and purchased by Lever in 1918 as *The Misses Paine* (fig.45) and the restoration of the figure of Mrs Paine, which is detectable in the condition of the paint, took place only in 1935.[7] A copy made for the Beaumont family by F. Spencer at the time of the sale of LL 3540 in 1906 (Ormesby Hall, Cleveland) originally contained the figure of Mrs Paine, implying that the desecration of LL 3540 took place in

the period 1906-1908; in 1929, however, Spencer was asked to remove Mrs Paine from the copy, and that canvas remains as a portrait of the two girls alone.[8]

PROVENANCE:
by descent in the family of Mrs Paine's brother, Richard Beaumont, to H.F. Beaumont; from whom bt. in 1906 by Charles Davis (£6,000); Agnew, March 1906; Sulley & Co., May 1906; ... C.J. Wertheimer by 1908;[8] Christie 30 May 1912 (65) bt. Agnew (£9,040); Christie 7 June 1918 (61) bt. Gooden & Fox for Lever (4,200 gns.).

EXHIBITIONS:
National Exhibition of Works of Art Leeds 1868 (1057); Huddersfield 1883 (24); *Old Masters* RA 1908 (147); Wembley 1925 (V.20); *Music and Painting* Norwich Castle Museum 1961 (25).

ENGRAVING:
R. Josey, 1878.

REFERENCES:
1. P. Leach: *James Paine* (1988) pp.23, 25; A. Graves and W.V. Cronin: *A History of the Works of Sir Joshua Reynolds P.R.A.* (1899-1901) Vol.II, p.718. Graves and Cronin also list sittings to Reynolds from 'Miss Pains' in December 1757 and 'Miss Payne' in March 1758; these sittings cannot have anything to do with LL 3540 and two portraits (*The Misses Paine*, engr. R. Bowles 1866, untraced; and *Miss Paine*, Wadsworth Atheneum, Hartford) exist which presumptively relate to them, (although it has to be said that neither of these is characteristic of Reynolds).
2. LL 3540 has also been described (in the sale catalogue, p.57) as the pendant of another version of *James Paine and his Son*, which was sold at Christie 3 April 1996 (56). In this the elder man plays a harpsichord. The resemblance of this figure to the elder Paine in the Ashmolean painting is tenuous, and the canvas size is only 35 × 27 in.; but the portrait has some claim to be an

autograph Reynolds and it could
conceivably be an abandoned earlier
version of the Ashmolean painting
(perhaps that for which 'Master Payne' is
recorded as having sat in January 1760,
Graves and Cronin, *loc. cit.*), whose
harpsichord motif Reynolds later
transferred to LL 3540 (David Mannings,
letter, 19 April 1996, gallery files).
3. *James Paine and his Son* was exhibited
at the Society of Artists in 1766; *Mrs.
Paine and the Misses Paine* is said by
Graves and Cronin, *loc. cit.*, to have been
shown at a special exhibition of the
Society of Artists held in September 1767;
however A. Graves: *The Society of Artists
and the Free Society* (1907) makes no
mention of this exhibition.
4.   Leach, *op. cit.* p.31.
5.   Charles Mould: 'The Broadwood
Books:2', *The English Harpsichord
Magazine*, Vol.1, No.2 (April 1974)
pp.49-50. The names of both Sir Joshua
Reynolds and Miss Paine appear
regularly in the Broadwood Journal 1771-
85 (Bodleian Library, Oxford).
6.   Lawrence Haward, letter, 1 March
1945, gallery files; a copy of the musical
score (inscribed: 'as sung by Miss Wright
at Vauxhall Gardens') is in the Rowe
Library, Kings College Cambridge.
7.   *The Times* (2 September 1935); see
also C.R. Grundy: 'The Obliteration of
Miss Paine', *Progress* (Autumn 1935)
pp.133-36.
8.   Mark Whyman, letter, 4 March 1985,
gallery files, enclosing cutting from *The
Times* (see note 7) annotated by [?]
H.R. Beaumont of Ormesby Hall.

Sir Joshua Reynolds
1723-1792

Venus Chiding Cupid for Learning to Cast Accounts
LL 3543 (WHL 620, H 23)
oil on canvas, 128 × 101.5 cm

Reynolds's first version of this
subject was exhibited at the Royal
Academy in 1771 (Iveagh Bequest,
Kenwood, fig.46). LL 3543 is a second
version which the artist painted for
Brooke Boothby (in 1776, according

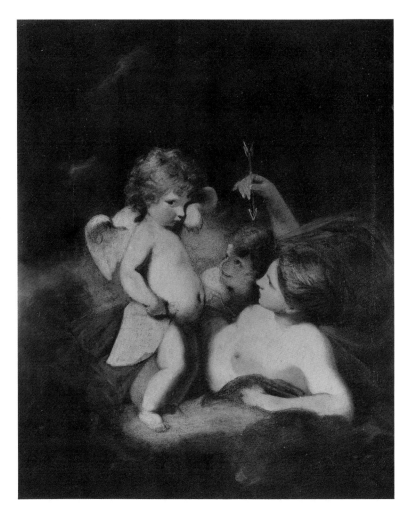

Sir J. Reynolds: *Venus Chiding Cupid for Learning to Cast Accounts*
LL 3543

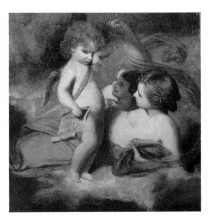

Fig.46
Sir J. Reynolds:
*Venus Chiding Cupid
for Learning to Cast Accounts*
Iveagh Bequest, Kenwood. English Heritage Photo Library

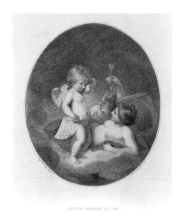

Fig.47
F. Bartolozzi, after Sir J. Reynolds:
*Venus Chiding Cupid
for Learning to Cast Accounts*
Lady Lever Art Gallery

to the catalogue of the 1813 Reynolds exhibition at the British Institution), and for which Boothby paid Reynolds the sum of £105 in 1784,[1] the year in which Bartolozzi's engraving (certainly after LL 3543 rather than the Kenwood picture; fig.47) was issued. Apart from the obvious differences between the two versions in the handling of paint, the respective colour schemes and the treatment of light, which give them an entirely distinct character, there are numerous more minor variations.[2] These include the repositioning of Venus's right arm and its flying drapery, the provision of Cupid with more substantial wings, and the alteration of the inscription on his scroll.[3] Cumulatively these changes suggest a conscious effort on Reynolds's part to improve on the 1771 canvas,[4] rather as he later envisaged doing with a second version of his *Venus and Piping Boy*.[5]

The 1771 painting has been described as 'one of the first works in which Reynolds consciously moved away from portraiture towards entirely imaginative compositions' and 'a demonstration of [his] commitment to European standards and conventions'.[6] The specific subject of Venus chiding Cupid does not derive from classical mythology, but had been popularised in 18th-century French art, notably by Etienne Falconet.[7] However, the idea of Cupid becoming money-conscious seems to have been Reynolds's own – his moral perhaps being the loveless nature of marriages made for money (as is suggested by the placing of the blunted dart at the centre of the design). His chief compositional source has been identified as a detail from the *Madonna of the Rosary* by Alessandro Tiarini (1577-1668), which he had sketched in Bologna many years previously.[8] The

influence generally of Correggio, Murillo and Boucher has also been adduced,[9] although the presence of the latter in particular is much less evident in LL 3543 than it is in the more florid and Rococo first version.

PROVENANCE:
Sir Brooke Boothby (c.1745-1824); sold by him to Thomas Bernard in 1794; bt. from Lady Bernard by Thomas Wright 1823; Christie 7 June 1845 (57) bt. Smith (505 gns.) for John Baring;[10] by descent in the Baring family to the 1st Earl of Northbrook by 1884;[11] bt. from him privately about 1893 by Sir J.D. Linton, in partnership with Mr Lawrie and James Orrock; Christie 8 July 1910 (40) bt. Tooth (£210);[12] re-purchased by Orrock and Linton; from whom bt. by Lever September 1910.[13]

EXHIBITIONS:
BI 1813 (87); RA 1872 (120); Grosvenor Gallery 1884 (88); *Old Masters* RA 1894 (4); Grafton Gallery 1895 (102).

ENGRAVINGS:
F. Bartolozzi 1784 (stipple); J.R. Collyer 1786; S.W. Reynolds[14].

REFERENCES:
1. A. Graves and W.V. Cronin: *A History of the Works of Sir Joshua Reynolds P.R.A.* (1899-1901) Vol.III, p.1225. Reynolds painted Boothby's portrait in 1784.
2. Two further differences visible today may not have existed originally: (i) from the odd placing of the figures in the Kenwood painting it seems possible that the canvas has been cut down, and was originally the same size as LL 3543; (ii) Venus's left breast was perhaps originally covered in LL 3543 and bared later – possibly on the occasion of Bartolozzi's engraving (as suggested by Martin Postle, verbally, 20 September 1990); or else was originally bare and subsequently overpainted in the Kenwood version.
3. The inscription on the Kenwood painting today reads: *Addition / C3-10 / x / 12 01 / 678*. According to C.R. Leslie and T. Taylor: *The Life and Times of Sir Joshua Reynolds* (1865) Vol.I, p.399 it once read *£. s. d.* and *pinmoney*, but they may have been relying on Bartolozzi's engraving on which the word pinmoney does appear.

The inscription on LL 3543 is extremely faint but seems to represent an actual sum of amounts of money, possibly: *52-10* (50 guineas was Reynolds's standard price for a half-length canvas in the mid-1770s) / *36-15 / 8-5 / 97-10*. The first two sets of figures are also present on Bartolozzi's engraving.
4. The 1771 *Venus Chiding Cupid* had not been universally admired at the Royal Academy; see Graves and Cronin, *op. cit.*, Vol.III, pp.1224-5 and Vol.IV, pp.1464 and 1480 BBB.
5. Reynolds to Lord Ossory, letter, 17 July 1786, in F.W. Hilles: *The Letters of Sir Joshua Reynolds* (1929) p.156, cited by Martin Postle: *Sir Joshua Reynolds, The Subject Pictures* (1995) p.205.
6. Postle, *op. cit.*, pp.85-87.
7. *Iveagh Bequest, Kenwood, Catalogue of Paintings* (1978) p.26.
8. Postle, *loc. cit.*, citing R. Prochno: 'Sir Joshua Reynolds's use of Bolognese art' in 'Il luogo ed il ruolo della citta di Bologna tra Europa continentale e mediterranea', *Atti del colloquio CIHA* (1990) p.459 and note 7.
9. Postle, *loc. cit.*
10. It was seen in Baring's collection by Waagen who wrote (*Treasures of Art in Great Britain* (1854) Vol.II, p.188): 'A subject of Venus and Cupid with Amorini [sic] is very affected in the composition, devoid of modelling and hard in the outline'.
11. Lent by Lord Northbrook to the 1884 exhibition.
12. This sale appears to have been a scam contrived by Orrock and Linton to pay off Mr T. Lawrie, descendant of an original third partner in the picture, who lived in Paris. They later sold the painting to Lever with a 'Gainsborough' (LL 3690 above), presumably in case word got out about the price Lever had paid.
13. Receipt for Lever's purchase of LL 3543 together with LL 3690 (see above under Gainsborough) for £3000, dated 24 September 1910, gallery files. Linton originally asked a price of £5,100 (letter to Lever, 9 September 1910, gallery files.
14. Graves and Cronin, *loc. cit.*, list three unattributed engravings apart from those by Bartolozzi and S.W. Reynolds; it is not clear if one of these is Collyer's.

Sir JoshuaReynolds
1723-1792

Lady Gertrude Fitzpatrick
LL 3542 (WHL 174, H 52)
oil on canvas, 76 × 63 cm

Lady Gertrude Fitzpatrick was born in 1774, the second surviving daughter of John Fitzpatrick, 2nd Earl of Upper Ossory (1745-1818), one of Reynolds's most intimate patrons. She never married and passed her life quietly at the family estate of Farming Woods, Nottinghamshire, dying in 1841. Considerable confusion has arisen in the past as to whether LL 3542 is a portrait of her or of her elder sister, Lady Anne Fitzpatrick. At the time Lever purchased the work it was believed to represent the latter,[1] but the arguments in favour of this identification are untenable.[2] The most significant evidence is the inscription *Lady Gertrude Fitzpatrick* on the second state of J.R. Smith's engraving of LL 3542 which was published on 10 June 1780.[3] Horace Walpole was surely referring to this when he wrote to Lady Ossory, the sitter's mother on 23 June 1780: 'I have got the print of Lady Gertrude, but it is poorly executed and faint and unfinished – however, it is sweetly pretty, though it has not half the countenance of the original'.[4]

No record of any sittings or payments for LL 3542 survives. An explanation for this may be that Reynolds painted the portrait on a social visit to Lord Ossory at Farming Woods[5] (and conceivably undertook it as a fancy work, for his own pleasure). From the little girl's apparent age, it can perhaps be dated to the years 1777-78;[6] comparison with the much more securely documented portrait for which Lady Gertrude sat to Reynolds in April 1779 and May 1780 (Columbus

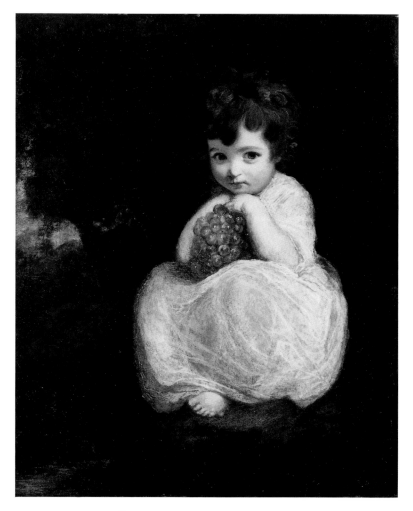

Sir J. Reynolds: *Lady Gertrude Fitzpatrick*
LL 3542

Museum of Art, Ohio, fig.48) suggests an age difference of a year or two but the resemblance is unmistakable.

The condition of LL 3542 is poor. It was damaged in an early re-lining and extensively repainted, and was again re-lined and retouched in the late 1960s.[7] A good quality copy, probably dating from the late 18th century,[8] is in a private collection, USA.

PROVENANCE:
Lord Ossory, the sitter's father, by 1813;[9] Hon. Robert Vernon-Smith (his son-in-law from his second marriage); by descent to Hon. Greville Vernon; sold by him to

Agnew in 1902;[10] bt. from Agnew by James Orrock 1903; Christie 4-6 June 1904 (128) bt. in; bt. from Orrock by Lever November 1904.[11]

EXHIBITIONS:
BI 1813 (19); BI 1844 (163); *The Portrait of a Lady: Sargent and Lady Agnew* National Gallery of Scotland, Edinburgh 1997 (46).

ENGRAVINGS:
J.R. Smith 1780; S.W. Reynolds; J. Richardson Jackson 1875.

REFERENCES:
1. A. Graves and W.V. Cronin: *A History of the Works of Sir Joshua Reynolds P.R.A.* (1899-1901) Vol.I, pp. 313-5 (followed by Christie's sale catalogue

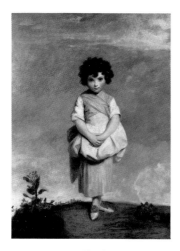

Fig.48
Sir J. Reynolds:
Lady Gertrude Fitzpatrick as 'Collina'
Columbus Museum of Art, Ohio:
Museum Purchase, Derby Fund

4-6 June 1904) identify LL 3542 as a portrait of Lady Anne Fitzpatrick.

2. Graves and Cronin, *loc. cit.*, argue that the payment recorded in Reynolds's ledger under 10 June 1775: 'Lord Ossory for Lady Anne Fitzpatrick £52.10.-; paid 25 more £26.15s' must relate to LL 3542 from the mistaken belief that Lady Anne was born in 1774, and Lady Gertrude 'about 1776'. In fact Lady Gertrude was born in 1774, Lady Anne on 23 August 1768 (see W.S. Lewis et al., eds.: *Horace Walpole's Correspondence* (1937-83) Vol.32, p.58, n.1). The canvas for which Lord Ossory paid Reynolds 50 guineas and 25 guineas more in 1775 is probably the portrait identified by Graves and Cronin (*op. cit.*, pp.315-6) as *Lady Gertrude Fitzpatrick as Sylvia*, now in the Museum of Fine Arts, Boston.

3. J. Chaloner-Smith: *British Mezzotinto Portraits* (1884) Vol.III, p.1267. Graves and Cronin, *op. cit.*, p.313 state that Smith's engraving omits the sitter's name; only the first state does so.

4. Lewis, *op. cit.*, Vol.33, p.201. An editorial note, depending on Graves and Cronin, argues that Walpole must have had an advance copy of J. Dean's engraving of *Lady Gertrude Fitzpatrick as Collina* after Reynolds (see main text above) which was published on 8 November 1780, but this scarcely seems likely.

5. 'The picture was painted during a visit to the Earl at Farming Woods, Notts., when the shy little girl hid beneath a marble-topped sideboard table on which was a silver dish of fruit; from this, after a time, she took a large bunch of grapes. A footman, resplendent in red plush, discovered her: 'Here is little miss'. 'Don't disturb her', said Sir Joshua, 'I will paint her just as she is' '. (S.L. Davison: 'The Work of Sir Joshua Reynolds', *Bebington News* (28 November 1936)). The source for this is apparently a family tradition, related in the course of a visit to the Lady Lever Art Gallery in 1932 by Lady Younghusband (note in gallery files). A variant of the same story, told by Emma Lady Lyveden to Helen Magniac, is recorded in family papers; quoted in *The Portrait of a Lady: Sargent and Lady Agnew*, exhibition catalogue, National Gallery of Scotland, Edinburgh (1997) p.87.

6. Reynolds's sitter-book for 1776 is missing, but the sitter is perhaps a little older than two.

7. 'The head appears to be reasonably free from damage but the rest of the painting is considerably damaged and some areas are completely overpainted, the overpainting covering original areas as well as damaged areas' (J.C. Witherop to R. Fastnedge, letter, 30 October 1965, gallery files).

8. M. Heslip, Paintings Conservator, Williamstown Regional Art Conservational Laboratory, verbally, 2 August 1990.

9. Lent by Lord Ossory to the 1813 exhibition.

10. Letter from W. Lockett Agnew to James Orrock, 9 June 1905, gallery files. According to Agnew's stockbooks however, the sale did not take place until the following year; Lockett Agnew may have been remembering the work's loan to an exhibition at Agnew in 1902 (information from David Mannings, letter, 26 June 1998, gallery files).

11. 1904 Inventory p.2, no.30.

Sir Joshua Reynolds
1723-1792

Mrs. Peter Beckford

LL 3125 (WHL 4094)
oil on canvas, 239 × 148 cm

Louisa Pitt, second daughter of George, 1st Baron Rivers, was born on 21 September 1754. Married in March 1773 to a Dorset neighbour, Peter Beckford of Steepleton, she had little interest in hunting and the rural pursuits which pre-occupied her husband[1] and between 1780 and 1782 had a passionate liaison with the latter's brilliant young cousin, William Beckford of Fonthill (1760-1844) during the most sensational phase of his life which witnessed the writing of his novel *Vathek* and his homosexual affair with William Courtenay. Soon abandoned by him and increasingly in poor health, Mrs Beckford declined in spirits; she died of tuberculosis at Florence on 30 April 1791.[2]

This portrait was painted when Mrs Beckford was in the throes of her infatuation with William; sittings were probably planned as a means of seeing him when he was in London. Two initial appointments with Reynolds were made on 7 June 1781,[3] shortly after William had returned to London from his Grand Tour, and another on 12 June. However, further sittings that summer were deferred firstly by her ill-health, which necessitated a visit to Tunbridge Wells, and then by Reynolds's departure for the Continent. Louisa wrote to Beckford on 28 July: 'As my looks are entirely recovered I intended to sit once or twice to Sir Joshua during my stay in Town but he is unfortunately gone abroad, so that I must wait till next year when I may perhaps look ill again'.[4] She finally sat fourteen times between March and May 1782, the bulk of the work being carried out in

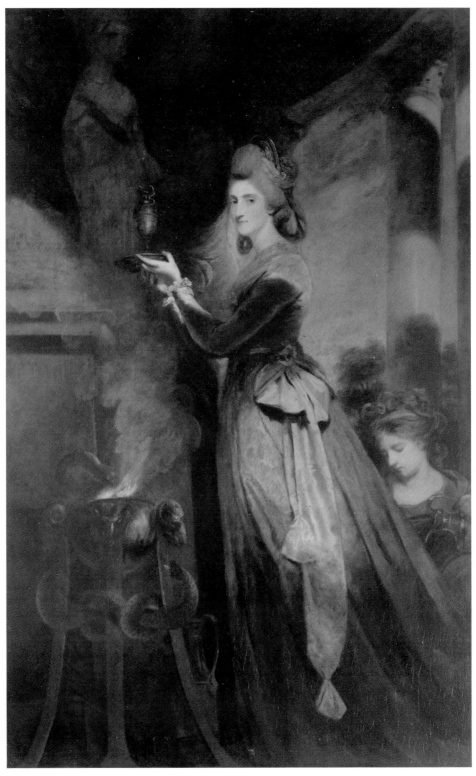

Sir J. Reynolds: *Mrs. Peter Beckford*
LL 3125

the course of six sittings between 27 April and 9 May.[5] The portrait may have been intended for that summer's Royal Academy exhibition (together with a bust portrait of William for which the latter had sat to Reynolds in January and February), but does not appear to have been ready in time.[6] Nevertheless, that Reynolds worked the painting up relatively quickly and fluently is confirmed by Beckford's recollection, many years later, that 'Sir Joshua took the greatest pleasure and delight in painting that picture, as it was left entirely to his own refined taste'.[7]

By 1838, the date of this remark, Beckford was the owner of LL 3125, but it is not clear, as has been claimed, that he commissioned the portrait;[8] and his words, although they suggest that he followed the progress of the work, give the lie to the idea that he helped to plan it.[9] It is true that the unusually lurid conception, with its smoke-laden atmosphere and unnatural contrasts of light and shadow, appears to owe something to the ambience of magic and necromancy which Beckford cultivated in his private amusements and in his writings at that time. All the same, the work is a characteristic example of Reynolds's theories of portraiture, whereby classical allusion both distances and ennobles the individual portrayed, and at the same time refers to specific biographical incident in the sitter's life. The consumptive Mrs Beckford is shown making a libation to the Greek goddess of health, Hygeia, a statue of whom, recalling a similar figure in Kneller's portrait of William Cheselden in the Royal College of Surgeons (fig.49),[10] which Reynolds may well have known, is dimly visible in the background; and whose attribute, a snake, decorates the smoking cauldron. The conception of the sacrifice, the setting of a peristyle

of a temple and the presence of a classically attired female attendant are all, moreover, taken up from one of Reynolds's seminal full-lengths of the 1760s, *Lady Sarah Bunbury Sacrificing to the Graces* (Art Institute of Chicago, fig.50). The major difference between LL 3125 and the earlier work lies in the treatment of hairstyle and costume: both here are much more obviously contemporary.[11] Neither Beckford, who liked to visualise Louisa 'in all the flow of your beautiful antique drapery',[12] nor Reynolds, for whom the costume in a Grand Manner portrait required 'something of the general air of the antique for the sake of dignity' as well as 'something of the modern for the sake of likeness'[13] seem likely to have prescribed the present dress; so Mrs Beckford must have done so herself. Steeped though she was in William Beckford's taste,[14] she and Reynolds alone were probably responsible for the final conception of the work.

PROVENANCE:
…William Beckford before 1838; his daughter, Susannah, Duchess of Hamilton; by descent in the collections of the Dukes of Hamilton; Christie

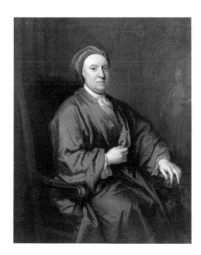
Fig.49
Sir G. Kneller: *William Cheselden*
Reproduced by kind permission
of the Royal College of Surgeons of England

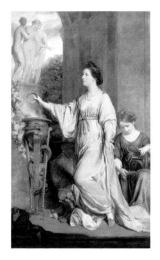
Fig.50
Sir J. Reynolds:
*Lady Sarah Bunbury
Sacrificing to the Graces*
Mr and Mrs W.W. Kimball Collection, Art Institute of
Chicago. Photograph © 1997 The Art Institute of Chicago.
All Rights Reserved.

6 November 1919 (50) bt. Gooden & Fox for Lever (6,800 gns.).

EXHIBITIONS:
[?RA 1782 (186)]; BI 1861 (183); Grosvenor Gallery 1883 (31); *Exhibition of Works by Old Masters and Scottish National Portraits* Edinburgh 1883 (154) and 1886 (1471); *Guelph Exhibition* New Gallery 1891 (159); *English Taste in the Eighteenth Century* RA 1955 (396); *Angelika Kauffman und ihre Zeitgenossen* Vorarlberger Landesmuseum Bregenz 1968 (400); *The Age of Neo-classicism* RA 1972 (219); *Lord Leverhulme* RA 1980 (32); *Reynolds* RA 1986 (132).

ENGRAVING:
F. Bromley 1861.

REFERENCES:
1. For Peter Beckford see especially A.H. Higginson: *Peter Beckford Esquire* (1937). He was the author of the classic *Thoughts on Hunting. In A Series of Letters to a Friend* (1781) but also travelled widely and cultivated literary and musical friendships with such figures as Clementi and Rousseau.
2. B. Fothergill: *Beckford of Fonthill* (1979) pp.73-141 *passim*.
3. Information from David Mannings,

letter, 2 July 1997, and not as given in N. Penny, ed.: *Reynolds*, exhibition catalogue, RA (1986) p.303.

4. Louisa Beckford to William Beckford, letter, quoted in J.W. Oliver: *The Life of William Beckford* (1932) p.73.

5. Mannings, *loc. cit.* The dates of the 1782 sittings were 2, 8, 27 and 28 (probably) March; 12, 27, and 29 April; and 1, 3, 6, 9, 11 (probably), 27 and 31 May; not as given in Penny, *loc. cit.*

6. That LL 3125 was no.186 in the 1782 exhibition is conjectured by Mannings in Penny, *op. cit.*, p.304; however Reynolds's exhibits are discussed e.g. in the *Public Advertiser* for 30 April 1782, and the *St. James's Chronicle* for 27-30 April 1782; neither mentions LL 3125, for which sittings continued to the end of May.

7. H.V. Lansdown: *Recollections of the Late William Beckford of Fonthill, Wilts and Lansdown, Bath* (1893) p.9.

8. E.g. J. Lees-Milne: *William Beckford* (1976), caption to plate between p.82 and p.83. It is noticeable that Reynolds's portraits of William and Louisa, although executed at the same time, are not pendants. By 1782 Romney had become William's preferred artist. It has been suggested by A.M. Clark: *Pompeo Batoni* (1985) p.302, cat.296, that LL 3125 was commissioned by Louisa's husband, Peter Beckford, as a pair to Batoni's full-length portrait of himself dating from 1766. But Clark seems to be in error in assuming that the 'companion picture of a lady in blue dress' which was sold with the Batoni at Sotheby, 29 November 1922 (190) was Reynolds's *Mrs. Beckford*: the sale catalogue does not state that this portrait was by Reynolds and implies that it was by Batoni.

9. Penny, *loc. cit.*, and see note 7 above.

10. J.D. Stewart: 'King William 'the Deliverer' and Shakespeare's 'Hopeful' Harry of Hereford – A Kneller Drawing Discovered and Elucidated', *Apollo* (November 1995) p.29.

11. See Penny, *op. cit.*, p.304 for a discussion of the costume, which suggests that although the dress is 'fashionable', it was invented by Reynolds.

12. William Beckford to Louisa, letter, 6 July 1781, quoted in Oliver, *op. cit.*, p.71.

13. Sir J. Reynolds: *Discourses on Art* ed. Wark (1975) p.140 (*7th Discourse*, lines 738-42).

14. 'Both shared an interest in magic, and their talk was full of references to spells, talismans, incantations, and sorcery' (Fothergill, *op. cit.*, p.73).

Sir Joshua Reynolds
1723-1792

Mrs. Seaforth and Child
LL 3544 (WHL 4250)
oil on canvas, 143 × 114 cm

Grozer's engraving of LL 3544 was published by W. Dickinson, under the title *A Lady and Child*, on 10 May 1787 (fig.51). That the engraving preserves the anonymity of the sitters lends credence to their identification as Mrs Seaforth,[1] a mistress of the celebrated Indian nabob Richard Barwell (1741-1805), and one of their children born out of wedlock (perhaps James Seaforth, baptised at Westbourne 10 October 1783[2]). Mrs Seaforth's black silk dress and the black edging to her hat indicate that she is in mourning; the undated etching by J. Jacquemart taken from the second version of LL 3544 (see below) is lettered *la veuve et l'enfant*.[3]

Mrs Seaforth is recorded as sitting

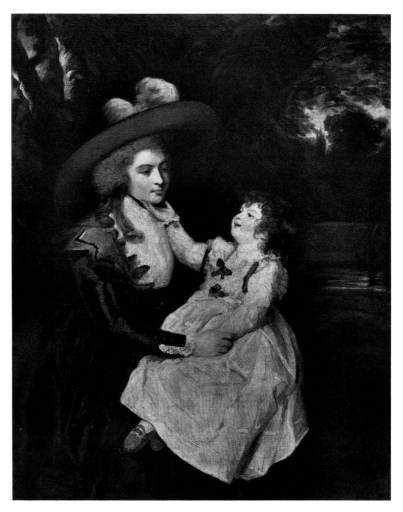

Sir J. Reynolds: *Mrs. Seaforth and Child*
LL 3544

to Reynolds twenty-three times between January and May 1786 and on two further occasions in December that year.[4] Reynolds's ledgers indicate that Richard Barwell paid for 'Mrs. Seaforth' between February and May 1787, a duplicate entry dating from the second half of 1786 confirming this picture to be *Mrs. Seaforth and Child* and the price as 200 guineas.[5] Reynolds had previously painted portraits of Barwell himself with his son, full length, and of his daughter; while Mrs Seaforth sat to Reynolds again, by herself, in June 1787,[6] perhaps for the fancy painting *Tuccia* (1787) which contemporaries identified as a portrait of her.[7]

To judge from the price of 200 guineas (the equivalent of two half-lengths) Reynolds was asked to provide two copies of the portrait. Another version formerly in the Wilson collection, Brussels and sold at the Secretan sale, Paris, 1889, was owned in 1903 by G. Harland Peck,[8] later the owner of LL 3544 (see provenance); this canvas is now untraced.

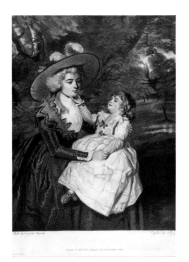

Fig.51
J. Grozer, after Sir J. Reynolds:
A Lady and Child
Yale Center for British Art, Paul Mellon Collection

PROVENANCE:
painted for Richard Barwell; by descent to 'Mrs. Barwell of Brighton';[9] Foster 8 November 1871 (lot number unknown) bt. Mrs Noseda (200 gns.);... C.R. Havell; Christie 17 December 1887 (210) bt. Lesser (73 gns.); Christie 10 February 1912 (29) bt. Leggatt (185 gns.);... G. Harland Peck; Christie 25 June 1920 (117) bt. Gooden & Fox for Lever (1,600 gns.).[10]

EXHIBITION:
Old Masters RA 1892 (134).[11]

ENGRAVINGS:
J. Grozer, 1787; S.W. Reynolds.

REFERENCES:
1. Lever bought LL 3544 as *Lady Seaforth and Child* (i.e. Mary Mackenzie, née Proby, whose husband was created Lord Seaforth in 1797 and who died in Edinburgh in 1829. Although her husband had succeeded to the Seaforth estates in 1783 Reynolds could not have referred to her as Mrs Seaforth in 1786; nor did she have any connection with Richard Barwell, who paid for LL 3544). This identification, given in the Harland Peck sale catalogue, follows that given by J. Chaloner Smith in *British Mezzotinto Portraits* (1878-83) Vol.II, pp.610-11; A. Graves and W.V. Cronin, in *A History of the Works of Sir Joshua Reynolds P.R.A.* (1899-1901) Vol.III, pp.871-3, had however already cast doubt on it. Harland Peck seems to have wished to obscure the identity of the not entirely reputable sitter, and there is some evidence that he defaced the exhibition label on LL 3544 in order to conceal his earlier ownership of the second version of the work (see note 11 below).
2. P. O'Neill, letter, 9 April 1997, gallery files. For Mrs Seaforth see also Martin Postle: *Sir Joshua Reynolds, The Subject Pictures* (1995) pp.48-9, 235-7. Postle's statement that Mrs Seaforth was only fifteen when she later married Barwell (p.49) is clearly incorrect.
3. Information from David Mannings, letter, 2 July 1997, gallery files.
4. Mannings, *loc. cit.* The sittings took place on 3, 6, 10, 16, 18, 21, 23 and 28 January, 2, 6, 11, 15, 17 and 22 February, 8 and 10 March, 18, 24 and 26 April, and 1, 8, 16 and 23 May. The later sittings took

place on 5 and 8 December.
5. M. Cormack: 'The Ledgers of Sir Joshua Reynolds', *Walpole Society*, Vol.XLII (1970) pp.147 and 164, quoted by Mannings, *loc. cit.*
6. Graves and Cronin, *loc. cit.*
7. Postle, *loc. cit.*
8. Julia Frankau: 'Mr. Harland Peck's Collection', *Connoisseur* (February 1903) pp.86-8.
9. The catalogue of the 1912 sale states that Barwell gave the portrait to Mrs Seaforth herself and it passed into the possession of her youngest daughter Matilda, with whom it remained until 1871. She offered for sale at Christie, 27 June 1863, a portrait of 'Mrs. Lyne, a member of the Seaforth family, in a black silk dress, nursing a child in a muslin frock', bt. in (450 gns.); the work was lined and cleaned for her in December of the same year by H. Graves & Co. (Graves and Cronin, *loc. cit.*) There seems no doubt, from the description, that that picture was LL 3544.
10. An unsuccessful attempt was made by the Trustees of the Lady Lever Art Gallery to sell the work privately through Agnew in 1958, gallery files.
11. Exhibition label on the back of LL 3544; owner's name removed. A Graves: *A Century of Loan Exhibitions 1813-1912* (1913-15) Vol.III, p.1064 records Lesser as the owner.

after
Sir Joshua Reynolds
1723-1792

Angelica Kauffman
LL 3677 (WHL 2004, HH 26)
oil on canvas, 76.5 × 64 cm

Angelica Kauffman (1740-1807), one of the best-known woman artists of the 18th century, lived in England from 1765 to 1781, and was a founder member of the Royal Academy, 1769.[1] She sat to Reynolds, who admired her, and with whom gossips linked her, in 1766, 1769 and 1777[2]. The 1777 sittings resulted in a head and shoulders portrait which was

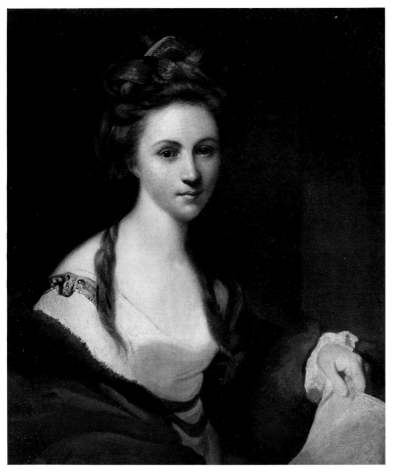

after Sir J. Reynolds: *Angelica Kauffman*
LL 3677

REFERENCES:
1. See W. Wassyng Roworth ed.: *Angelica Kauffman: A Continental Artist in Georgian England* (1992).
2. A. Graves and W. V. Cronin: *A History of the Works of Sir Joshua Reynolds P.R.A.* (1899-1901) Vol.II pp.533-4.
3. Graves and Cronin, *loc. cit.* Tatlock, p.64, incorrectly gives the dimensions of LL 3677 as 25½ × 22½ in., and identifies it as the version listed by Graves and Cronin as having been owned by D. Thwaites in 1885 and subsequently sold to or exchanged with Agnew. However, that version is described as having had a landscape background. The version on which LL 3677 appears to have been based, formerly at Althorp, was with Artemis 1980-1.
4. David Mannings, verbally, 20 September 1990.
5. 1910 Inventory p.32, valued at £400.

'Sir Joshua Reynolds'
1723-1792

A Boy
(called 'Master Lumsden')
LL 3545 (WHL 74, HH 20)
oil on canvas, 96 × 76 cm

Lever acquired LL 3545 as *Master Lumsden* by Sir Joshua Reynolds. Its stylistic resemblance to Reynolds's child portraiture is superficial, and there is no evidence for the identity of the boy. The work belongs less to the category of portraiture proper than to the genre of sentimental fancy pictures of poor children which became very popular in England in the period 1775-1800.[1] The subsequent attribution of LL 3545 to Richard Morton Paye (1750-1821),[2] who worked in such a vein from the mid-1780s, seems plausible. However, in view of the shortage of authenticated works by Paye, it must remain at present speculative.[3]

PROVENANCE:
...Mrs Dundas; James Orrock; bt. from Orrock by Lever 1910.[4]

engraved as an oval by Bartolozzi and published in 1780 (fig.52); LL 3677 is a version of that work. Numerous others are known.[3]

The very worn and considerably repainted condition of LL 3677 makes assessment of its original quality difficult, but the facial resemblance is not especially close to Bartolozzi's engraving, and the style suggests it is not from Reynolds's studio.[4] It probably dates from a considerably later period.

PROVENANCE:
...James Orrock; bt. from Orrock by Lever 1910.[5]

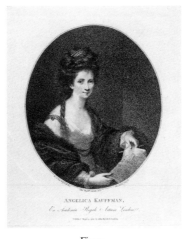

Fig.52
F. Bartolozzi, after Sir J. Reynolds:
Angelica Kauffman
© The British Museum

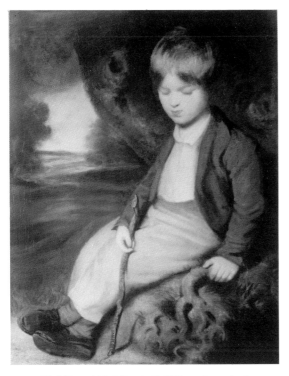

'Sir J. Reynolds': *A Boy (called 'Master Lumsden')*
LL 3545

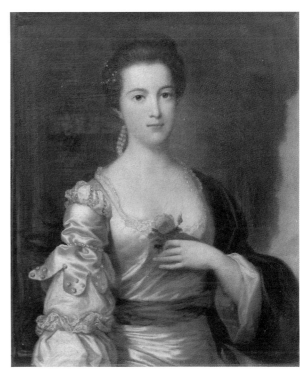

'Sir J. Reynolds': *Portrait of a Lady in a White Satin Dress*
LL 3665

REFERENCES:
1. For this see Martin Postle: *Angels and Urchins*, exhibition catalogue, Iveagh Bequest Kenwood House (1998).
2. Tatlock, p.59.
3. LL 3545 bears some stylistic resemblance to a work of unknown title signed by Paye last recorded at Taplow Park, and to an attributed but unsigned work titled *The Navy*, of unknown date, in a private collection (photographs in the Witt Library). See also E.W. Clayton: 'Richard Morton Paye', *Connoisseur* (December 1913) pp.229-36 in which twelve engraved works by Paye are illustrated; these however bear considerably less resemblance to LL 3545.
4. 1910 Inventory p.32, valued at £500. This gives the previous owner as Mrs Dundas. A note in gallery files gives the date of Orrock's acquisition of the work as 1906; the source of this information is unknown.

'Sir Joshua Reynolds'
1723-1792

Portrait of a Lady in a White Satin Dress
LL 3665 (WHL 2317, HH 127)
oil on canvas, 76.5 × 63.5 cm

Lever acquired LL 3665 as by Reynolds but its resemblance to his work extends no further than the very general facial type (which may be derived from the portrait of Mrs. Angelo, now in the Fitzwilliam Museum, Cambridge), and the motif of the rose at the sitter's breast.[1] The costume purports to date from the 1750s, but is an illogical mixture of motifs assembled from other portrait sources rather than something that would have been worn in real life.[2] The work is almost certainly a pastiche of mid 18th-century portraiture by a much later artist.

PROVENANCE:
…James Orrock; bt. from Orrock by Lever 1910.[3]

REFERENCES:
1. David Mannings, verbally, 20 September 1990.
2. Aileen Ribeiro, verbally, 26 February 1998.
3. 1910 Inventory p.52, valued at £60.

'Sir Joshua Reynolds'
1723-1792

Portrait of a Child
LL 3675 (WHL 59, H 75)
oil on canvas 37.5 × 32 cm

Lever acquired LL 3675 as by Reynolds. It bears a superficial resemblance to such works as the *Piping Shepherd*[1] in terms of the range of colour and effects of texture, and attempts to replicate the coy

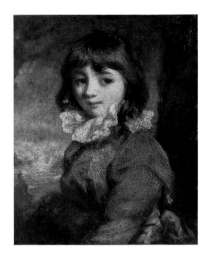

'Sir J. Reynolds': *Portrait of a Child*
LL 3675

Paris as a young man.[1] He was in France from August 1828 until May 1829[2] and is said to have lodged with Napoleon's former breeches-maker, who gave him graphic descriptions of the Emperor's appearance, as well as lending him a death mask of Napoleon which he owned, from which the portrait was made.[3]

This account of the work's gestation, however, is not easy to reconcile with the two dates of 1860 and 1875 inscribed on it, nor with its physical appearance. The painting consists of an original canvas measuring 85 × 68 cm on which the figure of Napoleon is painted to the waist, and an extension at the bottom and sides which brings it to its present size. On the back of the original canvas is a discarded portrait of a male academic (fig.53) whose presence (unless it is the 'spoiled' self-portrait Richmond is stated to have painted in Calais before travelling on to Paris[4]) is very hard to account for on a youthful work begun in France.[5] A more straightforward explanation is that the painting was begun on the back

charm of some of his child portraits. Although the worn and extensively repainted condition makes the original quality of the handling hard to judge, it can only be the work of an imitator. A later attribution to John Opie (1761-1807)[2] is not acceptable.

PROVENANCE:
...James Orrock; Christie 4-6 June 1904 (295) bt. in; bt. from Orrock by Lever November 1904.[3]

REFERENCES:
1. Martin Postle: *Angels and Urchins*, exhibition catalogue, Iveagh Bequest, Kenwood (1998) p.58, cat.4, and repr. pl.3.
2. Tatlock, p.58.
3. 1904 Inventory p.2, no.31.

George Richmond
1809-96

Napoleon Reading his Letter of Abdication

LL 3608 (WHL 107, TM 260)
oil on canvas, 113.5 × 88 cm
signed *GR pinx/1860 & 75* (bottom left)

According to the artist's son, John Richmond, LL 3608 was undertaken during George Richmond's stay in

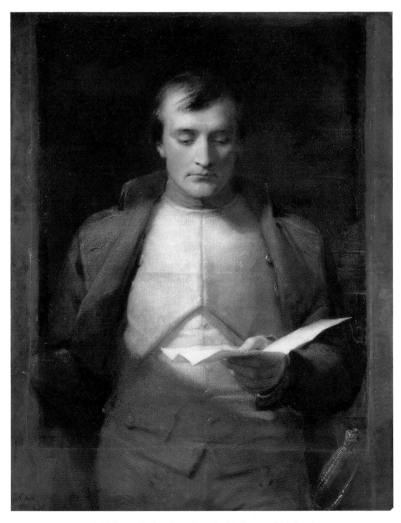

G. Richmond: *Napoleon Reading his Letter of Abdication*
LL 3608

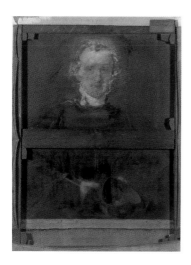

Fig.53
G. Richmond:
*Napoleon Reading His Letter
of Abdication*, reverse of painting
Lady Lever Art Gallery

of an abandoned portrait shortly before 1860,[6] and that Richmond extended the canvas to its present size in 1875.

John Richmond recalled that the painting was exhibited (on the above view, in its original, small, state) at the International Exhibition in London in 1862 and that it attracted a good deal of foreign attention; but in this his memory was apparently at fault.[7] Napoleon is represented reading the letter of abdication which he signed at Fontainebleau in 1814; and Richmond is said to have had in mind as a motto for the picture the words from Milton's *Paradise Lost*: 'care sat on his faded cheek', which are there used to describe Satan.[8]

PROVENANCE:
the artist; Christie 1 May 1897 (81) bt. Agnew; bt. from Agnew by Lever 3 July 1897 (£271.8.6).[9]

REFERENCES:
1. John Richmond to Lever, letter, 25 March 1914, gallery files, wrote: '…In 1830 [sic] my father studied Art & Anatomy in Paris, at a time when everything Napoleonic under the rule of Charles the 10th was under a cloud. It

happened however that Richmond saw much of the O'Mearas who were wine merchants in Paris whose connection with O'Meara the doctor at St. Helena was close, and was in an atmosphere of Bonapartist ideas. His student lodgings were over a shop in the Chaussée d'Antin kept by a man, who had been breeches maker to the Emperor, whose habit it was to have a new pair of nankeen breeches daily; & from this man Richmond got a graphic description of the appearance and habit of the Emperor as he was in the later years of the Empire. He spoke of him as having the colouring of a corpse, a waxy sallowness of complexion, of his rotundity, & of his habit of allowing rivers of snuff to run down his uniform. From these descriptions and built upon the death mask which he had my father constructed the portrait of the Emperor which you possess'.
2. R. Lister: *George Richmond* (1981) p.21.
3. See note 1 above.
4. Lister, *loc. cit.*
5. It is just possible that Richmond began the portrait of the academic on a previously abandoned work of 1829 which he then could not bring himself to write off. However, this seems uncharacteristic of his professionalism as a portrait painter. The portrait of the academic is on the same piece of canvas, i.e. is not on a lining canvas.
6. Lister, *op. cit.*, p.167 lists 'Napoleon 1 small half length oil' among Richmond's works of 1858.
7. Richmond, *loc. cit.* Its appearance at the exhibition is not recorded in A. Graves: *A Century of Loan Exhibitions 1813-1912* (1913-15) Vol III, p 1095
8. Richmond, *loc. cit.* The source is *Paradise Lost*, Book I, lines 601-2.
9. Lever's purchase of LL 3608 was uncharacteristic of his taste at this date and is almost certainly explained by his great admiration for Napoleon.

George Romney
1734-1802

Sarah Rodbard
LL 3539 (WHL 50, H 10)
oil on canvas, 240.5 × 148 cm

The sitter (*c.*1765-1795) was co-heiress with her sister Elizabeth of the London linen-draper John Rodbard (d.1780). However, she may not have been his daughter: by his will, dated 1774, John Rodbard left his property jointly to Sarah and Elizabeth Ellis.[1] On 8 November 1786 at the age of twenty one Sarah married Major (afterwards General Sir Eyre) Coote (1762-1823), to whom she bore three daughters, Susan, Sarah Anne and Catherine.[2] She died at Clifton on 30 October 1795.[3]

The portrait, one of the masterpieces of Romney's later years, was painted in 1784. John Romney, in his 'rough lists' of his father's works, noted 'Miss Rodbard, of Hackney, W.L. [whole length] for Mrs. Stratton' – and the latter – presumably a guardian – had appointments with Romney on 6, 13, 20 and 28 April and 5 May 1784. The last of these dates coincides with a first appointment for Miss Rodbard and others followed on 12 and 26 May, 2, 9 and 22 June and 2 July.[4] An entry in Romney's ledger for April 1786 reads 'Received of Mrs. Stratton for Miss Rodbard pictr full length – 84-0 Frame Allwood'.[5]

X-radiographs taken during cleaning in 1997 confirm that Romney originally intended to paint Miss Rodbard gazing to her proper right rather than towards the spectator, and to drape her in a cloak. He also reduced the size of the bow at her waist.[6]

PROVENANCE:
by descent to Eyre Coote, West Park, Salisbury; Christie 14 June 1902 (120) bt.

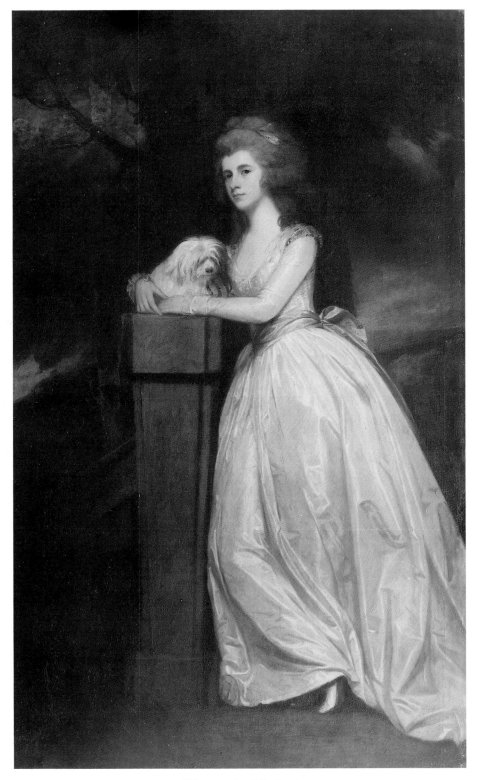

G. Romney: *Sarah Rodbard*
LL 3539

Agnew (10,500 gns.); bt. from Agnew by
Lever April 1903 (£12,000).[7]

EXHIBITIONS:
BI 1855 (160); *Winter Exhibition* RA 1908
(139).

REFERENCES:
1. *The Victoria History of the Counties of
England: A History of the County of
Somerset*, Vol III (1974) p.240. T. H. Ward
and W. Roberts: *Romney* (1904) Vol.II,
p.133, identify Sarah's father as John
Rodbard of Evercreech, Somerset; this
man, however, lived from 1759 to 1795
(information and genealogy supplied by
R. Robertson – Glasgow, letter, 29 August
1944, gallery files). It seems probable,
since the linen-draper is stated to have
owned property in Somerset, that the two
men were related.
2. Ms. label formerly on the reverse of
LL 3539, gallery files.
3. W. Roberts: 'Romney's Portrait of
Miss Rodbard', *Magazine of Art* (April
1903), p.261. Ward and Roberts, *loc. cit.*,
give the incorrect date 1796.
4. Ward and Roberts, *op. cit.*, Vol.II,
p.132. Cancelled appointments were on
19 May and 15 June; Ward and Roberts
omitted the 22 June sitting (Romney's
sitter book for 1784 (British Museum
Add. Ms.38083)).
5. The entry is reproduced in Roberts,
loc. cit. That LL 3539 retains the original
Allwood frame was confirmed by
M. Gregory, verbally, August 1994.
6. Conservation of LL 3539 has revealed
that the painting is carried out over
a cream-coloured ground on a medium-
weight twill-weave linen canvas; the
canvas is unlined and an indecipherable
stamp is present. The stretcher is not the
original. As with a number of Romney's
later works there is a significant amount
of drying-crackle, especially in the area
of the balustrade, which had been
extensively overpainted.
7. For the background to Lever's
'spectacular' purchase see *Lord
Leverhulme*, pp.17-21.

George Romney
1734-1802

Mrs. Mary Oliver
LL 3132 (WHL 76, H 28)
oil on canvas, 127 × 102 cm

Mary Shakespear who died aged 82
on 1 August 1845[1] was the youngest
daughter of John Shakespear,
a London rope maker and merchant,
of Stepney Causeway and 10 Billiter
Square, Alderman of the Aldgate
Ward, and supposedly a descendant
of William Shakespeare. She married
on 23 October 1785, Laver Oliver
(1740-1813), India merchant.[2]

The portrait was begun in 1785.
The sitter-book for this year is lost,
but the number allocated to the
portrait in Romney's ledger, No.53,
is consonant with this date. Six days
before her wedding, when work on it
was presumably advanced, the artist
was sent the following verse:[3]

TO MR ROMNEY
How great they art, O Romney,
   to portray
Nature's fair form – to catch
   the subtle ray
That plays in beauty's eye – to give
   a grace
To every feature of the female face!
But when a Shakespear's seated in
   thy Chair,

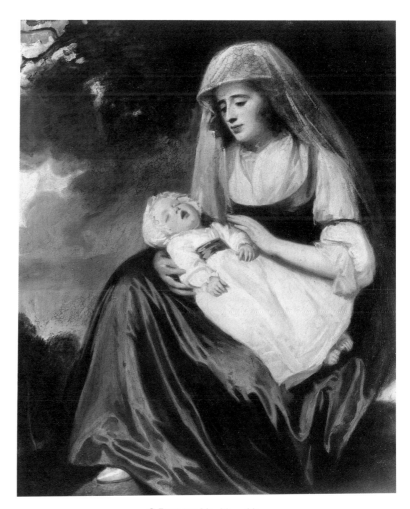

G. Romney: *Mrs. Mary Oliver*
LL 3132

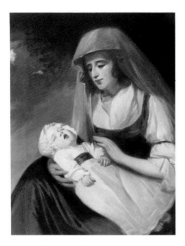

Fig.54
G. Romney: *Mrs. Oliver*
Bequest of John Ringling, Collection of the
John and Mable Ringling Museum of Art,
the State Art Museum of Florida

As angels lovely, and as Venus fair;
When with the charms of beauty
   are combin'd
The rare endowments of
   a virtuous mind;
Vain art they efforts, vain
   thy cunning art,
To trace the virtues which adorn
   her heart,
Sweet smiles and dimples may obey
   thy will,
But mental graces are beyond
   thy skill.
October 17th 1785
U.B.

Mrs Oliver sat to Romney eight
times between 20 May and 3 June
1787, a further four times between
March and October 1788 and finally
on 8 June 1791.[4] It is not clear which
of these sittings marks the occasion
on which Romney altered the
existing portrait to include Mrs
Oliver's first child 'in half an hour,
and with such truth of nature as to
impress the spectator with an idea
of hearing it respire'.[5] The identity
and date of birth of the child are
unknown;[6] however, the fact that in
the sitter book under 3 June 1788
Romney wrote 'Mrs. Oliver to be

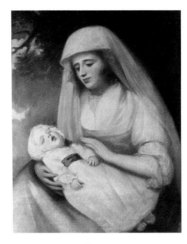

Fig.55
G. Romney: *Mrs. Oliver*
Private collection; photograph courtesy Sotheby's

finished' and under 6 October 1788
'Mrs. Oliver's hand finished' perhaps
implies that the baby was in position
before these dates. When LL 3132 was
sold at Christie's in 1896 (see below)
the auctioneer stated that the baby
had been painted in place of a fan;[7]
however, the consistently rapidly
brushed manner across the whole
surface of the picture suggests that
the re-modelling entailed by the
change was more thoroughgoing
and probably extended to the whole
pose, costume and background.
The portrait remained on Romney's
hands until it was sent to the Olivers
and paid for in June 1799.[8]

The Rev. John Romney's 'rough
lists' record two half-length portraits
of Mrs Oliver under the year 1787.[9]
What may be the second is the
36 × 28 in. version at the Ringling
Museum, Sarasota (fig.54); this is
stated to have been cut down at
the sides and top;[10] a further version,
now 35 × 27 in., but enlarged from
a 30 × 25 in. canvas, in which the sitter
is dressed in white (fig.55), was on the
London art market 1983-1991.[11]

PROVENANCE:
...Sir Julian Goldsmid; Christie 13 June
1896 (60)[12] bt. Agnew; bt. from Agnew by
Lever January 1899 (£3255).

EXHIBITIONS:
Second National Loan Exhibition
Grosvenor Galleries 1913 (14); *Lord
Leverhulme* RA 1980 (35).

REFERENCES:
1. *Gentleman's Magazine* (September
1845) p.325.
2. Letters from John Shakespear,
a collateral descendant of the sitter, 1 and
31 August 1927, gallery files.
3. Rev. John Romney: *Memoirs of
George Romney* (1830) p.196.
4. T.H. Ward and W. Roberts: *Romney*
(1904) Vol.I, p.112 (transcript of 1787
sitter books) and Vol.II, p.114, where the
last two sittings of 1 and 3 June 1787 are
conflated as 13 June.
5. Romney, *op. cit.*, p.165.
6. According to John Shakespear, letter,
31 August 1927 (*loc. cit.*) family records
state that the first child of the marriage
was a son, Richard Mansel Oliver. Ward
and Roberts, however, in discussing a
second version of the portrait (see note 4
above and note 11 below) describe the
baby as a daughter. C.R. Grundy: 'Lord
Leverhulme's Pictures at 'The Hill' ',
Connoisseur (December 1917) pp.186
and 188 says that Mrs Oliver returned
with her three month old child after the
painting had been in Romney's studio for
three years. He dated the work to 1787-91
and evidently assumed that the 8 June
1791 sitting (see above) was the occasion
when the child was inserted.
7. A.C.R. Carter: *Let Me Tell You* (1942)
p.49. No x-radiographs of LL 3132 have
been taken.
8. Ward and Roberts, *op. cit.*, Vol.II,
p.114. The portrait appears as no. 53 in
Romney's notebook listing portraits on
hand, 1791-96, V & A MSS.L.1456 25 iii
1957.
9. Ward and Roberts, *loc. cit.*
10. Peter Tomory, *Ringling Museums
Newsletter*, Vol.4, no.3 (1971); his
statement that this work has been cut
at the top (rather than the bottom) is
problematic, forcing him to make the
implausible suggestion that the Ringling
version was a preliminary half-figure trial
for LL 3132. The article was written while
the Sarasota painting was being
conserved, but that work's present
condition, following trimming and
relining, makes the statement impossible
to check (A. De Groft, Sarasota, letter,

12 August 1997, gallery files).

11. Most recently, Phillips, 30 April 1991
(59). This version, although it is unlikely
to be the second half-length listed by Rev.
John Romney, may well be the version
sold at Christie 10 July 1897, 36 × 28,
which Ward and Roberts (*loc. cit.*)
specifically state showed Mrs Oliver in
white. The latter cannot be the Ringling
Museum painting, as proposed by
Tomory, *loc. cit.*

12. A portrait of James Oliver by
Romney, 30 × 25 in., accompanied LL 3132
when it appeared at the Goldsmid sale,
but this man was unrelated to Mary
Oliver.

'George Romney'
1734-1802

The Reverend
William Humphry
LL 3563 (WHL 65, H 68)
oil on mahogany panel, 76 × 63.5 cm[1]

The sitter is identified by an
inscription on the reverse of the
panel.[2] William Humphry, born in
1743, was the younger brother of the
artist Ozias Humphry (1742-1810).
He became Vicar of Kemsing and
Rector of Birling in Kent,
preferments obtained from the Duke
of Dorset through Ozias; married
Elizabeth Woodgate in November
1778; was domestic chaplain to Lord
Amherst, and died in 1816.[3]

The attribution of LL 3563 to
Romney is extremely doubtful.
Romney very seldom if ever painted
on panel, and the thin, rather staid
handling lacks the breadth and
vigour of his style in the early 1770s,
when he was most closely associated
with Ozias Humphry.[4]

PROVENANCE:
[…?William Beckford[5]];…James Orrock
by 1903;[6] Christie 4-6 June 1904 (135) bt.
in; bt. from Orrock by Lever November
1904.[7]

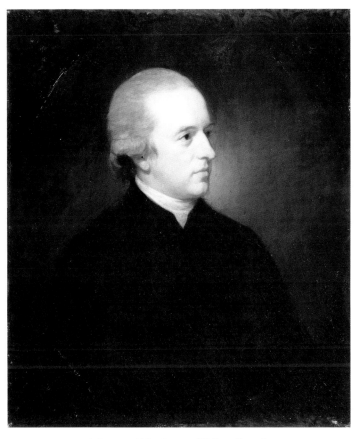

'G. Romney': *The Reverend William Humphry*
LL 3563

REFERENCES:
1. LL 3563 has been framed as if it was
a feigned oval, but does not seem to
have been painted as such.
2. The inscription reads: *G. Romney/
Rev. Humphrey brother of Ozias
Humphrey/miniature painter*. The writing
is not from the 18th century, and may be
Orrock's.
3. G.C. Williamson: *Life and Works of
Ozias Humphrey R.A.* (1918) especially
p. 10.
4. It is not certain that LL 3563 is a
painting of the late 18th century. The
selection of the profile pose may be a
clever allusion on the part of a later artist
to Romney's engraved portrait of Ozias
Humphry of 1772 which is the same size
and in which the sitter faces in the
opposite direction. This portrait was
owned by the Duke of Dorset, patron of
the Humphry brothers, in the late 18th

century. Conceivably, on the other hand,
LL 3563 is by Ozias himself: although best
known as a miniaturist and pastellist, he
concentrated on larger-scale portraits in
oils during the period 1777-83,
immediately after his return from Italy.
5. According to a label on the frame.
The source of this information is
unknown. The work has not been traced
in the Beckford sales of 1801, 1817 and
1845.
6. Repr. Webber, Vol. I, fp. 180.
7. 1904 Inventory p. 1, no. 19.

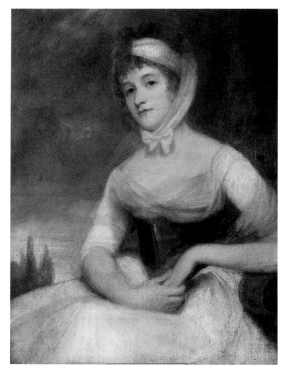

'G. Romney': *Mrs. Hugh Williams*
LL 3678

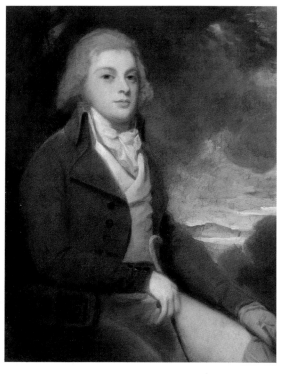

'G. Romney': *Mr. Hugh Williams*
LL 3679

'George Romney'
1734-1802

Mrs. Hugh Williams
LL 3678 (WHL 3571)
oil on canvas, 91.5 × 70.5 cm

Mr. Hugh Williams
LL 3679 (WHL 3574)
oil on canvas, 91.5 × 71 cm

The costumes indicate a date of about 1790 to 1795,[1] by which time Romney was regularly abandoning routine commissions; many of these were completed by his pupils and former rivals in imitation of his style. Although both works are in a very worn condition and have been considerably repainted, which makes their original quality hard to assess, such a scenario can tentatively be proposed for LL 3678-9.[2] There are noticeable pentimenti in both works, for example along the length of Mrs Williams's proper right shoulder and arm and Mr Williams's right hand.

However, it should be noted that there is no trace of Mr and Mrs Hugh Williams in Romney's ledgers and sitter books, which provide a reliable record of his output during the later part of his career.[3] It is possible that the true identity of the sitters became obscured at some point before the works' sale in 1918.

PROVENANCE:
…Sir Baldwyn Leighton Bt; (LL 3678) Christie 7 June 1918 (94) bt. Gooden & Fox for Lever (1700 gns.); (LL 3679) bt. privately from Leighton by Gooden & Fox for Lever 12 June 1918 (£717.10.-).

REFERENCES:
1. Aileen Ribeiro, verbally, 26 February 1998. Mrs Williams is costumed *à la paysanne*.
2. Both LL 3678 and LL 3679 are in frames whose style is associated with Romney (Jacob Simon, verbally, 13 August 1997).
3. T.H. Ward and W. Roberts: *Romney* (1904) do not list LL 3678-9. The sittings and portrait of Sir Hugh Williams Bt. (Vol.II, pp.171-2) are not related to LL 3679.

'George Romney'
1734-1802

Portrait of a Lady
LL 3695 (WHL 122, H 44)
oil on canvas, 76.5 × 64 cm

Lever acquired LL 3695 as by
Romney but it is not like his work.
The attribution may have been
prompted by the model's vague
resemblance to Emma Hart, later
Lady Hamilton, who was famously
associated with Romney. The hair
style and to a certain extent the
costume are uncharacteristic of the
late 18th century[2] and the painting
was probably executed shortly
before its purchase by Lever.

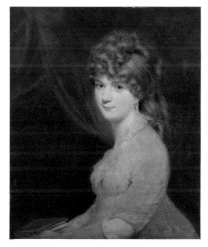

'G. Romney':
Portrait of a Lady
LL 3695

PROVENANCE:
…James Orrock; Christie 4-6 June 1904
(136) bt. in; bt. from Orrock by Lever
November 1904.[1]

REFERENCES:
1.   1904 Inventory p.2, no.35.
2.   Aileen Ribeiro, verbally, 26 February
1998.

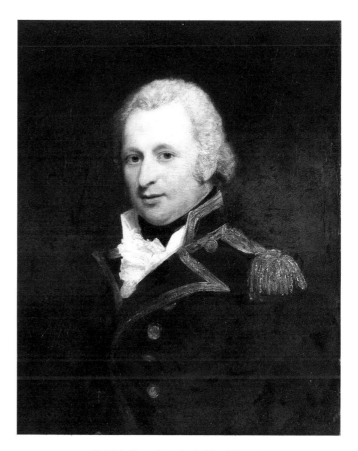

Sir M.A. Shee: *Portrait of a Naval Captain*
LL 3566

Sir Martin Archer Shee
1769-1850

Portrait of a Naval Captain
LL 3566 (WHL 705, H 21)
oil on canvas, 76 × 63 cm

The sitter wears the full dress
uniform of a naval captain in the
period 1795-1812.[1] His identity is
unknown. Lists of the artist's works
throw up two possibilities: the
Captain Dick whose portrait Shee
exhibited at the Royal Academy in
1808, but who is not certainly a naval
captain, and Sir W.G. Fairfax, Captain
of the *Venerable*, whose portrait was
shown in 1798.[2] Neither suggestion
can be more than tentative.

PROVENANCE:
[? Shee's studio sale, Christie 2 February
1855 (26) as *A Naval Officer*]; …James
Orrock; Christie 4-6 June 1904 (138) bt.
in; bt. from Orrock by Lever November
1904.[3]

REFERENCES:
1.   R. Quarm, National Maritime
Museum, letter, 23 October 1997, gallery
files.
2.   A. Graves: *The Royal Academy
Exhibitors 1769-1904* (1905-6) Vol.7,
pp.98-9; W.G. Strickland: *A Dictionary of
Irish Artists* (1913) Vol.II, pp.335-47.
3.   1904 Inventory p.3, no.79.

Henry Singleton
1766-1839

Flora

LL 3680 (WHL 1445, TM 39)

oil on oak panel, 31 × 23.5 cm

F.D. Soiron's engraving after LL 3680 (fig.56) was published on 1 June 1791, together with its companion, *Rosina* (fig.57), which had been engraved by C. Knight after a painting by Thomas Stothard (1755-1834). The painting was presumably commissioned from Singleton especially for the engraving and can therefore be dated to around 1790.

Soiron's print is inscribed as follows: *FLORA / Dans votre lit that bright Parterre / Should Flora bloom a Lilly fair. / A Smiling Jonquil I could be / To blow sweet Flow'r by side of thee. / Love in a Camp or Patrick in Prussia Act 1st.* A two-act play by John O'Keeffe, *Love in a Camp* was first performed at the Theatre Royal in 1785, with Mr Johnstone as Captain Patrick and Mrs Martyr as Flora. The play is about the adventures of two Irish gallants, Patrick and Darby, in a Prussian army camp near Breslau. Flora, a flower and fruit seller living in the camp, is serenaded in the second scene to the above words by the love-struck captain. The play was not published until 1800[1] and Soiron's print was presumably a marketing exercise to keep it in the public's favour.

PROVENANCE:

... Sir William Fraser 1st Bt. (d. 1878);[2] by descent to Sir William Augustus Fraser Bt.; Christie 3 December 1900 (71) bt. Agnew for Lever (45 gns.).[3]

ENGRAVING:

F.D. Soiron 1791.

REFERENCES:

1. Printed by A. Strahan for Longman and Rees, Paternoster Row, 1800.

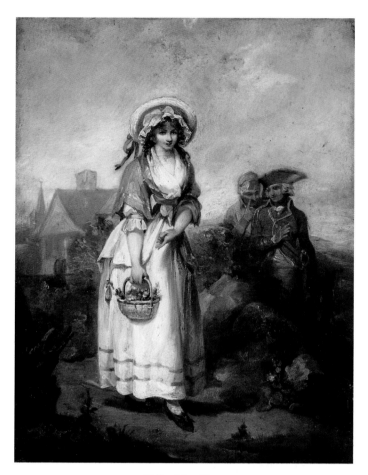

H. Singleton: *Flora*
LL 3680

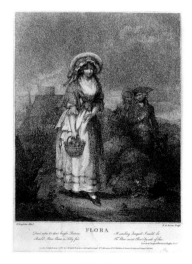

Fig.56
F.D. Soiron, after H. Singleton: *Flora*
© The British Museum

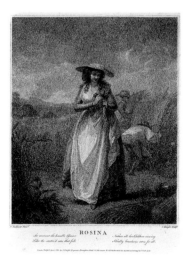

Fig.57
C. Knight, after T. Stothard: *Rosina*
© The British Museum

2.   The remains of a book plate stuck to the reverse of the panel were identified from the arms as belonging to Fraser by H.A.B. Lawson, Rothesay Herald, H.M. Register House, Edinburgh, letter to R. Fastnedge 10 January 1964, gallery files.

3.   Sold as *A Peasant Girl with a Basket of Flowers* by Francis Wheatley; Tatlock, p.68, retained the attribution but altered the title to *The Sailor's Lass*.

after
William Clarkson Stanfield
1793-1867

Wreckers off Fort Rouge
LL 3692 (WHL 1209)
oil on canvas, 124 × 150 cm

This is a reduced copy, with variations, of one of Clarkson Stanfield's best-known paintings, which was exhibited at the British Institution in 1828 and warmly received by the critics.[1] There are numerous differences with the original painting: the most prominent being that the sky is much less dark and stormy; the fort itself is replaced by a hulk in the middle of the composition; on the right, in place of the towers of Calais there is a more anonymous shorescape; and the nearest wrecker, sitting on the mast in the foreground, is missing.

Lever acquired LL 3692 as by John Sell Cotman but it bears no similarity to his work. The unknown copyist was presumably working from J.P. Quilley's engraving, which was published in 1829.

PROVENANCE:
…James Orrock; bt. from Orrock by Lever 1912.[2]

REFERENCES:
1.   P. van der Merwe: *Clarkson Stanfield 1793-1867*, exhibition catalogue, Rheinisches Landesmuseum Bonn and Sunderland Museum and Art Gallery (1979) pp.17 and 95, cat.135 (repr.).
2.   1912 Inventory p.13, valued at £300.

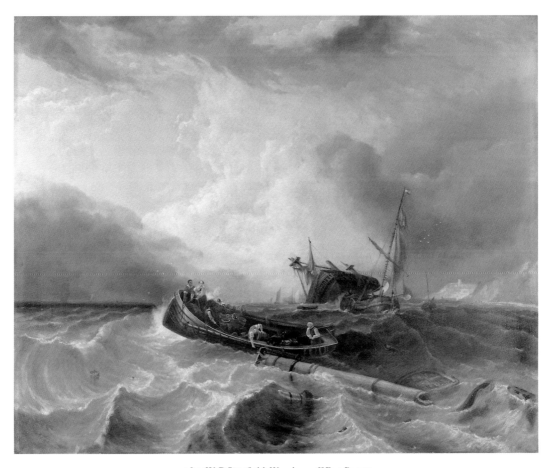

after W.C. Stanfield: *Wreckers off Fort Rouge*
LL 3692

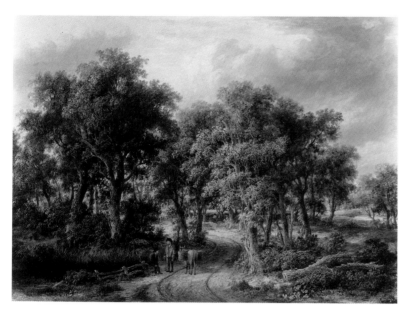

J. Stark: *A Wooded Landscape*
LL 3728

James Stark

1794-1859

A Wooded Landscape

LL 3728 (WHL 40, H I)
oil on panel, 40 × 55.5 cm

Stylistic comparison with LL 3729 (below) suggests that this work is autograph and can be dated to the period 1825-30. Stark's debt to Hobbema appears to have been most pronounced at this time.[1] Norfolk scenes were then predominant in Stark's work and that this is one is suggested by the existence of a Norwich framer's label on the reverse.[2] The generic nature of Stark's woodland landscapes, however, makes precise identification of such subjects impossible.

PROVENANCE:
…? bt. from Gooden & Fox by Lever July 1904.[3]

EXHIBITION:
Liverpool Autumn Exhibition Walker Art Gallery Liverpool 1933 (45).

REFERENCES:
1. W.F. Dickes: *The Norwich School of Painting* (1905) pp.459, 462 describes paintings of 1827 and about 1830 in terms of their similarity to Hobbema's work.
2. Framer's label of Freeman, Swan Lane, Norwich.

3. LL 3728 is likely to be, but cannot certainly be identified as, the unspecified Stark which Lever bought, with two Etty studies, for £400 from F.W. Fox on 27 July 1904. Fox wrote of this to Lever, 26 July 1904, gallery files: 'I would like you to have this picture being fully sure that it is one of the finest examples of the painter in existence'. Certainly none of the other Starks below seem such good candidates for Fox's encomium.

James Stark

1794-1859

Road Scene at Intwood

LL 3729 (WHL 3569)
oil on panel 35.5 × 43 cm

Lever acquired LL 3729 as *A Wooded Landscape with Peasant Driving Sheep*, but the title above has been given to the design, of which two upright variants are known, at least since 1905.[1] Intwood is a village three and a half miles south west of Norwich. LL 3729 can be dated to about 1830.[2] A closely related

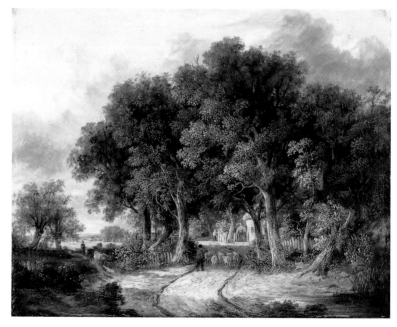

J. Stark: *Road Scene at Intwood*
LL 3729

treatment of the same scene forms the right-hand half of the larger subject *Postwick Reach*;[3] what was probably a version of this was exhibited by Stark as *Postwick Grove* at the British Institution in 1829.

PROVENANCE:
…W. Permain; bt. Agnew June 1906; W. Lockett Agnew; Christie 7 June 1918 (67) bt. Gooden & Fox for Lever (£183).

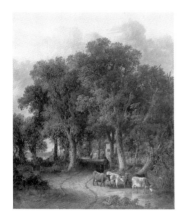

Fig.58
J. Stark: *Road Scene at Intwood*
Norfolk Museums Service (Norwich Castle Museum)

REFERENCES:
1. Both upright versions are in Norwich Castle Museum: (a) 19½ × 16 in., from the collection of Henry N. Holmes (fig.58); (b) 19½ × 16½ in., from the collection of Miss Wilson; reproduced in W.F. Dickes: *The Norwich School of Painting* (1905) p.464, with this title. A preparatory pencil drawing is in the British Museum (1932-12-20 231).
2. Dickes, *loc. cit.*, lists the Wilson picture (see note 1 above) under this date.
3. 24½ × 39½ in.; Sotheby 17 June 1981 (49). The *Postwick Grove* exhibited at the British Institution measured 40 × 53 in. (Dickes, *op. cit.*, p.461). Postwick is near Thorpe, south of Norwich.

James Stark
1794-1859

The Edge of a Wood
LL 3727 (WHL 575, H 89)
oil on panel, 26.5 × 20.5 cm

Although the handling of paint, particularly in the foliage, is not similar to that in LL 3728 and LL 3729 above, LL 3727 can be accepted as a work by Stark dating from his Windsor period, 1840-1850.[1] The work is of pot-boiler quality.

PROVENANCE:
…Fine Art Society; bt. by Lever March 1903 (£100).[2]

EXHIBITION:
Norwich School and Others Fine Art Society 1903 (25).

REFERENCES:
1. For a characteristic example of Stark's Windsor subjects see the *Milking Time* (RA 1845); *18th & 19th Century British Paintings*, Noortman & Brod, New York and London, exhibition catalogue (1983) cat.23; this larger work has a similar spattered treatment of foliage and brightly hatched tree trunks.
2. Copy of invoice, gallery files. The title of the work is here given as *The Road through the Woods*.

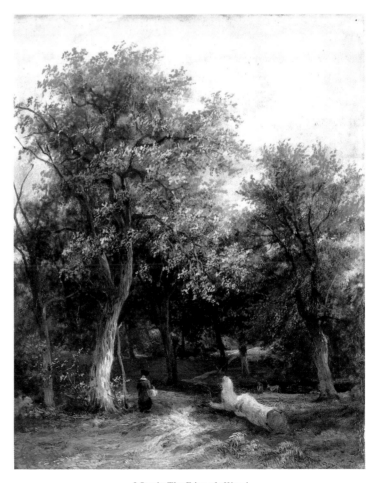

J. Stark: *The Edge of a Wood*
LL 3727

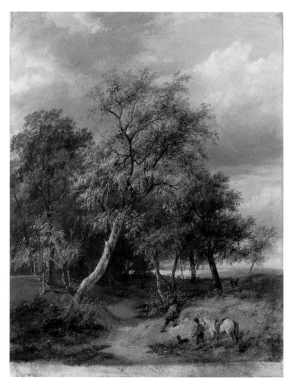

J. Stark: *Windsor Great Park, Near Bears' Rails*
LL 3567

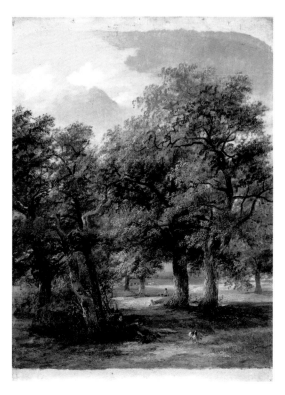

J. Stark: *Windsor Great Park, Near Middle Gates*
LL 3568

James Stark
1794-1859

*Windsor Great Park,
Near Bears' Rails*

LL 3567 (WHL 580, HH 129)
oil on canvas, 49.5 × 37.5 cm

*Windsor Great Park,
Near Middle Gates*

LL 3568 (WHL 581, HH 128)
oil on canvas, 52.5 × 37.5 cm

On both canvases there is an unpainted strip at the bottom, revealing an off-white ground, of approximately 3.5 cm. LL 3568 additionally has an unpainted strip of 2.5 cm, corresponding with the arched shape of the frame, at the top. This suggests that, although the two works were sold to Lever as a pair, they were not originally conceived as such. Rather, it seems likely that LL 3568, started on a slightly larger canvas, was left unfinished in order that the two works could be marketed as companions. Visible differences in technique, notably in the foliage, re-inforce this idea. Both works, however, seem generally characteristic of Stark's Windsor period, 1840-50; the handling in LL 3568 is closely comparable to that in LL 3727 above.

PROVENANCE:
...James Orrock; bt. from Orrock by Lever 1910.[1]

REFERENCE:
1. 1910 Inventory p.52, valued at £250 the pair.

'James Stark'
1794-1859

The Road Through a Wood

LL 3726 (WHL 3570)
oil on panel, 25.5 × 36.5 cm

Although many of Stark's characteristic motifs and stylistic mannerisms are present, such as the light hatchings on tree trunks and the curving, wide-rutted track with

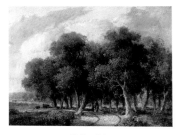

'J. Stark':
The Road Through a Wood
LL 3726

rather dumpy figures, there is a coarseness of touch which suggests that LL 3726 is a forgery. The handling of the foliage on the tree immediately to the right of the track is strongly reminiscent of the work of Joseph Paul (see above), who produced many imitation Norwich School paintings.[1]

PROVENANCE:
…Humphrey Roberts; Christie 7 June 1918 (68) bt. Gooden & Fox for Lever (£161.9.-.).

REFERENCE:
1. Norma Watt, Norwich Castle Museum, verbally, 20 April 1998, endorsed the opinion that LL 3726 was not an autograph Stark and was likely to be the work of Paul.

Thomas Stewardson
1781-1859

Mrs. Jane Romney
LL 3569 (WHL 645, H 9)
oil on canvas, 74.5 × 63.5 cm

Jane, daughter of John Kennel and Elizabeth Barrow, who married in 1782, was born in Kendal in 1786. She married the Rev. John Romney, son of the portraitist George Romney, at Colton on 21 November 1806. She died in 1861.[1]

Although it had been identified and attributed as above in the saleroom three years previously, LL 3569 was purchased by Lever as a portrait by George Romney of his wife, Mary Abbot.[2] The portrait was re-identified by a member of the Romney family when it was shown at the Royal Academy in 1907.[3] Given the work's provenance, the ascription to Stewardson, who is said to have been a pupil of George Romney during the latter's declining years in Kendal, 1799-1802, and who was employed by the Rev. John

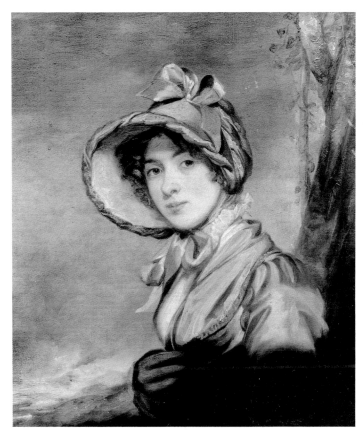

T. Stewardson: *Mrs. Jane Romney*
LL 3569

Romney to complete some of his father's portraits after the latter's death, is hard to question. It must nevertheless be said that the style of this portrait is quite unlike every other portrait securely attributed to Stewardson. It seems to have been tacitly assumed that the work dates from the period of Stewardson's closest association with the Romney family, namely the first half of the 1800s; conceivably (given that one of Jane's relations, William Kennel, acted as an amanuensis to the ailing George Romney[4]) from as early as 1802,[5] when Jane would have been only sixteen, and at any event from before her marriage in 1806. On this view, the untypical style is explicable in terms of Stewardson's youth and

artistic immaturity. However, the handling of paint in LL 3569, so far from being immature or provincial, is notably spirited and assured, while the costume seems less likely to date from the 1800s than from the mid to-later 1820s.[6] It seems preferable to propose, therefore, that LL 3569 is an affectionate and flattering portrait of Mrs Romney in her late thirties, executed by the mature Stewardson in an informal style, perhaps around 1825.

PROVENANCE:
by descent to the sitter's daughter, Miss Elizabeth Romney of Whitestock Hall Ulverston; Christie 24-25 May 1894 (153) bt. Shepherd (£31.10.-); …G. Donaldson; bt. by Agnew April 1897; bt. from Agnew by Lever 3 May 1897 (£500).

EXHIBITIONS:
International Exhibition Glasgow 1901 (76); *Old Masters* RA 1907 (99); *Four Kendal Portrait Painters* Abbot Hall Art Gallery, Kendal 1973 (57); *400 Years of Cumbrian Portrait Painting* Abbot Hall Art Gallery, Kendal 1982 (44).

REFERENCES:
1. Information from David Cross, verbally, 10 October 1996.
2. The portrait was included in T.H. Ward and W. Roberts: *Romney* (1904) Vol.II, p.135.
3. The correction appeared in later editions of the 1907 exhibition catalogue.
4. Cross, *ibid*.

5. C.R. Grundy: 'Romney's Last Pupil', *Connoisseur* (March 1933) p.192, followed by M. Burkett: *400 Years of Cumbrian Portrait Painting*, exhibition catalogue, Abbot Hall Art Gallery, Kendal (1982) p.12, cat.44. Stewardson was in London at least by 1803, which may have prompted this early dating of the portrait.
6. Pauline Rushton, verbally, 25 March 1998.

George Stubbs
1724-1806

The Farmer's Wife and the Raven

LL 3681 (WHL 2181)
enamel on Wedgwood biscuit earthenware, 72.5 × 94.5 cm
signed and dated: *Geo: Stubbs pinxit / 1782* (lower right)

This is Stubbs's first painted version of the subject, shown at the Royal Academy in 1782. It was one of the works with which Stubbs hoped to convince his fellow artists of the

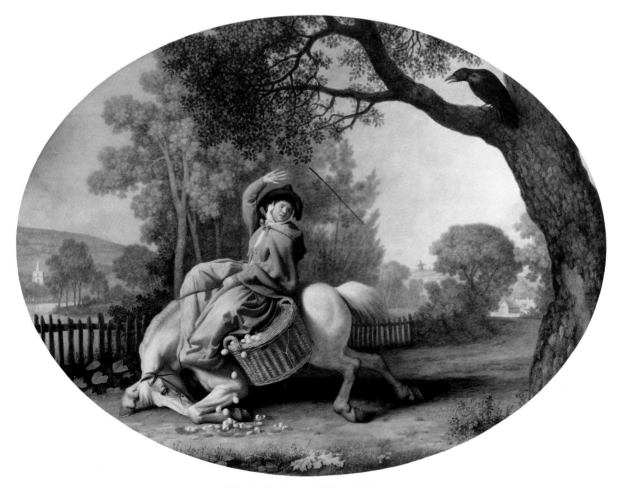

G. Stubbs: *The Farmer's Wife and the Raven*
LL 3681

viability of painting in enamels on ceramic plaques manufactured by Wedgwood, and whose indifferent reception at the exhibition, perhaps caused by their being badly hung, cemented his disaffection with the institution.[1] A second version in oil on panel, signed and dated 1783, is in a private collection; and a third, slightly smaller and with a less elaborate landscape background, also on panel, signed and dated 1786, is in the Yale Center for British Art, New Haven (fig.59). The latter was the basis of the etching published by Stubbs on 1 May 1788,[2] and may have been the version shown at the British Institution in 1806 (86).[3] Two related works are untraced: the 'original design' for the subject and the 'capital high finished coloured Drawing of the Farmer's Wife and Raven' which were both included in the artist's studio sale in 1807.[4]

Stubbs's design recalls, although it does not closely follow, Wootton's illustration of the subject for John Gay's *Fables*, engraved by B. Baron.[5] Gay's lines describe the scene as follows:

'That raven on yon left-hand oak
(Curse on his ill-betiding croak)
Bodes me no good. No more she said
When poor blind *Ball* with
    stumbling tread
Fell prone: o'erturned the pannier lay,
And her mash'd eggs bestrow'd
    the way.'

These lines (as far as 'prone') were inscribed on the 1788 print. The moral of the fable is that the farmer's wife ought to have used Dun, the old sure-footed mare, to transport her eggs, and has only herself to blame.

Stubbs's subscription proposal for his prints of *Haymakers* and *Reapers* dated 24 September 1788[6] provides evidence that by this date, the print of *The Farmer's Wife and the Raven* was being paired with the (as yet unfinished) print of *Labourers*. Stubbs had painted the latter subject in enamel for Wedgwood in 1781[7] but there is no evidence that he regarded the *Farmer's Wife and the Raven* as its pendant from the outset. His first version of *Labourers* had been painted as long before as 1767 and although the two enamels are the

same size the scale of the figures in each of them is noticeably different.[8]

At an unknown date LL 3681 broke into three portions, and the cracks remain visible on the painted surface; one running from the fence at left to the main branch of the tree at top centre, with a secondary one joining it from the sky at upper left. These were much more conspicuous before LL 3681 was restored in the middle of the 20th century.

PROVENANCE:
Mrs Armstead;[9] ... Dr Hawkins;[10] Christie 17 July 1880 (132) bt. Vokins (£22.1.-.); ... Sir Walter Gilbey; Christie at Elsenham Hall, 11 June 1915 (401) bt. Gooden & Fox for Lever (£105).

EXHIBITIONS:
RA 1782 (120); *First Hundred Years of the Royal Academy* RA 1951-52 (151); *Wedgwood* Iveagh Bequest, Kenwood 1954 (163); *Stubbs and Wedgwood* Tate Gallery 1974 (26).

REFERENCES:
1. For this see especially C. Parker: *Mr. Stubbs the Horse Painter* (1971) pp. 119-22. He had shown one work in enamel, *Fighting Stallions*, at the RA in 1781.
2. C. Lennox-Boyd, R. Dixon and T. Clayton: *George Stubbs, The Complete Engraved Works* (1989) pp. 184-85, cat.69. The fact that Stubbs did not use the enamel, with its more detailed background, as the basis for the print, suggests that LL 3681 had left his possession by the time he began work on it.
3. Lennox-Boyd, Dixon and Clayton, *op. cit.*, p.184, argue that the framed dimensions of this, as recorded at the British Institution, 36 × 48 in., make it incompatible with any of the other three painted versions. However, it could certainly be the Yale painting, whose unframed size is 26½ × 38½ in.
4. Coxe, 26-27 May 1807, 1st day lot 31 and 2nd day lot 37 respectively. A further item, lot 77 on the 2nd day, was described as *THE FARMER'S WIFE and raven, illustrative of that well-known*

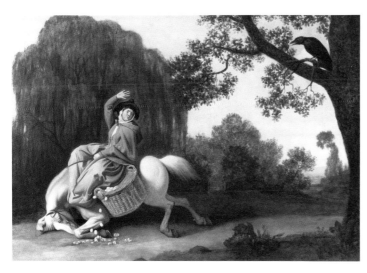

Fig.59
G. Stubbs:
The Farmer's Wife and the Raven
Yale Center for British Art, Paul Mellon Collection

subject in Gay's Fables – true to Nature and the Poet. The price fetched was 24 gns., indicating a relatively small work. Since the sale catalogue distinguishes enamels, it was certainly not LL 3681. It seems likely to have been the work shown at the BI the previous year (see note 3 above).

5. John Gay: *Fables*, Vol.I (1727) no.37; see Judy Egerton: *George Stubbs 1724-1806*, exhibition catalogue, Tate Gallery (1984) p.172, cat.129. B. Tattersall: *Stubbs and Wedgwood*, exhibition catalogue, Tate Gallery (1974) p.84, cat.26, following B. Taylor: *The Prints of George Stubbs* (1969) p.44 had previously identified the engraver as Van der Gucht.

6. repr. Lennox-Boyd, Dixon and Clayton, *op. cit.*, p.218.

7. Tattersall, *op. cit.*, pp.54-55, cat.11.

8. Judy Egerton: *British Sporting and Animal Paintings 1655-1867 in the Paul Mellon Collection* (1978) p.96 however points out that *Labourers* has a similarly moralistic content, being about 'the old men who 'fell into a dispute about putting the tailpiece into the cart' ' and observes that 'the two subjects ... have in common a bucolic, anecdotal quality not found elsewhere in Stubbs's work'.

9. J. Mayer: *Early Exhibitions of Art in Liverpool, with some notes for a Memoir of George Stubbs R.A.* (1876) p.125, states that Mrs Armstead (presumably the companion of Charles James Fox) bought LL 3681 for 100 gns.

10. Dr Hawkins's address is recorded as 146 Harley Street, London W1 (day books, Christie's archives).

George Stubbs
1724-1806

Self-Portrait on a White Hunter
LL 3684 (formerly H 3741)
enamel on Wedgwood biscuit
earthenware, 93 × 71 cm
signed and dated: *Geo. Stubbs pinxit / 1782* (lower right)

Lever purchased LL 3684 in 1905 as part of the Tweedmouth collection of Wedgwood ware, when it was

believed to be a portrait of Josiah Wedgwood himself. It was re-identified in 1957[2] as the self-portrait included in Stubbs's studio sale, second day, lot 97: 'Portrait of Mr. Stubbs seated on a white Hunter, an upright oval in enamel – a most excellent Likeness of this great Painter, and accompanied in the very Perfection and beauty of his art'. The sitter's features compare quite closely to other portraits of Stubbs,[3] notably a smaller self-portrait in enamel dated 1781, in which the

sitter is identified by an inscription on the reverse (National Portrait Gallery, fig.60). It has been demonstrated that LL 3684 follows in detail Stubbs's commissioned equestrian portrait of William Evelyn of St. Clere dated 1770 (private collection).[4] The horse is identical, as is the rider's pose and much of the landscape background. Nevertheless, since Wedgwood did not succeed in producing ceramic plaques for Stubbs's use until the late 1770s,[5] there is no real reason to

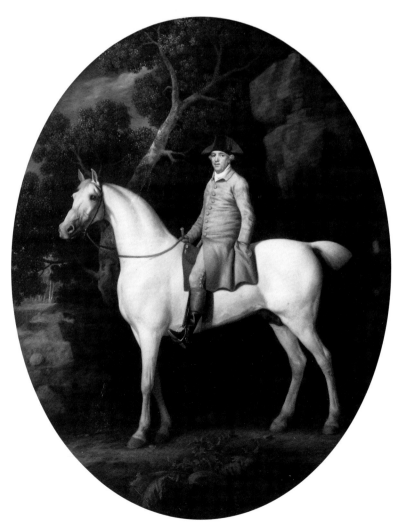

G. Stubbs: *Self-Portrait on a White Hunter*
LL 3684

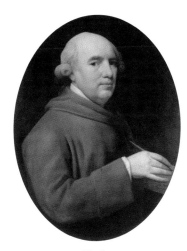

Fig.60
G. Stubbs: *Self-portrait*
Courtesy of the National Portrait Gallery, London

doubt the date inscribed on LL 3684. It has been suggested that Stubbs must have retained a study of the earlier portrait which he used as the basis for the work;[6] freeing him, perhaps, to concentrate on the technical difficulties presented by the medium. Technically the work was an outstanding success and remains one of the best-preserved of all Stubbs's enamels.

PROVENANCE:
Stubbs's studio sale, Coxe, 26-27 May 1807, 2nd day (97) bt. in by Isabella Saltonstall (210 gns.);[7] ...2nd Lord Tweedmouth;[8] Christie 3 June 1905 (47) bt. in (520 gns.); bt. from Charles Davis by Lever 30 June 1905 (£546).

EXHIBITIONS:
[? RA 1782 (173)[9]]; *Wedgwood Bi-centenary* Hanley and Victoria & Albert Museum 1930 (31); *George Stubbs 1724-1806* Whitechapel Art Gallery 1957 (14); *Face to Face: Three Centuries of Artists' Self-Portraiture* Walker Art Gallery Liverpool 1994 (33).

REFERENCES:
1. LL 3684 was never allocated a WHL number, being considered by Lever an integral part of the Tweedmouth Wedgwood collection.
2. B. Taylor: *George Stubbs 1724-1806*, exhibition catalogue, Whitechapel Art Gallery (1957) p.15, cat.14.

3. Taylor, *loc. cit.*
4. C. Parker: *Mr Stubbs the Horse-Painter* (1971) p.52; see also Judy Egerton: *George Stubbs 1724-1806*, exhibition catalogue, Tate Gallery (1984) p.152, cat.111, repr.
5. B. Tattersall: *Stubbs and Wedgwood*, exhibition catalogue, Tate Gallery (1974) pp.17-19.
6. Egerton, *loc. cit.*
7. The *Sporting Magazine*, November 1809, mentions that 'Miss Saltinstone [sic] possesses a great many of Stubbs pictures including several of the enamels, a portrait of himself on horseback among them'.
8. The Tweedmouth collection of Wedgwood had been purchased by Dudley Marjoribanks, 1st Baron Tweedmouth (1820-1894), at least in part, from Charles Darwin, Wedgwood's grandson (F. Rathbone: *The Collection of Old Wedgwood formed by Lord Tweedmouth*, exhibition catalogue, Charles Davis's Gallery, London (1905) pp.5-7); that LL 3684 was identified as a portrait of Josiah Wedgwood strongly suggests that it came from the same source.
9. This exhibit was titled *Portrait of an artist (Enamel)*. The *Public Examiner*, 1 May 1782, p.2, noted that 'Stubbs again exhibits several Performances in Enamel, and in a size so far beyond what has heretofore been practised in this part of the Art, that the improvement is nothing less than prodigious. The Portrait, as large as life, on this Enamel of Stubbs, is the Effigies of himself, and if the white had not been so cadaverous, it would have been a vera Effigies.' Traditionally the National Portrait Gallery self portrait is identified as the work in question, but since this measures only 26 × 20 in., there is the bare possibility that the larger LL 3684 was the exhibited work even though it is neither 'as large as life' itself nor obviously of an artist. On the other hand, J. Mayer: *Early Exhibitions of Art in Liverpool, with some notes for a Memoir of George Stubbs* (1876) p.125 describes the self-portrait 'painted for Mrs. Therold' (i.e. presumably the National Portrait Gallery enamel, which is inscribed on the reverse *Geo Stubbs painted by himself for his Friend Richd. Thorold*) as 'life-size'.

George Stubbs
1724-1806

Haymakers
LL 3682 (WHL 2179)
enamel on Wedgwood biscuit earthenware, 74.5 × 103.5 cm
signed and dated: *Geo Stubbs pinxit/1794* (lower right)

Haycarting
LL 3683 (WHL 2180)
enamel on Wedgwood biscuit earthenware, 77 × 105 cm
signed and dated: *Geo Stubbs pinx/1795* (lower right)

Together with *Reapers* (Yale Center for British Art, New Haven, fig.61), LL 3682-83 form a sequence of three scenes of rural labour which Stubbs painted in the mid-1790s on ceramic plaques manufactured by Josiah Wedgwood. The three paintings develop Stubbs's treatment of the theme in a pair of panel paintings of 1785, *Haymakers* and *Reapers* (Tate Gallery, figs. 62 and 63), which themselves elaborate upon an earlier pair, identically titled, dating from 1783 (Bearsted Collection, Upton House, National Trust, figs. 64 and 65). Stubbs is also known to have made drawings and figure studies for these works, now untraced.[1]

The importance of the 1785 paintings to Stubbs can be gauged from the fact that in 1786 he chose them to mark his return, after a four year absence, to exhibiting at the Royal Academy; the following year he also sent them to the Society for Promoting Painting and Design in Liverpool.[2] In September 1788 he issued subscription proposals for prints after the two works and the stipple engravings, which he executed himself, were finally published on 1 January 1791.[3] Nevertheless the precise reason for his return to the theme in 1794 (and

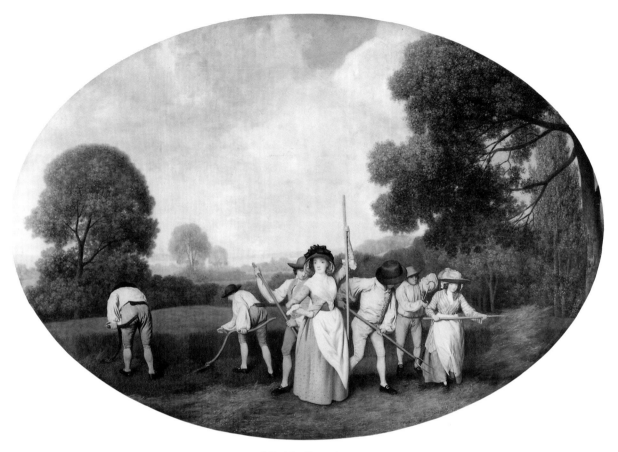

G. Stubbs: *Haymakers*
LL 3682

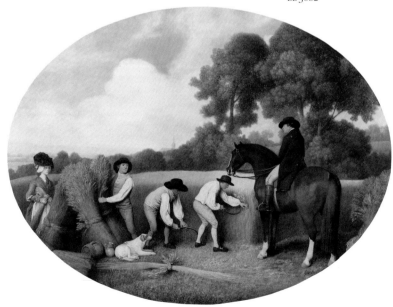

Fig.61
G. Stubbs: *Reapers*
Yale Center for British Art, Paul Mellon Collection

at the same time, to the enamel medium[4]) is unknown. The works do not appear to have been commissioned, since they remained in Stubbs's studio until his death. It may be significant that LL 3682, which the date indicates to be the earliest of the three, is a nearly new design, in which only the standing female figure in the centre has been re-used. The *Haycarting* and *Reapers* of 1795, on the other hand, are much more direct re-workings of the 1785 compositions. Stubbs appears to have made preliminary studies specifically for the two 1795 enamels,[5] which suggests that he had become dissatisfied with the 1785 designs. In the enamels the number

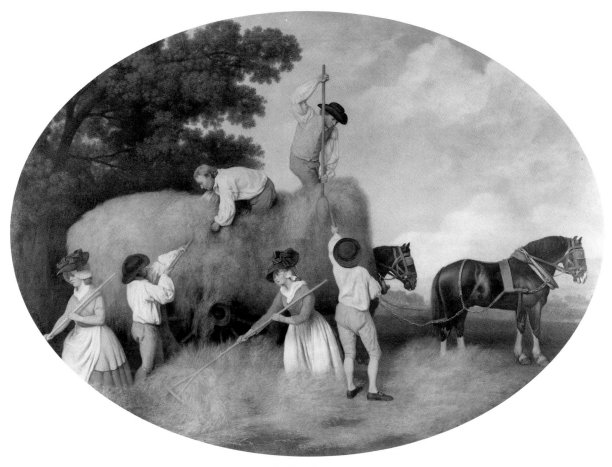

G. Stubbs: *Haycarting*
LL 3683

of figures has been reduced but their scale in relation to the picture area increased, while their previously frieze-like disposition has been replaced by a more concise and consciously formal treatment.

The contribution made by Stubbs's paintings to the iconography of rural labour in later 18th-century Britain has been much discussed. On the one hand, it has been pointed out that numerous similarities exist between his haymaking and haycarting scenes and Thomas Hearne's watercolour *A Landscape and Figures from Thomson's 'Seasons'* (Whitworth Art Gallery, University of Manchester, fig.66), which Stubbs could have seen at the Society of Artists exhibition in 1783; and the works consequently related to the fashion for painting scenes of idealised rustic labour inspired by Thomson's very popular poems.[6] Other interpretations have focused on the more distinctive or unique nature of Stubbs's vision and have seen the works as portraits of actual individuals,[7] as quasi-encyclopaedic illustrations of current farming methods[8] or as providing a critique of the changing social conditions of rural labour.[9] It cannot now be established whether the works show an actual place.[10]

Neither work is in the best condition. The former is suffering from numerous areas of discoloured retouching in the sky and in the trees at left; on the latter two cracks in the tablet are visible in the foliage of the trees at top left and in the sky to the right above the foremost horse. Both works are in their original frames.[11]

PROVENANCE:
Stubbs studio sale, Coxe, 26-27 May 1807 (LL 3682 as 2nd day lot 94, 100 gns.; LL 3683 as 2nd day lot 93, 100 gns.[12]); bt. in by Isabella Saltonstall;…William Millman; Christie 25 November 1890 (both works as lot 90);…Sir Walter Gilbey; Christie at Elsenham Hall, 11 June 1915 (LL 3682 as lot 394; LL 3683 as lot 395) bt. Gooden & Fox for Lever (150 gns. and 135 gns. respectively).

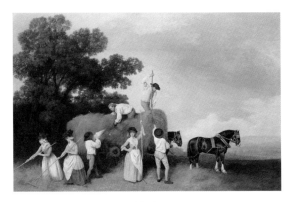

Fig.62
G. Stubbs: *Haymakers*
© Tate Gallery London

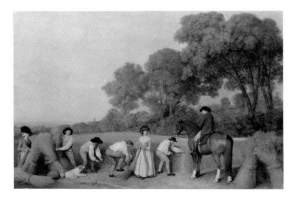

Fig.63
G. Stubbs: *Reapers*
© Tate Gallery London

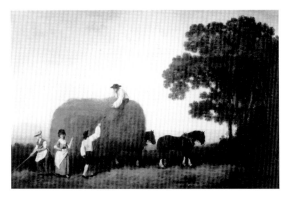

Fig.64
G. Stubbs: *Haymakers*
Upton House, The Bearsted Collection (The National Trust)
National Trust Photographic Library/Angelo Hornak

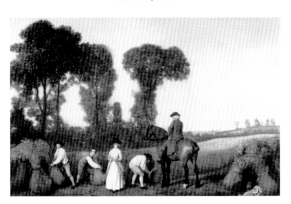

Fig.65
G. Stubbs: *Reapers*
Upton House, The Bearsted Collection (The National Trust)
National Trust Photographic Library/Angelo Hornak

EXHIBITIONS:
BI 1806 (LL 3682 as no.49; LL 3683 as
no.64); *George Stubbs* Walker Art Gallery
Liverpool 1951 (LL 3682 as no.61; LL 3683
as no.62); *George Stubbs 1724-1806*
Whitechapel Art Gallery 1957 (46)
(LL 3682 only).

REFERENCES:
1. Stubbs studio sale, Coxe, 26-27 May
1807; 1st day lots 17, 28, 30; 2nd day lot 31.
See also note 5 below.
2. Judy Egerton: *George Stubbs 1724-
1806*, exhibition catalogue, Tate Gallery,
(1984) p.168; see also C. Parker: *Mr
Stubbs the Horse Painter* (1971) p.128.
3. C. Lennox-Boyd, R. Dixon and T.
Clayton: *George Stubbs, The Complete
Engraved Works* (1989) pp.216-9,
cats. 89-90.

4. No works by Stubbs in enamel on
Wedgwood ceramic plaques dating from
between 1783 and 1793 are known except
for the solitary equestrian portrait of
Warren Hastings of 1791; B. Tattersall:
Stubbs and Wedgwood, exhibition
catalogue, Tate Gallery (1974) pp.22-3,
102-3. A close reading of Wedgwood's
oven-books reveals that between late
March 1783 and mid-September 1784 the
factory produced 28 large ceramic tablets,
of which no fewer than 24 were technical
failures; a rate which may explain why
their production seems to have been
abandoned after this date (Robin
Emmerson, verbally, 14 September 1998).
The four 'successful' tablets, each of
which measured roughly 42 inches in
its larger dimension, were clearly

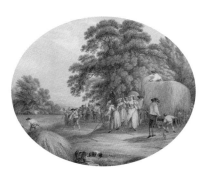

Fig.66
T. Hearne:
*A Landscape and Figures from Thomson's
'Seasons' (Summertime)*
The Whitworth Art Gallery, The University of Manchester

carefully husbanded by Stubbs, who must have known that no more would be forthcoming.

5. Stubbs studio sale, 2nd day, lots 69 and 72. Both are described in the catalogue as studies for the same subjects in enamel. Egerton, *op. cit.*, p.168 implies, however, that these are the 1785 paintings themselves. See also note 12 below.

6. Egerton, *loc. cit.*

7. B. Taylor: *Stubbs* (1971) p.40.

8. Lennox-Boyd, Dixon and Clayton, *op. cit.*, p.219.

9. For a discussion of this type of interpretation see especially J. Barrell: *The Dark Side of the Landscape* (1980) pp.25-31. Barrell justly points out that the composition of *Reapers* highlights a narrative centering on the man grasping the sheaves of corn, who appears to be intercepting an exchange of glances between the woman at his side and the man on horseback. The differences between the 1785 and 1795 versions of *Reapers* suggest that Stubbs's concern was to make this theme more explicit. However, there appears to be no such narrative content to the *Haycarting* and *Haymakers*; and its absence may well be a key element of the dynamic between the three works as Stubbs perceived it. See also the review by R. Simon of the exhibition *Toil and Plenty* in *Apollo* (March 1994) pp.47-9, which discusses a paper given by M. Rosenthal in a symposium at the Yale Center for British Art, January 1994. Rosenthal suggested that Stubbs in these works presented us with a contrast between old-style communal farming (*Haymakers* and *Haycarting*) and new capitalist farming, symbolised by the overseer on horseback (*Reapers*). See also M. Rosenthal, ed.: *Prospects for the Nation: Recent Essays in British Landscape 1750-1880* (1997) pp.49-56, where Rosenthal offers a similar view of these works.

10. Judy Egerton, in an unpublished catalogue entry for the Tate Gallery *Haymakers* (Tate Gallery files) has pointed out that R. Dodd's *North View of Highbury and Canonbury Places*, engraved by R. Pollard and F. Jukes, published in 1787, contains a group of haymakers which seems to be largely derived from Stubbs's work.

11. M. Gregory, letter, 18 July 1994, gallery files, identifies their maker as Thomas Allwood. Allwood is known to have carved two frames for Stubbs by April 1785 but it should be noted that no work by him after 1793 is known (*Dictionary of English Furniture Makers* (1986) p.11). Judy Egerton: *British Sporting and Animal Paintings 1655-1867: The Paul Mellon Collection* (1978) p.98 has offered evidence to the effect that the similar frame on the Yale *Reapers* is after the style of William Vile, of the firm Vile and Cobb.

12. LL 3683 has hitherto been identified (Tattersall, *op. cit.*, p.108) as lot 69 on the 2nd day of the Stubbs studio sale. The latter is described in the catalogue as *LANDSCAPE at the time of the Hay Harvest, representing a Hayfield, with Hay Makers loading a Haycart – a Study for the same Subject, in enamel*. It sold for 26 gns. The fact that it is described explicitly as a study, together with the low price, suggests it cannot be LL 3683. The comma after the word *Subject* is surely a misprint (compare the description of lot 72 as *LANDSCAPE, a Scene during the Corn Harvest, representing a Corn Field with Reapers, a study for the same Subject in enamel – painted from nature*). Lot 93 on the 2nd day sale, traditionally identified as the Yale *Reapers*, is described as *LANDSCAPE with Hay Field and Hay Makers, an oval in large enamels. This very extraordinary performance, not only the largest as a painting on enamel extant, but for finishing, beauty and perfection in all its parts, is a wonderful effort of ingenuity and success – capital*. It should be pointed out that LL 3683, at 77 × 105 cm, is in fact 3 cm wider than the *Reapers*; and it is significant that the description of lot 72 cited above clearly distinguishes the subject of *Reapers* as a corn harvest (an activity which takes place in a different season from haymaking); whereas the description of lot 93 explicitly does not mention corn harvesting or reaping. The fact that LL 3682 and LL 3683 have been together at least since 1890 tends to suggest that they were successive lots at the 1807 sale, especially since they fetched the same sum. The traditional identification of lot 93 with the Yale *Reapers* was initially questioned by Egerton, *op. cit.*, p.169.

Joseph Mallord William Turner
1775-1851

The Falls of the Clyde
LL 3584 (WHL 4708)
oil on canvas, 89 × 119.5 cm

This painting is one of a group of nine late oils in which Turner reworked compositions from his *Liber Studiorum*.[1] It is based on the *Drawing of the Clyde*,[2] published 29 March 1809 (fig.67), which in turn derived from the large watercolour *The Fall of the Clyde, Lanarkshire: Noon – vide Akenside's Hymn to the Naiads*, exhibited at the Royal Academy in 1802 (Walker Art Gallery Liverpool, fig.68). The view is of the upper fall of Bonnington Linn,[3] one of three falls on the Clyde near Lanark which had become a popular tourist attraction in the late 18th century. Turner, following in the footsteps of such artists as Paul Sandby, Jacob More and Joseph Farington, had sketched there on his second tour of Scotland in 1801. The composition of LL 3584 shows considerable differences from the *Liber Studiorum* print, which had in turn significantly altered the design of the 1802 watercolour. In this third version, the contained and picturesque aspects of the scene have been minimised in favour of a dramatic and sublime composition in which the human figures are dwarfed by the elemental forces of nature.[4]

The precise date of LL 3584 and of the other paintings in the group is uncertain and has been much discussed. It has been suggested that Turner's renewed interest in this particular subject (and that of *Norham Castle*, another work in the series) coincided with a visit to Scotland in 1831.[5] Turner returned to the Falls on this trip and made several sketches of them,[6] perhaps with a view to testing the colour and

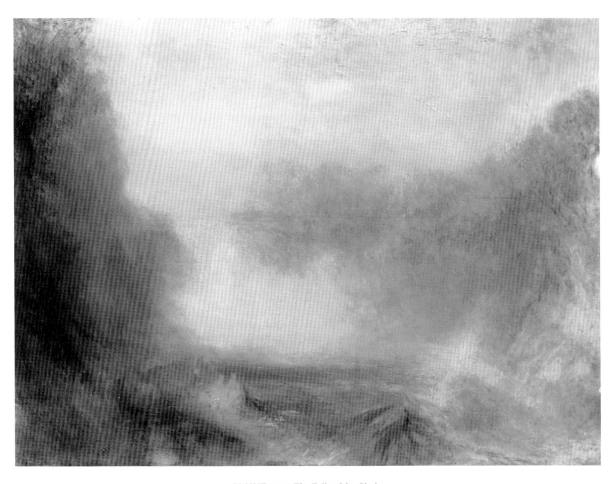

J.M.W. Turner: *The Falls of the Clyde*
LL 3584

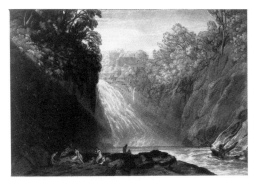

Fig.67
C. Turner, after J.M.W. Turner:
Drawing of the Clyde
© The British Museum

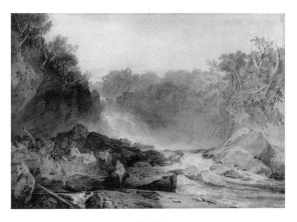

Fig.68
J.M.W. Turner:
*The Fall of the Clyde, Lanarkshire: Noon –
vide Akenside's Hymn to the Naiads*
Walker Art Gallery, Liverpool

light theories of Sir David Brewster, whom he had just met in Edinburgh.[7] The dominance of the primary colours in LL 3584 certainly does suggest an attempt on Turner's part to apply Brewster's ideas; but on the other hand, this is a feature of nearly all his later works, and none of the 1831 sketches of the Falls relates precisely to the compositional features of LL 3584, as distinct from its prototypes. The present consensus, based chiefly on the evidence from canvas stamps on other works in the group, is that LL 3584 dates from no earlier than 1840 and may be from considerably later in the 1840s.[8]

The painting has been described as unfinished and as being in the state in which Turner habitually left works before completing them on varnishing days,[9] implying that it is an intended exhibition picture whose appearance might well have undergone considerable future alteration. But elsewhere it has been proposed that the whole series of which the work forms part was painted as a conscious experiment in marketing more sketchily painted subjects.[10] Careful inspection of the surface of LL 3584, with its very delicate hatchings and highlights, and with its incorporation of watercolour,[11] does suggest that the painting is something more than a lay-in; that it is a fully worked-out conception in its own right.

PROVENANCE:
[…?John Pound[12]];… Rev. Thomas Prater; Christie 6 May 1871 (128) bt. Sir Hugh H. Campbell (340 gns.); Christie 2 May 1874 (125) bt. Agnew (330 gns.); William Houldsworth; Christie 23 May 1891 (58) bt. Agnew (290 gns.); Joseph Ruston; Christie 21 May 1898 (53) bt. Wallis (880 gns.); … Sir Joseph Robinson; Christie 6 July 1923 bt. Tooth (2400 gns.); bt. from Tooth by Lever September 1923.

EXHIBITIONS:
International Exhibition Glasgow 1888

(335); *J.M.W. Turner R.A. 1775-1851* Whitechapel Art Gallery 1953 (75); Glasgow Institute of Fine Arts 1957; *J.M.W. Turner R.A.* Leggatt 1960 (no cat.); *Landscape in Britain 1750-1850* Tate Gallery 1973 (218); *Turner 1775-1851* RA 1974-5 (621).

REFERENCES:
1.   For the other eight late oils based on *Liber Studiorum* subjects, together with two further stylistically similar oils usually grouped with them, but apparently not based on *Liber Studiorum* subjects, see M. Butlin and E. Joll: *The Paintings of J.M.W. Turner* (2nd. ed., 1984) pp.298-304, cats. 509-19. LL 3584 is Butlin and Joll cat.510.
2.   W.G. Rawlinson: *Turner's Liber Studiorum* (1906) cat.18. See also G. Forrester: *Turner's 'Drawing Book', The Liber Studiorum* (1996) pp.65-6.
3.   F. Milner: *Turner Paintings in Merseyside Collections* (1990) pp.19-20, correcting A. Wilton: *Turner and the Sublime* (1980) p.110, where it is stated that the view is of the fall of Corra Linn.
4.   Wilton, *loc. cit.*, notes that the treatment of light in LL 3584 is markedly different from that in the *Liber Studiorum* print. The latter's diagonal transparent rays are replaced by a more diffused, iridescent light. According to J. Gage: *Colour in Turner* (1969) p.41, this was intended by Turner as a direct visual expression of lines 45-49 in Akenside's *Hymn to the Naiads*.
5.   Gage, *op. cit.* p.143.
6.   In the 'Stirling and Edinburgh' sketchbook, TB CCLXIX, 1-12a.
7.   Gage, *loc. cit.*
8.   Butlin and Joll, *op. cit.* p.298. They point out also that Turner had renewed interest in his *Liber Studiorum* in 1845 when he had McQueen's run off fifteen new sets of the publication. In the first edition of *The Paintings of J.M.W. Turner* they had dated the whole series 1835-40. W. Armstrong: *Turner* (1902) p.220 had originally dated LL 3584 to 1840-45.
9.   Butlin and Joll, *loc. cit.*
10. Lawrence Gowing at the Turner Symposium at Johns Hopkins University, Baltimore USA, 1974 (Butlin and Joll, *loc. cit.*).
11. First noted in the *Turner 1775-1851* exhibition catalogue, RA (1974-5) p.170.

12. C.F. Bell: *The Exhibited Works of Turner* (1901) claimed that LL 3584 had been sold in the Mrs Booth/John Pound sale of 1865 (dated 1864 by Bell) but no work of this title can there be traced. Nevertheless, the vertical cracking on LL 3584, similar to that which appears on several other canvases in this group of works and suggesting that it was rolled up for removal from Turner's studio, is a feature often identified with Pound's ownership; Butlin and Joll, *op. cit.*, pp.299-300. The auctioneer's copy of the 1891 sale catalogue (see provenance above) is annotated 'Mrs. Pound's' [sic] and the 1923 Christie's catalogue also stated that the work was owned by John Pound. Armstrong, *loc. cit.*, following Bell, indicates the early existence of two versions of LL 3584; one owned by Houldsworth and Ruston which Armstrong stated (apparently erroneously) was owned by Henry Clay Frick in 1902; a second owned by Prater and Campbell which by 1902 was untraced. Butlin and Joll, *op. cit.*, p.300 convincingly argue that the two versions are in fact only one, and establish the provenance given above; it should however be noted that a second version of LL 3584 was recorded in a private collection in Australia (Graeme M. Cameron, Melbourne, letter, 25 May 1992, gallery files).

'Joseph Mallord William Turner'
1775-1851

A Town on the Rhine, with Bridge and Castle on a Height – Sunrise
LL 3698 (WHL 538, HH 176)
oil on canvas, 30 × 41 cm

The title used is that given to the work when it was bought by Lever. It is entirely fanciful, and the painting is a bizarre concoction of Turnerian motifs executed by a later pasticheur. The distant source for the work may have been the watercolour *Ehrenbreitstein from the Mosel*

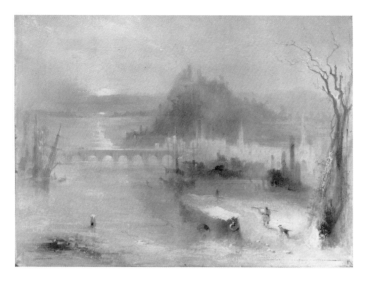

'J.M.W.Turner:'
A Town on the Rhine, with Bridge and Castle on a Height – Sunrise
LL 3698

The work is a very feeble copy of Turner's *San Benedetto, looking towards Fusina*, exhibited at the Royal Academy in 1843 (Tate Gallery, fig.70). Many of Turner's Venetian pictures were copied in the late 19th century when they hung in the National Gallery.[1]

PROVENANCE:
…James Orrock; bt. from Orrock by Lever 1912.[2]

REFERENCES:
1. Ian Warrell, letter, 19 February 1998, gallery files.
2. 1912 Inventory p.17, valued at £75.

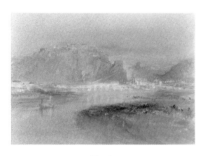

Fig.69
J.M.W.Turner:
Ehrenbreitstein from the Mosel
National Gallery of Scotland

after
Joseph Mallord William Turner
1775-1851

San Benedetto, looking towards Fusina
LL 3699 (WHL 69, H 433)
oil on panel, 26 × 39 cm

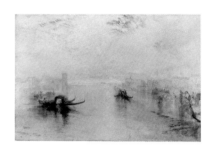

Fig.70
J.M.W.Turner:
San Benedetto, looking towards Fusina
© Tate Gallery London

(National Gallery of Scotland, fig.69) which Turner executed for the 1837 edition of Thomas Campbell's *Poetical Works*, where it illustrated the poem *Ode to the Germans: Ehrenbreitstein*.[1]

PROVENANCE:
…James Orrock; bt. from Orrock by Lever 1910.[2]

REFERENCES:
1. Ian Warrell, letter, 19 February 1998, gallery files.
2. 1910 Inventory p.56, valued at £40.

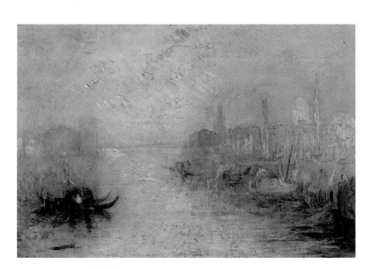

after J.M.W.Turner: *San Benedetto, looking towards Fusina*
LL 3699

'Joseph Mallord William Turner'

1775-1851

A Coast Scene: Sunrise

LL 3725 (WHL 2038, HH 145)
oil on panel, 27 × 38 cm

Lever acquired LL 3725 as by Turner, but the low value placed upon the work at the time would have indicated that it was not autograph. It bears no relation to any known work by Turner either in terms of style or of subject matter, and the very poor command of perspective raises doubts that it is by a trained artist. The painting has been damaged in an earlier cleaning and there are substantial losses and re-touchings, as well as odd shapes visible through the paint which suggest that a different subject exists under the present one. The work purports to date from the period 1825-1845 (but may be considerably later) and is perhaps intended to represent a scene on the coast of Devon.[1]

PROVENANCE:
...James Orrock; bt. from Orrock by Lever 1910.[2]

REFERENCES:
1. A very faint inscription on the reverse of the panel (possibly in Orrock's writing) appears to read: *On the Coast of Devon/Turner R.A.*
2. 1910 Inventory p 54, valued at £10.

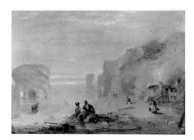

'J.M.W.Turner:' *A Coast Scene: Sunrise*
LL 3725

George Watson

1767-1837

Mrs. Peat and her Daughters

LL 3597 (WHL 4514)
oil on canvas, 129.5 × 99.5 cm

The sitters are Janet Ewart, who was born in Edinburgh in 1748 and married John Peat 'writer in St. Ninian's Row, in West Kirk parish' on 20 November 1768,[1] and their two youngest daughters, Janet, who was born on 22 June 1788, and Anne, who was christened at Edinburgh Parish Church on 7 August 1790. In later life, between 1854 and 1861, Anne published several volumes of poetry and she died in 1885 aged 95.[2] From the ages of the girls and the costumes, the portrait can be dated to about 1798-9, when Janet Ewart was fifty.

The work was bought by Lever as by Raeburn, but the later re-attribution to George Watson is convincing.[3] LL 3597 has however been badly damaged in the past (old tears remain visible on the mother's hand and dress and on the figure of the girl in white) and has been extensively restored.[4]

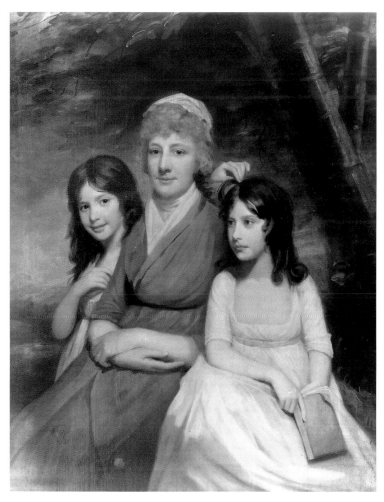

G. Watson: *Mrs. Peat and her Daughters*
LL 3597

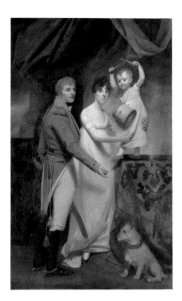

Fig. 71
G. Watson:
Lord Sinclair, his wife and child
Private collection; photograph courtesy
the Scottish National Portrait Gallery

PROVENANCE:
by descent to Rev. Alex C. Henderson,
B.D.;[5] bt. jointly by Agnew and Wallis &
Sons February 1902; bt. by J. Pierpont
Morgan June 1903; Agnew June 1905;
bt. by T. W. Wright, Liverpool December
1907; Christie 27 April 1923 (145) bt.
Gooden & Fox for Lever (£753.7.6).

REFERENCES:
1. F. J. Grant, ed.: 'Register of Marriages
of the City of Edinburgh 1751-1800',
Scottish Record Society (1922) Vol. 20,
p. 614.
2. Information from Alexander
Henderson, great-grandson of Janet
Ewart, vendor of the painting in 1902,
forwarded in a note from Wallis and Sons
to Agnew (Agnew's archives); see also
J. Greig: *Sir Henry Raeburn* (1911) p. 55.
3. Tatlock, p. 68; the attribution was
supported by L. Errington, letter,
24 September 1979, gallery files. The
traditional attribution to Raeburn, first
published by Greig, *loc. cit.*, was doubted
by W. G. Constable, note in gallery files,
and later by D. Mackie (note on a
photograph in the Yale Center for British
Art, New Haven). LL 3597 is stylistically
comparable to Watson's portrait of *Lord
Sinclair, his wife and child* (private
collection, fig. 71), among others.

4. F. W. Fox wrote to Lever just before
purchasing LL 3597 for him at Christie's
that 'it has suffered somewhat in the relining' (Fox to Lever, letter, 23 April 1923,
gallery files).
5. Not Alex C. H. Anderson as in Greig,
loc. cit.

Frederick Waters Watts
1800-1870

A Riverside
LL 3723 (WHL 643, HH 230)
oil on mahogany panel, 25.5 × 36 cm

Lever acquired LL 3723 as by
Constable, but the later re-
attribution to Watts is convincing.[1]
The loosely brushed technique is
characteristic of a group of works
dateable to the end of the 1820s
which are probably studies in the
open air painted from nature. Watts
is known, from inscriptions on the
back of some of these sketches, to
have worked at this period in Knole
Park, Kent, at Tadworth near
Epsom[2] and South Michelham near
Dorking,[3] both in Surrey, and along

the River Itchen in Hampshire[4].
LL 3723 may well represent this last
subject although no precise location
has been identified.

PROVENANCE:
…James Orrock; bt. from Orrock by
Lever 1910.[5]

REFERENCES:
1. Tatlock, p. 115. The attribution was
endorsed by C. Rhyne, letter, 10 October
1983, gallery files.
2. Christie 1 March 1977 (82) and
Sotheby 18 November 1981 (199) for
tree studies inscribed *Knole Park* and
Tadworth and dated *Sep. 1829.*
3. Paul Mellon collection; photographs
in the Paul Mellon Centre for Studies in
British Art.
4. I. Fleming Williams and L. Parris: *The
Discovery of Constable* (1984) p. 206; and
compare the letter from Watts to James
P. Ley of Bideford dated 1859 (Tate
Gallery archives) cited in L. Parris and
I. Fleming Williams: *Constable*, exhibition
catalogue, Tate Gallery (1976) p. 194,
cat. 348. Very similar sketches by Watts
include one at Christchurch Manor,
Ipswich and two at the Walker Art
Gallery Liverpool, each of which is the
same size as LL 3723.
5. 1910 Inventory p. 60, valued at £15.

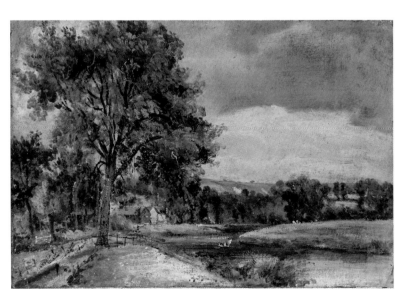

F. W. Watts: *A Riverside*
LL 3723

Richard Westall
1765-1836

Sappho
LL 3570 (WHL 115, H 132)
oil on canvas, 78 × 63.5 cm

Scriven's engraving (fig.72),
published on 1 January 1802, was
paired with H.B. Cook's engraving
titled *St. Cecilia*, after Westall's
portrait of *Lady Hamilton as St.
Cecilia* (untraced). The latter work,
which is the same size as LL 3570, was
presumably painted in about 1800-1
after Lady Hamilton's return to
England from Naples; LL 3570 must
date from the same time. It appears
to be a second version, painted for
the engraver, of an earlier composition, selected for its appropriateness
as a partner for the Lady Hamilton
portrait. The first version (formerly
in the collection of Sir Robert
Harvey, fig.73)[1] may originally have
been paired with an *Ariadne*
subject,[2] and conceivably dates from
some time before LL 3570, as Westall
exhibited a *Sappho in the Lesbian
Shades Chanting the Hymn of Love*
at the Royal Academy in 1796. That
Scriven's engraving follows LL 3570
rather than the Harvey canvas is
confirmed by the appearance in the
engraving of only one arm-band. The
lock of hair trailing over Sappho's
right shoulder is evidently a later
addition, although it is present in the
engravings by Sartain and Lightfoot
(see below) which suggests that it
was painted in not long after 1802.

The work has traditionally been
known as *The Artist's Wife as
Sappho*[3] but Westall never married.
The Harvey version was thought
in the past to represent Lady
Hamilton;[4] more recently it has been
suggested that the model was the
artist's sister Mary, who married the
artist William Daniell.[5] Another
likely candidate is his other sister
Anne (1770-1862) who was blind

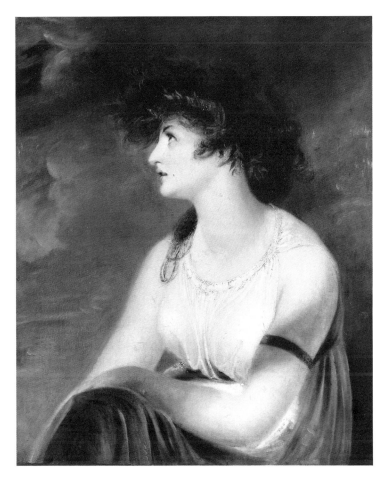

R. Westall: *Sappho*
LL 3570

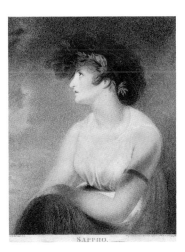

Fig.72
E. Scriven, after R. Westall: *Sappho*
Lady Lever Art Gallery

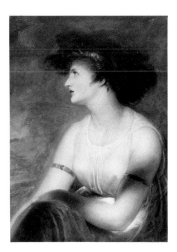

Fig.73
R. Westall: *Sappho*
Private collection; photograph courtesy Christie's

and remained unmarried; further possibilities are that she was the artist's stepmother or sister-in-law.[6]

PROVENANCE:
…Charles Neck; Christie 13 May 1905 (11) bt. Gooden & Fox for Lever (£94.10.-.).

EXHIBITIONS:
British Subject and Narrative Pictures 1800-1848 Arts Council, 1955 (40).

ENGRAVINGS:
Edward Scriven, stipple, published 1 January 1802; John or Emily Sartain, date unknown (unidentified volume in gallery files); P. Lightfoot, for Robert Bell: *Early Ballads* (1862).

REFERENCES:
1. About 79 × 55 cm; Christie 9 May 1980 (81), 28 February 1986 (141) and 22 July 1988 (223). Although the measurements given in the catalogues differ by 2 centimetres, the work seems to be the same one. It has apparently been cut down slightly at both sides, and originally is likely to have been the same size (or fractionally larger) than LL 3570.
2. 74.5 × 55 cm; Christie 12 April 1991 (133); this work may have been cut down fractionally on all sides.
3. Tatlock, p.68.
4. Compare J. Frankau: *The Story of Emma, Lady Hamilton* (1911) Vol.I, repr. following p.107 (Frankau's catalogue raisonné however omits Westall's painting and associated engravings at Vol.II, p.113); J. Turquan and J. D'Auriac: *A Great Adventuress: Lady Hamilton and the Revolution in Naples* (1914), fp.56.
5. R.J. Westall, letter, 18 May 1981, gallery files.
6. Family notes supplied by R.J. Westall, *loc. cit.* Westall remained interested in Sappho as a subject: he later painted her leaping off the Leucadian cliff (date unknown; reproduced in *The Poet and The Painter or Gems of Art and Song* (1869) p.68, illustrating *Sappho* by L.E. Landon).

'Francis Wheatley'
1747-1801

Cymon and Iphigenia
LL 3609 (WHL 2614)
oil on canvas, 26.5 × 30.5 cm

The title given to LL 3609 is traditional, but dates continuously only from the 20th century.[1] The story of the boorish Cymon, whose character was transformed by glimpsing Iphigenia asleep, is told on the fifth day of Boccaccio's *Decameron* but was probably more familiar to an 18th-century audience in the form of John Dryden's poem *Cymon and Iphigenia*.[2] Elements of Dryden's treatment, notably his description of the sleeping figure of Iphigenia, are closely followed in LL 3609, but in other respects (notably the presence of the sheep, which are not mentioned either by Dryden or Boccaccio) there are differences which suggest that the artist intended to represent another subject altogether.

The painting is closely comparable to four further ovals of horizontal format, similar in size, subject and style (though not certainly by the same hand), which have been recorded in a private collection in Derbyshire since 1778 and which have traditionally been attributed to George Morland.[3] If the latter paintings are by him they are very youthful productions, and the unconvincing handling of the girl's pose in LL 3609 strongly suggests that it too is an immature work. More recently, however, the privately-owned quartet has itself been re-attributed to Wheatley[4] (who was born in 1747) and the idea has been mooted that the subjects are from Thomson's *The Seasons*.[5] LL 3609 has been attributed to Wheatley since its appearance at Christie in 1882 (see below) and although it does not seem at all

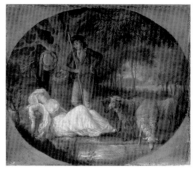

'F. Wheatley': *Cymon and Iphigenia*
LL 3609

characteristic of his work, at present consensus is lacking to support the work's re-attribution to the young Morland.[6]

PROVENANCE:
…J. Capron; Christie 7 January 1882 (96) bt. in (15 gns.); …Jeffery Whitehead; Christie 6 August 1915 (110) bt. Partridge for Lever (18 gns.).

REFERENCES:
1. At the Christie sale in 1882 it was titled *The Sleeping Shepherdess*; Lever, who liked to collect different paintings of the same subject, already owned treatments of *Cymon and Iphigenia* by Etty and Morland when he bought LL 3609 in 1915.
2. Edward Morris, verbally, October 1997.
3. Letter from the present owner, 2 July 1998, gallery files.
4. The circumstances of this re-attribution remain obscure and it is possible that acquaintanceship with LL 3609 was the reason. The present owner was not responsible (*ibid.*).
5. Annotations to photographs in the Witt Library.
6. Robert Mitchell, letter, 7 July 1998, gallery files, doubts the attribution to Morland.

Sir David Wilkie
1785-1841

Queen Victoria in Robes of State
LL 3598 (WHL 599, TM 334)
oil on canvas, 271.5 × 190.5 cm
signed and dated: *DAVID WILKIE of
LONDON 1840* (lower right, on base of
plinth)

Wilkie was appointed Queen
Victoria's Painter in Ordinary –
the same position that he had held
under William IV – shortly after
her accession in June 1837 and in
October he was asked by the Lord
Chamberlain to attend the Queen at
Brighton in order to begin work on
her portrait for foreign embassies.[1]
LL 3598 is the outcome of this
commission and was sent to the
British Embassy in Paris on 13 June
1840.[2]

At Brighton, the Queen sat
to Wilkie at regular two-day
intervals between 17 October and
1 November 1837;[3] but on the first of
these dates he was given a second
royal commission, for the *Queen's
First Council* (Royal Collection) and
this work, exhibited at the Royal
Academy in 1838, claimed his
immediate attention. He did manage
to obtain one full-face sitting for the
Embassy portrait (the *First Council*
sittings were in profile), and the
promise of further sittings at a future
date.[4] The first subsequent sitting
apparently took place at Windsor on
22 November 1838, when the artist
reported: 'Her Majesty has been very
gracious; she has given me a sitting
today, and I hope to have two more
sittings tomorrow and Saturday'.[5]
By this time, however, it is clear that
Wilkie had already devoted some
thought to the design of the portrait,
since one of a closely related group
of compositional sketches for it in
pen, ink and watercolour, is inscribed
October 15th 1838.[6] Another,

perhaps the most fully worked out
(National Portrait Gallery, fig.74),
shows the pose of the Queen and the
disposition of regalia already very
close to the finished work, with only
the treatment of the architectural
backdrop and billowing drapery
differing significantly from it.[7] By
24 December Wilkie wrote to the
Lord Chamberlain that he was
proceeding 'diligently' with the
portrait and submitted an estimate
of £200 for further copies.[8] Further
sittings took place at Windsor in
January 1839: a drawing for the train
of the Queen's Robes is dated to the
11th[9] and a study of the serpent
bracelet which she wears in the
finished portrait (Royal Collection,
fig.75) is perhaps also to be dated
from this time.[10] On 14 January
Wilkie wrote that the portrait would
not be ready for that summer's
Royal Academy exhibition,[11] but the
work does seem to have been well
advanced by the middle of March,
when Benjamin Robert Haydon saw
it in Wilkie's studio.[12] Two more
sittings took place on 8 and
22 August: on the second date Wilkie
wrote that a sitting of scarcely more
than half an hour had, with the
earlier sitting, enabled him to
improve the picture greatly.[13] The
following day he wrote to his sister:
'The picture of the Queen has just
come home; it appears to me very
like her, but no-one can tell how
likenesses strike other people'.[14]

The last remark suggests that
Wilkie was already feeling uneasy
about the work's reception. He may
already have sensed Haydon's
reaction: 'such a Queen! Kneller,
Hudson, Ramsay would have
disowned it!'[15] and (later)
'a slobbering muddle'.[16] The Queen
herself, primed by Lord Melbourne,
also disliked the work. She had noted
in her journal on 14 October 1838
(perhaps significantly, the day before
the date inscribed on Wilkie's

compositional sketch): 'spoke of the
necessity of my sitting to Wilkie for
these Ambassadors' Pictures, and
Lord M. said it was a great mistake
making Wilkie Portrait Painter, and
a very bad thing to send all these
bad pictures of me, all over the
Continent'; and on 20 March 1839
she wrote of 'the *too atrocious* full
length picture which Wilkie has
made of me, and which is put in the
Gallery, and which Lord M. is quite
schocked [sic] at; talked of the horror
of sending it to Paris; of it's being
such a mistake to make him Portrait
Painter.'[17] In the event, the work
lasted only seven years at the Paris
embassy before being replaced by
a copy of Winterhalter's Garter
portrait of 1843,[18] and it was donated
to the then Ambassador's wife, the
Marchioness of Normanby, a former
Lady of the Bedchamber. Many
years later, in 1899, when her
grandson, as Marquis of Normanby,
offered the work to the National
Portrait Gallery, the Queen
intervened to prevent it being
accepted.[19]

Wilkie's portrait was exhibited at
the Royal Academy in 1840. By this
time, however, there may have been
more than one version in existence,[20]
and there is evidence to suggest that
LL 3598 was not the exhibited canvas.
Lord Palmerston notified the Lord
Chamberlain on 30 May that the
Queen's portrait for Paris was ready
to be sent off,[21] and the Lord
Chamberlain's office records confirm
that the work was packed by 8 June
and shipped five days later;[22] the
Royal Academy exhibition,
however, had only opened on 4 May,
and continued until 15 July. The
version of the portrait exhibited
at the Royal Academy, which is not
known to have been removed from
the exhibition prematurely, was
badly mauled by the critics. The
politest form of response was to
pass over the work in silence – as

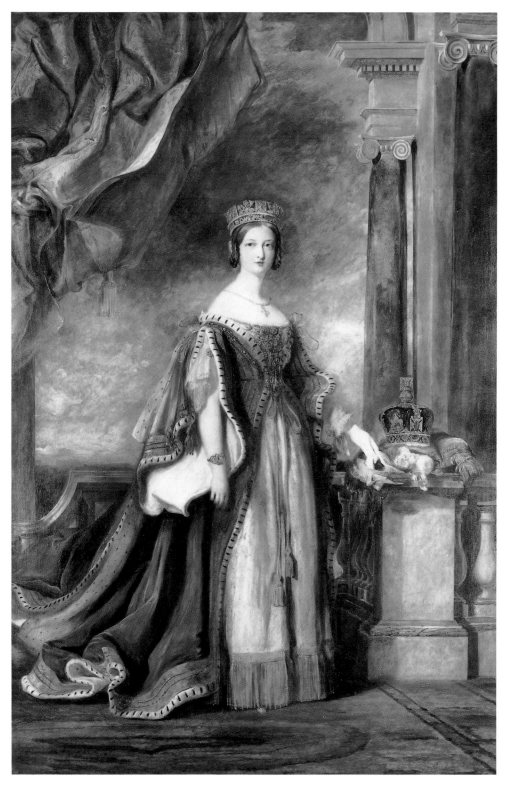

Sir D. Wilkie: *Queen Victoria in Robes of State*
LL 3598

the *Art Union* and *Athenaeum*
did – or to dismiss it as briefly as
possible. Thackeray, writing in
Fraser's Magazine as Michael Angelo
Titmarsh, observed in humorously
patriotic vein that 'the robes seem
as if they were cut out of British oak,
and the figure is as wooden as the
figurehead of one of your majesty's
men of war'; and later in the same
piece added that 'the Queen is as
bad a likeness and picture as we have
seen for many a day';[23] similarly brief
were the remarks of the *Examiner*
('Wilkie's portrait of the Queen
is execrable')[24] and the *Spectator*:
('a lamentable failure as a likeness,
and moreover, a bad picture: the
figure is stiff and graceless, like a
puppet clothed with the insignia
of royalty').[25] The critic of the
Observer, on the other hand, went
to town:

> 'The face is not that which gladdens
> the heart of these kingdoms – the face
> of one young, innocent and beautiful;
> the colour is not that transparent rose
> tint, the admiration of all beholders;
> the figure is not that *petite* but
> elegantly moulded form which amazes
> men from its singular combination of
> grace and beauty; nor is the expression
> of command in her queenly eye at all
> discoverable in this production. On
> the contrary, the countenance is
> wholly unlike that of our youthful
> and lovely sovereign; the colour, as
> compared with her fresh tints and
> blooming carnations, is as brick dust to
> rouge and pearl powder; the figure is
> dowdy and ungraceful, stiff without
> dignity, formal without the vestige of
> grandeur, and clumsy with not the
> least semblance of power and life. The
> hands and arms, which, in the original,
> are of a rare whiteness and delicacy,
> are here those of a nut-brown milk-
> maid, or some other rustic damsel of
> low degree, being at once dark-
> coloured, coarse-skinned, muscular
> and large to the uttermost point of
> ungainliness; and the feet, where
> discernible are made to match, at least
> in size and form. The drapery falls like
> logs of wood rudely hewn, the crown

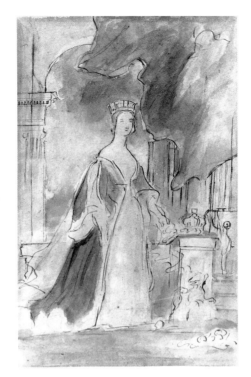

Fig. 74
Sir D. Wilkie:
*Study for the State Portrait
of Queen Victoria*
Courtesy of the National Portrait Gallery, London

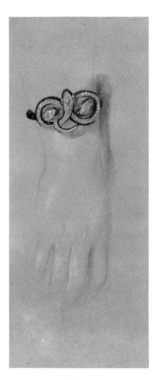

Fig. 75
Sir D. Wilkie:
*Study for the State Portrait of
Queen Victoria: Queen Victoria's
Hand with the Serpent Bracelet*
The Royal Collection
© Her Majesty Queen Elizabeth II

seems to oppress the royal brow which
it circles with its weight & in short, all
is rude & gross about the picture. It is
certain that the artist, enlightened
though he is, and high in his art though
he be, could never have read that most
popular of all text books, 'Burke on
the Sublime and Beautiful', or he
would never have painted such
a picture. Hear that great writer on
the subject: 'An air of robustness and
strength is very prejudicial to beauty.
An appearance of 'delicacy' and even
of fragility is almost essential to it …
The portrait',
the review concluded knowingly,
'will please neither her Majesty nor
her admirers'.[26]
Indeed, as Haydon observed the
following year, the work's failure
broke Wilkie at court, and made him
decide to go abroad.[27]

Wilkie's correspondence provides
an insight into his conception of the
sitter: …'She is eminently beautiful,
her features nicely formed, her skin
smooth, her hair worn close to her
face, in a most simple way; glossy
and clean-looking. Her manner,
though trained to act the Sovereign,
is yet simple and natural. She has
all the decision, thought, and self-
possession, of a queen of older years;
has all the buoyancy of youth, and
from the smile to the unrestrained
laugh, is a perfect child' …[28] 'The
regal power in so lovely a form is
perfectly new to us; it seems sent to
charm the disaffected by presenting
a settled government under the most
engaging aspect. Her Majesty is an
elegant person; seems to lose nothing
of her authority either by her youth

or delicacy; is approached with the same awe, and obeyed with the same promptitude, as the most commanding of her predecessors. She has all the buoyancy and singleness of heart of youth, with a wisdom and decision far beyond her years'.[29] In LL 3598 she is shown in the Robes of State worn at the opening of Parliament; she wears the George IV State Diadem of 1820, which she had worn for her coronation procession, and at her left hand is the Imperial state crown made for her coronation by Rundell, Bridge and Rundell.[30] Windsor Castle is visible in the background.

PROVENANCE:
Painted for the Lord Chamberlain's Office and sent to the British Embassy in Paris; on being replaced in 1847 given by the sitter to Maria, Marchioness of Normanby; by descent to her grandson Constantine Henry, 3rd Marquess of Normanby; … bt. by Lever shortly before November 1906.[31]

EXHIBITIONS:
[?RA 1840 (62)]; *Old Masters* Manchester 1909 (50); *Royal Treasures* 5 Great Stanhope Street, London 1937 (217).

REFERENCES:
1. Allan Cunningham: *Life of Sir David Wilkie* (1843), Vol.III, pp.228-9; PRO LC I/20 (1793).
2. PRO LC I/47 (21). The unusual form of signature was presumably devised by Wilkie to draw attention to the function of the portrait.
3. Cunningham, *op. cit.*, Vol.III, pp.226-9.
4. Letter of 6 November 1837; information from Hamish Miles, letter, 30 May 1998, gallery files.
5. Letter to his sister, 22 November 1838 (Cunningham, *op. cit.*, Vol.III, p.258). Queen Victoria's journal gives some indication of the conditions under which Wilkie laboured. *22 November 1838*: 'Sat to Wilkie for more than an hour. Daisy and Lady Barham, and Lord Conyngham [the Lord Chamberlain] with the children for a little while, as also Lady Barham's little boy'. *23 November*: 'Sat to Wilkie for an hour. Lady Barham and Daisy were

with me. Lady Barham's little boy came in towards the end of the sitting'.
24 November: 'Sat to Wilkie for an hour. Lady Barham and Daisy were in the room, as were also the dear little Conynghams who made us die with laughing; they are such dear, good, unaffected merry children …' (Royal Archives, Windsor Castle; extracts from Queen Victoria's journal are quoted by gracious permission of Her Majesty the Queen). The artist's private reaction to the sittings may perhaps be gauged from Haydon's later note, in his diary on 24 May 1840, that Wilkie felt 'unfairly treated' by the Queen, who 'sat to him half an hour & so forth, flurried him & pestered him, & then wonders why he does [not] make a fine work'; but this was after the vilification of the portrait at the Royal Academy (W.B. Pope, ed.: *The Diary of Benjamin Robert Haydon* (1960-63) Vol.4, p.31).
6. Sotheby 12 February 1964 (117).
7. Delia Millar: *The Victorian Watercolours and Drawings in the Collection of Her Majesty the Queen* (1995) Vol.2, pp.924-5, cat.5890, identifies a further study, of the Queen seated [RL 13592] as perhaps Wilkie's first idea for LL 3598, before he turned to a standing pose; A.P. Oppé: *English Drawings of the Stuart and Georgian Periods at Windsor Castle* (1950) p.103, cat.668, however, identified this as a study for *The Queen's First Council*.
8. PRO LC I/21 (1821).
9. Miles, *loc. cit.*
10. Millar, *op. cit.*, p.925, cat.5891; the bracelet is possibly the one set with diamonds and pink topazes given to Victoria for her birthday in 1837 by Queen Adelaide.
11. Miles, *loc. cit.*
12. Pope, *op. cit.*, Vol.4, p.547; entry for 17 March 1839.
13. Miles, *loc. cit.*
14. Cunningham, *op. cit.*, Vol.III, p.274.
15. Pope, *loc. cit.*
16. Pope, *op. cit.*, Vol.5, p.70; entry for 7 July 1841.
17. Queen Victoria's journal, Royal Archives, 14 October 1838 and 20 March 1839 (quoted by gracious permission of Her Majesty the Queen).
18. Royal Archives ADD.T.231, f.131; cited by Oliver Millar: *Victorian Pictures in the*

Collection of Her Majesty the Queen (1992) pp.287-8.
19. *Portraits of Queen Victoria*, a volume of letters in the archives of the National Portrait Gallery, *passim*; see also Royal Archives PP.Vic.1899/3401, 3643.
20. Cunningham, *op. cit.*, Vol.III, p.531 listed under the date 1840 a second full-length version of the portrait painted for Sir Charles Forbes. This remains untraced. A further full-length version, 269 × 174 cm, presented to the Government Art Collection in 1980, is stated to have been purchased at Wilkie's posthumous sale, Christie 30 April 1842 (658) by Sir Jamsetjee Jeejeebhoy of Bombay (D. Willey, Government Art Collection, verbally, 9 July 1998; at the time of writing this work is in store in New Delhi; from an indifferent photograph, which shows it to be in poor condition, it seems to be cruder and less assured in handling than LL 3598). R.S. Gower: *Sir David Wilkie* (1902) p.77 lists a half-length version at Glasgow; this is a mediocre copy of the figure of the queen, bust-length and with a plain dark background, not by Wilkie, now in Glasgow Art Gallery and Museum (cat.259). Also in Glasgow is a full-length portrait of Queen Victoria attributed to Wilkie which formerly hung in the City Chambers and later reverted to the care of Glasgow Art Gallery and Museum; from an old photograph this is not related to LL 3598. A further portrait of Queen Victoria by Wilkie measuring 30 × 25 in. was sold at Christie 2 May 1952 (184).
21. PRO LC I/47 (20).
22. PRO LC I/47 (21).
23. *Fraser's Magazine* (June 1840) pp.722, 729-30.
24. *Examiner* (3 May 1840) p.278.
25. *Spectator* (9 May 1840) p.452.
26. *Observer* (31 May 1840).
27. Pope, *op. cit.*, Vol.5, p.30, entry for 28 January 1841.
28. Wilkie to William Collins, letter, 12 November 1837 (Cunningham, *op. cit.*, Vol.III, p.229).
29. Cunningham, *op. cit.*, Vol.III, p.233.
30. R. Allison and S. Riddell, eds.: *The Royal Encyclopaedia* (1991) pp.133, 137, 272.
31. Recorded in an inventory of Thornton Manor made in November 1906; valued at £1500 (the figure supplied verbally by

Lever rather than derived from a dealer's invoice, suggesting that it was acquired privately); not present in an inventory of Thornton Manor made in May 1905.

Richard Wilson
1713-1782

*Lake Albano
and Castelgandolfo*
LL 3550 (WHL 2293, HH 57)
oil on canvas, 75.5 × 100 cm
Signed *RW* (monogram, R reversed, on stone bottom centre)

Lake Albano, eighteen miles southeast of Rome, was a site well-known to Grand Tourists thanks principally to Virgil's account in the *Aeneid* of the birth of Roman civilisation.[1] On its western shore is Castelgandolfo, the summer residence of the Popes. It is seen here from the north-east, replicating the viewpoint in a painting of the lake by Claude Lorrain which Wilson could have seen in the Barberini collection in Rome.[2]

Wilson's first treatment of the subject seems to have been a drawing of the far shore of the lake, with Castelgandolfo, presumably made on the spot not long after his arrival in Rome in 1752 (Victoria and Albert Museum, fig.76). In 1754 he worked up this essentially topographical study into a finished drawing for the Earl of Dartmouth,[3] adding an invented landscape foreground. His later painted versions of the subject[4] closely follow the design of the Dartmouth drawing.

The work can be dated to the later 1750s on stylistic grounds, and has good claim to be Wilson's first painted version. Neither of the other recorded versions has the two line Latin inscription on the fallen masonry at the lower left, which appears to be by Wilson himself rather than an addition; and the superior of the other two versions also lacks the church under the

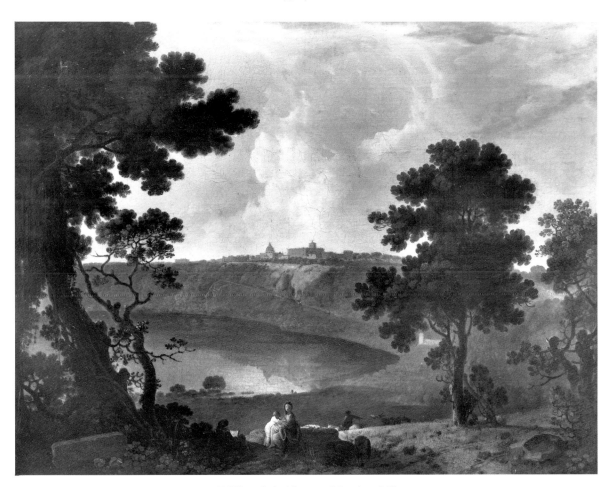

R. Wilson: *Lake Albano and Castelgandolfo*
LL 3550

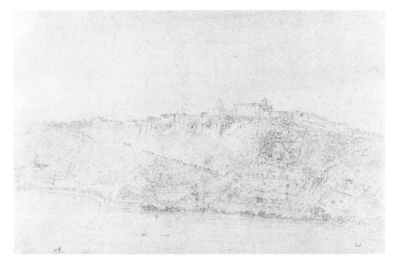

Fig.76
R.Wilson: *Castelgandolfo*
V & A Picture Library

foliage of the right-hand tree, which is present in the Dartmouth drawing. However, the chequered physical history of LL 3550 complicates assessment of its quality.[5]

The inscription on the masonry is no longer decipherable, but it was recorded in 1952 as *Qui Potentiora Egit, Qui Maiora Fecit* ('who did mightier deeds/who made greater works').[6] The masonry evidently purports to be the remains of an antique Roman monument, and Wilson presumably intended it to provide a counterpoint to the bucolic character of the scene in his own day, as conveyed through the peasant figures. He perhaps also intended the inscription as a comment on the moral authority of the Roman empire, as compared with that of the 18th-century Papacy.

PROVENANCE:
…James Orrock by 1908;[7] bt. from Orrock by Lever 1910.[8]

EXHIBITIONS:
Loan Exhibition of Works by Richard Wilson Tate Gallery 1925 (17); *Richard Wilson Loan Exhibition* Manchester City Art Gallery 1925 (67); *Peinture Anglaise* Musée d'Art Moderne Brussels 1929 (197); *Exhibition of Works by Richard Wilson* Ferens Art Gallery Hull 1936 (51); *Richard Wilson and His Circle* Birmingham Museum and Art Gallery 1948-9 (59) and Tate Gallery 1949 (58); *Art in the Georgian Home* Arts Council 1949 (7) *Le Paysage Anglais de Gainsborough à Turner* Paris 1953 (92); *Engelse Landschapschilders van Gainsborough tot Turner* Museum Boymans-van Beuningen Rotterdam 1955 (67); *British Painting in the Eighteenth Century* British Council 1957 (74); *Painting in Rome in the 18th Century* Rome (British Council) 1959 (no cat. no.); *W.B. Yeats Images of a Poet* Whitworth Art Gallery Manchester and the Building Centre Dublin 1961 (278); *English Landscape Painting of the 18th and 19th Centuries* Tokyo and Kyoto (British Council) 1970-1 (54).

REFERENCES:
1. D. Solkin: *Wilson*, exhibition catalogue, Tate Gallery (1982) p.170, cat.46.
2. Solkin, *loc. cit.*
3. Repr. Solkin, *loc. cit.*, and W.G. Constable: *Richard Wilson* (1953) pl.65b. The drawing is now in a private collection. Solkin is cautious about the chronological relationship between this drawing and the Victoria and Albert Museum drawing (*op. cit.*, p.161, cat.41) although he agrees

that the latter was studied from nature.
4. Constable, *op. cit.*, p.191, cat.64b. The other two recorded versions are a) 29½ × 39 in., with Gooden & Fox 1950, according to Constable perhaps painted in Italy; and b) Birmingham Museum and Art Gallery, described as a replica.
5. LL 3550 was repaired, cleaned and restored in 1959 after being damaged whilst on loan to the 1957 British Council exhibition (see above). Up until this point, the painting was disfigured by crude overpainting concealing damages in the sky and extensive cracking in the lower part of the work. Constable's negative assessment of LL 3550 (*loc. cit.*) reflects his having seen it in this condition.
6. Constable, *loc. cit.*; information conveyed by letter from S.L. Davison through Brinsley Ford, 1952.
7. B. Fletcher: *Richard Wilson R.A.* (1908) repr. fp. 152 (as *Lake Nemi*, in the Orrock collection). A note made by A.C. Tait of inscriptions on the reverse of LL 3550 (dateable to between 1925 and 1952, gallery files) records an old written label: *Mrs. J.G. Orrie from Bush Hill*. This has been taken (Constable, *loc. cit.*) to refer to a previous owner although the suspicion remains that the first part is a misreading of *Mr. James Orrock*. The same note records a chalk inscription on the stretcher crossbar indicating that the work was in the Orrock sale at Christie in 1904. Neither inscription has survived.
8. 1910 Inventory p.36, valued at £150.

Richard Wilson
1713-1782

Landscape with Diana and Callisto
LL 3122 (WHL 641, H 35)
oil on canvas, 103 × 139 cm
Signed: *RW* (monogram; the *R* reversed; on the stone at lower right)

The story of Diana and Callisto is related in Book II of Ovid's *Metamorphoses* (lines 401-530); the goddess, having discovered her attendant's pregnancy, is banishing

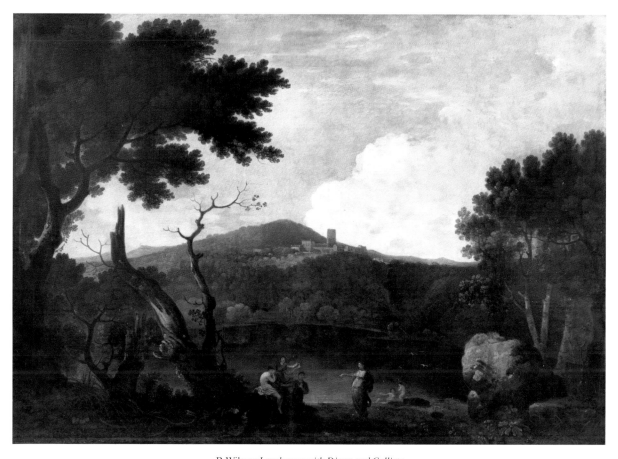

R.Wilson: *Landscape with Diana and Callisto*
LL 3122

her. Callisto's child will be the forefather of the Arcadian people. The theme had been popular with artists since the Renaissance[1] and Wilson probably consciously borrowed the pose of Diana's outstretched arm and pointing finger from Titian's famous painting of the subject (Duke of Sutherland, on loan to the National Gallery of Scotland, Edinburgh).[2] However, Wilson's figures are dwarfed by the landscape, a view of Lake Nemi, twelve miles east of Rome, with the town of Nemi above it and Monte Calvarone behind. Wilson made on-the-spot drawings of the lake about 1754 during his stay in Italy,[3] but none is known which precisely replicates this viewpoint, and essentially the design

is an adaptation of one of his first Italian landscapes, for which a work by Gaspard Dughet had been the model.[4]

Lake Nemi was commonly known as 'Speculum Dianae' (the Mirror of Diana) and Ariccia, situated in the woods below the town, was the goddess's most celebrated shrine.[5] It has been pointed out that the association of myth and specific landscape in this painting is unique in Wilson's work and argued that this reflects the taste of Henry Hoare of Stourhead, who bought a smaller version of the painting for £30 in 1758.[6] The handling of LL 3122 is entirely characteristic of Wilson's work of the late 1750s and this canvas, which is the largest known

version of the design, may well be the *Lake Nemi* which Wilson exhibited, with 'its companion', at the Society of Artists in 1761. At least by 1832, and perhaps much earlier, it was paired with an identically sized version of *Diana and Actaeon*, a subject which Wilson had first painted in Rome around 1754.[7] When it was sold in 1859, LL 3122 was described in the catalogue as 'the famous picture'.

Besides LL 3122 and the Stourhead painting, two further autograph versions of the work which include the figures of Diana and Callisto are known,[8] together with several versions of the landscape with different figures.[9] In addition, Wilson painted the Diana and Callisto episode set against the landscape of Dolbadarn Castle and Snowdon. It seems likely that that work, one of a set of four large upright canvases commissioned by Henry Blundell in the mid-1760s,[10] was Wilson's last treatment of the theme.

PROVENANCE:
…Lord Northwick by 1832;[11] Phillips at Thirlestaine House 26 July 1859 (1195) bt. J. Daubeney; W. Daubeney; Christie 27 June 1881 (91) bt. in;…James Orrock and Sir J.D. Linton; Christie 25-27 April 1895 (322)[12] bt. in; Christie 4-6 June 1904 (147) bt. in; bt. from Orrock by Lever November 1904.[13]

EXHIBITIONS:
[?Society of Artists 1761 (137)]; Society of British Artists, Suffolk Street 1832 (34); *Loan Exhibition of Works by Richard Wilson* Tate Gallery 1925 (24); *Richard Wilson Loan Exhibition* Manchester City Art Gallery 1925 (55); *Peinture Anglaise* Musée d'Art Moderne Brussels 1929 (196); *Lord Leverhulme* RA 1980 (41).

REFERENCES:
1. See J.D. Reid: *The Oxford Guide to Classical Mythology in the Arts 1300-1990s* (1993) Vol.I, pp.281-5.
2. *Lord Leverhulme*, p.81.
3. e.g. *Monte Cavo* (Huntington Art Collections, San Marino); *Lake Nemi with Gensano* (Victoria and Albert Museum, repr. W.G. Constable: *Richard Wilson* (1953) pl.94a).
4. D. Solkin: 'Richard Wilson's Variations on a Theme by Gaspard Dughet', *Burlington Magazine* (July 1981) pp.410-4.
5. LL 3122 is unusual in lacking the shrine, which is visible in other versions of the work.
6. Solkin, *op. cit.*, and *Wilson*, exhibition catalogue, Tate Gallery (1982) p.192, cat.77, repr.
7. Constable, *op. cit.*, p.160, cat.17a.
8. Constable, *op. cit.*, pp.164-5, cat.24a: a) 30 × 39 in., West collection; b) 28 × 52 in., Leon collection. The latter, which Wilson originally painted for Standlynch, the house of Sir William Young, was sold at Sotheby 6 July 1977 (143).
9. Constable, *op. cit.*, p.208, cat.93a-93b.
10. Constable, *op. cit.*, p.164, cat.23b, now in Bristol Museum and Art Gallery.

11. Lent by Lord Northwick to the 1832 exhibition.
12. Described in the catalogue as from the collection of 'Lord Northbrook'.
13. 1904 Inventory p.1, no.12.

Richard Wilson
1713-1782

The Villa of Maecenas, Tivoli
LL 3548 (WHL 598, H 36)
oil on canvas, 124.5 × 171.5 cm
signed: *RW* (monogram; on rock by figures)

This is a version of the painting thought to have been commissioned from Wilson by the 8th Earl of Thanet following their visit to Tivoli in 1754 with the Earls of Pembroke and Essex and Viscount Bolingbroke (Tate Gallery, fig.77). A nearly contemporary memorandum which relates this occasion also describes the scene in some detail:

'The Ruins of Maecenas's Villa at Tivoli on the Bank of the River Anio which runs into the Tibur 20 miles distant from Rome. The building to the right of it among the Cypress Trees in a Convent of Jesuits. The Temple beneath that was built in honour to the God Tusis. The Spring which issues out of the Rock on the Left is the Fons Blandae of Horace whose Villa stood between the trees on the left fronting Maecenas's'.[1]

According to the artist's pupil, Joseph Farington, Wilson began the Thanet painting in Italy and completed it in England.[2] The composition became one of his most celebrated and it was the basis of numerous versions and variants.[3] LL 3548 has the same dimensions as its prototype and is virtually identical to it in design (even down to the treatment of the large rock in the right foreground and the fall of the light on the facade of the villa), arguing that it may have been undertaken as a straightforward copy. The relatively mechanical handling of the foliage and the uncharacteristically slick figures, which are perhaps not by Wilson, support this view. Other areas, however, seem of higher quality and

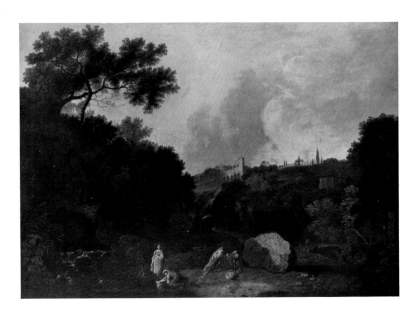

R. Wilson: *The Villa of Maecenas, Tivoli*
LL 3548

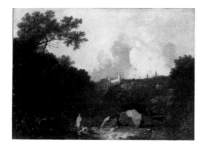

Fig.77
R.Wilson:
The Villa of Maecenas, Tivoli
© Tate Gallery London

they, together with the monogram, suggest that the work was supervised by Wilson and is at least partially autograph. One theory is that LL 3548 may have been made as a reference copy when the Thanet version was still in Wilson's studio, and that it served as the basis for the freer versions and those of different sizes which he and his assistants made in the mid-1760s and early 1770s.[4]

The so-called Villa of Maecenas, situated outside the Porta del Colle on the western edge of Tivoli, is thought to have been part of a temple of Hercules Victor dating from the 1st century BC. Its traditional association with the celebrated Roman patron of the arts

gave it particular appeal to Grand Tourists and Wilson introduced it into other Tivoli subjects and Italian capriccii without concern for topographical accuracy.[5] The memorandum referred to above implies that the present subject was based on a drawing which Wilson made on the spot; this drawing has not been identified but the two likeliest candidates appear to be a topographically moderately accurate distant view of the whole site with the river in the foreground (Tate Gallery, fig.78)[6] and a more fanciful design which, however, contains in the foreground what may be a group of visiting milordi and an artist sketching (Victoria and Albert Museum, fig.79).[7] These works suggest that Wilson changed the scenery considerably in the painting in order to classicise the composition.[8] Photographs of the view confirm that in reality, the slope is higher and steeper, and that the villa is situated below its crest, not upon it.

PROVENANCE:
…James Orrock by 1895;[9] Christie 25-27 April 1895 (306) bt. in; Christie 4 June 1904 (145), bt. in; bt. from Orrock by Lever November 1904.[10]

EXHIBITIONS:
Loan Exhibition of Works by Richard Wilson Tate Gallery 1925 (38); *Richard Wilson Loan Exhibition* Manchester City Art Gallery 1925 (56); *Richard Wilson and his Circle* Birmingham Museum and Art Gallery 1948-9 (58) and Tate Gallery 1949 (57).

REFERENCES:
1. W.G.Constable: *Richard Wilson* (1953) p.226 cites this memorandum in full. It was apparently written by Wilson's friend F. Macklay, for whom Wilson painted a smaller version of the subject (Brinsley Ford Collection). However, according to Anna Jameson: *Handbook to the Public Galleries* (1842) Vol.I, p.117, the memorandum was written by Wilson himself and given to Macklay.
2. K.Garlick, A. Macintyre and K. Cave, eds.: *The Diary of Joseph Farington* (1978-84) Vol.I, p.214; entry for 15 July 1794.
3. Constable, *loc. cit.*, lists a large number, some of which, however, may refer to a different *Villa of Maecenas* composition; to these should be added the version in the Sheldon Swope Art Museum, Terre Haute, Indiana USA (69.44). This painting's dimensions (47 × 56 in.) are different from all the versions cited by Constable; although (from a photograph) it may have been cut down at the sides and have originally measured the same as LL 3548 and other versions.

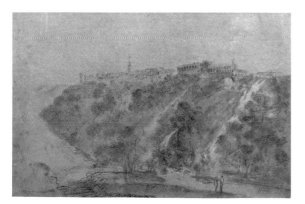

Fig.78
R.Wilson:
The Villa of Maecenas, Tivoli
© Tate Gallery London

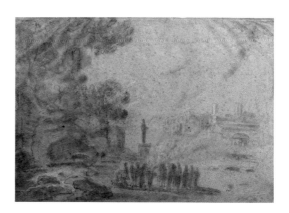

Fig.79
R.Wilson:
The Villa of Maecenas, Tivoli
V & A Picture Library

4. The upright version of the picture commissioned by Henry Blundell of Ince was worked on 1763-67; the version in Birmingham Museum and Art Gallery, which is the same size as LL 3548 is dated 1767; and Thomas Hastings's later etching of the smaller Ford version is inscribed *Painted by R. Wilson 1771* (Constable, *loc. cit.*).

5. For example *Tivoli, The Cascatelle*, repr. Constable, *op. cit.* pl.117a and *Landscape Capriccio with the Tomb of the Horatii and Curiatii and the Villa of Maecenas at Tivoli*, repr. D. Solkin: *Wilson*, exhibition catalogue, Tate Gallery (1982) p.188, cat.72.

6. Constable, *op. cit.*, pl.118a. M. Davies: *National Gallery Catalogues: The British School* (1946) p.174 observes that this work 'may be' the drawing made on the spot 'but has apparently not been claimed to be so'. Solkin, *op. cit.*, p.165 suggests that the drawing made on the spot may in fact be the study of a large tree, p.12 of Wilson's Italian sketchbook in the Yale Center for British Art, New Haven.

7. Constable, *op. cit.*, pl.118b.

8. Solkin, *op. cit.*, p.192 observes that '[Wilson's] classical design ultimately derives from the works of Gaspard Dughet (though perhaps with Claude-Joseph Vernet as an intermediary) and it is this clearly structured formula, rather than the actual topography, which has determined his arrangement of motifs'. He adds that the foreground and middle ground appears to be entirely invented.

9. The earlier provenance of LL 3548 cannot definitively be established. Farington, in his diary, 4 March and 8 May 1801, refers to a version measuring 4 ft. 10 × 6 ft. 5 framed (i.e. the size of LL 3548 with a 5-in. wide frame) being sold by Dr John Purling on 16 February 1801 and as having been sold by Wilson himself to Captain Baillie; but this might refer to several of the versions which are the same size as LL 3548. The painting was bought at the 1801 sale for £246.15.- by 'Sherlock [or] Leader Junior the Coachmaker' (B. Fredericksen, ed.: *The Index of Paintings Sold in the British Isles in the Nineteenth Century* (1988-present) Part 1, p.831); this is presumably the W. Leader who lent a painting of the subject to the BI in 1814 (114). A *Villa of Maecenas* ('The Ruins of a Fortress on a Rock, at a foot of which a river flows from a waterfall in the foreground, women are getting water at a cascade, near some fragments of sculpture – a beautiful, clear, picture') was in the Thomas Wright sale, Christie 7 June 1845 (48) bt. Burland (136 gns.). LL 3548 bears a label stating that it was formerly in Arthur Sanderson's collection; a version of the work was in Sanderson's sale at Christie, 3 July 1908 (87) 'from the collection of A. Andrews Esq 1888' and was bt. Tooth (100 gns.); however, by this date LL 3548 was already in Lever's possession. It is nevertheless perhaps worth observing that Orrock and Sanderson were close friends and Orrock and Andrews neighbours in Bedford Square.

10. 1904 Inventory p.1, no.15.

Richard Wilson
1713-1782

The Unransomed
LL 3549 (WHL 638, H 46)
oil on canvas, 101.5 × 127 cm

The Unransomed is a painting of uncertain date, one of a number of banditti subjects loosely derived from the works of Salvator Rosa. Two of the figures, the kneeling woman and the corpse beside her, appear in what is thought to be the first work in this sequence, *The Murder*, which Wilson painted for Ralph Howard, later Viscount Wicklow, in 1752 (National Museum and Gallery of Wales, Cardiff; fig.80). They recur, and the two figures at the left appear, in another early composition, the *Landscape with Banditti* of about 1754.[1] In its general handling, however, LL 3549 appears stylistically closer to a number of Wilson's dramatic mythological works of the second half of the 1760s, especially *Meleager and Atalanta* (Tate Gallery, fig.81).

In terms of design, LL 3549 is especially closely related to a smaller sketch, also undated, now in the collection of Brinsley Ford (fig.82). The latter was engraved as *The Murder* by Thomas Hastings with the

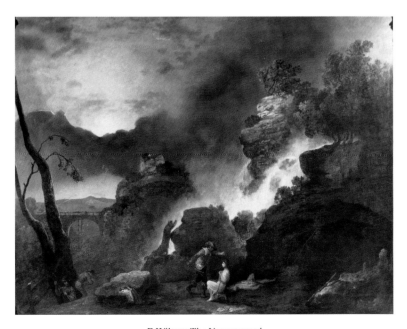

R. Wilson: *The Unransomed*
LL 3548

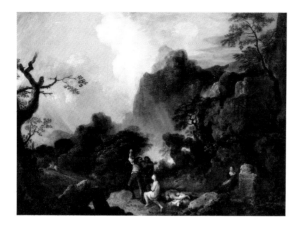

Fig.80
R. Wilson: *The Murder*
National Museums and Galleries of Wales

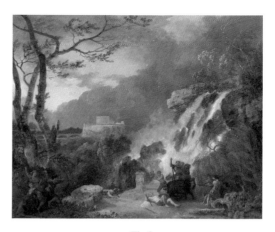

Fig.81
R. Wilson: *Meleager and Atalanta*
© Tate Gallery London

inscription 'This composition gave rise to the well-known one of Meleager'.[2] The phrase 'gave rise', together with Hastings's description of the work as 'a sketch for after consideration'[3] perhaps indicate his belief that there was a substantial lapse of time between it and the *Meleager*. If the precise interval remains open to question, it nevertheless seems fair to argue that the Ford sketch and LL 3549 represent an intermediate stage in the development of the *Meleager* composition from the banditti scenes of the early 1750s.[4] Of the two works, it seems certain that the sketch pre-dates LL3549; in the former the

central group of the 1752 *Murder* appears virtually intact, whereas in LL 3549 the bandit wielding the sword is a newly-invented figure which does not occur in any related work. How closely the two works resembled each other in terms of the handling of paint is now hard to judge owing to LL 3549's extensively restored condition.[5]

The picture's present, now traditional, title was apparently first given to it at the 1906 Royal Academy exhibition.

PROVENANCE:
…James Orrock by 1895; Christie 25-27 April 1895 (323) bt. in; Christie 4-6 June 1904 (146) bt. in; bt. from Orrock by Lever November 1904.[6]

EXHIBITIONS:
[?BI 1817 (20) *Storm with Banditti*, lent by Sir A. Hume]; [?Liverpool Royal Institution 1823 (112): *Fall of Narni, Banditti*, lent by Winstanley]; *Old Masters* RA 1906 (85); *Richard Wilson and His Circle* Birmingham Museum and Art Gallery 1948-49 (56) and Tate Gallery 1949 (55).

REFERENCES:
1. Repr. W.G. Constable: *Richard Wilson* (1953) pl.13a; the figures are not visible in this illustration but do show up in a photograph of a version unrecorded by Constable, in the Ulster Museum, Belfast.

Wilson's related drawing of this subject (*op. cit.*, pl.13b), now in the National Museum and Gallery of Wales, Cardiff, was made for the Earl of Dartmouth in 1754.
2. Thomas Hastings: *Etchings from the Works of Richard Wilson, with some Memoirs of his Life &c …* (1825) pl.32; quoted by Constable, *op. cit.*, p.158.
3. Constable, *loc. cit.*
4. When Brinsley Ford first published his painting, he suggested that its stylistic and colouristic affinities to the work of Sebastiano Ricci, to which Wilson had been exposed in Venice in 1751, marked it as one of the first paintings that Wilson made in Rome and as a trial for the 1752 *Murder*. (B. Ford: 'Richard Wilson in Rome 1 – The Wicklow Wilsons', *Burlington Magazine* (May 1951) pp.157-67). Subsequently (ms. catalogue notes on his *Murder*, unpublished, copy in gallery files) Ford adopted the view also taken by W.G. Constable (*loc. cit.*) that it postdates the banditti subjects of the early 1750s.
5. 'The painting has been executed over an asphaltum imprimatura, more pronounced in the lower half of the picture. This underpainting probably caused some trouble, in the appearance of brown cracks, quite early in the life of the painting. The main damage was undoubtedly done, however, when the painting was re-lined. The impasto, forming the waterfall, draperies, etc. had been pressed down; the asphaltum, under the action of heat would assist in this.

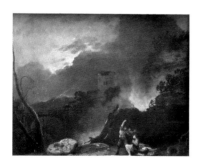

Fig.82
R. Wilson: *The Murder*
Sir Brinsley Ford; photograph courtesy
Courtauld Institute of Art

The thinly painted areas of the sky and vapour from the waterfall had been worn away from countless small areas by excessive pressure, again assisted by the asphaltum under the action of heat. These areas were completely overpainted and had become very dark and discoloured. I have revived the impasto as far as possible, and have restored the damage in each individual damaged area' … (J. Coburn Witherop to R. Fastnedge, letter, 18 November 1961, gallery files).

6.   1904 Inventory p.1, no.13.

after
Richard Wilson
1713-1782

On the River Arno
LL 3575 (WHL 141, H 104)
oil on canvas, 64 × 77 cm

This is a close copy, of respectable quality but not by Wilson himself, of a subject which exists in four chief types and many versions.[1] What may have been the prime version of this type (Petworth House, National

Trust, fig.83) was lent by the Earl of Egremont in 1814 to the British Institution, whose exhibitions were frequented by copyists. Wilson's earliest version of the subject may well have been the upright work supposedly commissioned by Thomas Worsley of Platt Hall Manchester, which is signed and dated 1764.[2]

The precise location of Wilson's view has not been identified. Thomas Hastings seems to have been the first to state that it was on the Arno, but he titled his etching of the subject (which has a few variations in the foreground) *View in Italy*.[3] It has also been known, less plausibly, as *On the Tiber*, and (without any justification) as *Lake Nemi* (see below) and *Tivoli*.[4]

PROVENANCE:
…James Orrock (? by 1895 and certainly by 1903[5]); Christie 4-6 June 1904 (151) bt. in; bt. from Orrock by Lever November 1904.[6]

REFERENCES:
1.   W. G. Constable: *Richard Wilson* (1953) pp. 213-215.

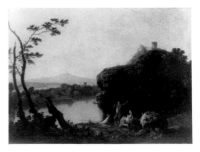

2.   Constable, *loc. cit.*, and pl.101a. This version is stated to have been based on a sketch made by Wilson on the spot during his visit to Italy.
3.   Thomas Hastings: *Etchings from the Works of Richard Wilson with some Memoirs of His Life &c* … (1825) pp.11-12 and pl.9.
4.   Constable, *op. cit.*, p.215.
5.   LL 3575 was probably lot 90 in the Orrock-Linton sale, Christie 25-27 April 1895, titled *Lake Nemi*, bt. in (52 gns.). This work is listed by Constable, *op. cit.*, p.209, under Wilson's recorded *Lake Nemi* compositions and identified as probably the work measuring 24 × 30 in. which Orrock lent to the *Old Masters* exhibition at the RA 1884 (57). However, the description there, 'The lake is seen through an opening in the trees on a height overlooking it; beyond are wooded heights and buildings, with the Campagna and Rome in the distance; sunset sky' cannot be regarded as conclusive proof that it is LL3575. What was presumably the same work was lent by Orrock to Edinburgh in 1888 and the Grosvenor Gallery 1889. LL 3575 was given the title *Lake Nemi* when reproduced in Webber, Vol.1, fp. 158.
6.   1904 Inventory p.1, no.18.

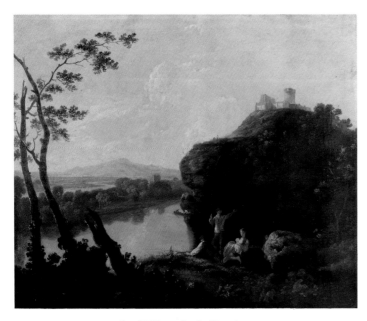

after R. Wilson: *On the River Arno*
LL3575

Johann Zoffany
1733-1810

Robert Baddeley as Moses in 'The School for Scandal'
LL 3535 (LP 32)
oil on canvas, 76.5 × 61 cm

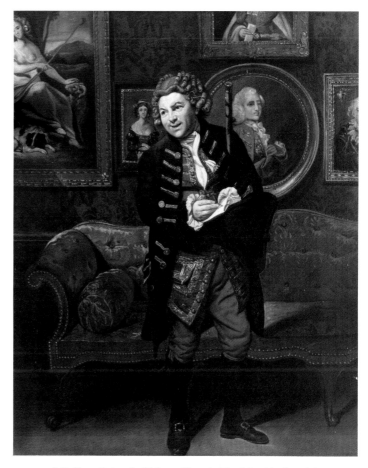

J. Zoffany: *Robert Baddeley as Moses in 'The School for Scandal'*
LL 3535

In Act IV scene I of Sheridan's play, the impecunious Charles Surface, assisted by his friend Careless, sells his family portraits in order to raise money to pay his debts to the money-lender Moses. Moses has brought along a likely buyer, Master Premium – in reality Charles's nabob uncle Oliver.

The part of Moses, drawn by Sheridan primarily from a Jewish money-lender, Jacob Nathan Moses, to whom he himself owed money,[1] was created by the actor Robert Baddeley (1733-1794). Formerly in the entourage of the actor-manager Samuel Foote and noted for his assumption of low comic roles, Baddeley played Moses over two hundred times at Drury Lane between the play's opening night on 8 May 1777 and his death. It was the rôle with which he was most closely identified.[2]

That Baddeley is represented in LL 3535 is indicated both by the work's provenance (see below) and from comparison of the actor's features with other portraits of him.[3] It is less certain that he actually commissioned the work. It is noteworthy that a scene is repre-sented in which Moses effectively has no more than a watching brief, but one which would allow Zoffany imaginatively to re-create the paintings described by Sheridan.[4] In the scene concerned Moses does not act as the auctioneer nor indeed take centre-stage at all. Nevertheless, it is possible that the portrait reflects elements of Baddeley's inter-pretation of the part in terms of stage business (here he seems to be carrying the rolled parchment Surface family tree which is used as an auctioneer's hammer, and ticking off works in a catalogue[5]); and more particularly in terms of costume. This, compared with what Moses has traditionally worn in later productions, is unusually rich and elegant,[6] but Baddeley was notoriously dandyish[7] and Zoffany probably accurately depicts what he wore in the part.

The present canvas has traditionally been identified as the painting exhibited by Zoffany at the Royal Academy in 1781, where it was titled *A Character In the School for Scandal*.[8] The work was widely admired in the press: typical was the notice in the *Morning Chronicle and London Advertiser*, which said that 'Baddely, in the School for Scandal, by Mr Zoffany, is full of expression and humour, as well as correct painting, in which department and close imitation, Mr Z has no rival'; while the critic of the *St. James's Chronicle* wrote: 'I am glad to see this artist come back again to his old favourite stile, and draw from the English Stage subjects for his pencil'.[9] That the exhibited work was LL 3535, however, is far from clear, for mentioned in a list drawn up by Baddeley's executors and dated 22 January 1795, of the *Books, Paintings, Drawings, Prints, & c bequeathed by the late Mr Robert*

*Baddeley (In Future) to the
Theatrical Fund, incorporated at the
Theatre Royal, Drury Lane,* is *Mr
Baddeley in the Character of Moses, a
Copy, from Zophany.*[10] No such copy
is now traceable at Drury Lane
Theatre,[11] and moreover, LL 3535 is
stated to have been presented by
Baddeley's executors to an official of
the theatre (see provenance below);
so that although no other version of
the portrait has come to light it is
distinctly possible that LL 3535 is
a copy rather than Zoffany's
original.[12] On the other hand,
the undoubtedly rather wooden
handling of the figure in LL 3535 may
simply be indicative of Zoffany's
declining interest in the genre of
theatrical portraiture: the portrait of
Baddeley was his last work of this
type before his departure for India
in 1783.[13]

PROVENANCE:
Robert Baddeley; presented by his
executors to William Dunn (1783-1835),
Treasurer and Secretary of the
Committee and Proprietors of Drury
Lane Theatre; given by him to Thomas
Field Savory (d. 1847); his nephew
John Savory;[14] by descent to Keith
Hutchison;[15] Christie 12 December 1930
(130) bt. Gooden & Fox for the Trustees
of the Lady Lever Art Gallery
(£639.19.6).

EXHIBITIONS:
[?RA 1781 (246)]; *Spring Exhibition*
Whitechapel Art Gallery 1906 (122);
Shakespeare Exhibition Whitechapel Art
Gallery 1910 (50); *Liverpool Autumn
Exhibition* Walker Art Gallery, Liverpool
1933 (31); *Johann Zoffany* Arts Council
1960-61 (17); *The Painter and the Stage*
Chichester 1962 (79); *The Georgian
Playhouse* Arts Council 1975 (32).

REFERENCES:
1. C. Price, ed.: *The Dramatic Works of
Richard Brinsley Sheridan* (1973) Vol.1,
pp.302-3. Sheridan was widely thought to
have based the character on Benjamin
Hopkins, Chamberlain of the City of
London and a well-known money lender
(Price, *op. cit.*, pp.300-2).

2. For Baddeley see especially
P.H. Highfill Jr, K.A. Burnim and
E.A. Langhans: *A Biographical
Dictionary of Actors, Actresses, Musicians,
Dancers, Managers, and Other Stage
Personnel in London, 1660-1800* (1973-
93) Vol.1, pp.196-202.
3. G. Ashton, K.A. Burnim and
A. Wilton: *Pictures in the Garrick Club*
(1997) pp.13-15 reproduces five further
portraits, by Zoffany and Samuel de
Wilde among others.
4. The paintings are, from left to right:
'My Great Aunt Deborah done by
Kneller thought to be in his best manner;
and a very formidable likeness – There
She is you See – A Shepherdess feeding
her flock – you shall have her for five
pounds Ten – the Sheep are worth the
Money'; a lady cousin of Deborah's 'done
some time ago-when Beaux wore Wigs,
and the Ladies wore their own Hair'; an
oval portrait of Uncle Oliver himself
('that ill-looking little Fellow over the
Settee'), with above it 'a Grandfather of
my Mother's, a learned judge, well known
on the Western Circuit'; and finally 'my
Great uncle Sir Richard Raviline –
a Marvellous good General in his Day
I assure you – He served in all the Duke
of Marlborough's Wars; and got that cut
over his Eye at the Battle of Malplaquet'.
For further notes and references on the
scene see Price, *op. cit.*, pp.404-9.
5. E. Morris and M. Evans: *Lady Lever
Art Gallery Port Sunlight: Catalogue of
Foreign Works* (1983), p.25.
6. B. Shuttleworth, quoted in the
editorial, *Theatre Notebook*, Vol.6, no.1
(October – December 1951) p.1.
7. Highfill, Burnim and Langhans, *op.
cit.*, p.197.
8. The identification of the painting
exhibited at the 1781 Royal Academy as a
portrait of Baddeley was apparently first
made by A. Graves: *The Royal Academy
Exhibitors 1769-1904* (1905-6), Vol.8,
p.413.
9. *Morning Chronicle and London
Advertiser* (10 May 1781) p.2; *St. James's
Chronicle* (5-8 May 1781) p.4. See also
*The London Courant and Westminster
Chronicle* (8 May 1781), the *Whitehall
Evening Post* (1-3 May 1781) p.2 and the
Public Advertiser (2 May 1781) for brief
reviews of Zoffany's painting.
10. Information from J. Bisset, Secretary

of the Drury Lane Theatrical Fund, letter,
24 October 1995, gallery files.
11. Bisset, *loc. cit.*
12. Highfill, Burnim and Langhans, *op.
cit.*, p.201 state that the exhibited picture
is 'now [i.e. in 1973] the property of the
family of Mrs Keith Hutchison, whose
ancestor received it from the Treasurer of
Drury Lane Theatre', but this may simply
be a confusion with LL 3535. Another
painting bequeathed by Baddeley to the
Drury Lane Theatrical fund; but actually
disposed of privately by William Dunn, is
Zoffany's unfinished portrait of David
Garrick (Garrick Club) (Ashton, Burnim
and Wilton *op. cit.*, p.138, cat.249).
13. *The Georgian Playhouse*, exhibition
catalogue, Arts Council (1975) cat.32.
14. The provenance this far is given in
a letter from E.T. Smith of Drury Lane
Theatre to *The Era*, written 28 and
printed 29 January 1854. A cutting of it
is pasted to the back of LL 3535.
P. Fitzgerald: *History of the Garrick Club*
(1904), p.154 stated however only that
'Baddeley gave his portrait by Zoffany
to a member of the Savory family'.
15. That the Hutchisons were descended
from the Savory family is stated in the
Christie sale catalogue, 12 December
1930, p.30.

British School

A Man in Armour

LL 3159 (WHL 3785)
oil on canvas, 76 × 63.5 cm

The work was purchased by Lever
as a portrait of King William III by
Godfried Schalken dating from 1688.
Comparison of the sitter's features
with those in the Royal portraits by
Lely and Wissing casts doubt on this
identification, and current opinion is
the work is English, of an unknown
sitter, painted in the period 1690-
1700.[1] The original oval painted
edge has been extended all round by
a later hand.

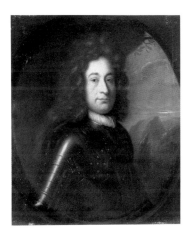

British School:
A Man in Armour
LL 3159

PROVENANCE:
… H.J. Gaunt; Christie 28 April 1919 (134)
bt. Gooden & Fox for Lever (22 gns.).

REFERENCE:
1. M. Rogers, letter, 20 October 1980,
gallery files.

British School

Portrait of a Lady in a Brown Dress

LL 3164 (WHL 2859)
oil on canvas, 53 × 39.5 cm

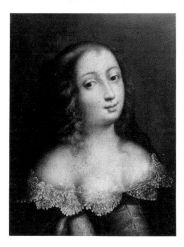

British School:
Portrait of a Lady in a Brown Dress
LL 3164

Lever purchased LL 3164 without
attribution. Although the handling of
paint is crude, there is no real reason
to doubt that the work is an authentic
seventeenth-century picture. It has
been dated to the period 1640-1660.[1]
The black mourning veil which the
sitter wears with her rather extreme
décolletage suggests the work is
a *vanitas* painting rather than
a portrait proper. LL 3164 has been
accepted as possibly British[2]
although it is not certainly so, and
a label on the reverse describes it
as 'French school'.

PROVENANCE:
… Mrs Milbank; Christie 14 July 1916
(141, part); bt. Gooden & Fox for Lever
(£23.2.-).

REFERENCES:
1. Aileen Ribeiro, verbally,
26 February 1998.
2. Ribeiro, *ibid*.

British School

A Young Girl Gathering Honeysuckle

LL 3166 (WHL 64, HH 27)
oil on canvas, 119 × 93.5 cm

When acquired by Lever, the work
was called 'Early English'. On its
transfer to the gallery it was ascribed
to Gainsborough,[1] and it was later
re-attributed to Prince Hoare (1755-
1834).[2] On stylistic grounds, the
former attribution is unacceptable;
the attribution to Hoare has been
described as 'very plausible'[3] but in
the current state of knowledge of his
work it must remain conjectural. The
costume suggests a date of the late
1770s or early 1780s[4] when Hoare
was briefly active as a portraitist.[5]

The painting was cleaned and
restored in 1959. It may have been
cut down, either at this time or
previously, since the dimensions
are not those of a standard portrait
canvas and the figure seems
awkwardly placed and over-large in
the design. The work may be by more
than one hand, for the face is quite
delicately painted whereas the

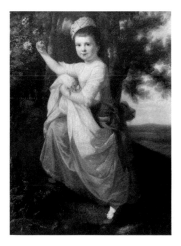

British School:
A Young Girl Gathering Honeysuckle
LL 3166

remainder (especially the hat) has the air of an afterthought and is much more coarse in execution.

PROVENANCE:
…James Orrock; bought from Orrock by Lever 1910.[6]

REFERENCES:
1. The authorship of this attribution is unknown.
2. Tatlock, p.54.
3. Evelyn Newby, letter, 7 July 1998, gallery files.
4. Aileen Ribeiro, verbally, 26 February 1998.
5. For an outline of Hoare's career, see Ellis Waterhouse: *Dictionary of British 18th Century Painters* (1981) pp.172-3. It has to be said that the portrait reproduced by Waterhouse is not at all like LL3166, and nor are the portraits by Hoare at Stourhead. An alternative possibility is that LL3166 is by the Rev. Matthew William Peters (1742-1814), who is noted for is portraits of young girls and also for his richly-worked surfaces.
6. 1910 Inventory p.32, valued at £750.

British School

St. James's Palace and Pall Mall
LL 3564 (WHL 2349, TM 146)
oil on canvas, 59 × 95.5 cm

The view is eastwards up Pall Mall, laid out in the late 17th century. At the far end, the spire of the church of St. Martin's-in-the-Fields, rebuilt by James Gibbs in 1722-6, is visible. To the right is the main gatehouse of St. James's Palace, built for Henry VIII in 1532-40. The changing of the guard is being witnessed by groups of onlookers.

Lever acquired the work and its companion, *Queen Square, Bloomsbury* (later sold), as by 'Hayes'. This artist is unidentified, and the name is probably a misprint for Dayes,[1] and intended for the topographical watercolourist Edward Dayes (1763-1804), who however, cannot have been responsible for LL 3564. Subsequently the work was ascribed to Samuel Scott (1702-72),[2] whose name was a catch-all for this type of painting in the general period 1920-70; it is not characteristic of his work either. LL 3564 is almost certainly by the same hand as LL 3565 (below), which is based on an engraving by Thomas Bowles after a work by Canaletto and is probably by one of the latter's English followers.[3] LL 3564 seems also to derive from a print by Bowles,[4] and probably too dates from the mid-1750s.

PROVENANCE:
…Sir William Augustus Fraser; Christie 3 December 1900 (62) bt. Agnew for Lever (42 gns. with companion).

REFERENCES:
1. This is suggested by a correction in the auctioneer's copy of the 1900 sale catalogue (Christie's archives).
2. The companion view was sold as by Scott (see Appendix 1), and LL 3564 has hitherto been regarded as by Scott within the gallery. Tatlock did not catalogue the painting.
3. The name most frequently associated with this type of work is William James (flourished 1754-1771), for whom see M. Liversedge and J. Farrington, eds.: *Canaletto & England*, exhibition catalogue, Birmingham Museum and Art Gallery (1993-94) pp.130-1, cat.57. The work by James discussed here, *Horse Guards Parade from St. James's Park*, is stylistically close to LL 3564. Other artists whose names are sometimes applied to topographical scenes of this type include Daniel Turner (flourished 1782-1817) and Sir John Paul (1775-1857).
4. Photograph in the Witt Library; however, no copy of the print itself has been traced.

British School

Northumberland House, Charing Cross
LL 3565 (WHL 111)
oil on canvas, 75.5 × 126 cm

The view is eastwards up the Strand, from a point today close to Landseer's Lions in Trafalgar

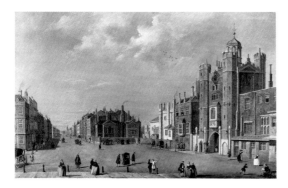

British School: *St James's Palace and Pall Mall*
LL 3564

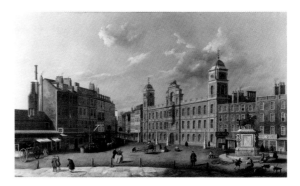

British School: *Northumberland House, Charing Cross*
LL 3565

Square. The facade of Northumberland House, during the 17th and 18th centuries the London residence of the Dukes of Northumberland, but demolished in 1873 in order to accommodate Northumberland Avenue, dominates the right-hand side of the view. This façade was erected in 1748-1752[1] and LL 3565 was probably painted shortly afterwards. The equestrian statue is Le Sueur's *Charles I*, erected on the site in 1675-77. To the left is the Golden Cross coaching inn.[2]

Lever acquired LL 3565, without attribution, amongst a group of topographical items. Shortly after its arrival at the gallery it and a companion picture, titled *Old London Bridge* (later sold) were ascribed to Samuel Scott (1702-1772).[3] The wooden and pedestrian handling of LL 3565 argues against it being an autograph work by Scott, and it is almost certainly copied from the engraving by T. Bowles, published in 1753, of Canaletto's *Northumberland House* (1752-53; Dukes of Northumberland, Alnwick Castle; fig.84). Other artists identified with this subject include Joseph Nickolls (active 1726-55) whose known works are of finer quality than LL 3565;[4] and Canaletto's supposed follower William James (active 1754-1771).[5]

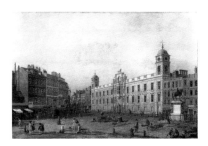

Fig.84
A. Canaletto:
Northumberland House
Duke of Northumberland;
photograph Courtauld Institute of Art

PROVENANCE:
…[? William Morris, of Newhaven, Sussex, March 1906[6]];… B.T. Batsford, London; bt. by Lever September 1913 (£60 with companion).

REFERENCES:
1. R. Dorment: *British Painting in the Philadelphia Museum of Art* (1986) p.438, cat.121.
2. Today No.8 Duncannon Street is known as Golden Cross House.
3. Scott is known to have exhibited London Bridge subjects; another version of LL 3565, attributed to Scott, was published in *Connoisseur* (August 1923) pp.191-4; then owned by the Marquess of Sligo.
4. A version of Nickolls's *A View of Charing Cross and Northumberland House*, 20 × 30 in., said to be signed and dated 1746 (but see text above and footnote 1) was exhibited in *Manners and Morals*, Tate Gallery 1987 (115); a larger version is in the Yale Center for British Art, New Haven.
5. For James see above, under LL 3564, note 3. A 29 × 46 in. canvas very close to LL 3565 and replicating the foreground figures and incidents, attributed to him (but dated 1750, i.e. before the completion of the façade) was reproduced in *Apollo* (May 1942); what is apparently the same work was reproduced in *Connoisseur* (September 1966) p.40. Another version attributed to James, 12 × 16 in., is in the Yale Center for British Art, New Haven. A further version, 22½ × 35½ in., also very close to LL 3565 although with some differences in the figures and in the positioning of Le Sueur's statue, is in the Philadelphia Museum of Art. This work entered the Philadelphia collection with a companion *Old Somerset House from the River Thames*, a direct copy of a painting by Canaletto; both these works are catalogued at Philadelphia as 'English School after Canaletto' (Dorment, *loc. cit.*). For a full list of versions of the design see W.G. Constable and J.G. Links: *Canaletto* (2nd ed., 1976) Vol.2, pp.412-13.
6. On the reverse of LL 3565 is a stencil referring to property of William Morris consigned to Christie in March 1906; not sold by Christie but forwarded to Messrs Foster's.

British School

Windmills on a Dutch River
LL 3693 (WHL 2888, HH 32)
oil on canvas, 156 × 106.5 cm

Lever acquired LL 3693 as 'Cotman school'. The painting resembles the work of neither John Sell Cotman (1782-1842)[1] nor his son Miles Edmund Cotman (1810-58) and is probably not by any Norwich artist.[2] It is, nevertheless, a work of considerable proficiency. The draughtsmanship of the mill interior is highly accomplished, and the whole scene is well-observed in detail. The work, for which no convincing attribution has emerged,[3] can be dated about 1830-50.

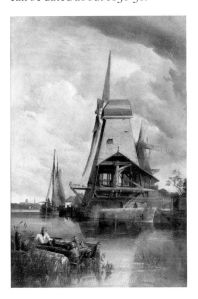

British School:
Windmills on a Dutch River
LL 3693

PROVENANCE:
…James Orrock; bt. from Orrock by Lever 1910.[4]

REFERENCES:
1. Tatlock, p.90, called LL 3693 'after Cotman'; W.G. Constable (note in gallery files) described it as 'not by Cotman; a large empty pastiche on his work'.

2. Norma Watt, Norwich Castle Museum, verbally, 20 April 1998.

3. One very speculative suggestion is that LL 3693 is the work of George Balmer (for whom see LL 2909 and LL 3700 above); Orrock seems to have had access to Balmer's work and Balmer exhibited numerous Dutch river scenes at the Society of British Artists, Suffolk Street, between 1835 and 1840 including *On the Lower Rhine Emmerich* and *On the Old Rhine near Leyden* in the former year and *Dutch River Scene* in the latter one.

4. 1910 Inventory p.33, valued at £60.

British School

Portrait of a Man (called 'Lord Melbourne')

LL 3717 (WHL 2304, HH 80)
oil on millboard, 32 × 26.5 cm (oval)

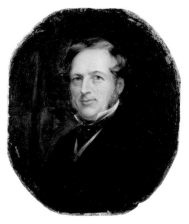

British School:
*Portrait of a Man
(called 'Lord Melbourne')*
LL 3717

When acquired by Lever, LL 3717 was called 'Lawrence school' and said to represent William Lamb, 2nd Viscount Melbourne (1779-1848). The work is not related to any of the known portraits of Melbourne by Lawrence[1] and its stylistic resemblance to Lawrence's portraiture is minimal. The sitter's resemblance to

Lord Melbourne as portrayed in later life by Landseer (1836; National Portrait Gallery), Hayter (1838; formerly collection of Lord Brocket), and Partridge (1844; National Portrait Gallery) – who are alike in giving him a square head and notably bushy eyebrows – is tenuous and largely confined to the prominent side-whiskers.[2] LL 3717 can be dated to the period 1841-57 on the basis of the wording of a Winsor & Newton label on the reverse.[3] The edges of the curved sections of the millboard are noticeably rough and suggest that the support has been cut down, but the painting may have been executed originally as an oval. No satisfactory attribution has emerged.

PROVENANCE:
…James Orrock; bt. from Orrock by Lever 1910.[4]

REFERENCES:
1. K. Garlick: *Sir Thomas Lawrence, a Complete Catalogue* (1989) p.218, cats. 459 a-c.
2. For a full iconography of Lord Melbourne see R. Ormond: *Early Victorian Portraits* (1973) Vol.I, pp.310-15.
3. I.K. Garrett, Technical Director, Winsor & Newton, letter, 8 April 1998, gallery files.
4. 1910 Inventory p.38, valued at £10.

British School

Portrait of a Gentleman in a Black Coat[1]

LL 3732 (WHL 610, HH 271)
oil (on canvas?) 67.5 × 54.5 cm

The painting was purchased by Lever without attribution. It is described as a head and shoulders portrait of a man with dark hair and side whiskers facing three-quarters to the left, wearing a high-collared coat and white cravat. The portrait dates from the early 19th century.[2]

PROVENANCE:
…James Orrock; bt. from Orrock by Lever 1910.[3]

REFERENCES:
1. The painting was last recorded on loan in 1937 and has not been traced. No photograph is available.
2. Note by A.C. Tait, gallery files.
3. 1910 Inventory p.65, valued at £20.

Appendix I

*Paintings by British artists born before 1810
formerly owned by Lever but not now in the Lady Lever Art Gallery*

This list has been compiled from the so-called WHL inventory, begun by Lever in 1913 to replace and incorporate his various existing inventories, and thereafter used for all new fine art acquisitions up until his death in 1925. Early British oils which Lever disposed of before 1913 have also been included, where it has been possible to trace these.

Attributions are those given to the works in Lever's time, except where the attribution was changed from a foreign to a British artist after Lever's death. In a number of cases titles have been simplified or given in the form used at the work's disposal, rather than its acquisition. The method of disposal is given where this is in the public domain. By far the majority of the works were sold by Lever's executors in a series of sales held in Lancashire, London and New York in 1925-26, and by the Trustees of the Lady Lever Art Gallery in 1958 and 1961.

Works are listed alphabetically by artist and then in inventory order number. Sizes are given in inches where they are known. A number of unattributed works have been included where the description or other circumstantial evidence indicates they are early British oils; those works where a reasonable element of doubt exists have been excluded.

Thomas Barker
1769-1847

*Quarrymen: in
a Wooded Landscape*
WHL 571
10 × 11 in.
Sold Christie 21 April 1961 (141)

*A Wooded Lane with a Peasant
Approaching a House*
WHL 2305
5½ × 6 in.
Sold Christie 21 April 1961 (142)

Charles Baxter
1809-1879

*A Bacchante (A Fancy Portrait
of Miss Ellen Coles)*
WHL 4397
23½ × 19½ in.
Sold Knight, Frank & Rutley
16 November 1925 (1069)

Sir William Beechey
1753-1839

Portrait of a Woman
WHL 670
30 × 24 in.
Sold Christie 14 April 1961 (140)

**'P. Bendixon'
[? S. Bendixen**
1786-1864]

The Flower Stall
WHL 4248
11½ × 9½ in.
Sold Anderson Galleries
11 May 1926 (3)

Richard Parkes Bonington
1802-1828

Waggon on the Sands, Normandy
WHL 93
7 × 10 in.
Sold Anderson Galleries
17 February 1926 (6)

A View on the Seine
WHL 128
11 × 15½ in.
Sold Anderson Galleries
17 February 1926 (5)

*Château of the Duchesse
De Berri from the Garonne*
WHL 129
9½ × 14¾ in.
Sold Anderson Galleries
17 February 1926 (7)

*Shore Scene with Small
Sailing Craft*
WHL 558
6¾ × 8¾ in.
Sold Christie 7 April 1961
(192 part)

*Coast Scene with Boats
and Figures*
WHL 585
6¾ × 8¾ in.
Sold Christie 7 April 1961
(192 part)

*A Moored Sailing Barge
with Figures at a Repast*
WHL 611
20 × 29½ in.
Sold Christie 21 April 1961 (82)

*A Quay Scene with Boats,
View of a City in the Distance*
WHL 690
17 × 30 in.
Sold Knight, Frank & Rutley
15 June 1926 (4)

A Woman in a Low Neck Dress
WHL 2032
4¾ × 3¾ in.
Sold Knight, Frank & Rutley,
14 July 1926 (3)

A Woman in a Low Neck Dress
WHL 2033
4¾ × 3¾ in.
Sold Knight, Frank & Rutley,
14 July 1926 (2)

A Woman in a Low Neck Dress
WHL 2034
4¾ × 3¾ in.
Sold Knight, Frank & Rutley
14 July 1926 (1)

*Large and Small Sailing Craft
Offshore*
WHL 2313
27½ × 36 in.
Sold Christie 21 April 1961 (140)

A Lady Standing at a Table
WHL 2316
4¾ × 6¾ in.
Sold Knight, Frank & Rutley
14 July 1926 (4)

Scene in a Painter's Studio
WHL 2325
8½ × 7¼ in.
Sold Knight, Frank & Rutley
14 July 1926 (5)

Hay Barges on Calm Water
WHL 2337
24 × 36 in.
Sold Knight, Frank & Rutley
15 June 1926 (10)

An Old Lady, Seated
WHL 2341
11½ × 9½ in.
Sold Knight, Frank & Rutley
14 July 1926 (11)

Two Fisherwomen
WHL 4526
12½ × 17¼ in.
Sold Anderson Galleries
17 February 1926 (8)

Sir Augustus Wall Callcott
1779-1844

A Coast Scene
WHL 92
6¼ × 8¼ in.
Sold Christie 6 June 1958 (102)

*A Riverside Farm, with Boys
Sailing Boat*
WHL 2338
32 × 42 in.
Sold Christie 6 June 1958 (101)

George Cattermole
1800-1868

Entrance to an Abbey
WHL 2303
19 × 30 in.

Alfred Edward Chalon
1780-1860

*Queen Victoria
in Coronation Robes*
WHL 3055
Presented to Hall i'th'Wood,
Bolton

George Chambers
1803-1840

*A Fishing Smack off
Scarborough Castle*
WHL 600
48 × 66 in.
Sold Christie 6 June 1958 (103)

The Barge
WHL 2324
8¼ × 11¼ in.
Sold Christie 6 June 1958 (104)

Giovanni Batista Cipriani
1727-1785

Paris and Oenone
WHL 4399
77 × 56 in.
Sold Anderson Galleries
17 February 1926 (18a)

William Collins
1788-1847

Out of School
WHL.182
10½ × 15½ in.
Sold Anderson Galleries
17 February 1926 (21)

Trying on Father's Sea Boots
WHL 633
25½ × 32 in.
Sold Christie 6 June 1958 (105)

John Constable
1776-1837

A Riverside Village
WHL 41
7½ × 11¾ in.
Sold Anderson Galleries
17 February 1926 (39)

A Lane with Overhanging Trees
WHL 43
7½ × 5½ in.
Sold Anderson Galleries
17 February 1926 (25)

A Study of Trees
WHL 44
6 × 4¾ in.
Sold Anderson Galleries
17 February 1926 (36)

A Woody Landscape
WHL 56
7½ × 5¾ in.
Sold Anderson Galleries
17 February 1926 (41)

A Country Lane
WHL 57
5½ × 4 in.
Sold Anderson Galleries
17 February 1926 (28)

A Study of a Common
WHL 89
5 × 6¾ in.
Sold Anderson Galleries
17 February 1926 (35)

The Ruins of Netley Abbey
WHL 94
11 × 8½ in.
Sold Anderson Galleries
17 February 1926 (24)

The Edge of a Wood
WHL 98
6¾ × 5 in.
Sold Anderson Galleries
17 February 1926 (37)

A Farm Scene
WHL 99
10½ × 8 in.
Sold Anderson Galleries
17 February 1926 (32)

*A Mansion and Park
at East Bergholt, Suffolk*
WHL 116
19½ × 29½ in.
Sold Christie 7 April 1961 (111)

The Hay Wain
WHL 123
24 × 29 in.
Sold Christie 21 April 1961 (81)

River Scene with Punt
WHL 140
11 × 9 in.
Sold Bonham 20 April 1961
(167 part)

A Cottage by the River
WHL 190
7½ × 12 in.
Sold Anderson Galleries
17 February 1926 (23)

Landscape
WHL 197
3¾ × 6½ in.
Sold Anderson Galleries
17 February 1926 (31)

A Study of Two Horses
WHL 198
4¾ × 6 in.
Sold Anderson Galleries
17 February 1926 (40)

A Woody River Scene
WHL 239
7½ × 11½ in.
Sold Anderson Galleries
17 February 1926 (34)

A Landscape
WHL 242
6¾ × 10¾ in.
Sold Anderson Galleries
17 February 1926 (29)

Woody Landscape
WHL 251
6½ × 9 in.
Sold Anderson Galleries
17 February 1926 (30)

Autumn Landscape
WHL 252
6¾ × 9 in.
Sold Anderson Galleries
17 February 1926 (33)

Caravan Scene
WHL 254
6¾ × 5 in.
Sold Anderson Galleries
17 February 1926 (38)

Salisbury Cathedral
WHL 535
22½ × 27½ in.
Sold Christie 7 April 1961 (188)

Landscape
WHL 537
3½ × 9½ in.
Sold Knight, Frank & Rutley
15 June 1926 (36)

Moorland Scene
WHL 543
6 × 8½ in.
Sold Knight, Frank & Rutley
15 June 1926 (37)

The Glebe Farm
WHL 551
40 × 35 in.
Sold Bonham 20 April 1961 (143)

*Hampstead Heath
Looking Towards Harrow*
WHL 553
28 × 34 in.
Sold Christie 7 April 1961 (137)

*A Wooded River with a Bridge
and an Angler*
WHL 554
3 × 4 in.
Sold Christie 21 April 1961 (149)

Hampstead Heath
WHL 577
24½ × 29½ in.
Sold Christie 7 April 1961 (112)

Stormy Landscape
WHL 579
10 × 17 in.
Sold Bonham 20 April 1961 (37)

*A River Scene
with a Distant Windmill*
WHL 586
8½ × 10 in.
Sold Christie 7 April 1961 (115)

*River Scene with Lock
and Cottage*
WHL 591
10 × 9 in.
Sold Bonham 20 April 1961
(39 part)

*Wooded Landscape
with Dark Trees*
WHL 607
11¾ × 9¾ in.
Sold Bonham 20 April 1961
(unidentified part lot)

On the Stour Near Flatford Mill
WHL 623
27 × 36 in.
Sold Christie 21 April 1961 (139)

Lock on the Stour
WHL 646
27 × 30 in.
Sold Knight, Frank & Rutley
15 June 1926 (30)

*River Scene with Windmills
in Moonlight*
WHL 647
10½ × 14½ in.
Sold Bonham 20 April 1961
(166 part)

Riders by an Inn
WHL 656
5 × 7 in.
Sold Bonham 20 April 1961 (182)

*View from Hampstead Heath,
Stormy Day*
WHL 657
11 × 13½ in.
Sold Knight, Frank & Rutley
15 June 1926 (38)

*A Riverside with Sailing Barges,
Horse and Cart*
WHL 661
6 × 7 in.
Sold Knight, Frank & Rutley
15 June 1926 (39)

Arundel
WHL 669
44 × 55½ in.
Sold Anderson Galleries
11 May 1926 (80)

*A Cottage in the Home Counties,
with Figures*
WHL 2001
6½ × 8½ in.
Sold Knight, Frank & Rutley
15 June 1926 (40)

The Edge of a Wood
WHL 2010
13½ × 20 in.
Sold Bonham 20 April 1961 (168)

A Boat House on a Wooded Bank
WHL 2011
6 × 5½ in.
Sold Christie 7 April 1961 (116)

Woodland Scene, with Donkeys and Figures
WHL 2013
18 × 14 in.
Sold Knight, Frank & Rutley
15 June 1926 (41)

Landscape with Figures, a Cart and Windmill
WHL 2021
8½ × 11 in.
Sold Bonham 20 April 1961
(161 part)

Landscape with Cattle and Figures - Passing Showers
WHL 2023
8 × 11 in.
Sold Bonham 20 April 1961
(unidentified part lot)

Landscape with Cottage and Donkey at a Gate
WHL 2039
10¼ × 9¼ in.
Sold Bonham 20 April 1961
(unidentified part lot)

The Windmill
WHL 2047
9¼ × 11½ in.
Sold Bonham 20 April 1961
(unidentified part lot)

River Scene with Watermill and Figures in a Boat
WHL 2050
6½ × 7¾ in.
Sold Bonham 20 April 1961
(unidentified part lot)

Cow in a Green Pasture: A Sketch
WHL 2051
3¼ × 4½ in.
Sold Knight, Frank & Rutley
15 June 1926 (42)

A Lock in the River, with Barge and Horse
WHL 2054
9¼ × 12¼ in.
Sold Knight, Frank & Rutley
15 June 1926 (43)

A Dark Landscape with Horse and Church Tower
WHL 2055
6½ × 10 in.
Sold Bonham 20 April 1961 (162)

A Wooded River Landscape
WHL 2056
6 × 8 in.
Sold Christie 21 April 1961 (144)

Three Small Sketches of Landscapes in One Frame
WHL 2057
Sold Knight, Frank & Rutley
15 June 1926 (44)

Three Small Sketches in One Frame
WHL 2057A
Sold Knight, Frank & Rutley
15 June 1926 (45)

Three Small Sketches in One Frame
WHL 2057B
Sold Knight, Frank & Rutley
15 June 1926 (46)

A Storm Over Hampstead Heath
WHL 2059
19 × 23 in.
Sold Christie 21 April 1961 (90)

A Landscape with Sandy Banks
WHL 2061
9½ × 12 in.
Sold Bonham 20 April 1961
(unidentified part lot)

A Duck Pond
WHL 2065
8¾ × 11¾ in.
Sold Bonham 20 April 1961
(unidentified part lot)

The Edge of a Wood
WHL 2066
8¾ × 11¾ in.
Sold Bonham 20 April 1961
(unidentified part lot)

Woody Lake Scene
WHL 2067
8¾ × 11¾ in.
Sold Bonham 20 April 1961
(unidentified part lot)

A Mountain Landscape with a Horseman
WHL 2069
22 × 18½ in.
Sold Christie 21 April 1961 (84)

Wood Scene, with Stream and Boy Fishing
WHL 2286
19 × 29 in.
Sold Knight, Frank & Rutley
15 June 1926 (47)

An Extensive Landscape, with Factory and Other Buildings
WHL 2331
14½ × 21½ in.
Sold Knight, Frank & Rutley
15 June 1926 (48)

Near East Bergholt
WHL 4240
8¾ × 11 in.
Sold Anderson Galleries
17 February 1926 (26)

Abraham Cooper
1787-1868

Portraits of Copenhagen and Marengo, the Horses Ridden by Wellington and Bonaparte at Waterloo
WHL 2177
27½ × 34½ in.
Sold Knight, Frank & Rutley
15 June 1926 (49)

Francis Cotes
1725-1770

Portrait of a Lady, with her Two Daughters
WHL 246
35 × 25½ in.
Sold Christie 28 April 1961 (119)

Miss Constance Simpson
WHL 2332
6¼ × 4¼ in.
Sold Knight, Frank & Rutley
14 July 1926 (12)

Countess of Shannon
WHL 2671
88 × 50 in.
Sold Anderson Galleries
7 February 1926 (45)

Portrait of a Lady
WHL 3536
35 × 28 in.
Sold Anderson Galleries
11 May 1926 (81)

Lady Melbourne
WHL 4495
50 × 40 in.
Sold Anderson Galleries
17 February 1926 (44)

Portrait of James, Second Earl of Fife
WHL 4771
93½ × 56½ in.
Sold Anderson Galleries
17 February 1926 (43)

John Sell Cotman
1782-1842

Fishing Boats and Figures
4½ × 5 in.
WHL 184
Sold Anderson Galleries
17 February 1926 (47)

A Seascape
WHL 189
9¾ × 11¾ in.
Sold Anderson Galleries
17 February 1926 (48)

The Mouth of a River
WHL 549
17 × 21¾ in.
Sold Knight, Frank & Rutley
15 June 1926 (52)

Small Craft and Hulks off Portsmouth
WHL 550
29 × 38 in.
Sold Christie 7 April 1961 (110)

Small Fishing Craft in a Squall Offshore
WHL 694
23½ × 35½ in.
Sold Christie 21 April 1961 (80)

Sailing Craft in a Choppy Sea Near a Lighthouse
WHL 2287
19½ × 26 in.
Sold Christie 21 April 1961 (86)

Fishing Craft Hauling in their Nets Offshore
WHL 2312
27 × 35 in.
Sold Christie 7 April 1961 (189)

Small Sailing Craft in a Fresh Wind
WHL 2322
4 × 7½ in.
Sold Christie 21 April 1961 (146)

Cromer Beach, Cottage, Boats, and Figures in Foreground
WHL 2339
12 × 15¼ in.
Sold Knight, Frank & Rutley
15 June 1926 (58)

David Cox
1783-1859

Tossing the Hay
WHL 6
18½ × 28 in.
Sold Knight, Frank & Rutley
14 July 1926 (49)

Peace and War
WHL 9
18½ × 24 in.
Sold Anderson Galleries
17 February 1926 (52)

A Cloudy Landscape with a Windmill
WHL 86
7 × 10½ in.
Sold Anderson Galleries
17 February 1926 (51)

A Heath Landscape with a Shepherd and a Herdsman
WHL 145
8½ × 13½ in.
Sold Christie 7 April 1961 (140)

Rustic Figures
WHL 150
7½ × 11 in.
Sold Anderson Galleries
17 February 1926 (50)

A Hayfield
WHL 187
9½ × 15½ in.
Sold Anderson Galleries
17 February 1926 (49)

A Common, with Cows
WHL 536
4¾ × 6½ in.
Sold Knight, Frank & Rutley
15 June 1926 (54)

*A View of Bolton Abbey
with Figures and Cattle*
WHL 541
9¾ × 13¾ in.

Ploughing the Uplands
WHL 593
13½ × 17 in.
Sold Christie 17 March 1961 (74)

Going to the Hayfield
WHL 597
11 × 15 in.
Sold Knight, Frank & Rutley
14 July 1926 (13)

Changing Pastures
WHL 603
10 × 14 in.
Sold Christie 21 April 1961 (143)

*A Mountain Landscape
with Welsh Peasants*
WHL 636
19 × 13 in.
Sold Christie 17 March 1961 (75)

Going to the Hayfield
WHL 650
12½ × 16½ in.
Sold Christie 6 June 1958 (106)

*A View of Bolton Abbey
with Figures and Cattle*
WHL 659
12 × 15 in.
Sold Christie 7 April 1961 (190)

Wooded Landscape with Figures
WHL 667
12 × 16 in.
Sold Bonham 20 April 1961
(163 part)

Coast Scene with Figures
WHL 2048
6¾ × 10¾ in.
Sold Bonham 20 April 1961
(149 part)

Farmer Watering Horses
WHL 2052
6 × 9 in.
Sold Bonham 20 April 1961
(149 part)

A Mountain Landscape
WHL 2320
17½ × 24 in.
Sold Knight, Frank & Rutley
15 June 1926 (181)

*The Welsh Coast:
Crossing the Sands*
WHL 2327
11½ × 17 in.
Sold Christie 7 April 1961 (113)

Charles Cranmer
1780-1841

Returning from the Market
WHL 3319
24 × 18 in.
Sold Knight, Frank & Rutley
14 July 1926 (14)

View at The Hague
WHL 3321
22 × 23 in.
Sold Knight, Frank & Rutley
14 July 1926 (15)

John Crome
1768-1821

A View in Norfolk
WHL 34
3¾ × 6¾ in.
Sold Anderson Galleries
17 February 1926 (59)

*A Woodland Path with a Woman
and a Dog*
WHL 36
24 × 19 in.
Sold Christie 21 April 1961 (83)

A Scene in Norwich
WHL 39
25½ × 21 in.
Sold Knight, Frank & Rutley
15 June 1926 (53)

A View Near Whittingham
WHL 83
29½ × 39 in.
Sold Christie 6 June 1958 (107)

A View in Norfolk
WHL 118
23 × 18½ in.
Sold Anderson Galleries
17 February 1926 (54)

A River Estuary
WHL 133
11 × 15½ in.
Sold Anderson Galleries
17 February 1926 (57)

A Study of Cattle Watering
WHL 188
8½ × 10½ in.
Sold Anderson Galleries
17 February 1926 (55)

A Landscape
WHL 244
14 × 23½ in.
Sold Anderson Galleries
17 February 1926 (56)

*A Wooded Landscape with
Two Figures Under a Dying Oak*
WHL 532
39 × 49 in.
Sold Christie 7 April 1961 (136)

*An Estuary Overlooked by a
Castle on a Cliff*
WHL 552
18 × 25 in.
Sold Christie 21 April 1961 (89)

The Edge of a Forest
WHL 561
7 × 9 in.
Sold Bonham 20 April 1961 (147)

A Dark Pool Shaded by Trees
WHL 604
21 × 32 in.
Sold Christie 21 April 1961 (79)

A Town on a River, Moonlight
WHL 614
18½ × 26 in.
Sold Knight, Frank & Rutley
14 July 1926 (16)

*A Wooded River Scene
with an Angler in a Rowing Boat*
WHL 634
16½ × 21 in.
Sold Christie 21 April 1961 (91)

The Edge of a Wood
WHL 635
17½ × 23½ in.
Sold Knight, Frank & Rutley
14 July 1926 (17)

A Road Through a Wood
WHL 655
5 × 4 in.
Sold Christie 21 April 1961 (147)

Woody Lane Scene
WHL 2000
8¾ × 12 in.
Sold Bonham 20 April 1961
(161 part)

*Wooded River Landscape
with Cottages*
WHL 2019
3 × 4 in.
Sold Christie 21 April 1961
(148 part)

*Wooded River Landscape
with Cottage*
WHL 2020
3 × 4½ in.
Sold Christie 21 April 1961
(148 part)

*A Wood Scene with a Pool
and a Woman Beside a Fence*
WHL 2044
8½ × 12 in.
Sold Knight, Frank & Rutley
15 June 1926 (61)

Cottage at the End of a Wood
WHL 2290
14 × 23 in.
Sold Bonham 20 April 1961
(lot 169 part)

*A Woody Landscape With
Cottages and a Pool of Water*
WHL 2329
20½ × 24½ in.
Sold Knight, Frank & Rutley
15 June 1926 (62)

The Edge of a Wood
WHL 4241
15½ × 11½ in.
Sold Anderson Galleries
17 February 1926 (58)

Thomas Daniell
1749-1840

*Fishing Village Under Cliff,
Clovelly*
WHL 2022
17 × 28½ in.
Sold Knight, Frank & Rutley
15 June 1926 (65)

Peter De Wint
1784-1849

Lincoln Cathedral
WHL 119
14½ × 21½ in.
Sold Anderson Galleries
17 February 1926 (64)

William Etty
1787-1849

Cymon and Iphigenia
15 × 19 in.

A Figure Reposing
17 × 21 in.
Presented to York City Art Gallery
1911

A Banquet of the Gods
WHL 95
11 × 25 in.
Sold Knight, Frank & Rutley
15 June 1926 (70)

Cupid Appealing to Jupiter
WHL 96
11 × 25 in.
Sold Knight, Frank & Rutley
15 June 1926 (71)

A Girl Watering Flowers
WHL 159
20 × 14 in.

A Female Figure Reposing
WHL 160
15 × 19 in.
Sold Anderson Galleries
17 February 1926 (293)

*Cupid and Psyche Reclining
on the Clouds*
WHL 161
11½ × 13½ in.
Sold Christie 6 June 1958 (118)

The Reading Magdalen
WHL 162
12 × 14 in.
Sold Anderson Galleries
17 February 1926 (80)

A Female Figure Seated
WHL 163
12½ in. (diam.)
Sold Anderson Galleries
17 February 1926 (87)

Venus, Cupid and Mars
WHL 166
20½ × 25½ in.
Sold Anderson Galleries
17 February 1926 (78)

A Male Figure Seated
WHL 167
22½ × 18 in.
Sold Anderson Galleries
17 February 1926 (84)

Cupid
WHL 168
21 × 13 in.
Sold Anderson Galleries
17 February 1926 (82)

An Allegory of Plenty
WHL 171
27½ × 34½ in.
Sold Anderson Galleries
17 February 1926 (79)

Venus and Cupid
WHL 172
27 × 20½ in.
Sold Anderson Galleries
17 February 1926 (77)

A Group of Three Female Figures
WHL 173
27½ × 22½ in.
Sold Anderson Galleries
17 February 1926 (90)

A Reclining Female Nude
WHL 584
17 × 23 in.
Sold Christie 7 April 1961 (114)

Female Study
WHL 590
10½ × 8 in.
Sold Knight, Frank & Rutley
15 June 1926 (72)

A Bacchanalian Dance
WHL 637
24 × 18½ in.
Sold Knight, Frank & Rutley
14 July 1926 (50)

*A Male Figure, Seated,
Study From Life*
WHL 640
26 × 19½ in.
Sold Knight, Frank & Rutley
15 June 1926 (73)

A Seated Female Figure
WHL 2029
27 × 18 in.
Sold Anderson Galleries
17 February 1926 (91)

*Pandora Crowned
by the Four Seasons*
WHL 2070
11 × 16½ in.
Sold Anderson Galleries
17 February 1926 (81)

*A Sketch for the Rape
of the Sabines*
WHL 2648
8½ × 10½ in.
Sold Anderson Galleries
17 February 1926 (83)

Female Figure
WHL 2852
23½ × 15½ in.
Sold Anderson Galleries
17 February 1926 (89)

Female Figure Kneeling
WHL 2853
25 × 18½ in.
Sold Anderson Galleries
17 February 1926 (86)

A Seated Nymph
WHL 2888
27½ × 15½ in.
Sold Anderson Galleries
17 February 1926 (88)

A Reclining Nymph
WHL 3065
20 × 12 in.

The Bathers
WHL 3305
26 × 20 in.
Sold Anderson Galleries
17 February 1926 (92)

*Cymochles and Phaedra
on the Idle Lake*
WHL 3306
24½ × 30 in.
Sold Christie 6 June 1958 (117)

Venus Disarming Cupid
WHL 3307
20½ × 16½ in.
Sold Anderson Galleries
17 February 1926 (76)

Venus and Cupid
WHL 3401
25½ × 19 in.
Presented to the Tate Gallery 1925

A Youth Asleep Beside the Sea
WHL 3546
25 × 18½ in.
Sold Anderson Galleries
17 February 1926 (75)

Britomart Redeems Faire Amoret
WHL 4031
35 × 25 in.
Sold Christie 6 June 1958 (116)

The Lake
WHL 4123
26 in. (diam.)

A Female Figure Seated
WHL 4529
23 × 17½ in.
Sold Anderson Galleries
17 February 1926 (85)

Anthony Vandyke Copley Fielding
1787-1855

A Flat Landscape
WHL 186
10½ × 14½ in.
Sold Anderson Galleries
17 February 1926 (94)

Alexander Fraser
1786-1865

Fishmonger's Shop
WHL 4425
23½ × 20 in.

William Edward Frost
1810-1877

Ariadne
WHL 3123

Melpomene
WHL 3123A

Terpsichore
WHL 3123B

Thomas Gainsborough
1727-1788

The White Horse
WHL 125
25½ × 20½ in.
Sold Knight, Frank & Rutley
15 June 1926 (75)

Portrait of a Young Girl
WHL 534
29 × 24 in.
Sold Anderson Galleries
17 February 1926 (105)

The Market Cart
WHL 567
33 × 28 in.
Sold Christie 28 April 1961 (120)

Miss Ogle
WHL 570
27 × 22
Sold privately through Agnew
1958

*Portrait of a Lady,
said to be Miss Coghlan*
WHL 573
27½ × 22½ in.
Sold Christie 14 April 1961 (6)

*Cattle Watering
at a Woodland Pool*
WHL 609
29 × 39 in.
Sold Christie 14 April 1961 (186)

Portrait of a Lady
WHL 612
58 × 41 in.
Sold Christie 28 April 1961 (117)

Portrait of a Gentleman
WHL 2026
29 × 24 in.
Sold Anderson Galleries
17 February 1926 (107)

A River Scene
WHL 2031
29 × 44½ in.
Sold Anderson Galleries
17 February 1926 (108)

Portrait of a Gentleman
WHL 2291
21 × 17 in.
Sold Christie 14 April 1961 (8)

Mr Nuthall
WHL 4243
30 × 25 in.
Sold Anderson Galleries
17 February 1926 (106)

Duke of Cumberland
WHL 4244
29 × 24 in.
Sold Anderson Galleries
17 February 1926 (104)

**Marcus Gheeraerts
(the elder)**
c.1525-c.1590

*Portrait of Robert Devereux,
Second Earl of Essex*
WHL 4103
22 × 16½ in.
Sold Anderson Galleries
17 February 1926 (109)

Portrait of a Lady
WHL 4770
44 × 31 in.
Sold Anderson Galleries
17 February 1926 (110)

Thomas Girtin
1775-1802

A Coast Scene
WHL 151
9 × 14½ in.
Sold Anderson Galleries
17 February 1926 (115)

Hugh Douglas Hamilton
1734-1806

Portrait of a Lady
WHL 3440
11 × 9 in.
Sold Anderson Galleries
17 February 1926 (121)

William Hamilton
1751-1801

Portrait of a Lady
WHL 2882
14 × 10 in.
Sold Knight, Frank & Rutley
15 June 1926 (78)

Portrait of a Boy
WHL 2883
14 × 10 in. (oval)
Sold Knight, Frank & Rutley
15 June 1926 (79)

Portrait of a Boy
WHL 2884
14 × 10 in.
Sold Knight, Frank & Rutley
15 June 1926 (80)

William Havell
1782-1857

A Wayside Shrine
WHL 97
7 × 5 in.
Sold Anderson Galleries
17 February 1926 (122)

Sir George Hayter
1792-1871

*Portrait of Queen Victoria
in Garter Robes*
WHL 3441
11½ × 9¼ in.

Charles Cooper Henderson
1803-1877

The Continental Mail
WHL 3222
24 × 30 in.
Sold Knight, Frank & Rutley
15 June 1926 (81)

William Hogarth
1697-1764

*Miniature Portrait
of a Gentleman*
WHL 3126
4 × 3 in.
Sold Anderson Galleries
17 February 1926 (134)

James Holland
1799-1870

The Colleoni Monument, Venice
WHL 80
38 × 49 in.
Sold Christie 6 June 1958 (128)

Cathedral of St Stephen's, Vienna
WHL 127
10½ × 23 in.
Sold Anderson Galleries
17 February 1926 (136)

Venice
WHL 177
9 × 20 in.
Sold Anderson Galleries
17 February 1926 (135)

*Venice, with Gondolas
and Figures*
WHL 629
28 × 20 in.
Sold Knight, Frank & Rutley
15 June 1926 (82)

Venice
WHL 654
9½ × 13½ in.
Sold Christie 6 June 1958 (130)

Venice
WHL 2063
13½ × 16½ in.
Sold Christie 6 June 1968 (129)

Lighthouse and Rough Sea
WHL 2850

Bridge Over Canal, Venice
WHL 2851

Seascape and Ship
WHL 2851A

Venice
WHL 2851B

Landscape
WHL 2851C

Mountain Scene with Sheep
WHL 2851D

Seascape
WHL 2851E

*The Painted Hall,
Greenwich Hospital*
WHL 2880
Sold Knight, Frank & Rutley
14 July 1926 (22)

Church of the Jesuits, Venice
WHL 3308
10 × 23¾ in.
Sold Anderson Galleries
17 February 1926 (137)

*Venice, Gondolas in Foreground
with Figures on Quay*
WHL 3566
9½ in. (diam.)
Sold Knight, Frank & Rutley
14 July 1926 (23)

Greenwich Hospital
WHL 4124
6 × 10¾ in.
Sold Anderson Galleries
17 February 1926 (138)

John Hoppner
1758-1810

Portrait of the Misses Fanning
42 × 33 in.
returned to James Orrock 1908

The Misses Hollingworth
WHL 82
42 × 33 in.

Portrait of a Lady
WHL 589
35 × 28½ in.
Sold Anderson Galleries
17 February 1926 (149)

*A Gentleman, Seated, Holding a
Book which a Child is Reading*
WHL 592
17 × 13 in.
Sold Knight, Frank & Rutley
15 June 1926 (105)

*Lady in Grey Dress with
Orange Scarf*
WHL 2002
30 × 24 in.
Destroyed in the Lady Lever Art
Gallery 1961

Boy with Hoop and Dog
WHL 2007
49 × 40 in.
Sold Anderson Galleries
17 February 1926 (71)

*A Girl's Head, with Curls
Escaping Beneath Her Cap*
WHL 2045
10 × 8 in.
Sold Knight, Frank & Rutley
15 June 1926 (106)

Lucius Concannon
WHL 2173
50 × 40 in.
Sold Anderson Galleries
17 February 1926 (148)

*A Lady in a White Dress, her Hair
Bound with a Blue Riband*
WHL 2294
10 × 8½ in.
Sold Knight, Frank & Rutley
15 June 1926 (107)

A Child Seated Nursing a Doll
WHL 2335
30 × 24 in.
Sold Knight, Frank & Rutley
15 June 1926 (108)

Squire Cholmley
WHL 3129
30 × 25 in.
Sold Anderson Galleries
17 February 1926 (146)

Mrs. O'Hara
WHL 4245
30 × 25 in.
Sold Anderson Galleries
17 February 1926 (145)

Miss Mary Rycroft
WHL 4246
30 × 25 in.
Sold Anderson Galleries
17 February 1926 (147)

Cornelius Johnson
1593-1661

*Portrait of the Duke of
Buckingham*
WHL 2636
Presented to Hall I'th'Wood,
Bolton

John Hampden
WHL 2891
25½ × 21½ in.
Presented to Hall i'th'Wood,
Bolton

Portrait of a Lady
WHL 3445
29½ × 24½ in.

Angelica Kauffman
1741-1807

The Judgment of Paris
WHL 707
25 × 25 in.
Sold Knight, Frank & Rutley
15 June 1926 (188)

Rinaldo and Armida
WHL 2229
17 × 13 in.
Sold Christie 14 April 1961 (10)

Diana and Nymph
WHL 2230
25½ in. (diam.)
Sold Knight, Frank & Rutley
15 June 1926 (110)

*Youth in Red, Placing a Crown
of Laurels on a Female Figure*
WHL 2231
25½ in. (diam.)
Sold Knight, Frank & Rutley
15 June 1926 (111)

Paris and Helen
WHL 3444
25 × 25 in.
Sold Knight, Frank & Rutley
15 June 1926 (189)

Ariadne
WHL 3835
10¼ × 7½ in.

Sir Godfrey Kneller
1646-1723

Lady in Orange and Blue Robe
WHL 666
Sold Knight, Frank & Rutley
15 June 1926 (113)

Portrait of a Lady in a Blue Dress
WHL 1447
29 × 24 in.

Portrait of a Divine
WHL 1448
29 × 24 in.

Portrait of a Lady in a Blue Robe
WHL 1463
29 × 24 in.
Sold Knight, Frank & Rutley
9 November 1925 (295 part)

A Young Cavalier
WHL 2043
13 × 11 in.
Sold Bonham 20 April 1961
(163 part)

Queen Mary II
WHL 2226
49 × 39 in.
Presented to Hall i'th'Wood,
Bolton

George Lance
1802-1864

Two Pears
WHL 2938
6 × 11 in.
Sold Knight, Frank & Rutley
9 November 1925 (1121)

Sir Edwin Landseer
1802-1873

*Black Dog, with Landscape
in Background*
WHL 2014
10 × 11½ in.
Sold Knight, Frank & Rutley
15 June 1926 (115)

A King Charles Spaniel
WHL 3393
22½ × 18½ in.

*Pony, Donkey and Dog
in Landscape*
WHL 3832
15 × 17½ in.
Sold Knight, Frank & Rutley
9 November 1925 (1122)

Sir Thomas Lawrence
1769-1830

Portrait of a Lady
WHL 70
13½ × 11½ in.
Sold Christie 7 April 1961 (141)

John Philip Kemble as Hamlet
WHL 79
77 × 44 in.
Sold Anderson Galleries
17 February 1926 (156)

Portrait of a Lady
WHL 250
11 × 7½ in.
Sold Anderson Galleries
11 May 1926 (27)

Mrs. Newte and Her Daughter
WHL 533
35 × 25 in.
Sold Anderson Galleries
17 February 1926 (160)

Miss Phelps in Black Dress
WHL 613
29 × 24 in.
Sold Bonham 20 April 1961
(145 part)

Portrait of a Lady in White
WHL 616
29 × 24 in.
Sold Bonham 20 April 1961
(145 part)

Lady Elizabeth Skeffington
WHL 626
49½ × 39½ in.
Sold Anderson Galleries
17 February 1926 (157)

Lady Trimlestown
WHL 631
89 × 57 in.
Sold Anderson Galleries
17 February 1926 (159)

*Portrait of a Lady
in a White Robe*
WHL 2025
29 × 24½ in.
Sold Christie 21 April 1961 (87)

Portrait of a Lady in Black Dress
WHL 2062
30 × 24 in.
Sold Christie 21 April 1961
(94 part)

Portrait of a Lady in Red Turban
WHL 2308
29 × 23 in.
Sold Anderson Galleries
17 February 1926 (161)

*Mary Timbery, Portrait of a
Young Woman with a Rose*
WHL 2314
35 × 27 in.
Sold Bonham 20 April 1961 (144)

Portrait of a Lady
WHL 2673
30 × 24 in.
Sold Christie 21 April 1961
(94 part)

Marquise de Blaisel and Child
WHL 3567
36 × 28 in.
Sold Anderson Galleries
17 February 1926 (155)

Head of Prince Hoare
WHL 4070
24 × 20 in.
Sold Anderson Galleries
17 February 1926 (158)

James Mathews Leigh
1808-1860

A Bacchante
WHL 170
50 × 40 in.
Sold Anderson Galleries
17 February 1926 (165)

Sir Peter Lely
1618-1680

Nell Gwynn
WHL 1
49 × 37 in.

Charles II
WHL 2873
Presented to Hall i'th'Wood,
Bolton

James II in Garter Robes
WHL 2876
Presented to Hall I'th'Wood,
Bolton

*Portrait of a Lady in Yellow Dress
and Blue Scarf*
WHL 4035
30 × 24 in.

John Frederick Lewis
1805-1876

The Bezestein Bazaar, Cairo
WHL 3793
44 × 34 in.
Sold Knight, Frank & Rutley
9 November 1925 (1119)

*The Courtyard of the
Coptic Patriarch's House, Cairo*
WHL 4752
43½ × 42 in.
Sold Anderson Galleries
17 February 1926 (171)

John Linnell
1792-1882

A Sunset Landscape
WHL 101
6½ × 8½ in.
Sold Anderson Galleries
17 February 1926 (175)

Arcadian Shepherds
WHL 114
26½ × 35 in.
Sold Anderson Galleries
17 February 1926 (174)

Milking Time, Autumn
WHL 583
11½ × 18½ in.
Sold Knight, Frank & Rutley
14 July 1926 (26)

A Woodland Stream
WHL 2018
9½ × 13½ in.
Sold Christie 31 July 1958 (135)

Changing Pastures
WHL 2058
14½ × 22½ in.
Sold Christie 6 June 1958 (136)

*Portrait of a Lady
said to be Mrs. Trimmer*
WHL 2346
24 × 19½ in.
Sold Christie 7 April 1961 (197)

The Barley Harvest
WHL 2788
19 × 23¾ in.

Portrait of Benjamin Flint
WHL 3770
14½ × 11 in.
Sold Anderson Galleries
17 February 1926 (172)

Portrait of Mrs. Flint
WHL 3771
14½ × 11 in.
Sold Anderson Galleries
17 February 1926 (173)

George Morland
1763-1804

The Slate Quarry
WHL 37
19½ × 25½ in.
Sold Anderson Galleries
17 February 1926 (189)

Selling the Pet Lamb
WHL 47
21½ × 18 in.
Sold Anderson Galleries
17 February 1926 (190)

The Wreckers
WHL 49
39 × 55 in.
Sold Knight, Frank & Rutley
15 June 1926 (94)

The Recruits
WHL 72
23½ × 35½ in.
Sold Christie 14 April 1961 (179)

Riding to Hounds
WHL 104
10¾ × 14½ in.
Sold Christie 14 April 1961 (99)

A Country Inn
WHL 106
11½ × 14¾ in.
Sold Anderson Galleries
17 February 1926 (193)

The Morning Ride
WHL 121
24 × 29 in.
Sold Christie 28 April 1961 (114)

Cymon and Iphigenia
WHL 131
9½ × 11½ in.
Sold Anderson Galleries
17 February 1926 (194)

*A Ship in a Storm
off a Rocky Coast*
WHL 143
9½ × 11½ in.
Sold Anderson Galleries
17 February 1926 (199)

A Coast Scene - 'The Look Out'
WHL 144
9½ × 11¾ in.
Sold Anderson Galleries
17 February 1926 (196)

The Bear Hunt
WHL 148
8 × 10 in.
Sold Anderson Galleries
17 February 1926 (192)

Landscape with Coursing Scene
WHL 539
10½ × 13½ in.
Sold Knight, Frank & Rutley
15 June 1926 (95)

The Fair Angler
WHL 548
7 × 5½ in.
Sold Christie 14 April 1961 (181)

Peasants by a Cottage
WHL 559
9 × 11 in.
Sold Bonham 20 April 1961 (36)

Selling Fish on the Coast
WHL 560
9¾ in. (diam.)
Sold Knight, Frank & Rutley
15 June 1926 (96)

Feeding the Pigs
WHL 563
27 × 35 in.
Sold Knight, Frank & Rutley
15 June 1926 (103)

The Alms Giver
WHL 572
17½ × 14 in.
Sold Christie 14 April 1961 (155)

The Elegant Angler
WHL 576
17½ × 14 in.
Sold Christie 14 April 1961 (154)

The Shipwreck
WHL 601
9¾ × 11¾ in.
Sold Christie 14 April 1961 (98)

*Gamekeeper with Gun
and Three Dogs*
WHL 606
22 × 16 in.
Sold Knight, Frank & Rutley
15 June 1926 (104)

A Shore Scene with a Jetty
WHL 608
9¼ × 11½ in.
Sold Christie 14 April 1961
(100, 157 or 180)

Selling the Catch
WHL 617
14 × 18½ in.
Sold Christie 14 April 1961 (139)

The Turnpike Gate
WHL 632
35 × 45 in.
Sold Anderson Galleries
17 February 1926 (188)

At the Stable Door
WHL 648
13½ × 17 in.
Sold Knight, Frank & Rutley
15 June 1926 (97)

Setters in a Wood
WHL 662
14 × 17 in.
Sold Bonham 20 April 1961
(148 part)

Pointers in a Wood
WHL 663
14 × 17 in.
Sold Bonham 20 April 1961
(148 part)

Selling the Sucking Pig
WHL 2003
20 × 28 in.
Sold Knight, Frank & Rutley
15 June 1926 (98)

*A Mounted Huntsman
Leading a Saddled Horse*
WHL 2030
25 × 33 in.

*Coast Scene with Jetty,
Two Figures in a Boat*
WHL 2040
9½ × 11½ in.
Sold Christie 14 April 1961
(100, 157 or 180)

*Coast Scene with Jetty,
Four Figures and Boat*
WHL 2041
9½ × 12½ in.
Sold Christie 14 April 1961
(100, 157 or 180)

*A Winter Landscape with Figures
and a Dead Tree*
WHL 2053
9 × 11½ in.
Sold Christie 14 April 1961 (159)

The Shipwreck
WHL 2072
13½ × 16½ in.
Sold Christie 14 April 1961 (9)

Scene on a Common
WHL 2284
7 × 10 in.
Sold Bonham 20 April 1961
(unidentified part lot)

The Lesson
WHL 2319
29½ × 24½ in.
Sold Knight, Frank & Rutley
15 June 1926 (99)

The Butcher Taking Refreshment
WHL 2334
24½ × 29½ in.
Sold Knight, Frank & Rutley
15 June 1926 (100)

Buying Fish
WHL 2845
11¾ × 13¾ in.
Sold Christie 6 June 1958 (141)

The Fisherman's Hut
WHL 2846
20 × 19 in.
Sold Knight, Frank & Rutley
15 June 1926 (101)

The Market Woman
WHL 3446
14½ × 11½ in.
Sold Anderson Galleries
17 February 1926 (200)

*Selling Fish, View of the Coast
in the Isle of Wight*
WHL 3686
40 × 54 in.
Sold Knight, Frank & Rutley
15 June 1926 (102)

The Gypsies' Camp
WHL 3800
17 × 23½ in.
Sold Anderson Galleries
17 February 1926 (191)

African Hospitality
WHL 3844
34 × 48 in.
Sold Knight, Frank & Rutley
15 June 1926 (87)

The Slave Trade
WHL 3845
34 × 48 in.
Sold Knight, Frank & Rutley
15 June 1926 (88)

Gypsies
WHL 4036
16½ × 20 in.
Sold Anderson Galleries
17 February 1926 (195)

*The Farmer's Visit
to his Married Daughter*
WHL 4100
12 in. (diam.)
Sold Anderson Galleries
17 February 1926 (197)

Louisa
WHL 4247
9½ × 7½ in.
Sold Anderson Galleries
17 February 1926 (198)

Selling Fish in the Isle of Wight
WHL 4512
25 × 38½ in.
Sold Knight, Frank & Rutley
9 November 1925 (1130)

Patrick Nasmyth
1787-1831

Woody Landscape
WHL 91
7½ × 9½ in.
Sold Anderson Galleries
17 February 1926 (205)

A Country Road
WHL 4513
18 × 24 in.
Sold Anderson Galleries
17 February 1926 (206)

John Opie
1761-1807

Children of William Smith, M.P.
WHL 4527
30 × 25 in.
Sold Anderson Galleries
17 February 1926 (209)

'John Parry'
[?Joseph Parry
1744-1826]

The Fortune Teller
WHL 1429
34½ × 26½ in.
Sold Christie 6 June 1958 (146)

Richard Morton Paye
1750-1821

Puss in Durance
WHL 3180
Sold Knight, Frank & Rutley
14 July 1926 (30)

Sir John Dean Paul
1775-1857

The Strand Looking Towards Temple Bar
WHL 3758
15 × 23 in.
Sold Christie 17 March 1961 (80)

Old Northumberland House
WHL 3759
15½ × 23 in.
Sold Christie 17 March 1961 (79)

Whitehall, Looking Towards the Holbein Gate, with the Banqueting House on the Left
WHL 3760
15½ × 23½ in.
Sold Christie 17 March 1961 (78)

Westminster Hall
WHL 4052
24½ × 29½ in.
Sold Anderson Galleries
17 February 1926 (213)

Rev. Matthew William Peters
1742-1814

Portrait of a Girl
WHL 3157
23 × 19 in.
Sold Anderson Galleries
17 February 1926 (212)

Portrait of a Child, in White Dress, Sitting Holding an Apple
WHL 3221
27 × 23½ in.
Sold Christie 6 June 1958 (147)

Robert Edge Pine
c.1730-1788

King George II
WHL 2890
17½ × 14 in.
Presented to Hall i'th'Wood, Bolton

Sir Henry Raeburn
1756-1823

Portrait of a Lady, said to be Mrs. Balfour
WHL 124
30 × 25 in.
Sold Christie 21 April 1961 (93)

Mrs. Campbell, in Black Dress with White Yoke and Cap
WHL 547
9½ × 7½ in.
Sold Knight, Frank & Rutley
15 June 1926 (547)

Portrait of a Lady, said to be Mrs. Emily Dutton
WHL 587
36 × 27 in.
Sold Christie 21 April 1961 (92)

An Old Lady in Black Dress and White Cap
WHL 2035
28 × 23 in.
Sold Bonham 20 April 1961
(unidentified part lot)

A Group of Three Children
WHL 2296
56 × 44 in.
Sold Anderson Galleries
17 February 1926 (221)

Portrait of Balafre, Scottish Archer
WHL 2333
26½ × 22 in.
Sold Christie 21 April 1961 (88)

Sir Brooke Boothby, Bart
WHL 3834
36½ × 27½ in.
Sold Anderson Galleries
17 February 1926 (220)

Allan Ramsay
1713-1784

Mrs. Madan
WHL 3592
49 × 39 in.

Sir Joshua Reynolds
1723-1792

Lady and Spaniel
WHL 60
48 × 38 in.
Sold Anderson Galleries
17 February 1926 (70)

Portrait of William Jones and His Wife Elizabeth
WHL 63
39 × 48 in.
Sold Christie 17 March 1961 (81)

Countess of Thanet
WHL 67
41 × 32½ in.
Sold Anderson Galleries
17 February 1926 (224)

Portrait of a Lady
WHL 84
30 × 25 in.
Sold Anderson Galleries
17 February 1926 (231)

Collina
WHL 245
19½ × 15½ in.

Two Children with a Bird's Nest
WHL 588
48 × 40 in.
Sold Anderson Galleries
17 February 1926 (69)

A Wooded River Landscape with a Distant Town
WHL 628
49 × 62 in.
Sold Christie 14 April 1961 (178)

Portrait of a Lady in a White Robe
WHL 2005
29 × 24 in.
Sold Christie 14 April 1961 (136)

Portrait of Miss Dobbs
WHL 2006
20 × 16 in.
Sold Christie 14 April 1961 (158)

Sketch of a Lady
WHL 2046
8 × 7 in.
Sold Knight, Frank & Rutley
14 July 1926 (33)

The Infant Hercules Strangling Serpents
WHL 2071
13½ × 10½ in.
Sold Knight, Frank & Rutley
14 July 1926 (34)

Portrait of Miss Sarah Ann Falkiner
WHL 2336
35 × 27 in.
Sold Anderson Galleries
17 February 1926 (229)

Sarah, Lady Mexborough
WHL 3073
Returned to E. Cremetti 1917

Portrait of Mrs. Payne Gallwey and Child
WHL 3122
29 × 24 in.
Sold Anderson Galleries
17 February 1926 (232)

King George III
WHL 3374
93 × 57 in.
Sold Anderson Galleries
17 February 1926 (228)

Queen Charlotte
WHL 3375
93 × 57 in.
Sold Anderson Galleries
17 February 1926 (227)

The Infant Academy
WHL 4249
27½ × 34 in.
Sold Anderson Galleries
17 February 1926 (223)

The Age of Innocence
WHL 4394

A Gypsy Boy
WHL 4496
33 × 27 in.
Sold Anderson Galleries
17 February 1926 (230)

Margaret Oxenden
WHL 4768
35½ × 45 in.
Sold Anderson Galleries
17 February 1926 (226)

Self Portrait
WHL 4772
24 × 19½ in.

Venus and Cupid
WHL 4773
49 × 39 in.
Sold Anderson Galleries
17 February 1926 (225)

George Romney
1734-1802

Mrs. Butler (Miss Carwardine)
WHL 51
27½ × 21½ in.
Sold Anderson Galleries
17 February 1926 (233)

Portrait of a Gentleman
WHL 103
16½ × 11½ in.
Sold Anderson Galleries
17 February 1926 (235)

Portrait of a Lady
WHL 195
29½ × 24½ in.
Sold Anderson Galleries
17 February 1926 (236)

Portrait of a Lady
WHL 253
11¾ × 9¾ in.
Sold Anderson Galleries
17 February 1926 (234)

Head of a Lady
WHL 564
8 × 6¼ in.
Sold Knight, Frank & Rutley
15 June 1926 (129)

Portrait Bust of a Young Woman
WHL 566
17 × 14 in.
Sold Bonham 8 June 1961
(123 part)

Head of a Lady
WHL 2036
11½ × 9½ in.
Sold Knight, Frank & Rutley
15 June 1926 (130)

Gentleman with Powdered Hair
WHL 2037
11¼ × 9½ in.
Sold Knight, Frank & Rutley
15 June 1926 (131)

Portrait of a Lady
(said to be Mrs. Close)
WHL 2131
31½ × 25 in.
Sold Christie 14 April 1961 (141)

Miss Strachan
WHL 2318
29½ × 24½ in.
Sold Knight, Frank & Rutley
15 June 1926 (132)

Mrs. Ann Baldwin
WHL 4236
29 × 24 in.

John Nost Sartorius
1759-1828

The Hunt: nine small hunting scenes in one frame
WHL 3331
each 4 in. (diam.)
Sold Christie 17 March 1961 (82)

The Hunt: nine small hunting scenes in one frame
WHL 3332
each 4 in. (diam.)
Sold Christie 17 March 1961 (83)

Samuel Scott
1710-1772

Old London Bridge
WHL 112
30 × 49 in.
Sold Knight, Frank & Rutley
15 June 1926 (165)

Richmond
WHL 247
30½ × 38 in.
Sold Knight, Frank & Rutley
15 June 1926 (133)

View of Westminster
WHL 248
23 × 43 in.
Sold Knight, Frank & Rutley
15 June 1926 (134)

View of Queen's Square Bloomsbury
WHL 2350
Sold Knight, Frank & Rutley
15 June 1926 (135)

Westminster from Lambeth Palace
WHL 3324
20 × 34 in.
Sold Knight, Frank & Rutley
15 June 1926 (136)

Westminster from Hungerford Bridge
WHL 3325
20 × 34 in.
Sold Knight, Frank & Rutley
15 June 1926 (137)

William Shayer
1787-1879

Landscape, with Mill
WHL 1439
9½ × 11½ in.
Sold Knight, Frank & Rutley
15 June 1926 (138)

Sir Martin Archer Shee
1769-1850

Miss Lee as Ophelia
WHL 4497
92 × 56½ in.
Sold Anderson Galleries
17 February 1926 (246)

The Annesley Children
WHL 4693
71 × 47 in.
Sold Anderson Galleries
17 February 1926 (245)

Henry Singleton
1766-1839

George IV and Mrs. Fitzherbert
WHL 194
23½ × 19 in.
Sold Anderson Galleries
17 February 1926 (247)

Peace in the Old Home
WHL 3395
30 × 24 in.
Sold Knight, Frank & Rutley
15 June 1926 (140)

A Settler Attacked by Natives
WHL 3396
30 × 24 in.
Sold Knight, Frank & Rutley
14 July 1926 (36)

W. Clarkson Stanfield
1793-1867

A Coast Scene with Fisherfolk
WHL 691
21 × 30 in.
Sold Christie 6 June 1958 (159)

James Stark
1794-1859

The Edge of a Wood
WHL 71
12¾ × 10½ in.
Sold Anderson Galleries
17 February 1926 (250)

A Woody Landscape
WHL 100
9½ × 7½ in.
Sold Anderson Galleries
17 February 1926 (251)

Wooded Landscape with Figures
WHL 602
10 × 16 in.
Sold Bonham 20 April 1961 (165)

The Woodman's Cottage
WHL 3182
11½ × 9 in.
Sold Anderson Galleries
17 February 1926 (248)

A Woodland Scene
WHL 3772
9½ × 13½ in.
Sold Anderson Galleries
17 February 1926 (249)

A Landscape
WHL 4071
18 × 24 in.
Sold Anderson Galleries
17 February 1926 (252)

Thomas Stothard
1755-1834

Garden Scene: Figures in a Grotto
WHL 240
9 × 6 in.

Garden Scene: Nymphs Bathing
WHL 241
9 × 6 in.

A Scene from the Arabian Nights
WHL 542
8½ × 6¼ in.
Sold Bonham 20 April 1961 (170)

'David Turner'
[? Daniel Turner]
fl. 1782-1817]

The Horse Guards Parade, Whitehall
WHL 3460
24 × 30 in.
Sold Knight, Frank & Rutley
15 June 1926 (155)

Joseph Mallord William Turner
1775-1851

Off the Nore
WHL 58
11½ × 17½ in.
Sold Anderson Galleries
17 February 1926 (271)

Ulysses Deriding Polyphemus
WHL 75
26 × 43 in.
Sold Christie 7 April 1961 (187)

Hurley House
WHL 117
15½ × 25 in.
Sold Anderson Galleries
17 February 1926 (269)

Among the Cumberland Hills
WHL 126
15 × 18 in.
Sold Anderson Galleries
17 February 1926 (270)

Castle on Mount by the Sea
WHL 132
9½ × 13½ in.
Sold Bonham 20 April 1961
(unidentified part lot)

The Top of the Knoll
WHL 147
15½ × 20½ in.
Sold Anderson Galleries
17 February 1926 (272)

The Valhalla
WHL 545
30 × 38 in.
Sold Knight, Frank & Rutley
14 July 1926 (42)

*A View of Greenwich
from the North Bank*
WHL 605
7½ × 10½ in.
Sold Christie 7 April 1961 (142)

Queen Mab's Grotto
WHL 688
12 × 22 in.
Sold Bonham 20 April 1961 (181)

*Lake Scene, Horsemen and Boy
Driving Cattle*
WHL 1998
9½ × 12 in.
Sold Bonham 20 April 1961
(unidentified part lot)

Classical River Scene, Sunset
WHL 1999
7 × 10½ in.
Sold Bonham 20 April 1961
(unidentified part lot)

The Battle of Trafalgar
WHL 2016
24 × 34 in.

The Blowing up of L'Orient
WHL 2017
21 × 34 in.

*View of a Town with Bridges
Spanning a River*
WHL 2042
7 × 11 in.
Sold Bonham 20 April 1961
(164 part)

Wreck of the Minotaur
WHL 2049
15 × 23½ in.
Sold Knight, Frank & Rutley
15 June 1926 (157)

Ulysses Deriding Polyphemus
WHL 4396
26 × 39 in.
Sold Knight, Frank & Rutley
15 June 1926 (158)

John Varley
1778-1842

A Lake Scene with Boats
WHL 191
9½ × 13½ in.
Sold Anderson Galleries
17 February 1926 (276)

George Vincent
1796-1832

*A Coast Scene with Figures
and Boats*
22 × 34 in.
Sold Knight, Frank & Rutley
24 September 1926 (278)

Road Through the Woods
WHL 53
21½ × 17½ in.
Sold Anderson Galleries
17 February 1926 (277)

River Scene with Cattle
WHL 2899
18 × 23 in.
Sold Knight, Frank & Rutley
15 June 1926 (160)

Robert Walker
c.1607-c.1658

Oliver Cromwell
WHL 2877
Presented to Hall i'th'Wood,
Bolton

Frederick Waters Watts
1800-1870

*A Mountainous Landscape,
with Peasants and Animals
Near a Lake*
WHL 108
24 × 29 in.
Sold Christie 6 June 1958 (169)

Thomas Webster
1800-1886

The Slide
WHL 3549
29½ × 60 in.
Sold Christie 6 June 1958 (171)

Francis Wheatley
1747-1801

Distress
WHL 3416
13 in. (diam.)
Sold Anderson Galleries
17 February 1926 (286)

Primroses
WHL 4263
13¼ × 10¼ in.
Sold Anderson Galleries
17 February 1926 (285)

Richard Wilson
1713-1782

A Village Green
WHL 35
4½ × 5¾ in.
Sold Anderson Galleries
17 February 1926 (290)

*A Wooded River with a Castle
on an Overhanging Bluff*
WHL 55
27½ × 35½ in.
Sold Christie 28 April 1961 (118)

Ruins on a Rock and Stream
WHL 102
12 × 10 in.
Sold Anderson Galleries
17 February 1926 (291)

An Italian Landscape
WHL 146
11½ × 15 in.
Sold Anderson Galleries
17 February 1926 (289)

A Woody River Scene
WHL 152
12 × 16½ in.
Sold Anderson Galleries
17 February 1926 (292)

*River Scene with Crucifix
and Figures*
WHL 178
12½ × 18½ in.
Sold Anderson Galleries
17 February 1926 (287)

A Woody Landscape
WHL 199
13 × 15½ in.
Sold Anderson Galleries
17 February 1926 (288)

The White Monk
WHL 243
25 × 31½ in.
Sold Christie 28 April 1961 (116)

Landscape with Cattle
WHL 578
28 × 49 in.
Sold Christie 14 April 1961 (177)

The White Monk
WHL 627
26 × 31½ in.
 Sold privately through Agnew
1958

A Small Landscape
WHL 660
5 × 6½ in.
Sold Knight, Frank & Rutley
15 June 1926 (161)

A Small Landscape
WHL 665
5 × 6½ in.
Sold Knight, Frank & Rutley
15 June 1926 (162)

Catacombs with Figures
WHL 2012
18 × 16 in.
Sold Christie 14 April 1961 (182)

*Italian Landscape with a Lake
and Figures*
WHL 2028
19 × 25¼ in.
Sold Christie 14 April 1961 (138)

The Bridge at Rimini
WHL 2285
19 × 23½ in.
Sold Christie 14 April 1961 (135)

*An Italian Landscape with Ruins,
Figures and Animals*
WHL 2289
24 × 29 in.
Sold Christie 14 April 1961 (137)

*Italian River Landscape with
Bathers and a Distant Hill Town*
WHL 2311
24 × 29 in.
Sold Christie 14 April 1961 (134)

Johann Zoffany
1733-1810

Portrait of Lord Keith
WHL 1476
11 × 9 in.
Sold Knight, Frank & Rutley
15 June 1926 (164)

British School

Dead Game, Partridges and Hare
11½ × 19 in.
Sold Knight, Frank & Rutley
24 September 1926 (274 part)

*Painting on Glass: A Landscape
with a Mounted Officer
discovering a Seated Soldier*
Sold Knight, Frank & Rutley
9 November 1925 (8)

Portrait of a Child, with Monkey
Sold Knight, Frank & Rutley
24 September 1926 (295 part)

Sheep in a Landscape
6 × 8 in.
Sold Knight, Frank & Rutley
24 September 1926 (274 part)

The Seven Deadly Sins
WHL 664
26 × 20½ in.
Sold Knight, Frank & Rutley
15 June 1926 (166)

The Duchess of Hamilton
WHL 1446
17½ × 14½ in.

Portrait of a Girl
in a Maroon Dress
WHL 1472
19 × 15 in.
Sold Bonham 20 April 1961
(163 part)

Lady Placing Flowers
in a Blue Vase
WHL 1482
10½ × 8 in.

A Girl with Pleated Hair
WHL 1490

Portrait of a Lady
in a White Dress, with a
Landscape Background
WHL 2068
35½ × 27½ in.
Sold Knight, Frank & Rutley
15 June 1926 (174)

Lady in White Low Neck Dress
WHL 2073
10½ × 8½ in.
Sold Knight, Frank & Rutley
14 July 1926 (46)

Portrait on Glass of a Lady
in a Grey Wig with
Three Tricolour Plumes
WHL 2184
Sold Knight, Frank & Rutley
9 November 1925 (4)

Portrait on Glass of a Lady
in a Grey Mantilla
WHL 2185
Sold Knight, Frank & Rutley
9 November 1925 (5)

Portrait on Glass of an Officer
on a white horse with a
red saddle-cloth
WHL 2186
Sold Knight, Frank & Rutley
9 November 1925 (6)

Portrait on Glass of an Officer
on a white horse with a
blue saddle-cloth
WHL 2187
Sold Knight, Frank & Rutley
9 November 1925 (7)

Portrait of a Gentleman
WHL 2298
24 × 19½ in.
Sold Christie 14 April 1961 (156)

A Gentleman in a Blue Coat
and White Waistcoat
WHL 2326
12 × 9½ in.
Sold Knight, Frank & Rutley
14 July 1926 (47)

A Lady in a Green Dress
WHL 2340
26 × 21 in.
Sold Christie 21 April 1961 (85)

Portrait of a Gentleman
WHL 2625

Portrait of a Lady
WHL 2626

The Pilkington Picture
WHL 2687
43 × 63½ in.
Presented to Rivington Grammar
School

Ships in a Storm
WHL 2715
23 × 36 in.
Sold Christie 6 June 1958 (150)

A Cricket Match
WHL 2752
25 × 28 in.
Sold Christie 17 March 1961 (76)

King Charles I
WHL 2856
Presented to Hall i'Th' Wood,
Bolton

Lord Sandwich
WHL 2857
Presented to Hall i'Th' Wood,
Bolton

The Earl of Morton
WHL 2860
Presented to Hall i'Th' Wood,
Bolton

Portrait of a Gentleman
WHL 2861
9 × 6¾ in.
Sold Anderson Galleries
17 February 1926 (68)

Portrait of a Lady
WHL 2862

Portrait of a Gentleman
WHL 2863

Appendix II

Paintings omitted from the Lady Lever Art Gallery Foreign Schools catalogue (1983)
in the belief that they were British, and which have now been re-designated as foreign works

Dutch or German school
mid 18th century

Portrait of a Man with a Book
LL 3162 (WHL 2708)
oil on canvas
96.5 × 77.5 cm

Dutch or German school
mid 18th century

Portrait of a Man with a Parrot
LL 3163 (WHL 2707)
oil on canvas
96.5 × 77.5 cm

A. de Lelie
(1755-1820)

The Sculpture Gallery of
the Felix Meritis Society,
Amsterdam
LL 3571 (LP 70)
oil on canvas
41.5 × 53.5 cm

French school
mid 19th century

Children at Play
LL 3574 (WHL 3320)
oil on canvas
54 × 40.5cm

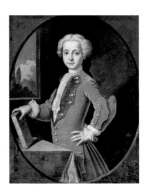
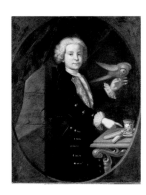
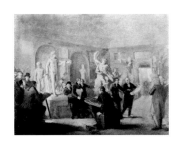
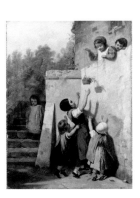

Index of Names and Places